Over! Academy

1

Vol.1
Story & Art by
Maki Minami

TECHNICAL ADVISORS
Yoichi Kato, Kaori Kagami, Ayumi Hashidate,
Ayako Harino and Touko Fujitani

Vol. 1

Chapter 1	4
Chapter 2	71
Chapter 3	107
Chapter 4	137
Chapter 5	167
Bonus Pages	197
End Notes	199

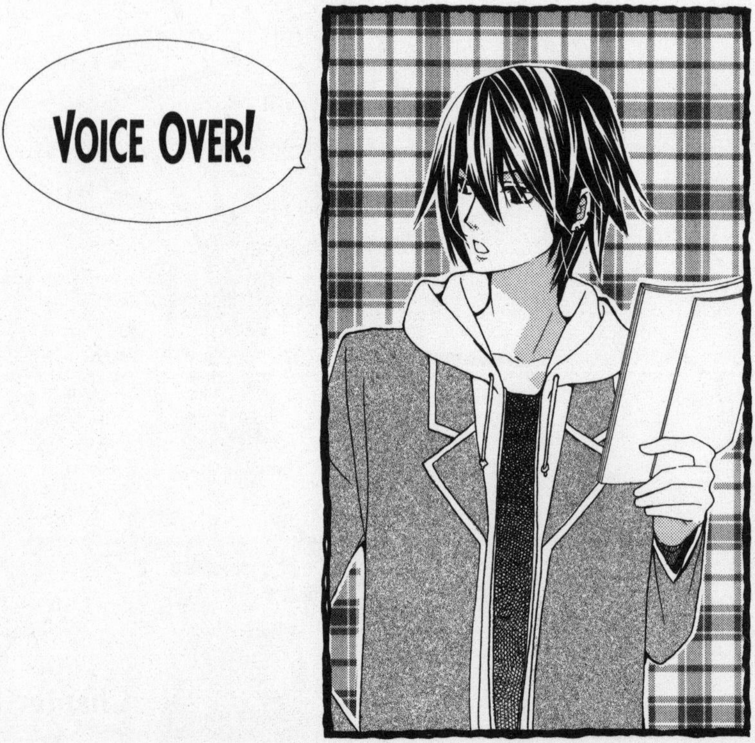
VOICE OVER!

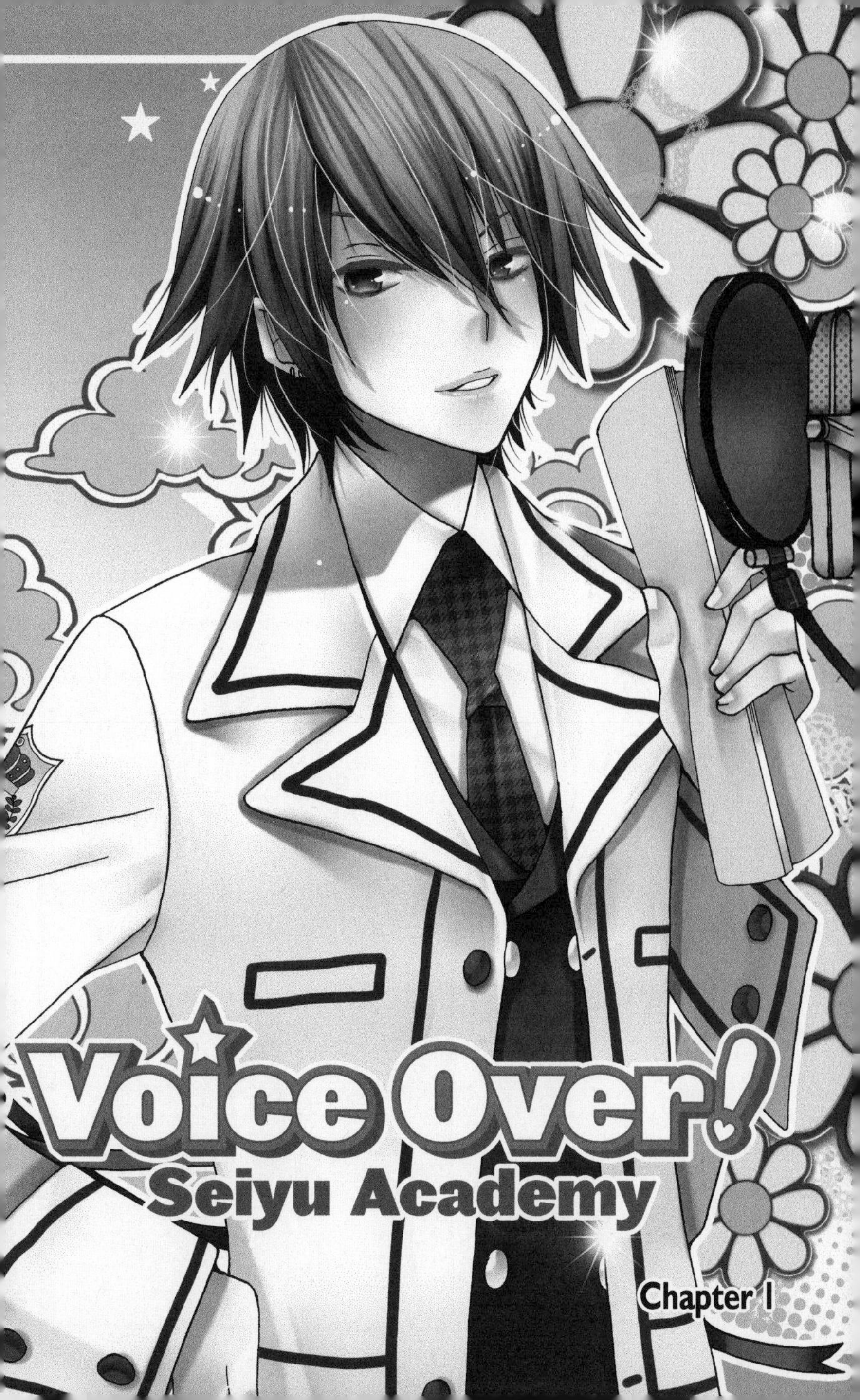
Voice Over!
Seiyu Academy
Chapter 1

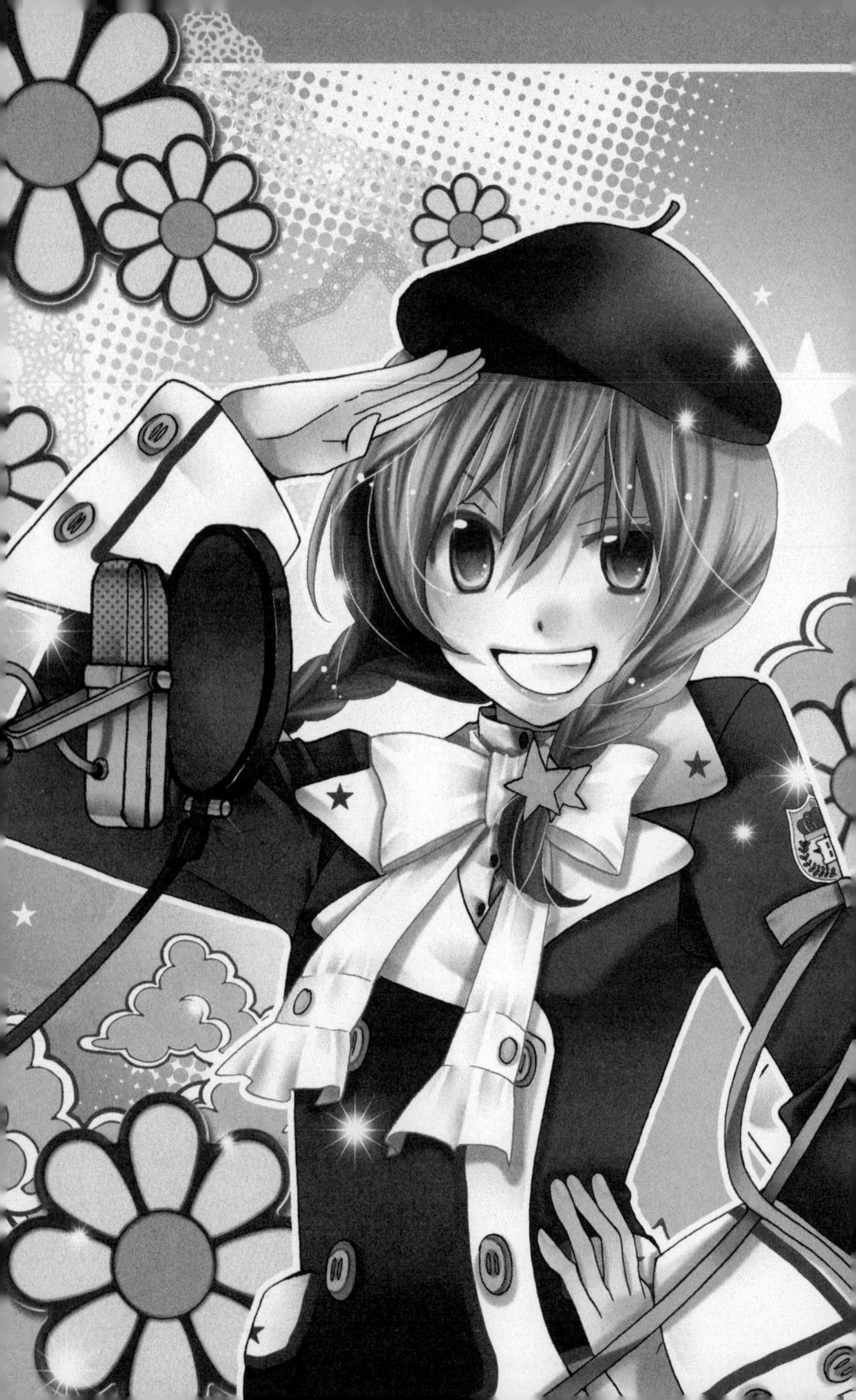

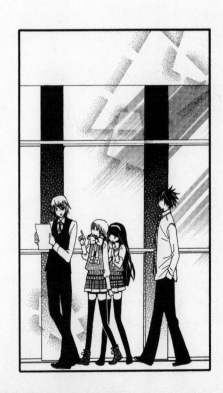

VOICE OVER!

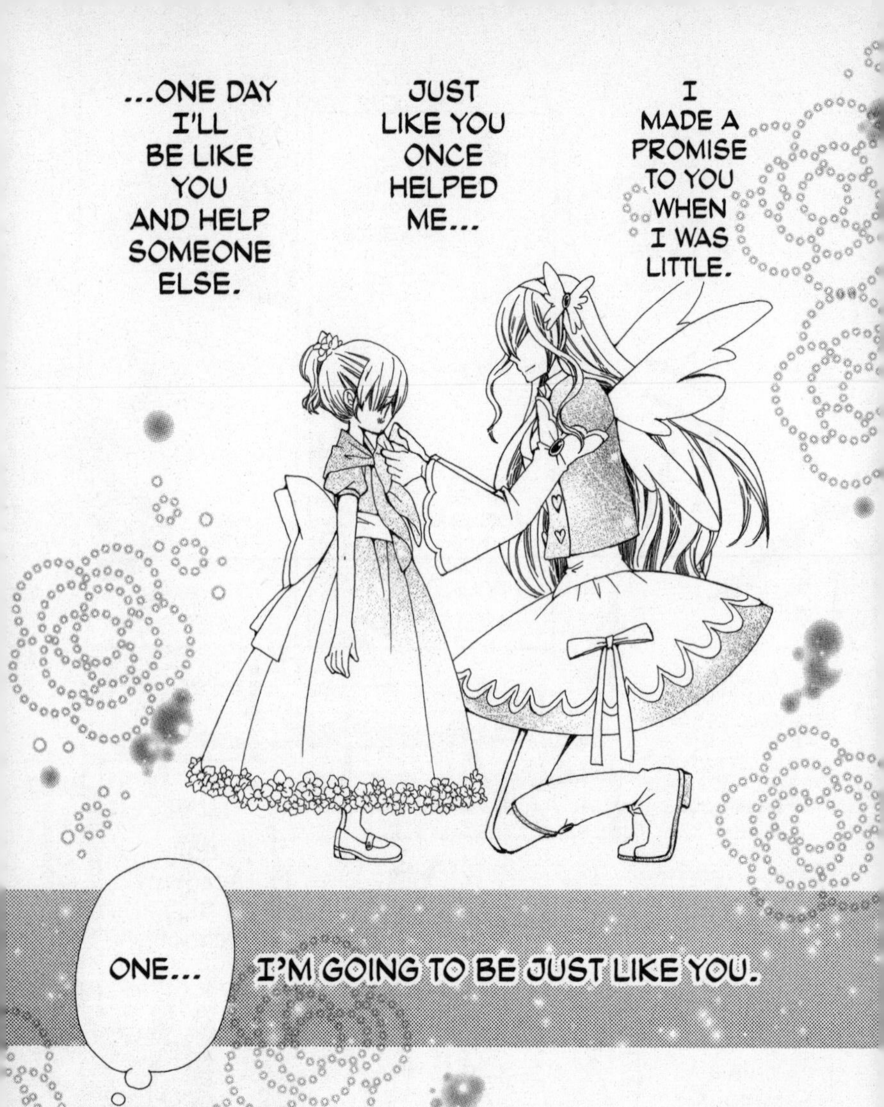
I MADE A PROMISE TO YOU WHEN I WAS LITTLE.
JUST LIKE YOU ONCE HELPED ME...
...ONE DAY I'LL BE LIKE YOU AND HELP SOMEONE ELSE.
I'M GOING TO BE JUST LIKE YOU.
ONE...

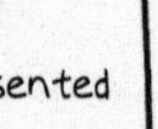

• *Voice Over!* 1

• *Voice Over!: Seiyu Academy* is my first new series since *S.A.* *S.A.* branched into other media, so I got to observe voice actors at work several times and thought it was really neat work, so I began this series. I hope you enjoy it!! Thank you!

• My editor and I decided on the school uniform designs together. When I presented a few designs, my editor said:

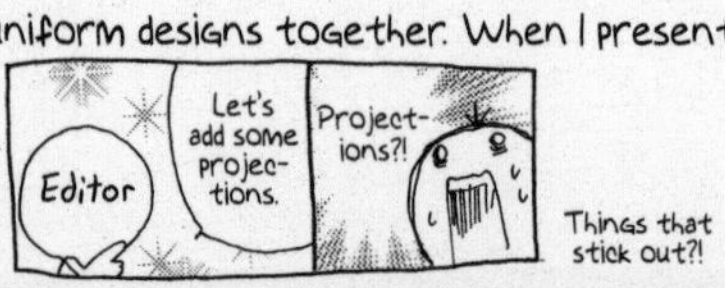
Projections?!
Things that stick out?!
Editor
Let's add some projections.

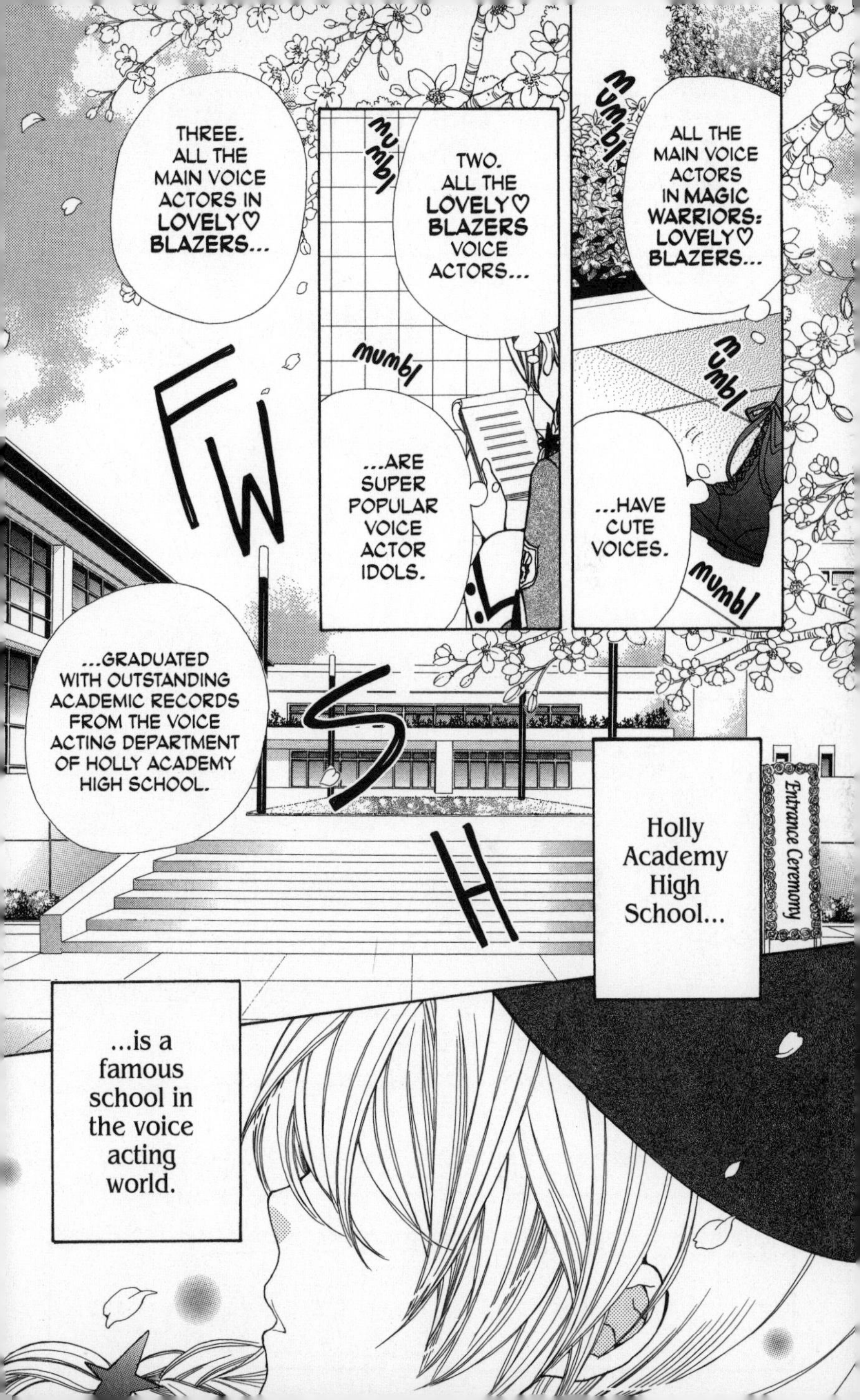
mumbl
ALL THE MAIN VOICE ACTORS IN MAGIC WARRIORS: LOVELY♡ BLAZERS...
mumbl
...HAVE CUTE VOICES.
mumbl
mumbl
TWO. ALL THE LOVELY♡ BLAZERS VOICE ACTORS...
mumbl
...ARE SUPER POPULAR VOICE ACTOR IDOLS.
THREE. ALL THE MAIN VOICE ACTORS IN LOVELY♡ BLAZERS...
...GRADUATED WITH OUTSTANDING ACADEMIC RECORDS FROM THE VOICE ACTING DEPARTMENT OF HOLLY ACADEMY HIGH SCHOOL.
FWISH
Entrance Ceremony
Holly Academy High School...
...is a famous school in the voice acting world.

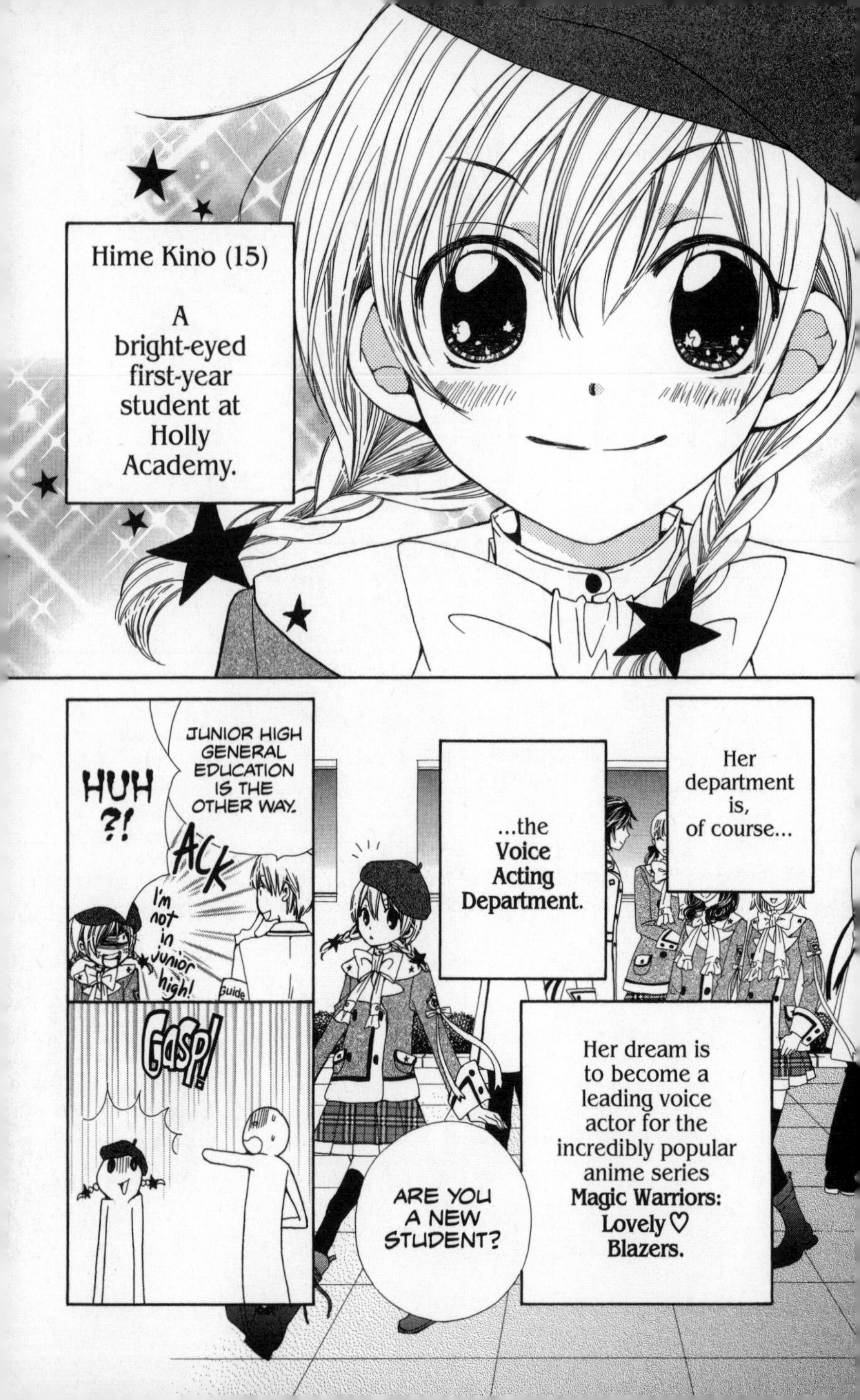
Hime Kino (15)
A bright-eyed first-year student at Holly Academy.
Her department is, of course...
...the Voice Acting Department.
Her dream is to become a leading voice actor for the incredibly popular anime series Magic Warriors: Lovely ♡ Blazers.
ARE YOU A NEW STUDENT?
JUNIOR HIGH GENERAL EDUCATION IS THE OTHER WAY.
HUH ?!
ACK
I'm not in junior high!
Guide
GASP!

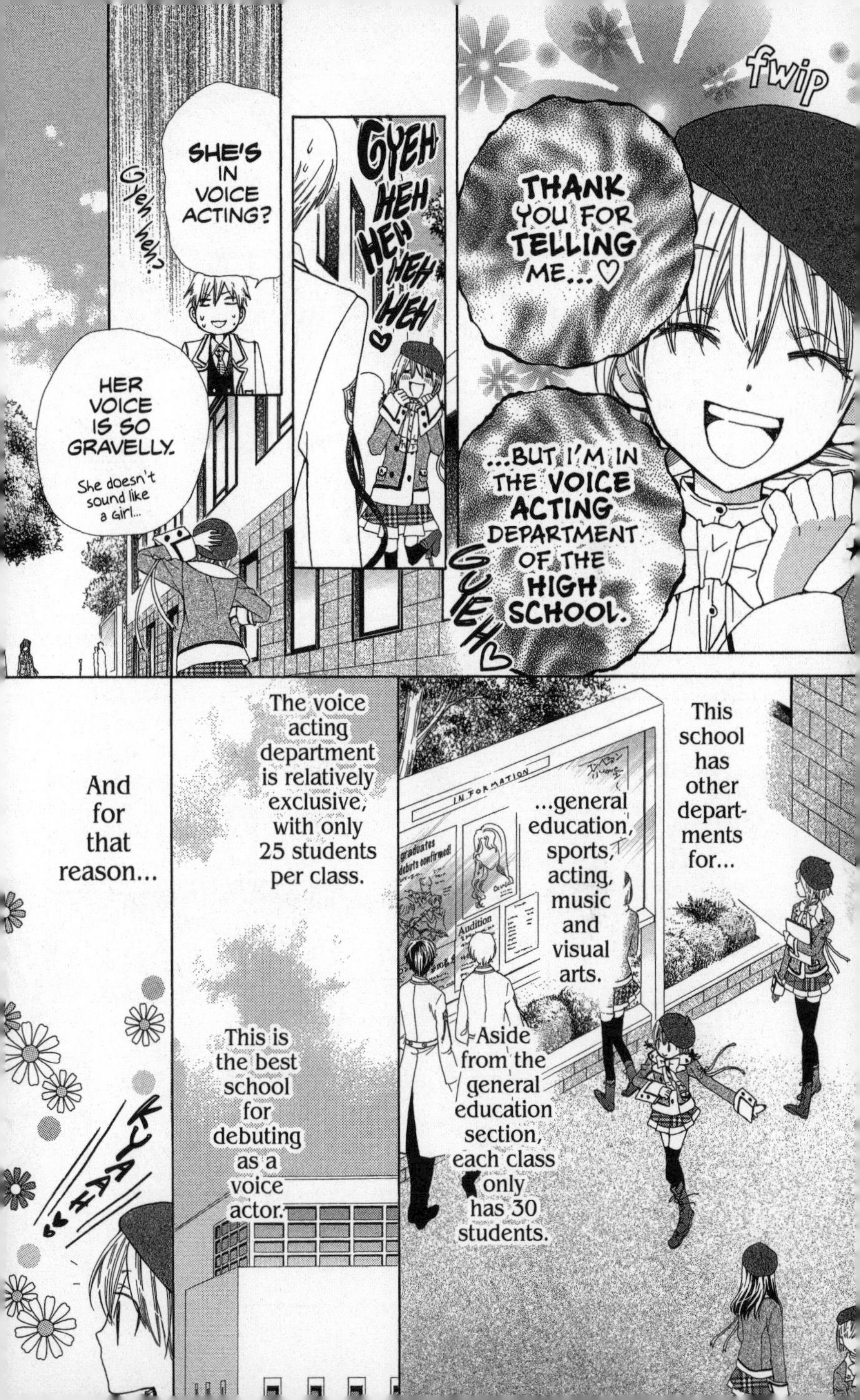
fwip
THANK YOU FOR TELLING ME...♡
...BUT I'M IN THE VOICE ACTING DEPARTMENT OF THE HIGH SCHOOL.
GYEH♡
GYEH HEH HEH HEH HEH
SHE'S IN VOICE ACTING?
Gyeh heh?
HER VOICE IS SO GRAVELLY.
She doesn't sound like a girl...
This school has other depart- ments for...
...general education, sports, acting, music and visual arts.
INFORMATION
graduates debuts confirmed!
Audition
Aside from the general education section, each class only has 30 students.
The voice acting department is relatively exclusive, with only 25 students per class.
This is the best school for debuting as a voice actor.
And for that reason...
KYAAH

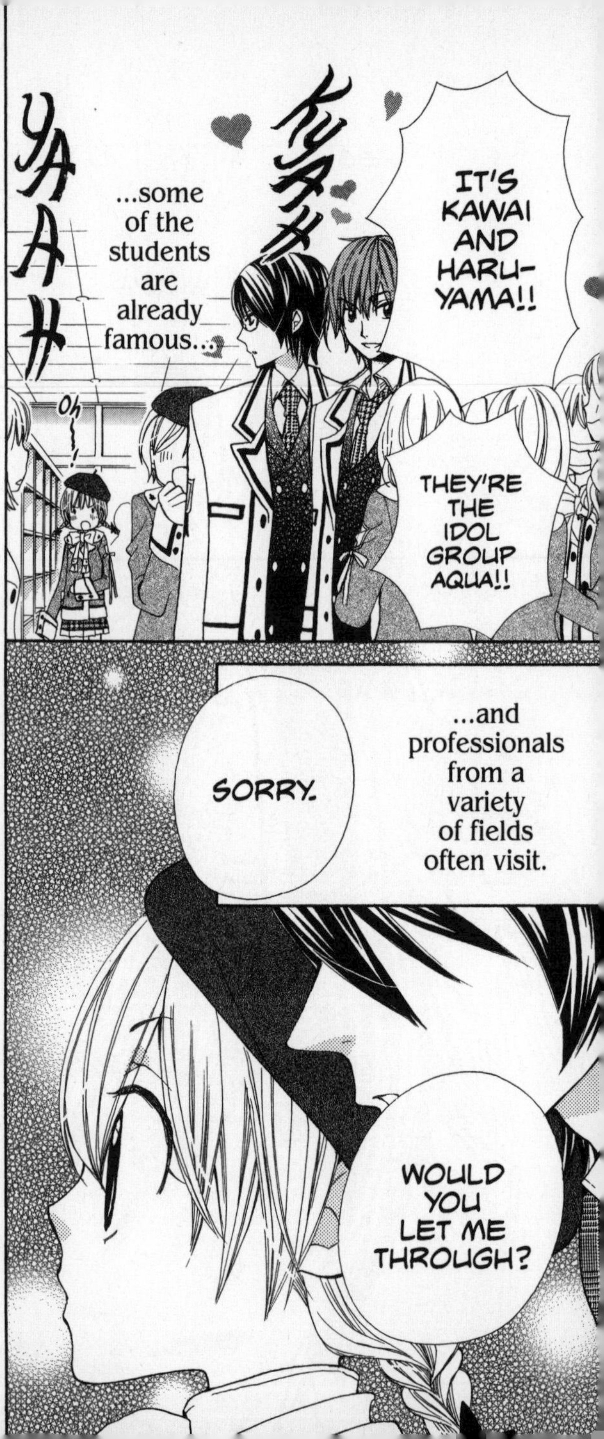
IT'S KAWAI AND HARU-YAMA!!
KYAAH
...some of the students are already famous...
YAAH
THEY'RE THE IDOL GROUP AQUA!!
Oh—!
...and professionals from a variety of fields often visit.
SORRY.
WOULD YOU LET ME THROUGH?

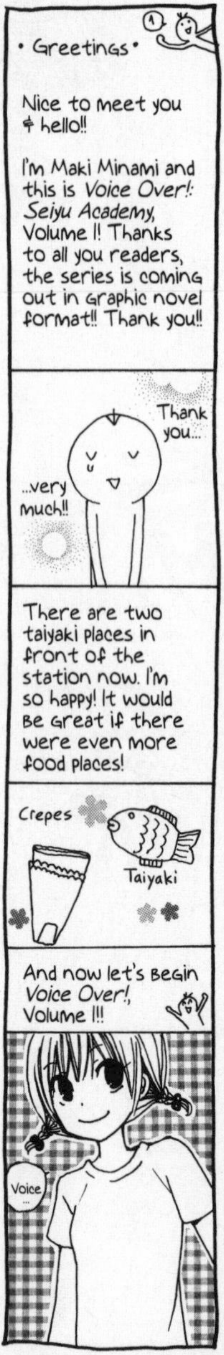
1
• Greetings •
Nice to meet you & hello!!
I'm Maki Minami and this is Voice Over!: Seiyu Academy, Volume 1! Thanks to all you readers, the series is coming out in graphic novel format!! Thank you!!
Thank you...
...very much!!
There are two taiyaki places in front of the station now. I'm so happy! It would be great if there were even more food places!
Crepes
Taiyaki
And now let's begin Voice Over!, Volume 1!!
Voice ...

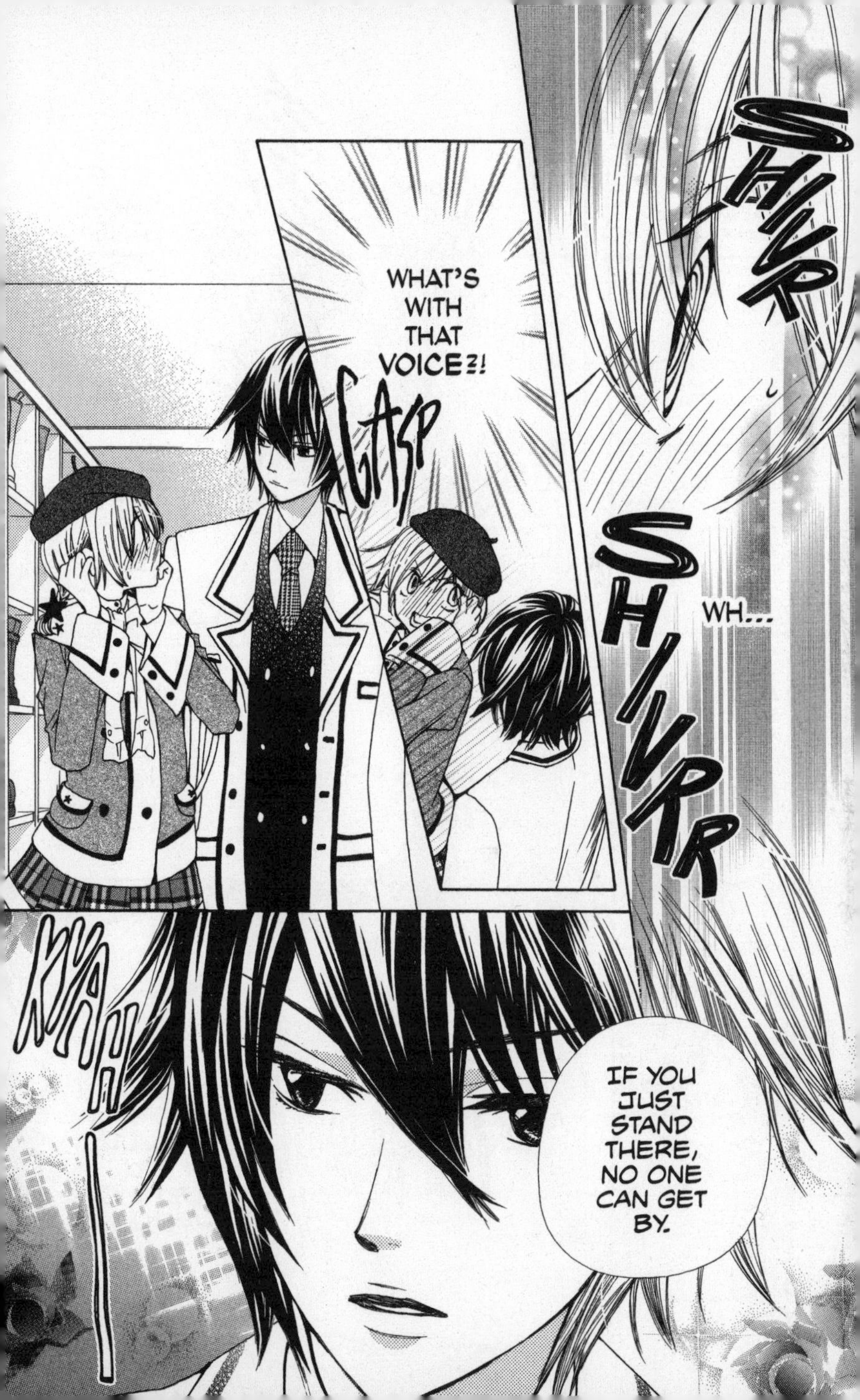
SHIVR
SHIVRR
WH...
WHAT'S WITH THAT VOICE?!
GASP
IF YOU JUST STAND THERE, NO ONE CAN GET BY.
KYAAH!

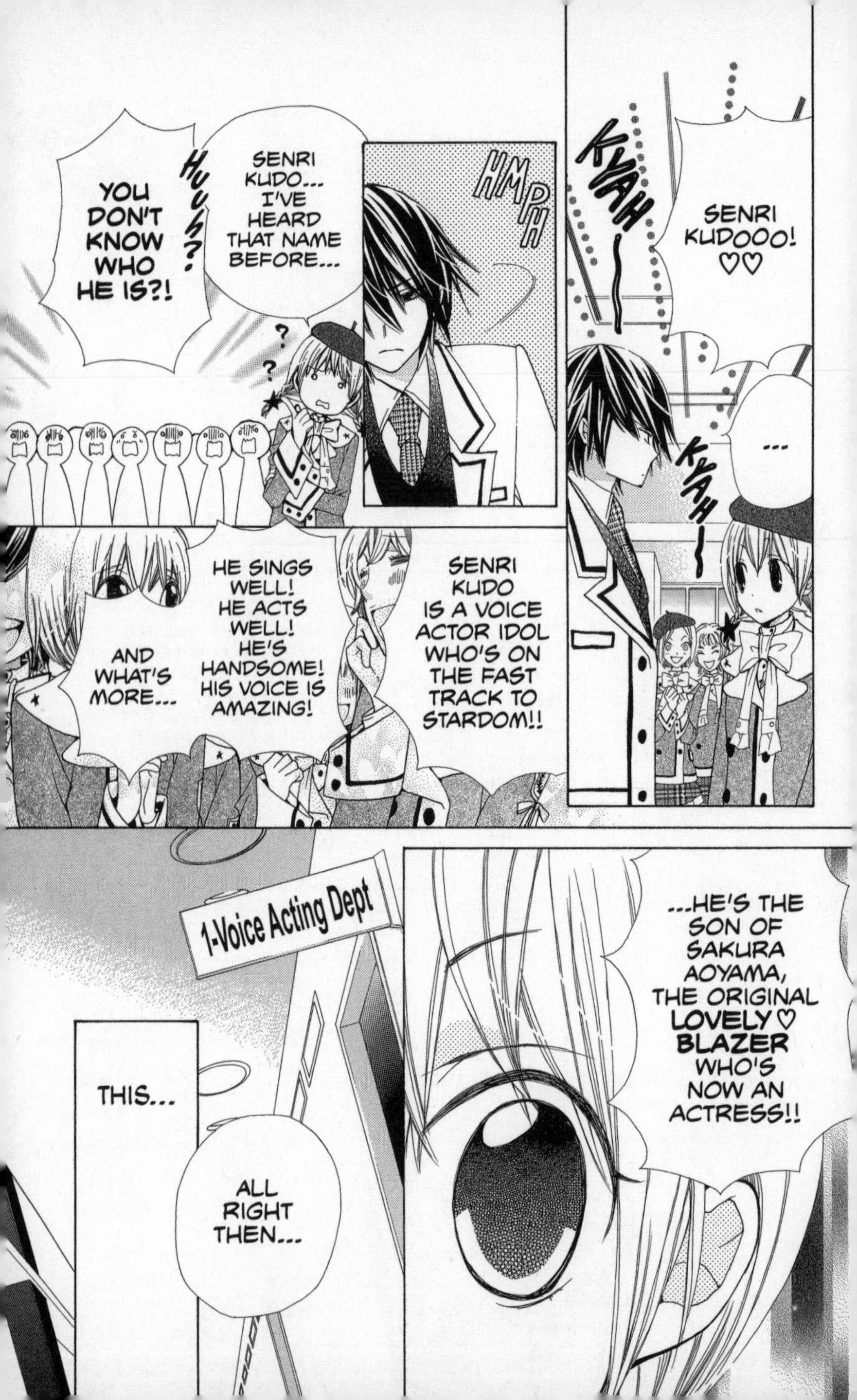
SENRI KUDOOO! ♡♡
KYAH~~
KYAH~~
...
HMPH
SENRI KUDO... I'VE HEARD THAT NAME BEFORE...
HUUH?
??
YOU DON'T KNOW WHO HE IS?!
SENRI KUDO IS A VOICE ACTOR IDOL WHO'S ON THE FAST TRACK TO STARDOM!!
HE SINGS WELL! HE ACTS WELL! HE'S HANDSOME! HIS VOICE IS AMAZING!
AND WHAT'S MORE...
...HE'S THE SON OF SAKURA AOYAMA, THE ORIGINAL LOVELY♡ BLAZER WHO'S NOW AN ACTRESS!!
1-Voice Acting Dept
THIS...
ALL RIGHT THEN...

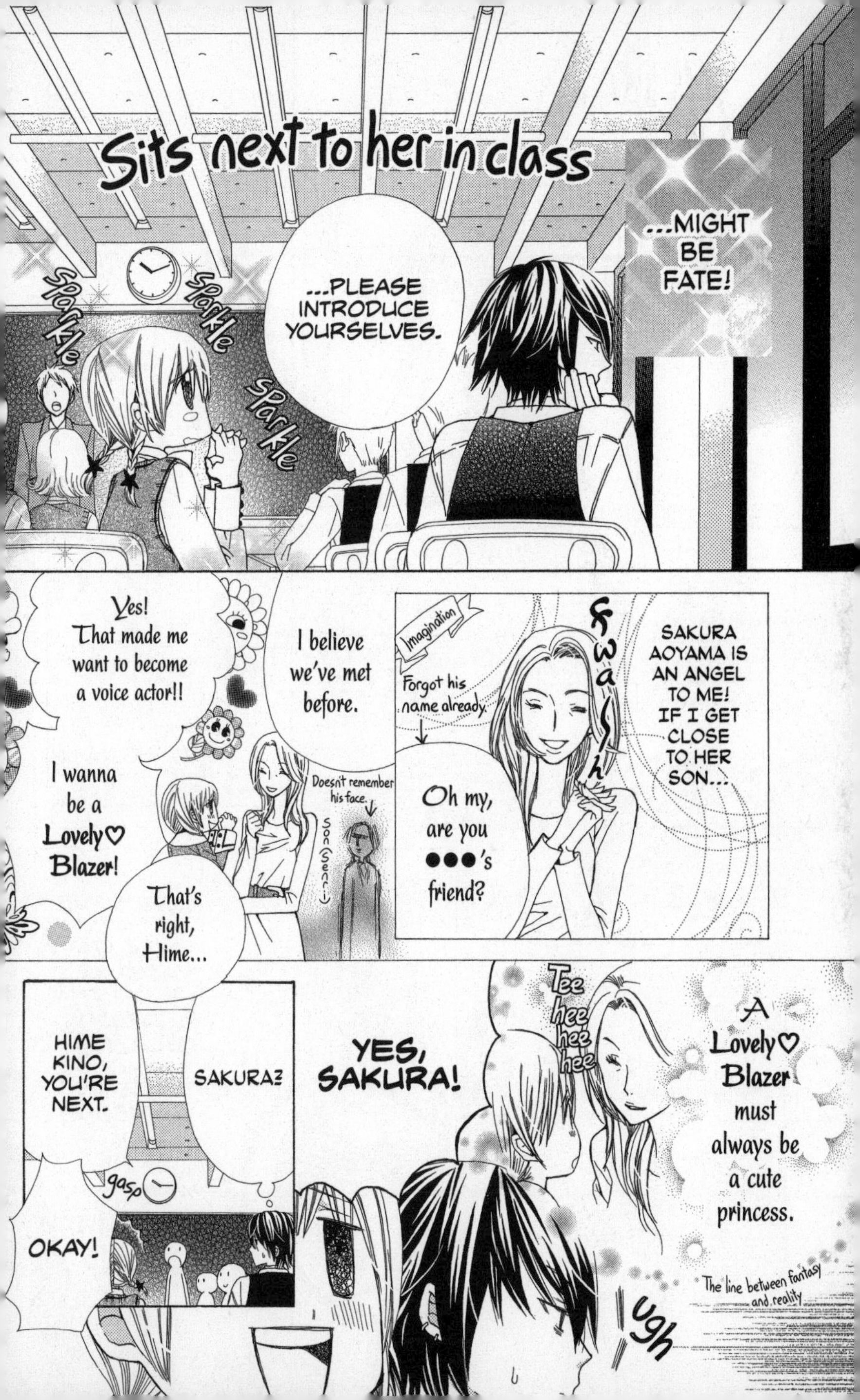
Sits next to her in class
...MIGHT BE FATE!
...PLEASE INTRODUCE YOURSELVES.
Sparkle
Sparkle
Sparkle
SAKURA AOYAMA IS AN ANGEL TO ME! IF I GET CLOSE TO HER SON...
fwash
Imagination
Forgot his name already.
Oh my, are you ●●●'s friend?
I believe we've met before.
Doesn't remember his face.
Son (Senri)
Yes! That made me want to become a voice actor!!
I wanna be a Lovely♡ Blazer!
That's right, Hime...
A Lovely♡ Blazer must always be a cute princess.
Tee hee hee hee
YES, SAKURA!
The line between fantasy and reality
ugh
SAKURA?
HIME KINO, YOU'RE NEXT.
gasp
OKAY!

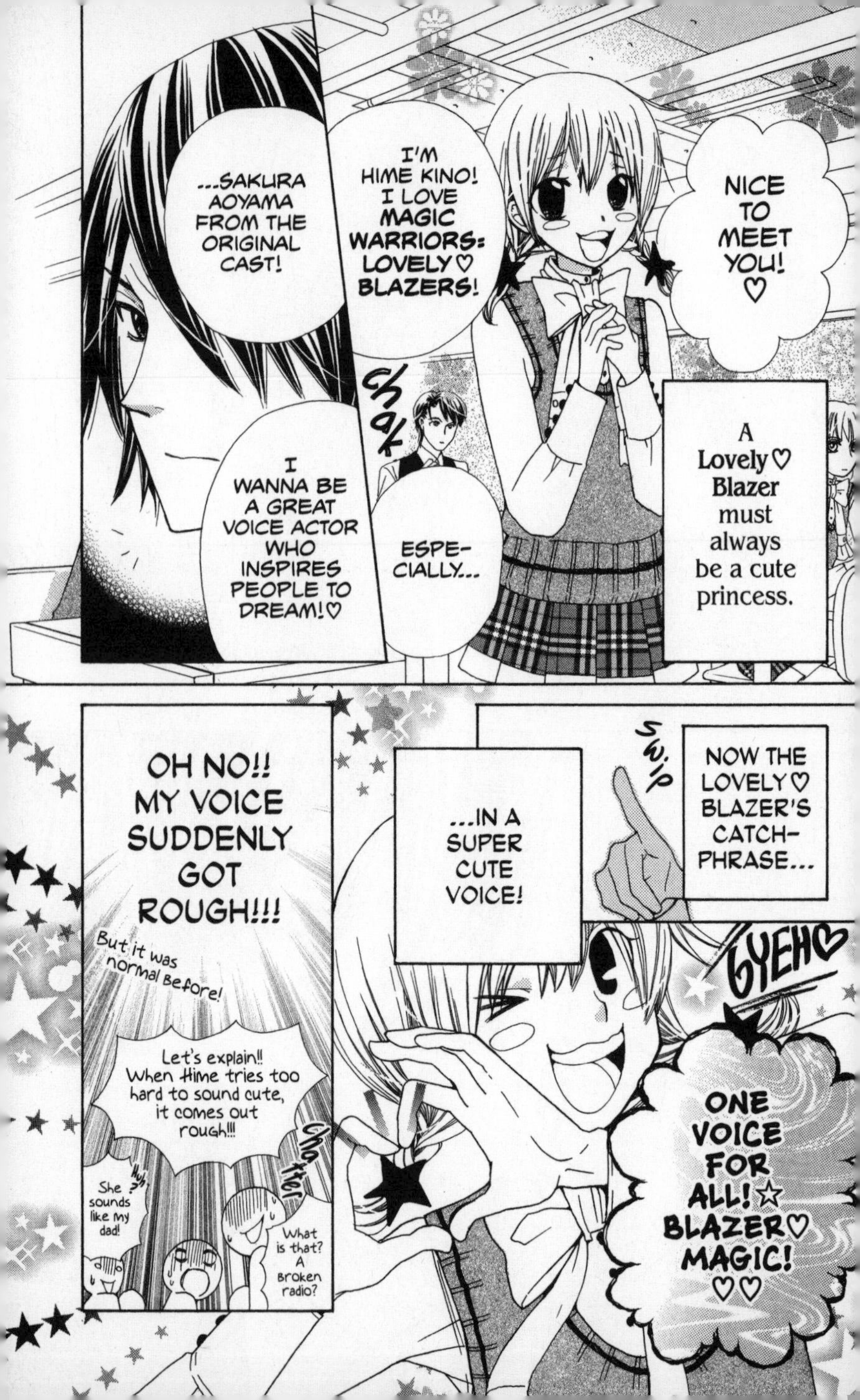
NICE TO MEET YOU! ♡
I'M HIME KINO! I LOVE MAGIC WARRIORS: LOVELY♡ BLAZERS!
...SAKURA AOYAMA FROM THE ORIGINAL CAST!
A Lovely♡ Blazer must always be a cute princess.
chak
ESPE-CIALLY...
I WANNA BE A GREAT VOICE ACTOR WHO INSPIRES PEOPLE TO DREAM!♡
swip
NOW THE LOVELY♡ BLAZER'S CATCH-PHRASE...
...IN A SUPER CUTE VOICE!
GYEH♡
ONE VOICE FOR ALL!☆ BLAZER♡ MAGIC! ♡♡
OH NO!! MY VOICE SUDDENLY GOT ROUGH!!!
But it was normal before!
Let's explain!! When Hime tries too hard to sound cute, it comes out rough!!!
Chatter
Huh?
She sounds like my dad!
What is that? A broken radio?

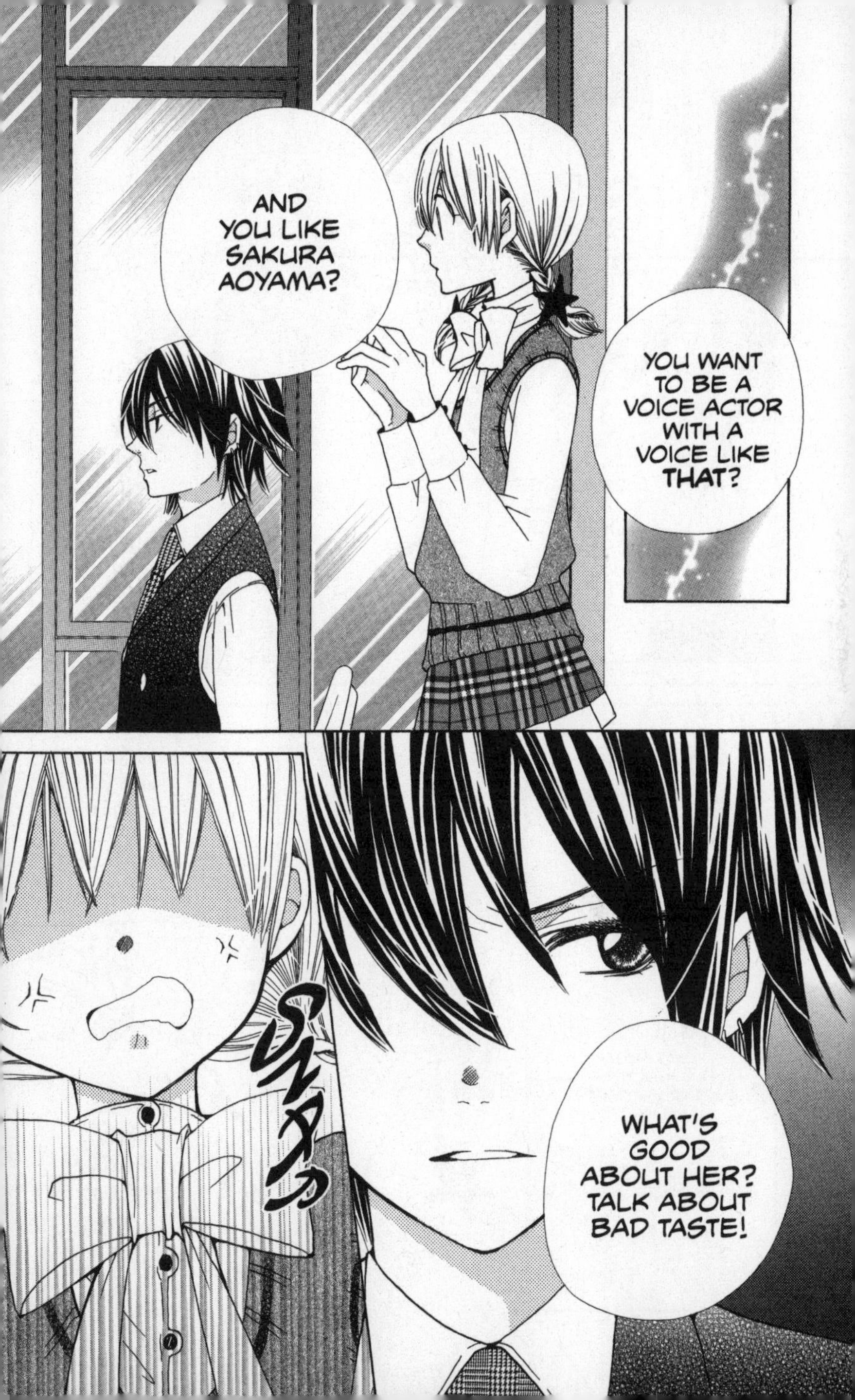

YOU WANT TO BE A VOICE ACTOR WITH A VOICE LIKE THAT?
AND YOU LIKE SAKURA AOYAMA?
WHAT'S GOOD ABOUT HER? TALK ABOUT BAD TASTE!
SNAP

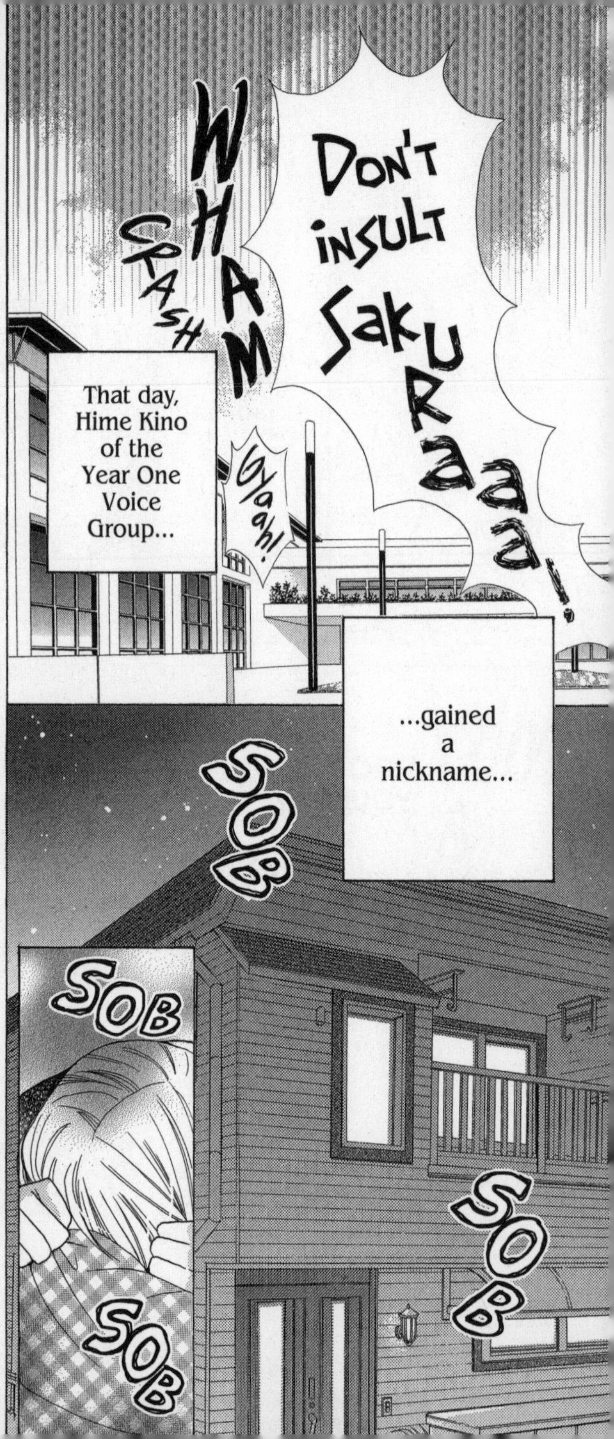
Don't insult Sakuraaaa!
WHAM
CRASH
That day, Hime Kino of the Year One Voice Group...
Gyaah!
...gained a nickname...
SOB
SOB
SOB
SOB

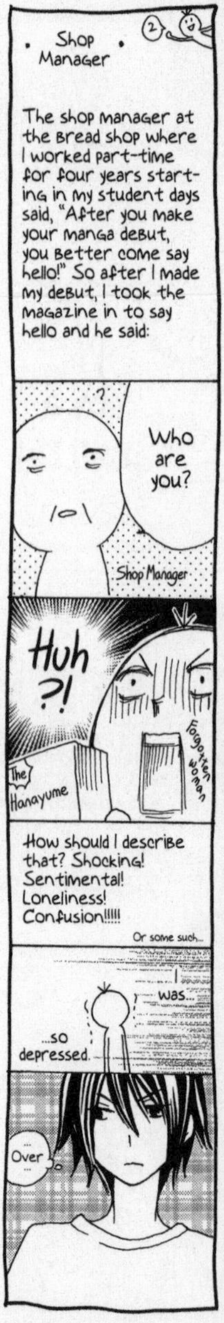
• Shop Manager •
2
The shop manager at the bread shop where I worked part-time for four years starting in my student days said, "After you make your manga debut, you better come say hello!" So after I made my debut, I took the magazine in to say hello and he said:
?
Who are you?
Shop Manager
Huh?!
The Hanayume
Forgotten woman
How should I describe that? Shocking! Sentimental! Loneliness! Confusion!!!!!
Or some such...
I was...
...so depressed.
...Over...

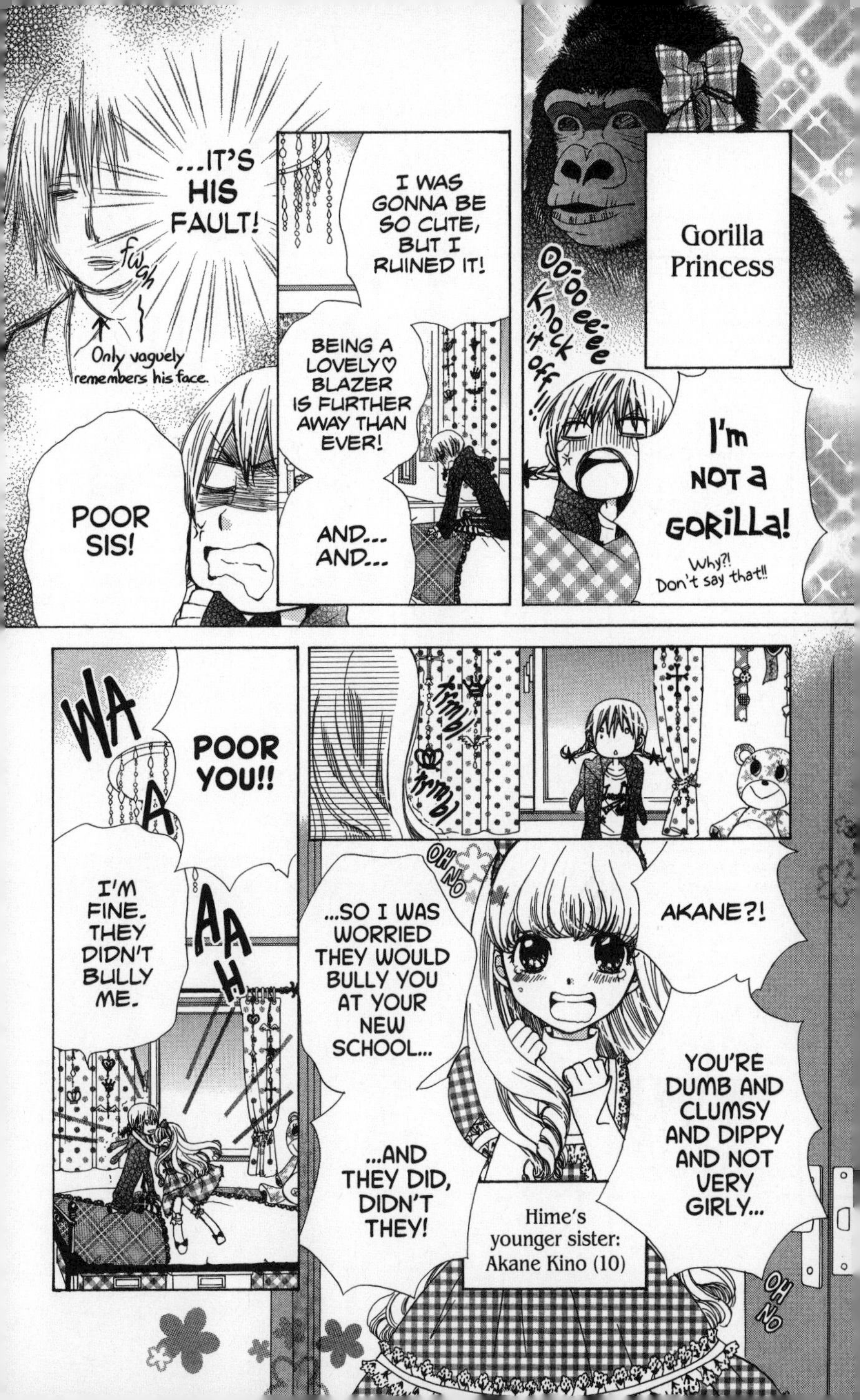
Gorilla Princess
Oo-oo eeeee
Knock it off!!!
I'm NOT a GORILLA!
Why?! Don't say that!!
I WAS GONNA BE SO CUTE, BUT I RUINED IT!
BEING A LOVELY♡ BLAZER IS FURTHER AWAY THAN EVER!
AND... AND...
...IT'S HIS FAULT!
fwah
Only vaguely remembers his face.
POOR SIS!
AKANE?!
OH NO
YOU'RE DUMB AND CLUMSY AND DIPPY AND NOT VERY GIRLY...
...SO I WAS WORRIED THEY WOULD BULLY YOU AT YOUR NEW SCHOOL...
...AND THEY DID, DIDN'T THEY!
Hime's younger sister: Akane Kino (10)
OH NO
WAAAH
POOR YOU!!
I'M FINE. THEY DIDN'T BULLY ME.

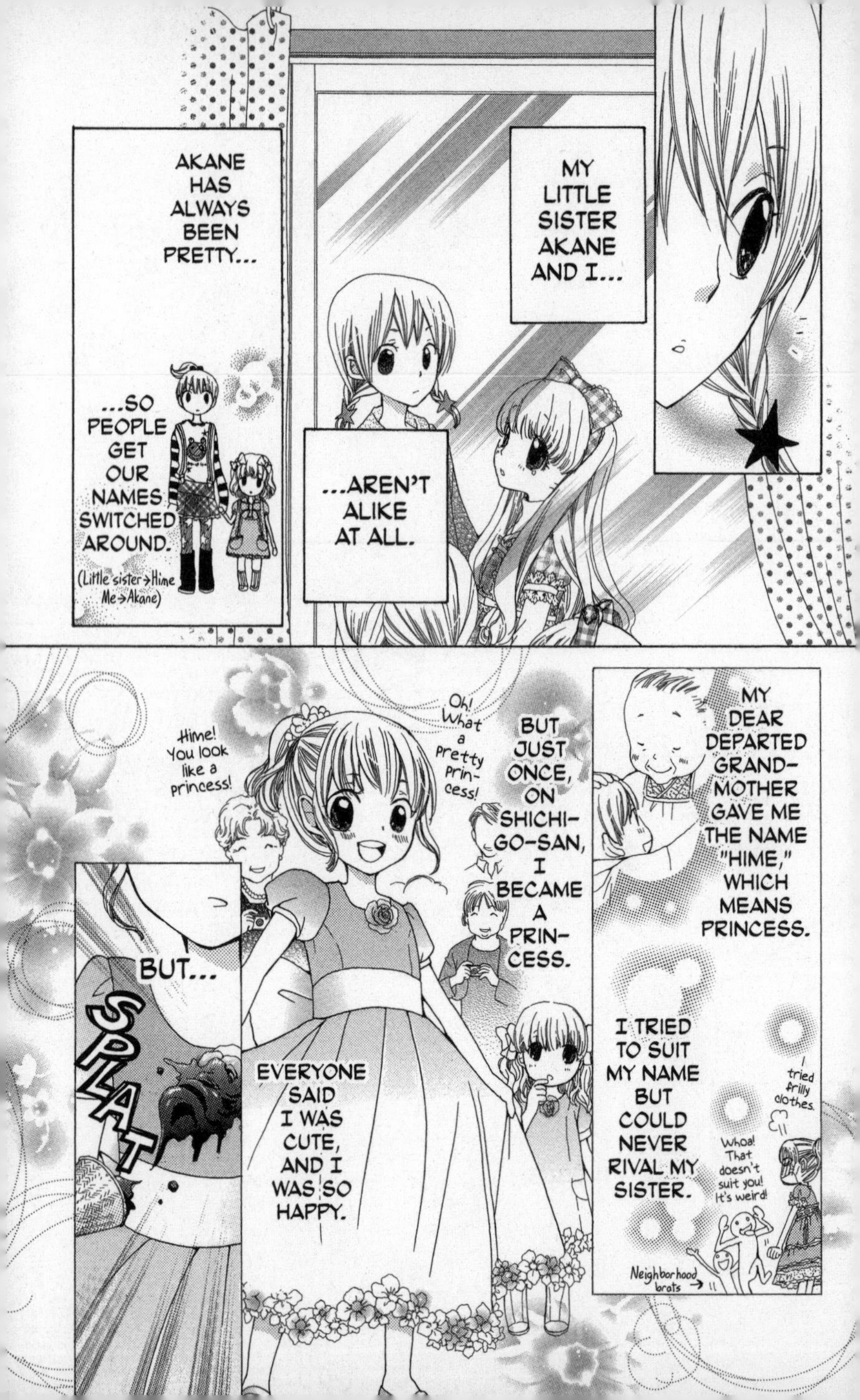
MY LITTLE SISTER AKANE AND I...
...AREN'T ALIKE AT ALL.
AKANE HAS ALWAYS BEEN PRETTY...
...SO PEOPLE GET OUR NAMES SWITCHED AROUND.
(Little sister→Hime Me→Akane)
MY DEAR DEPARTED GRANDMOTHER GAVE ME THE NAME "HIME," WHICH MEANS PRINCESS.
I TRIED TO SUIT MY NAME BUT COULD NEVER RIVAL MY SISTER.
I tried frilly clothes.
Whoa! That doesn't suit you! It's weird!
Neighborhood brats
BUT JUST ONCE, ON SHICHI-GO-SAN, I BECAME A PRINCESS.
Oh! What a pretty princess!
Hime! You look like a princess!
EVERYONE SAID I WAS CUTE, AND I WAS SO HAPPY.
BUT...
SPLAT

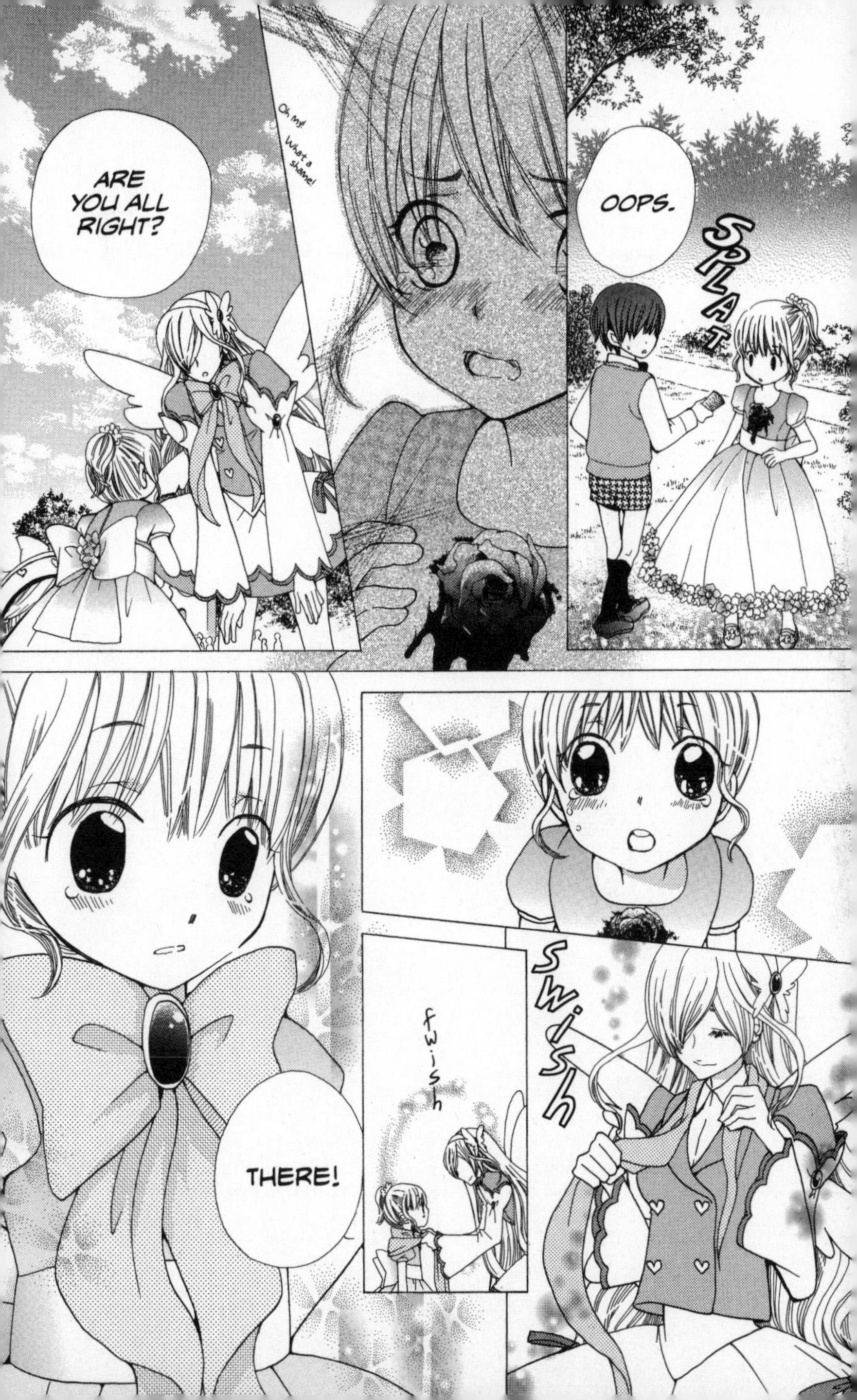
OOPS.
SPLAT
Oh my! What a shame!
ARE YOU ALL RIGHT?
SWISH
fwish
THERE!

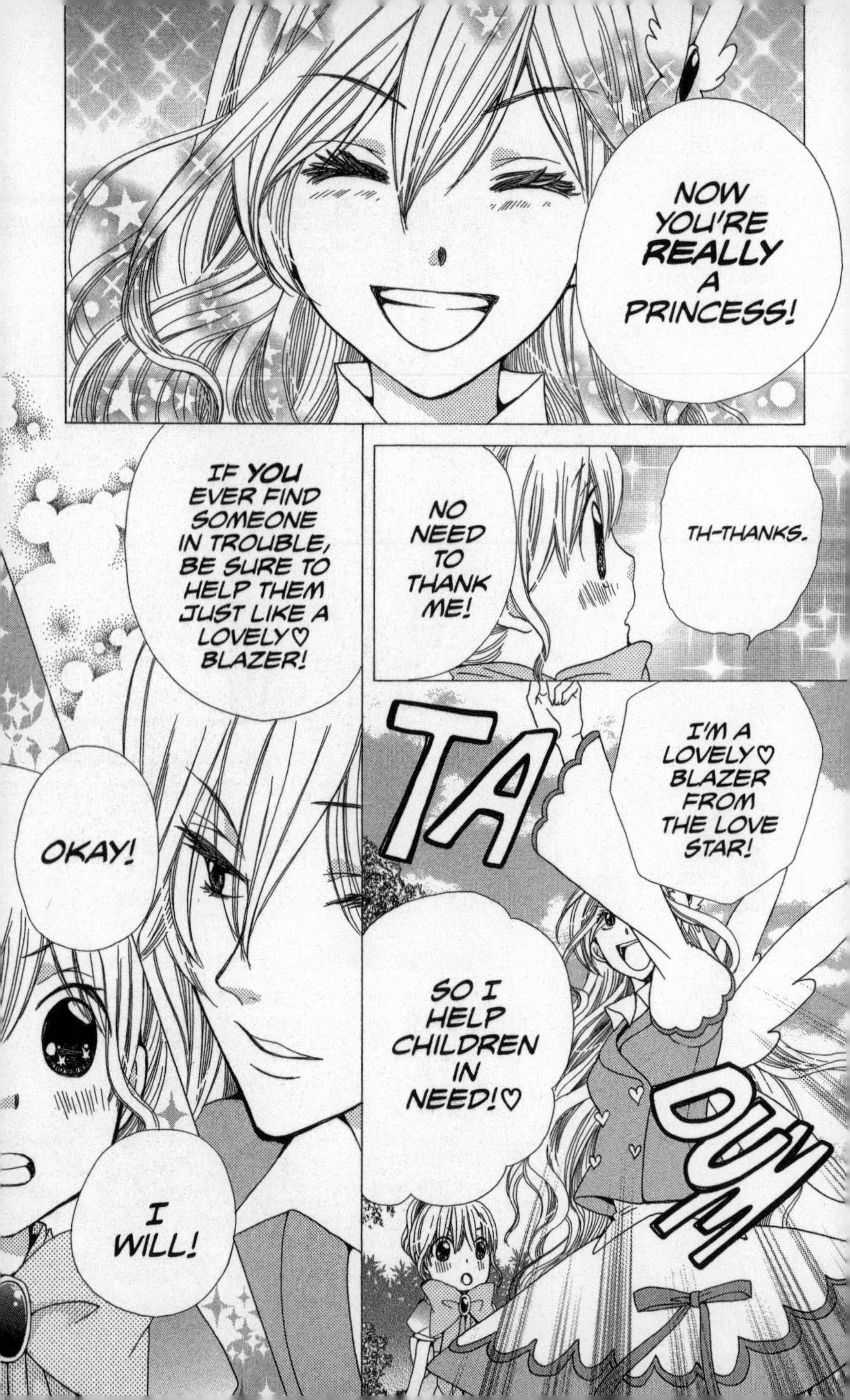
NOW YOU'RE REALLY A PRINCESS!
TH-THANKS.
NO NEED TO THANK ME!
TA
I'M A LOVELY♡ BLAZER FROM THE LOVE STAR!
SO I HELP CHILDREN IN NEED!♡
DUM
IF YOU EVER FIND SOMEONE IN TROUBLE, BE SURE TO HELP THEM JUST LIKE A LOVELY♡ BLAZER!
OKAY!
I WILL!

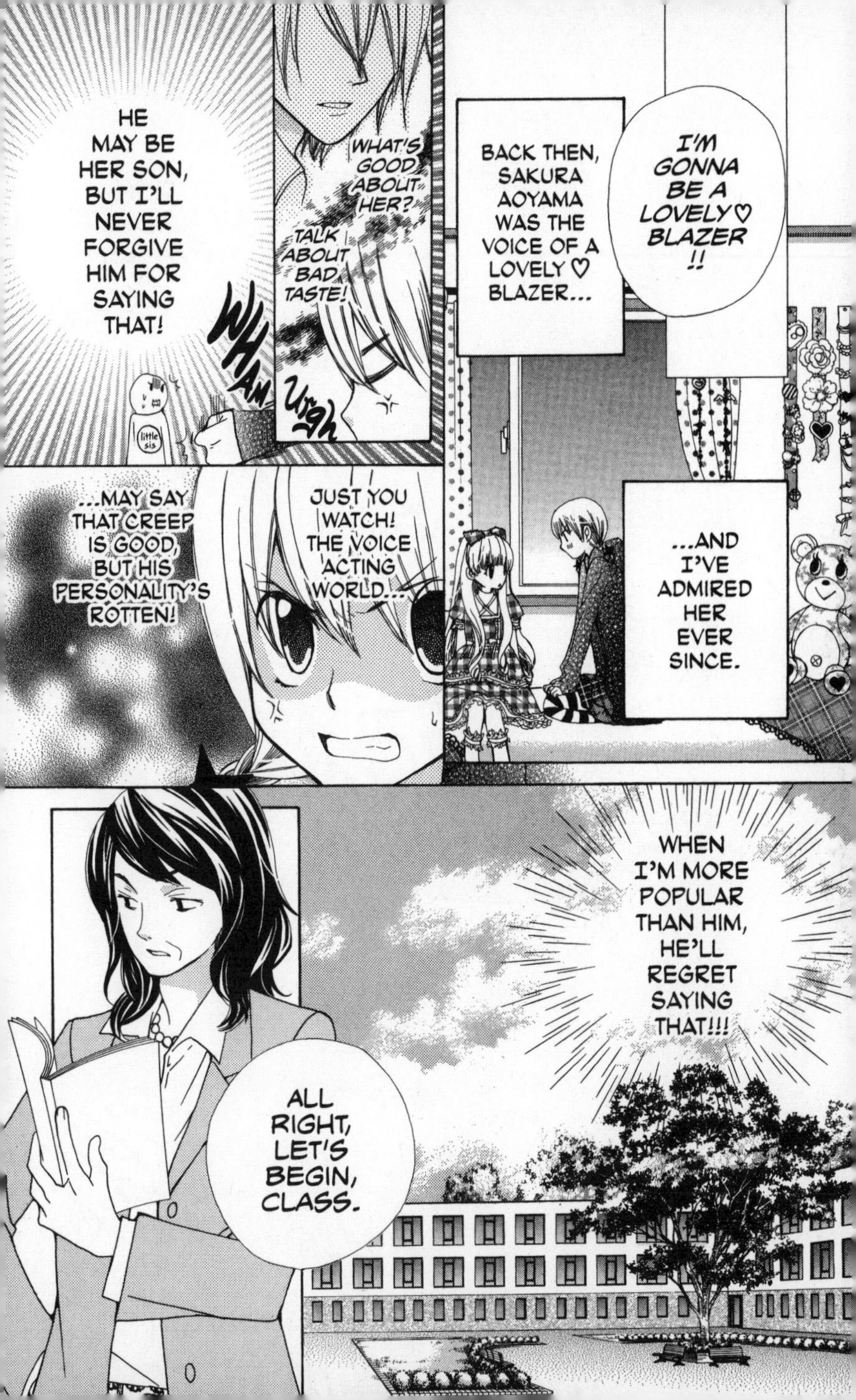
I'M GONNA BE A LOVELY♡ BLAZER!!
BACK THEN, SAKURA AOYAMA WAS THE VOICE OF A LOVELY♡ BLAZER...
...AND I'VE ADMIRED HER EVER SINCE.
WHAT'S GOOD ABOUT HER?
TALK ABOUT BAD TASTE!
Urgh
HE MAY BE HER SON, BUT I'LL NEVER FORGIVE HIM FOR SAYING THAT!
WHAM
little sis
JUST YOU WATCH! THE VOICE ACTING WORLD...
...MAY SAY THAT CREEP IS GOOD, BUT HIS PERSONALITY'S ROTTEN!
WHEN I'M MORE POPULAR THAN HIM, HE'LL REGRET SAYING THAT!!!
ALL RIGHT, LET'S BEGIN, CLASS.

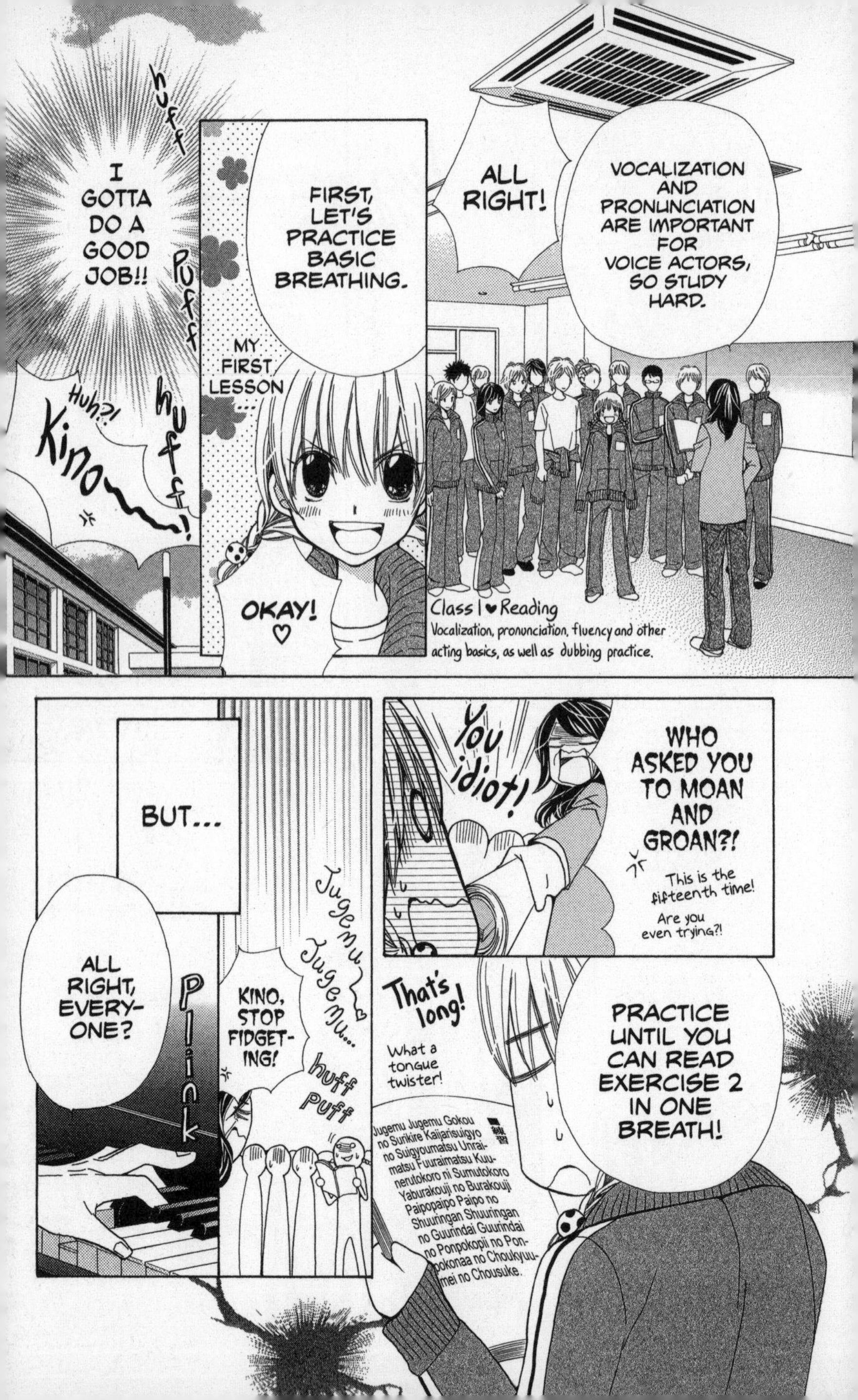
VOCALIZATION AND PRONUNCIATION ARE IMPORTANT FOR VOICE ACTORS, SO STUDY HARD.
ALL RIGHT!
FIRST, LET'S PRACTICE BASIC BREATHING.
MY FIRST LESSON...
OKAY! ♡
Class 1 ♥ Reading
Vocalization, pronunciation, fluency and other acting basics, as well as dubbing practice.
I GOTTA DO A GOOD JOB!!
huff puff huff huff!
Huh?!
Kino~!
WHO ASKED YOU TO MOAN AND GROAN?!
You idiot!
This is the fifteenth time!
Are you even trying?!
PRACTICE UNTIL YOU CAN READ EXERCISE 2 IN ONE BREATH!
That's long!
What a tongue twister!
Jugemu Jugemu Gokou no Surikire Kaijarisuigyo no Suigyoumatsu Unraimatsu Fuuraimatsu Kuunerutokoro ni Sumutokoro Yaburakouji no Burakouji Paipopaipo Paipo no Shuuringan Shuuringan no Guurindai Guurindai no Ponpokopii no Ponpokonaa no Choukyuumei no Chousuke.
Jugemu Jugemu...
KINO, STOP FIDGETING!
huff puff
BUT...
ALL RIGHT, EVERYONE?
Plink

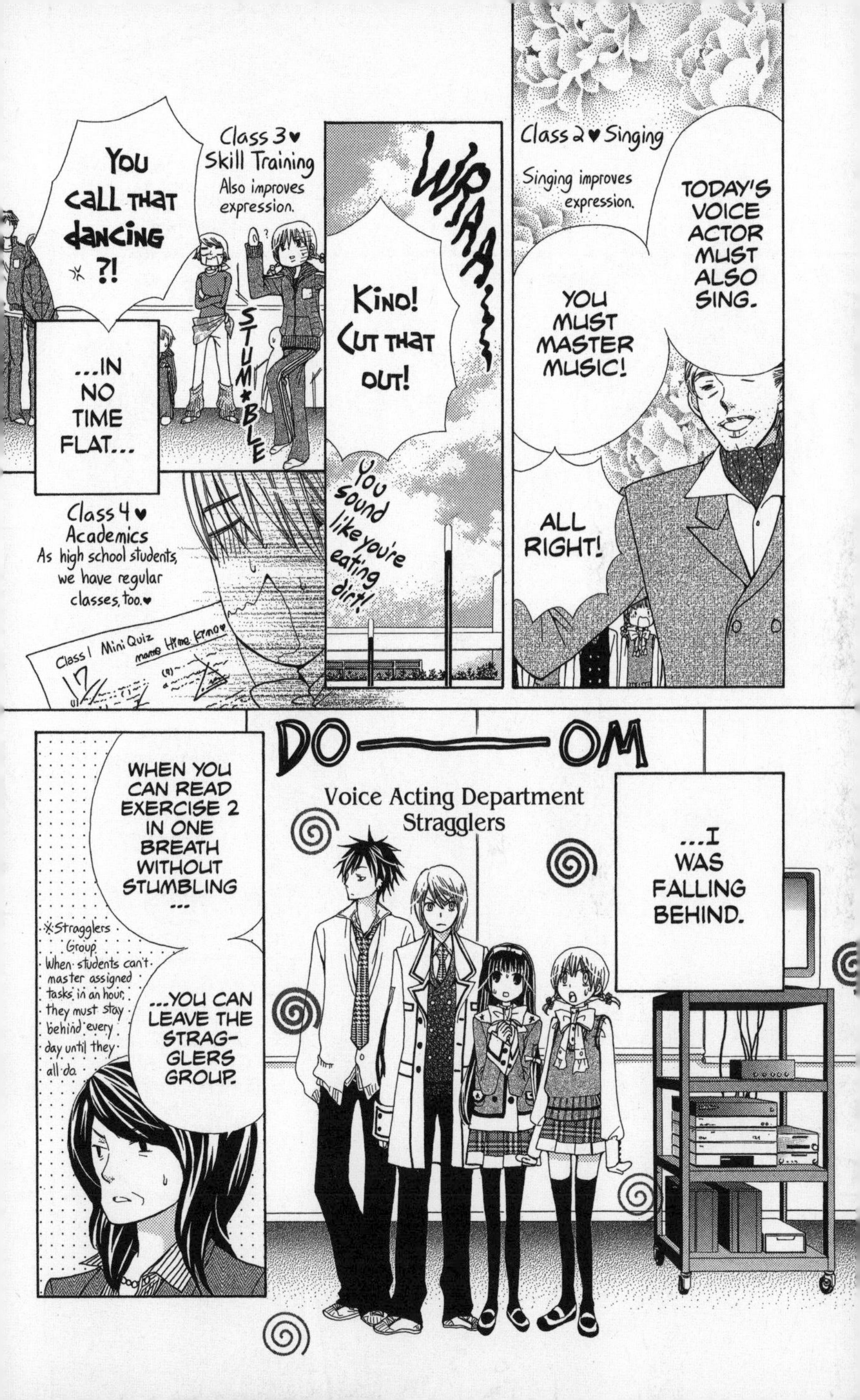
Class 2 ♥ Singing
Singing improves expression.
TODAY'S VOICE ACTOR MUST ALSO SING.
YOU MUST MASTER MUSIC!
ALL RIGHT!
WRAA~~
Kino! Cut that out!
You sound like you're eating dirt!
Class 3 ♥ Skill Training
Also improves expression.
YOU CALL THAT DANCING ※ ?!
STUMBLE
...IN NO TIME FLAT...
Class 4 ♥ Academics
As high school students, we have regular classes, too. ♥
Class 1 Mini Quiz
name Hime Kino ♥
17
DO———OM
Voice Acting Department Stragglers
...I WAS FALLING BEHIND.
WHEN YOU CAN READ EXERCISE 2 IN ONE BREATH WITHOUT STUMBLING...
※Stragglers Group
When students can't master assigned tasks in an hour, they must stay behind every day until they all do.
...YOU CAN LEAVE THE STRAG-GLERS GROUP.

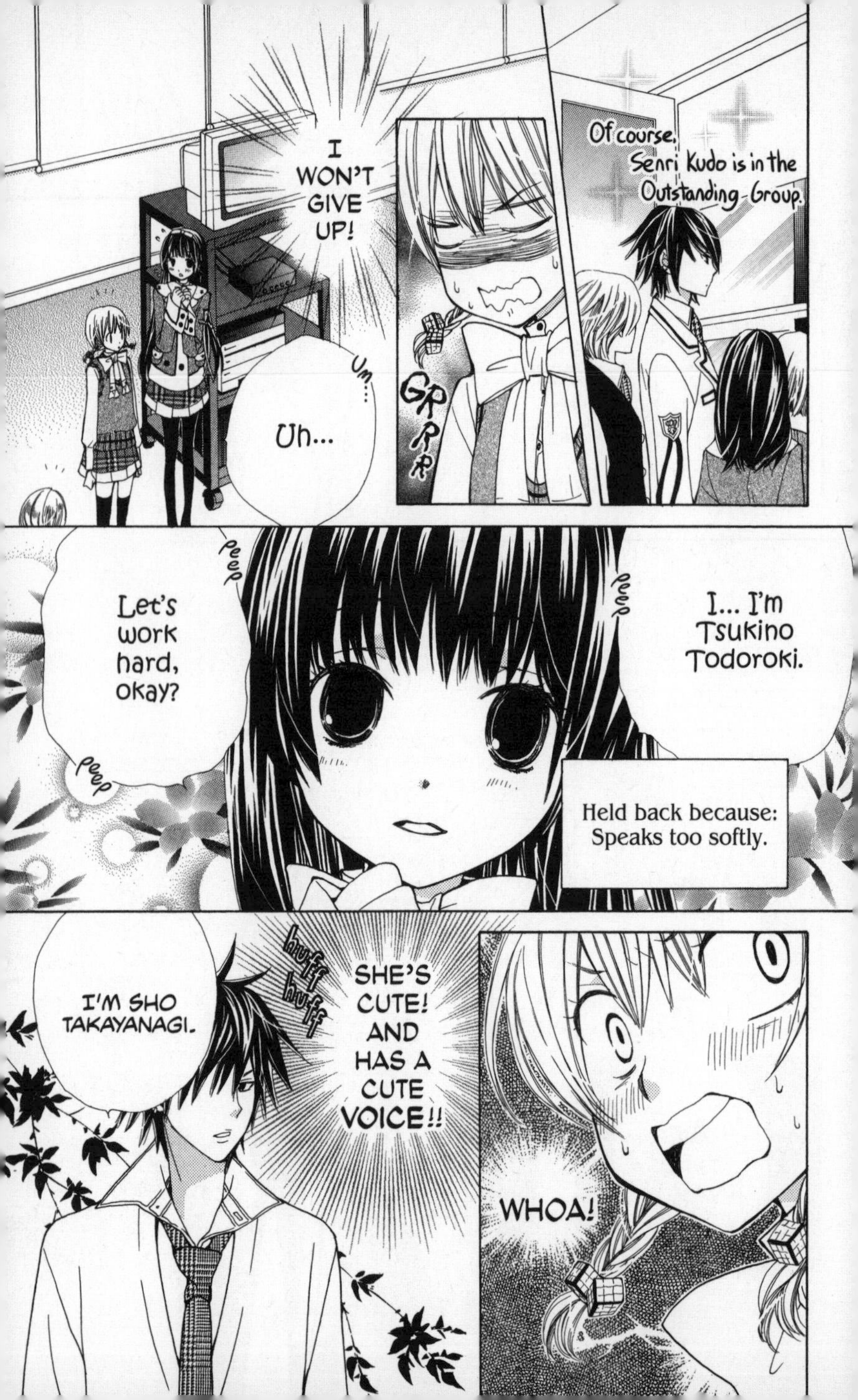

Of course, Senri Kudo is in the Outstanding-Group.
GRRR
I WON'T GIVE UP!
Um...
Uh...
peep
I... I'm Tsukino Todoroki.
Held back because: Speaks too softly.
peep
Let's work hard, okay?
peep
WHOA!
SHE'S CUTE! AND HAS A CUTE VOICE!!
huff huff
I'M SHO TAKAYANAGI.

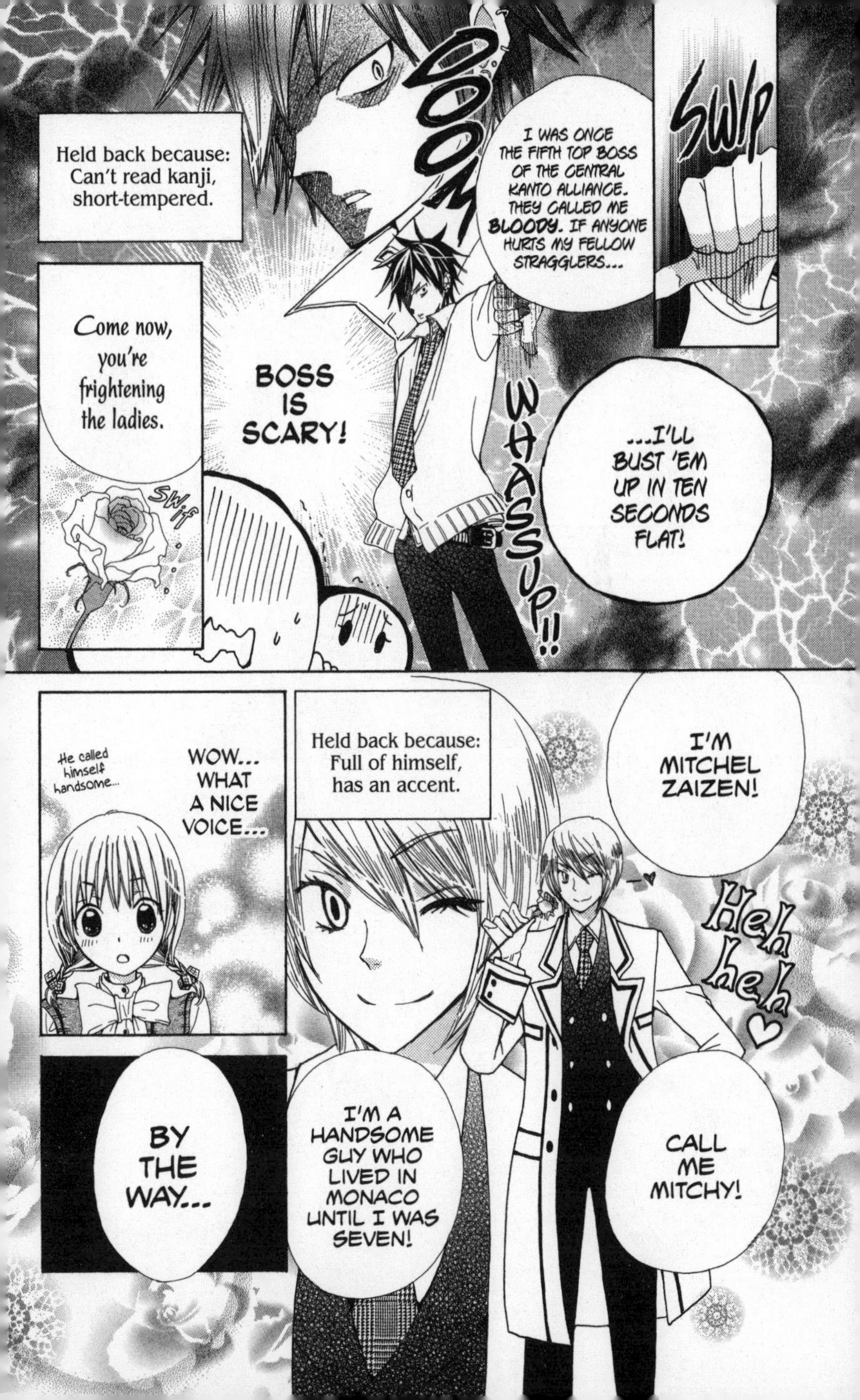
SWIP
DOOOM
I WAS ONCE THE FIFTH TOP BOSS OF THE CENTRAL KANTO ALLIANCE. THEY CALLED ME BLOODY. IF ANYONE HURTS MY FELLOW STRAGGLERS...
Held back because: Can't read kanji, short-tempered.
...I'LL BUST 'EM UP IN TEN SECONDS FLAT!
WHASSUP!!
BOSS IS SCARY!
Come now, you're frightening the ladies.
SWif
I'M MITCHEL ZAIZEN!
Held back because: Full of himself, has an accent.
Heh heh ♥
CALL ME MITCHY!
BY THE WAY...
I'M A HANDSOME GUY WHO LIVED IN MONACO UNTIL I WAS SEVEN!
WOW... WHAT A NICE VOICE...
He called himself handsome...

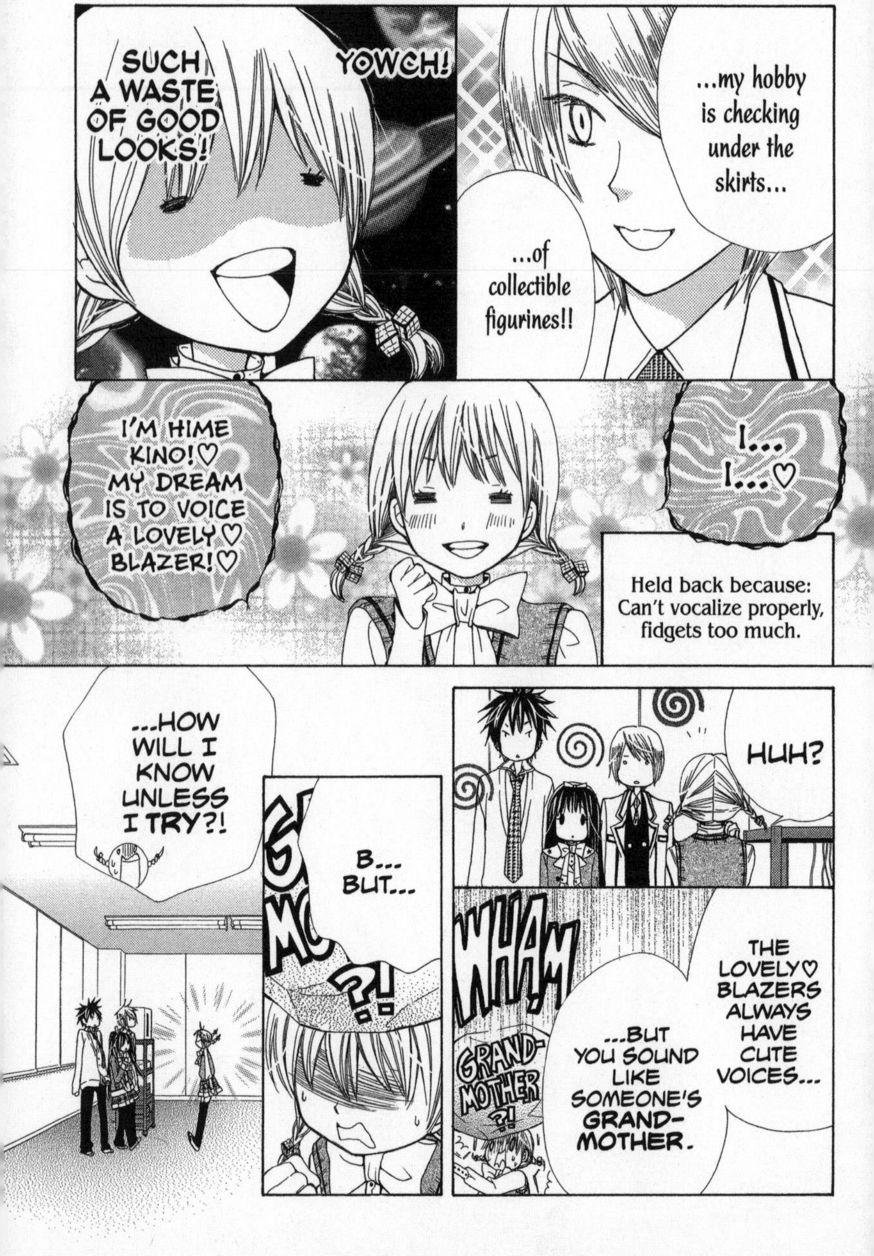
...my hobby is checking under the skirts...
...of collectible figurines!!
YOWCH!
SUCH A WASTE OF GOOD LOOKS!
I... I...♡
I'M HIME KINO!♡ MY DREAM IS TO VOICE A LOVELY♡ BLAZER!♡
Held back because: Can't vocalize properly, fidgets too much.
HUH?
WHAM
THE LOVELY♡ BLAZERS ALWAYS HAVE CUTE VOICES...
...BUT YOU SOUND LIKE SOMEONE'S GRANDMOTHER.
GRANDMOTHER?!
?!
B... BUT...
...HOW WILL I KNOW UNLESS I TRY?!

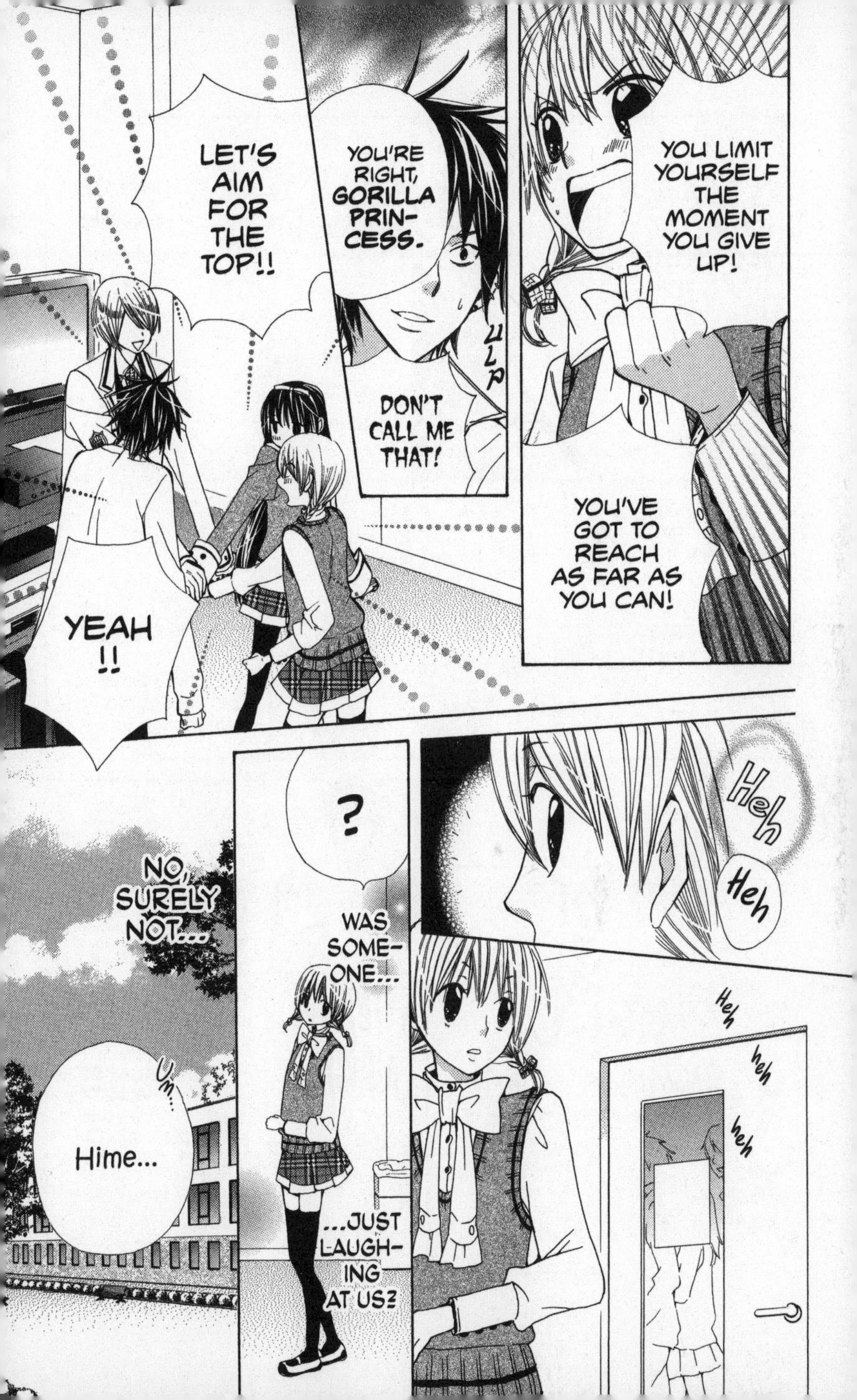
YOU LIMIT YOURSELF THE MOMENT YOU GIVE UP!
YOU'VE GOT TO REACH AS FAR AS YOU CAN!
YOU'RE RIGHT, GORILLA PRIN-CESS.
ULP
DON'T CALL ME THAT!
LET'S AIM FOR THE TOP!!
YEAH!!
Heh
Heh
Heh
heh
heh
?
WAS SOME-ONE...
...JUST LAUGH-ING AT US?
NO, SURELY NOT...
Um...
Hime...

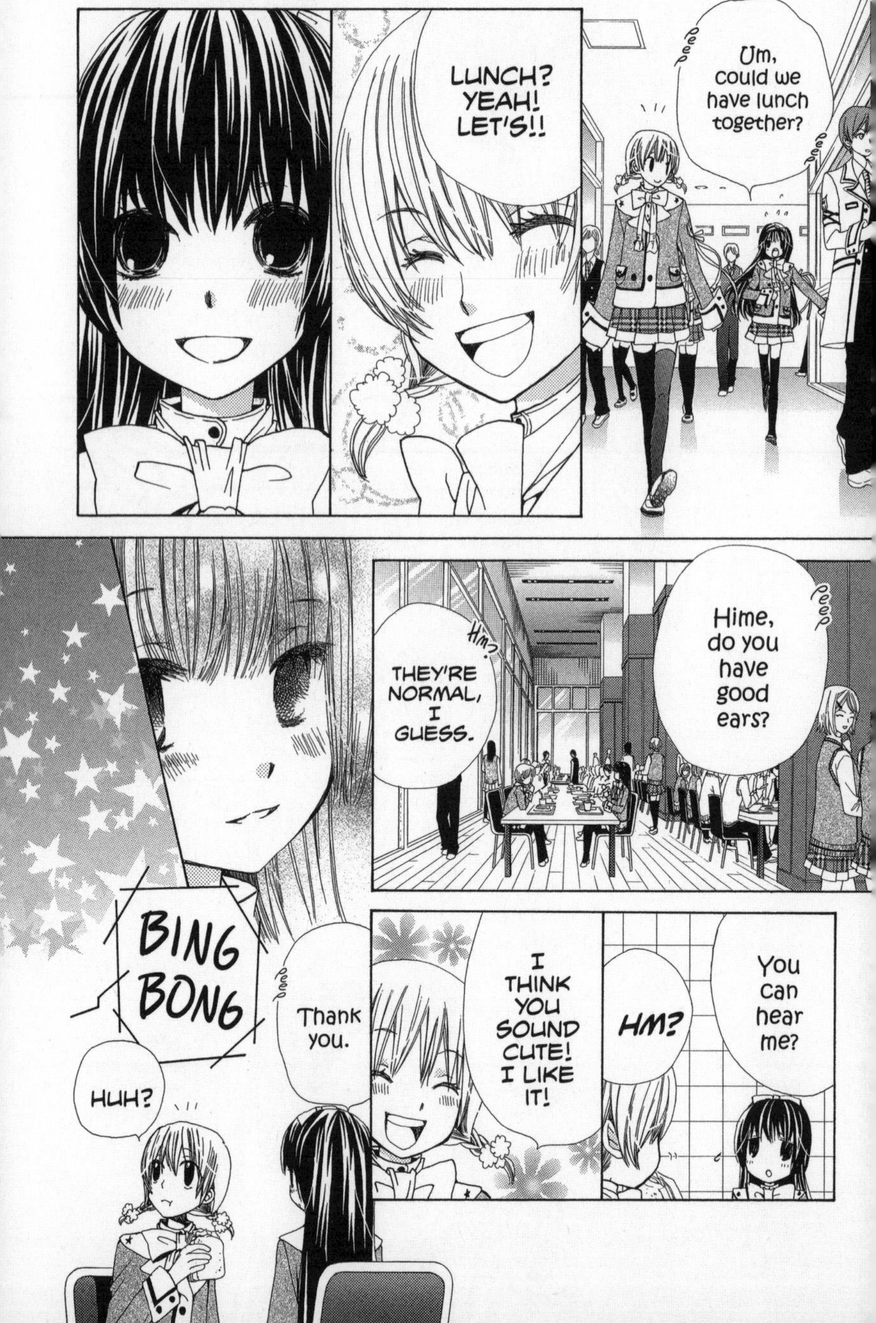
Um, could we have lunch together?
LUNCH? YEAH! LET'S!!
Hime, do you have good ears?
Hm?
THEY'RE NORMAL, I GUESS.
You can hear me?
HM?
I THINK YOU SOUND CUTE! I LIKE IT!
BING BONG
Thank you.
HUH?

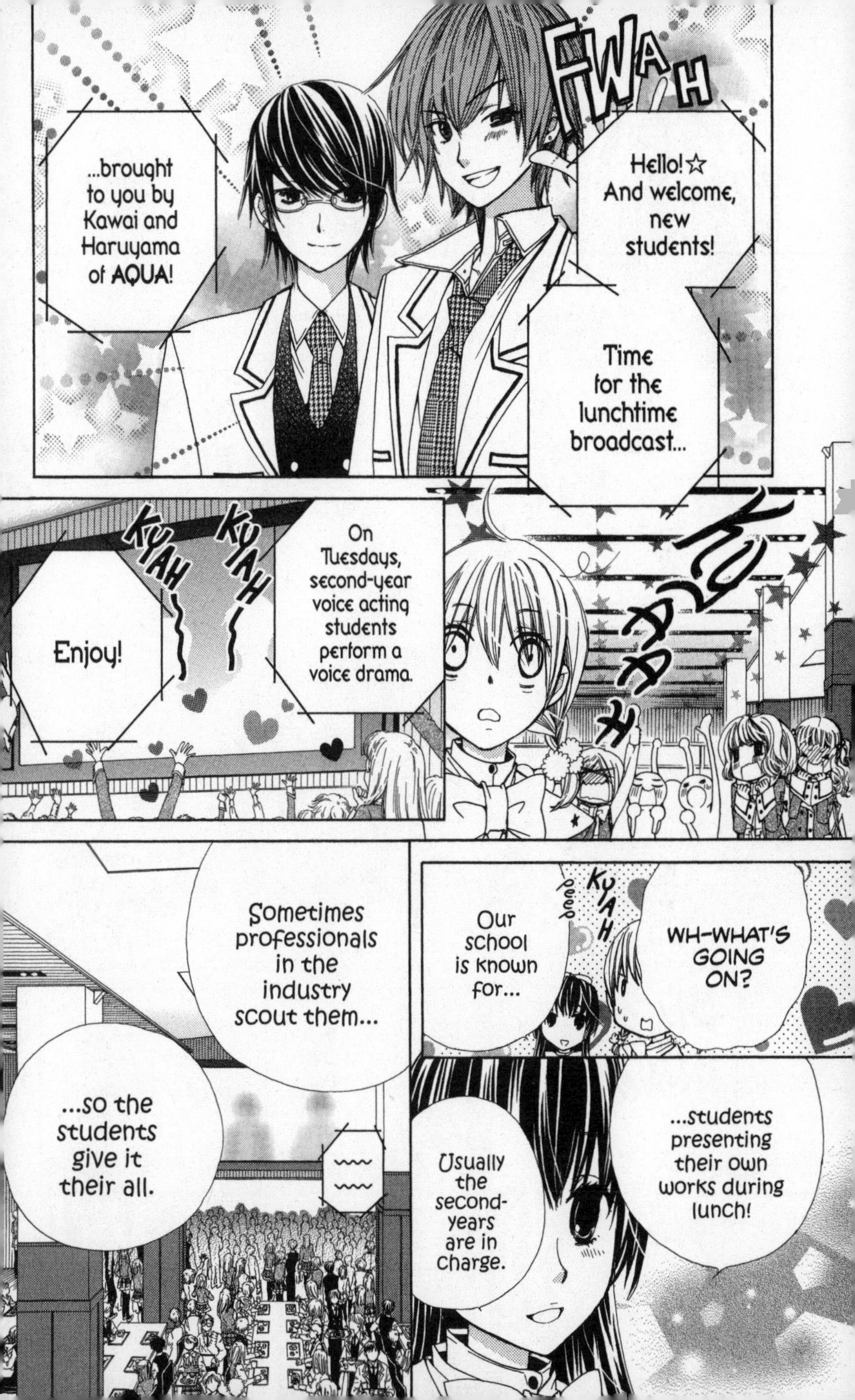
FWAH
Hello!☆ And welcome, new students!
Time for the lunchtime broadcast...
...brought to you by Kawai and Haruyama of AQUA!
KYAAAH
On Tuesdays, second-year voice acting students perform a voice drama.
KYAH
KYAH
Enjoy!
WH-WHAT'S GOING ON?
KYAH
Our school is known for...
...students presenting their own works during lunch!
Usually the second-years are in charge.
Sometimes professionals in the industry scout them...
~~~ ~~~
...so the students give it their all.
~~~

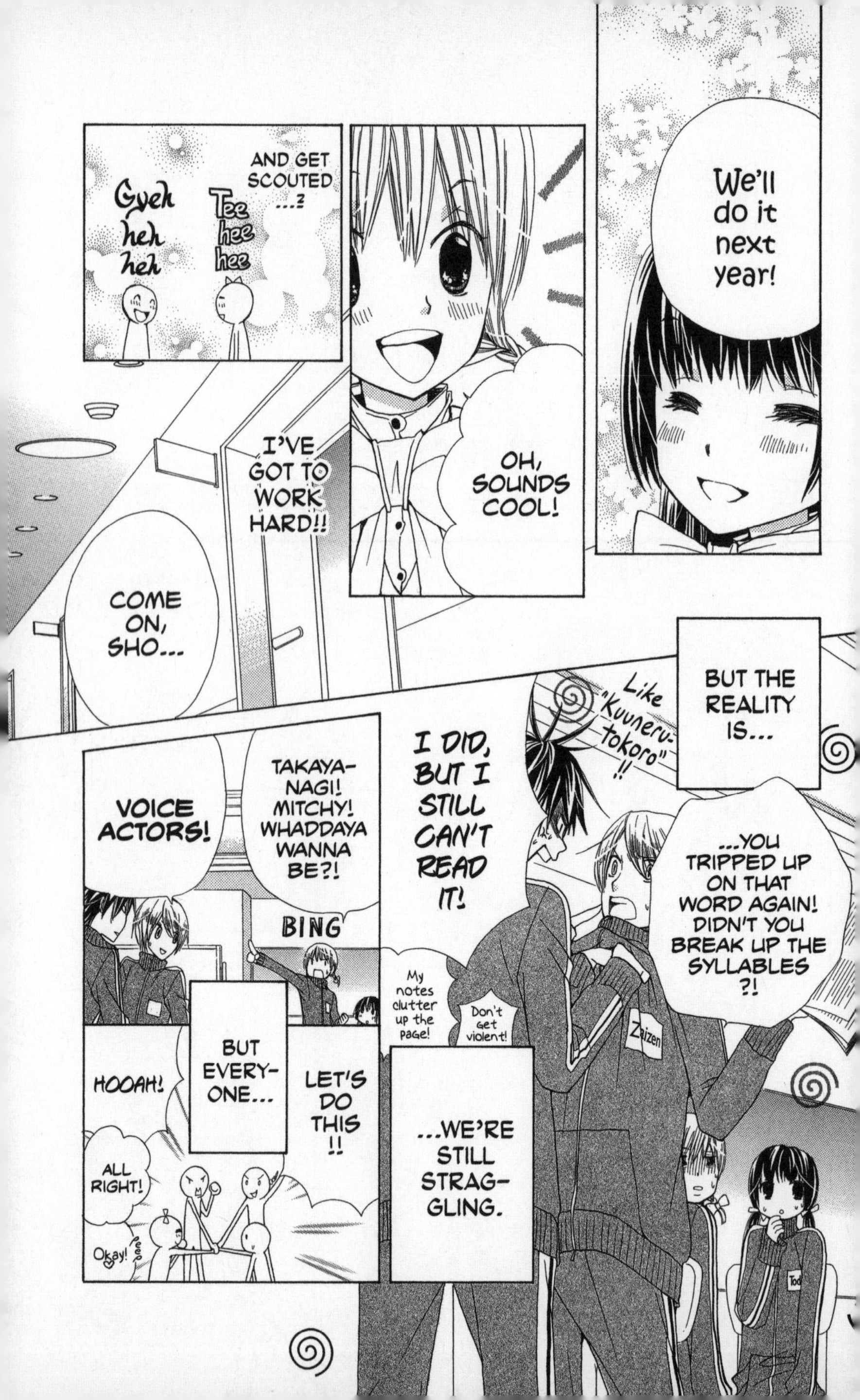
We'll do it next year!
OH, SOUNDS COOL!
I'VE GOT TO WORK HARD!!
AND GET SCOUTED ...?
Tee hee hee
Gyeh heh heh
COME ON, SHO...
BUT THE REALITY IS...
...YOU TRIPPED UP ON THAT WORD AGAIN! DIDN'T YOU BREAK UP THE SYLLABLES?!
Like "Kuuneru-tokoro"!!
I DID, BUT I STILL CAN'T READ IT!
My notes clutter up the page!
Don't get violent!
...WE'RE STILL STRAG-GLING.
TAKAYA-NAGI! MITCHY! WHADDAYA WANNA BE?!
VOICE ACTORS!
BING
LET'S DO THIS!!
BUT EVERY-ONE...
HOOAH!
ALL RIGHT!
Okay!
Peep

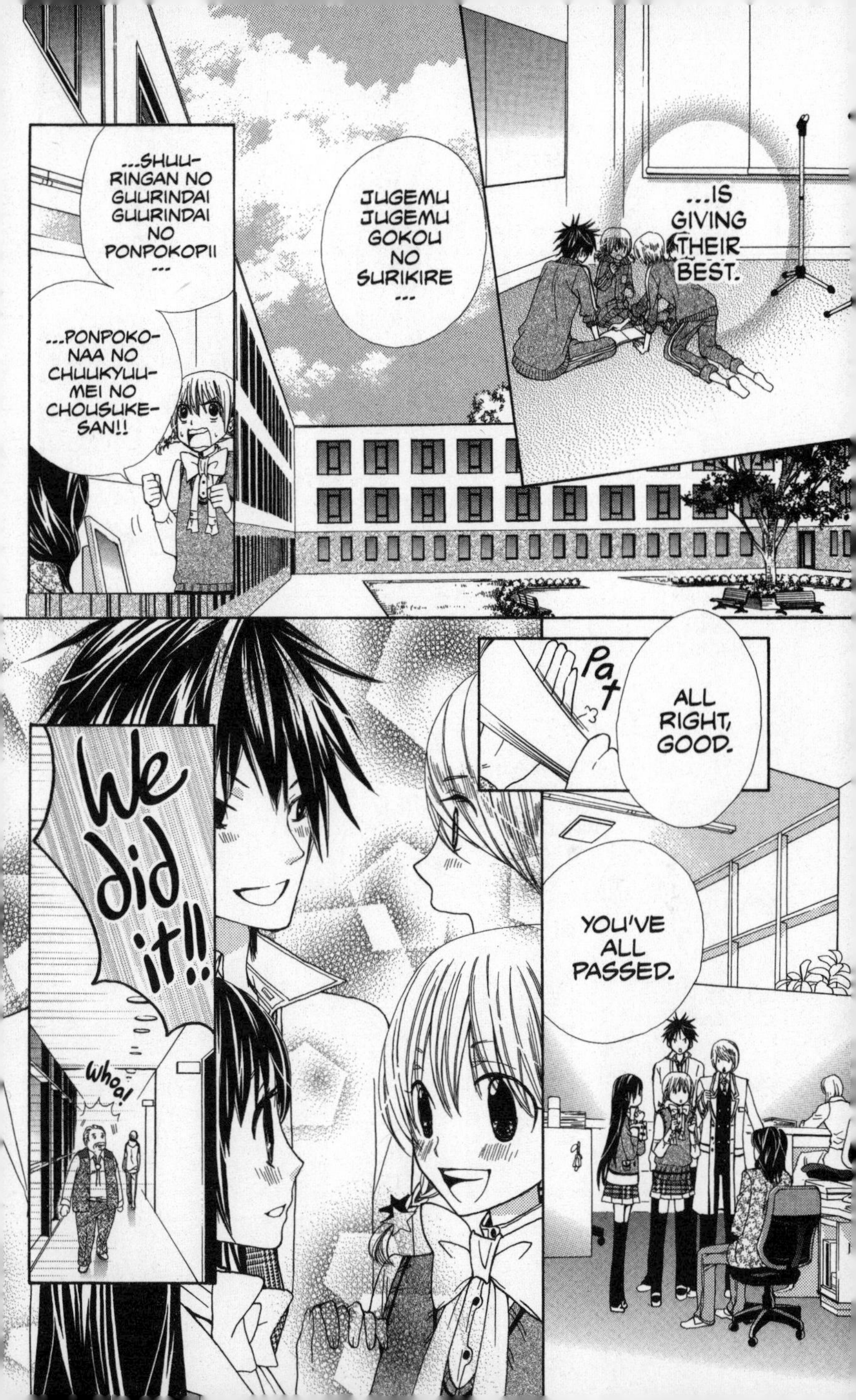
...IS GIVING THEIR BEST.
JUGEMU JUGEMU GOKOU NO SURIKIRE ---
...SHUU-RINGAN NO GUURINDAI GUURINDAI NO PONPOKOPII ---
...PONPOKO-NAA NO CHUUKYUU-MEI NO CHOUSUKE-SAN!!
ALL RIGHT, GOOD.
Pat
YOU'VE ALL PASSED.
We did it!!
Whoa!

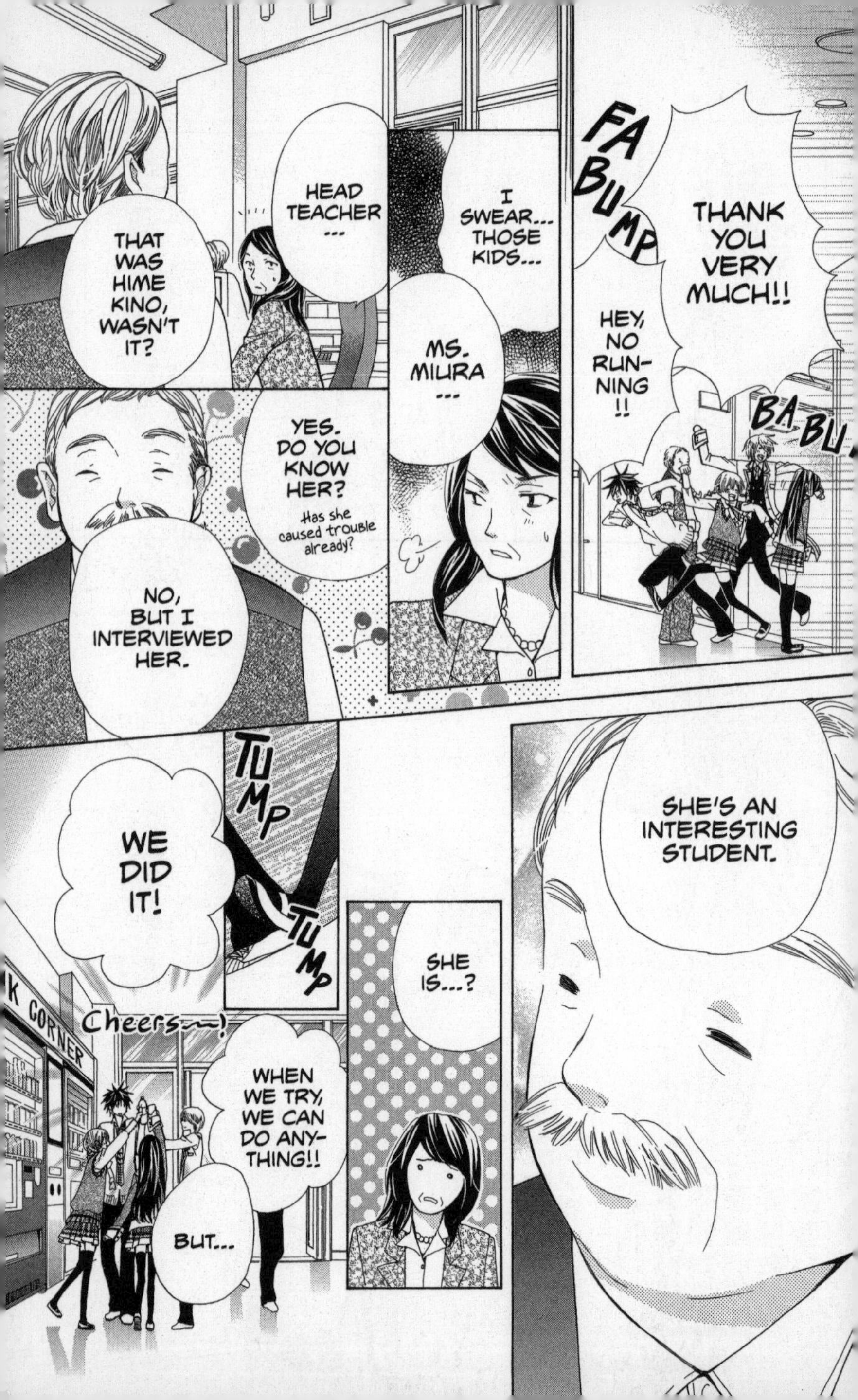
THANK YOU VERY MUCH!!
FABUMP
HEY, NO RUN-NING!!
BABU
I SWEAR... THOSE KIDS...
MS. MIURA...
HEAD TEACHER...
THAT WAS HIME KINO, WASN'T IT?
YES. DO YOU KNOW HER?
Has she caused trouble already?
NO, BUT I INTERVIEWED HER.
SHE'S AN INTERESTING STUDENT.
SHE IS...?
TUMP
TUMP
WE DID IT!
K CORNER
Cheers~!
WHEN WE TRY, WE CAN DO ANY-THING!!
BUT...

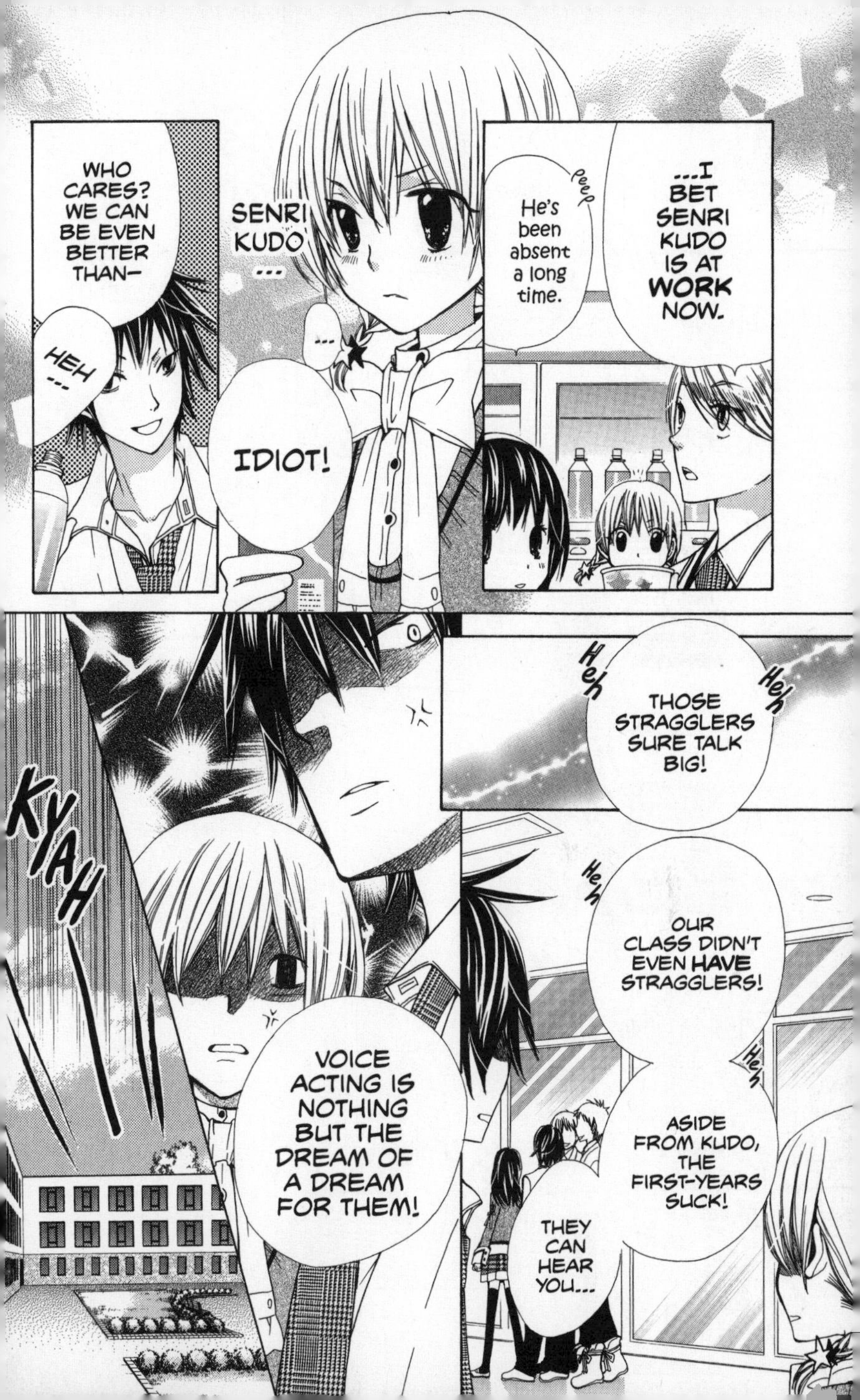
...I BET SENRI KUDO IS AT WORK NOW.
Peep
He's been absent a long time.
SENRI KUDO ...
...
IDIOT!
WHO CARES? WE CAN BE EVEN BETTER THAN—
HEH ...
Heh Heh
THOSE STRAGGLERS SURE TALK BIG!
Heh
OUR CLASS DIDN'T EVEN HAVE STRAGGLERS!
Heh
ASIDE FROM KUDO, THE FIRST-YEARS SUCK!
THEY CAN HEAR YOU...
KYAH
VOICE ACTING IS NOTHING BUT THE DREAM OF A DREAM FOR THEM!

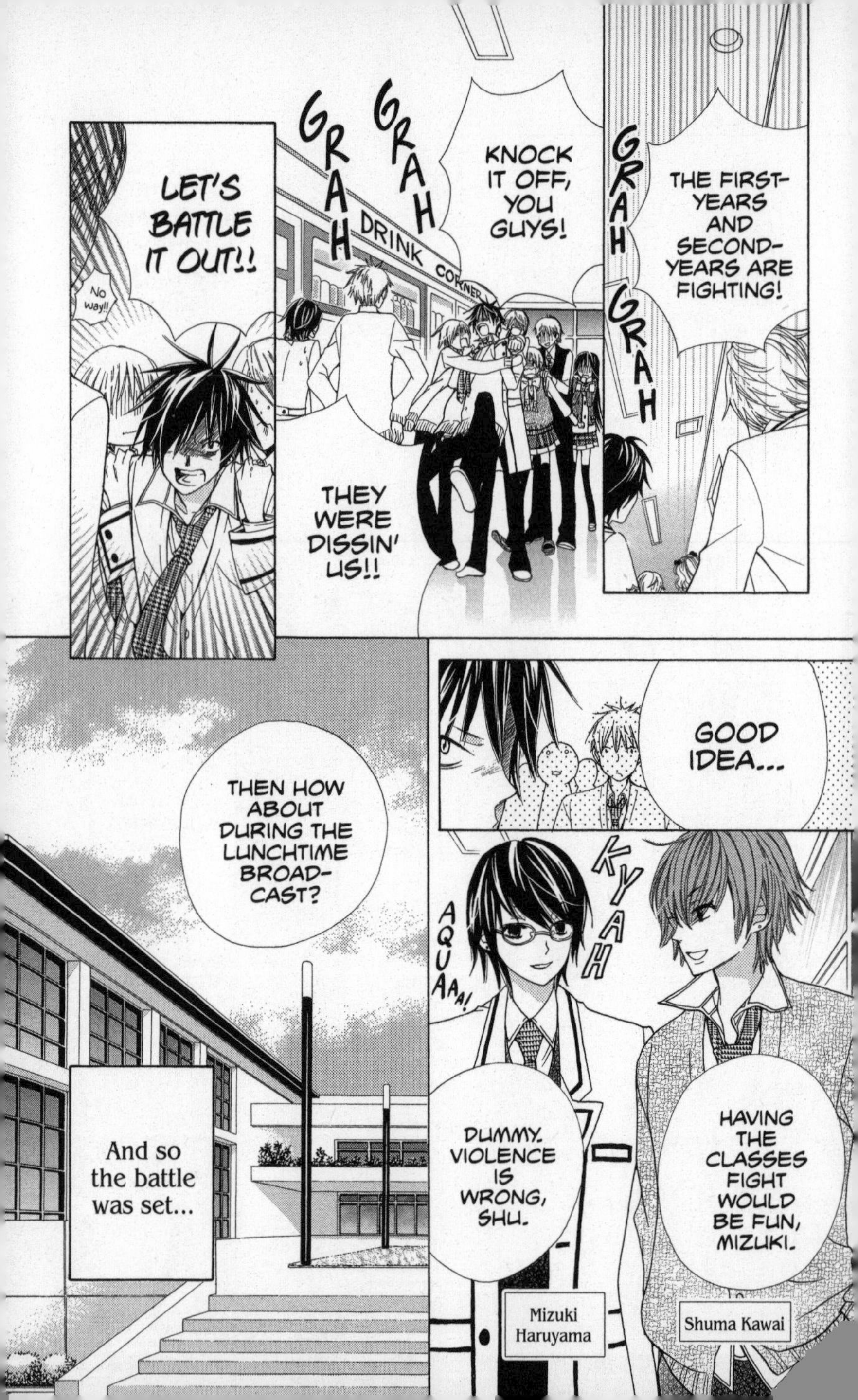
THE FIRST-YEARS AND SECOND-YEARS ARE FIGHTING!
GRAH GRAH
KNOCK IT OFF, YOU GUYS!
GRAH GRAH
DRINK CORNER
THEY WERE DISSIN' US!!
LET'S BATTLE IT OUT!!
No way!!
GOOD IDEA...
KYAH
AQUAAAA!
HAVING THE CLASSES FIGHT WOULD BE FUN, MIZUKI.
DUMMY. VIOLENCE IS WRONG, SHU.
Shuma Kawai
Mizuki Haruyama
THEN HOW ABOUT DURING THE LUNCHTIME BROADCAST?
And so the battle was set...

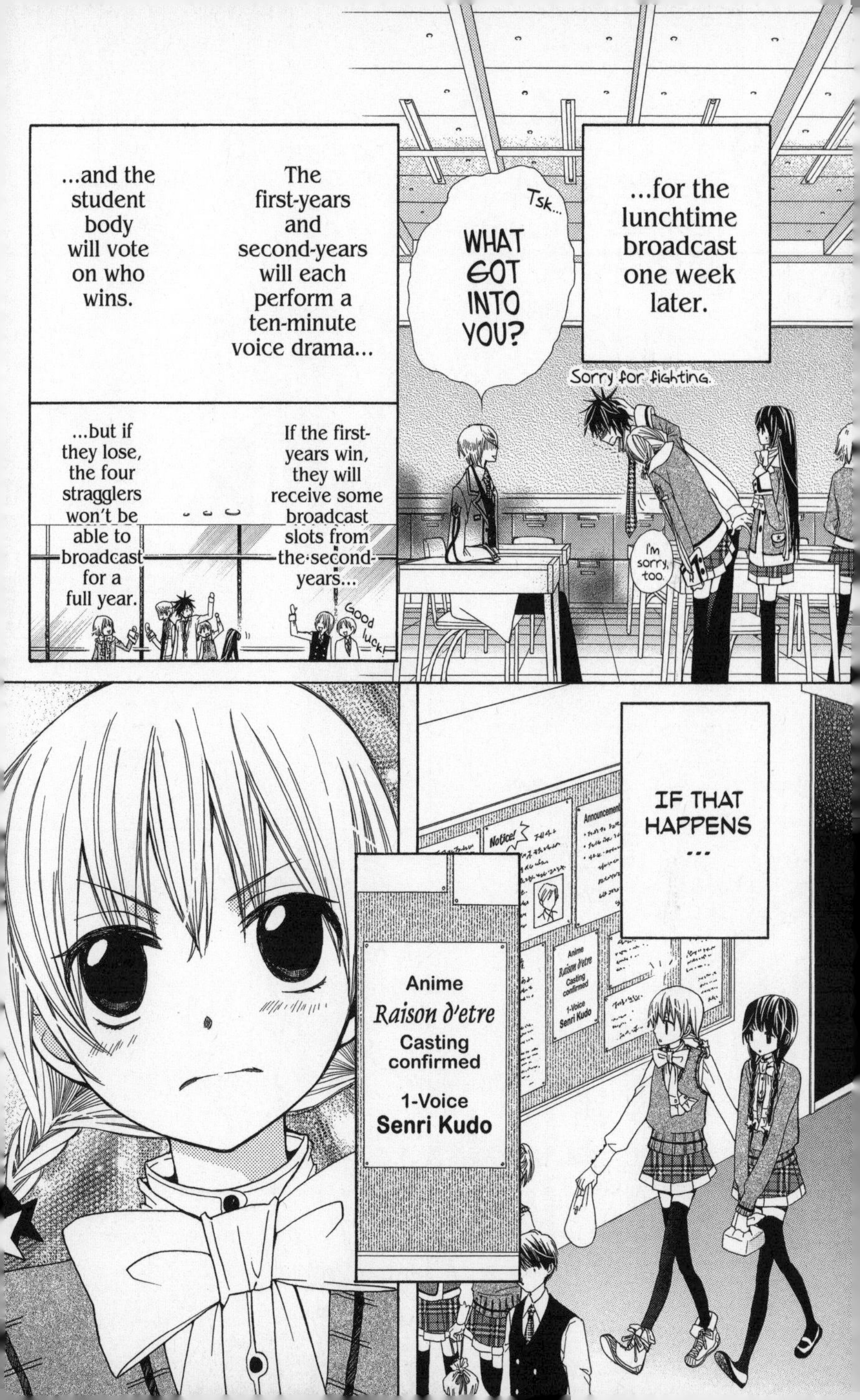

...for the lunchtime broadcast one week later.
Tsk...
WHAT GOT INTO YOU?
Sorry for fighting.
I'm sorry, too.
The first-years and second-years will each perform a ten-minute voice drama...
...and the student body will vote on who wins.
If the first-years win, they will receive some broadcast slots from the second-years...
Good luck!
...but if they lose, the four stragglers won't be able to broadcast for a full year.
IF THAT HAPPENS...
Notice!
Announcement
Anime Raison d'etre Casting confirmed 1-Voice Senri Kudo
Anime
Raison d'etre
Casting confirmed
1-Voice
Senri Kudo

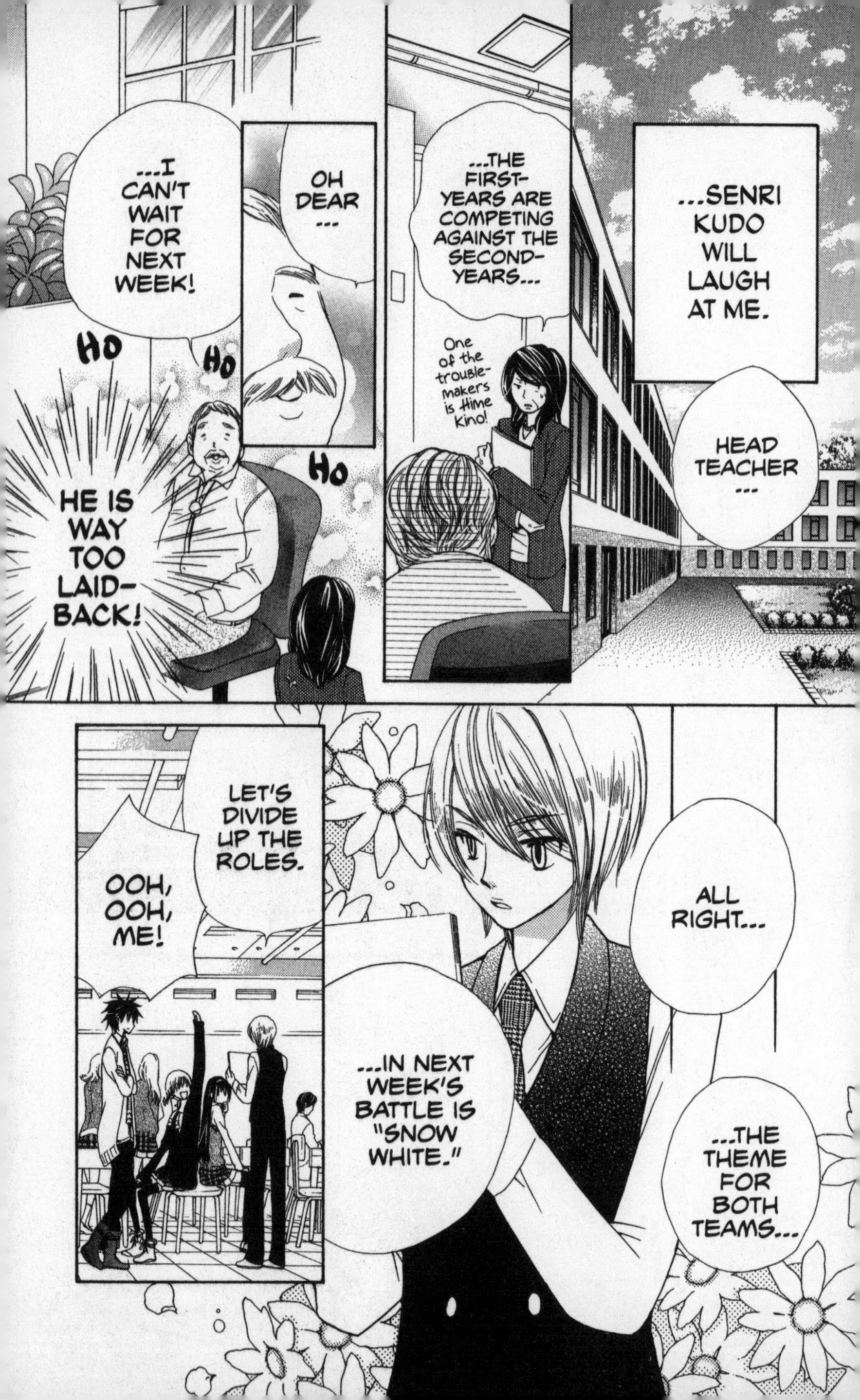
...SENRI KUDO WILL LAUGH AT ME.
HEAD TEACHER...
...THE FIRST-YEARS ARE COMPETING AGAINST THE SECOND-YEARS...
One of the trouble-makers is Hime Kino!
OH DEAR...
...I CAN'T WAIT FOR NEXT WEEK!
HO
HO
HO
HE IS WAY TOO LAID-BACK!
ALL RIGHT...
...THE THEME FOR BOTH TEAMS...
...IN NEXT WEEK'S BATTLE IS "SNOW WHITE."
LET'S DIVIDE UP THE ROLES.
OOH, OOH, ME!

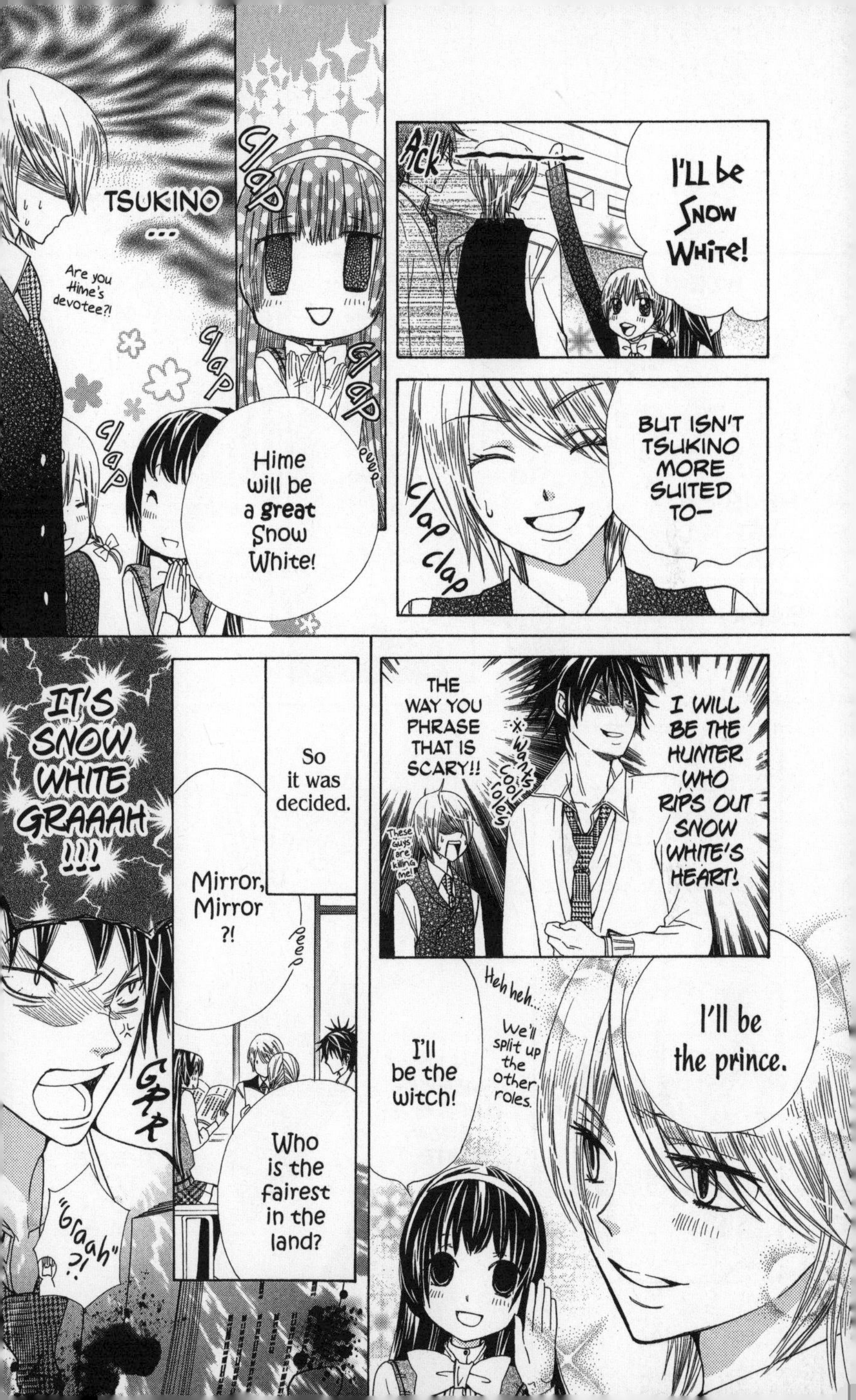

Ack
I'LL be Snow White!
BUT ISN'T TSUKINO MORE SUITED TO—
clap clap
clap clap clap clap
Hime will be a great Snow White!
peep
TSUKINO ...
Are you Hime's devotee?!
I WILL BE THE HUNTER WHO RIPS OUT SNOW WHITE'S HEART!
THE WAY YOU PHRASE THAT IS SCARY!!
*Wants cool roles
These guys are killing me!
I'll be the prince.
Heh heh...
We'll split up the other roles.
I'll be the witch!
So it was decided.
Mirror, Mirror ?!
peep
Who is the fairest in the land?
IT'S SNOW WHITE GRAAAH !!!
GRR
"graah" ?!

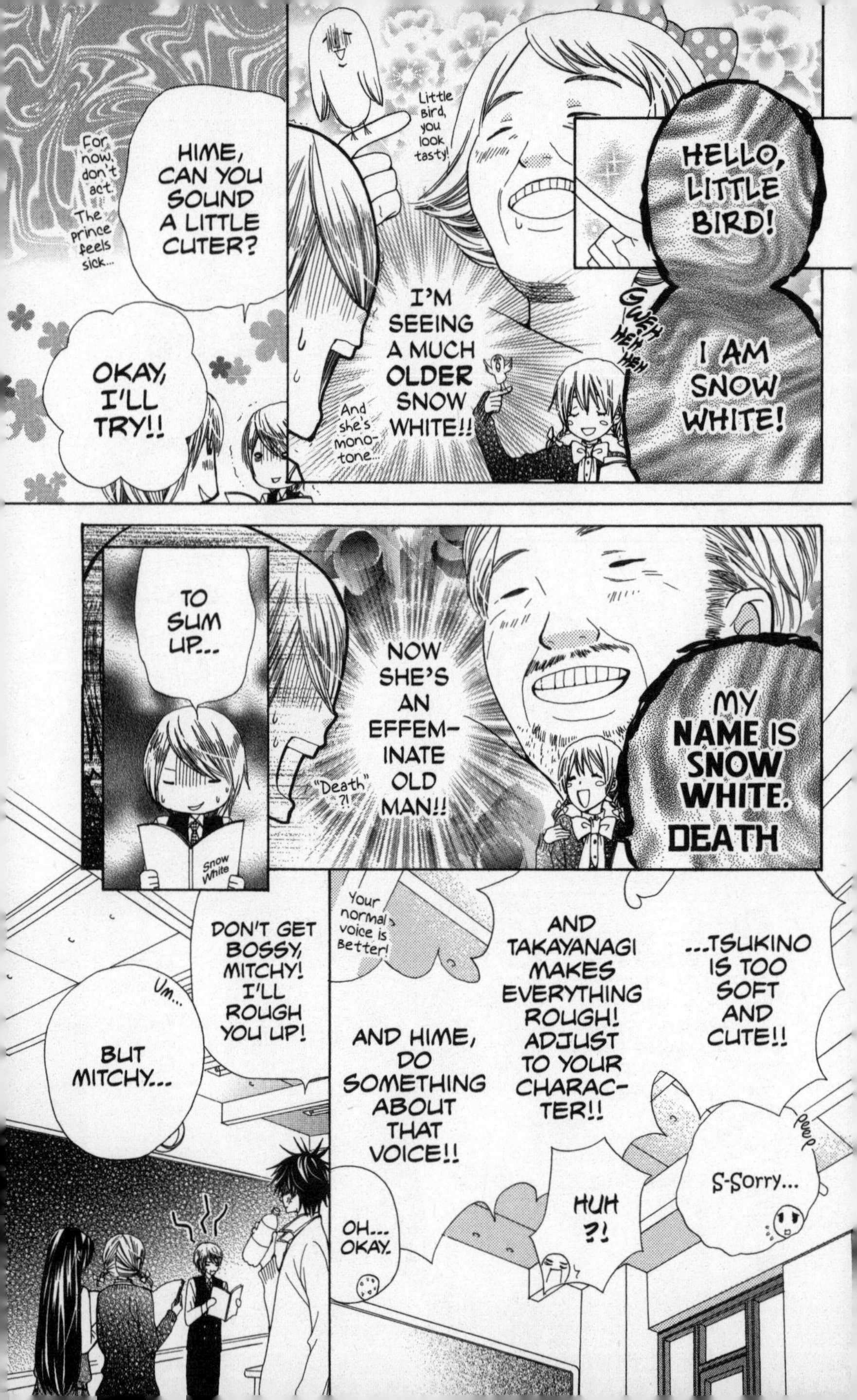
HELLO, LITTLE BIRD!
Little Bird, you look tasty!
GWEH HEH HEH
I AM SNOW WHITE!
I'M SEEING A MUCH OLDER SNOW WHITE!!
And she's monotone...
HIME, CAN YOU SOUND A LITTLE CUTER?
For now, don't act. The prince feels sick...
OKAY, I'LL TRY!!
MY NAME IS SNOW WHITE. DEATH
NOW SHE'S AN EFFEMINATE OLD MAN!!
"Death" ?!
TO SUM UP...
Snow White
...TSUKINO IS TOO SOFT AND CUTE!!
AND TAKAYANAGI MAKES EVERYTHING ROUGH! ADJUST TO YOUR CHARACTER!!
Your normal voice is better!
AND HIME, DO SOMETHING ABOUT THAT VOICE!!
Peep
S-Sorry...
HUH ?!
OH... OKAY.
DON'T GET BOSSY, MITCHY! I'LL ROUGH YOU UP!
Um...
BUT MITCHY...

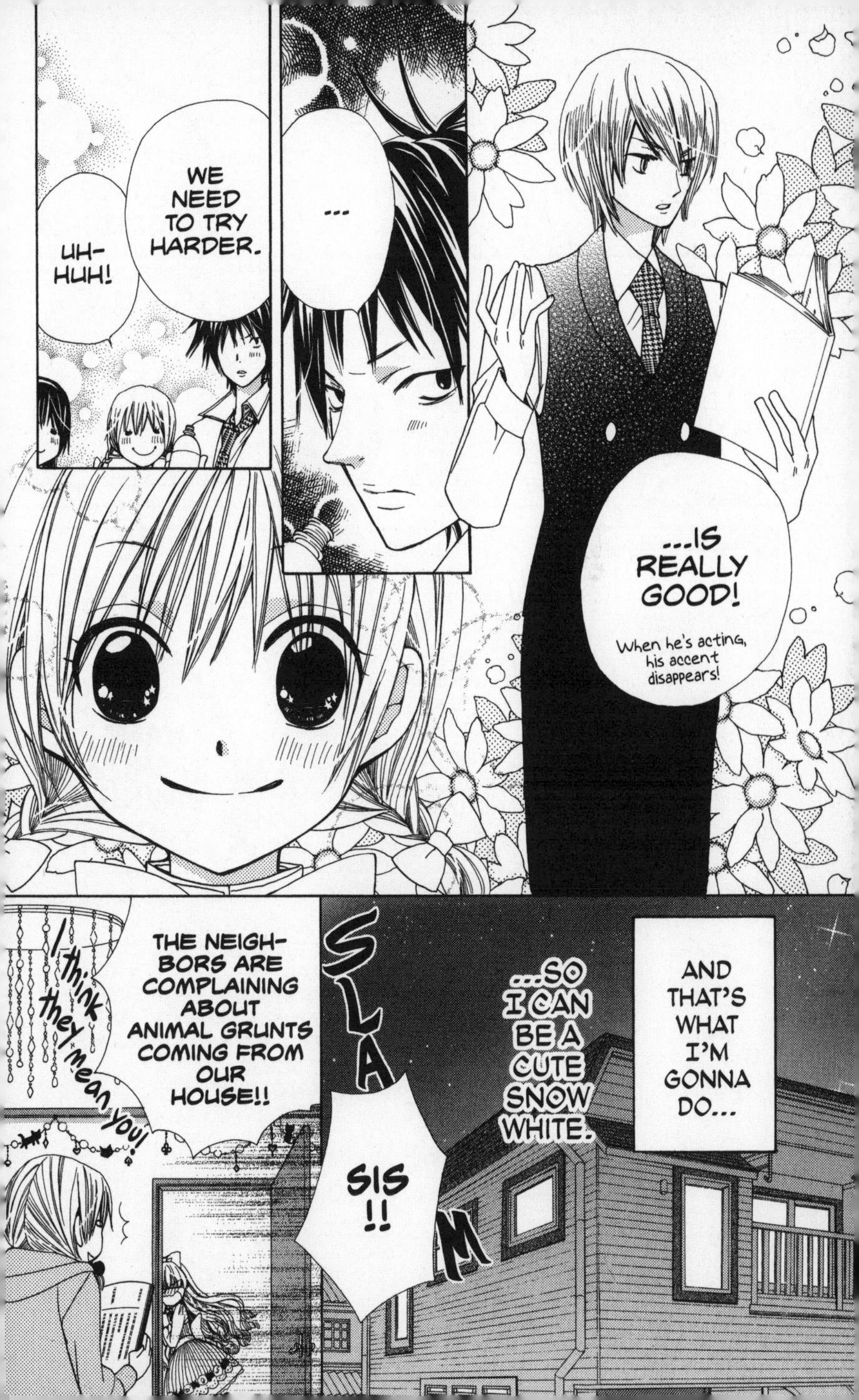

...IS REALLY GOOD!
When he's acting, his accent disappears!
...
WE NEED TO TRY HARDER.
UH-HUH!
AND THAT'S WHAT I'M GONNA DO...
...SO I CAN BE A CUTE SNOW WHITE.
SLAM
SIS!!
THE NEIGHBORS ARE COMPLAINING ABOUT ANIMAL GRUNTS COMING FROM OUR HOUSE!!
I think they mean you!

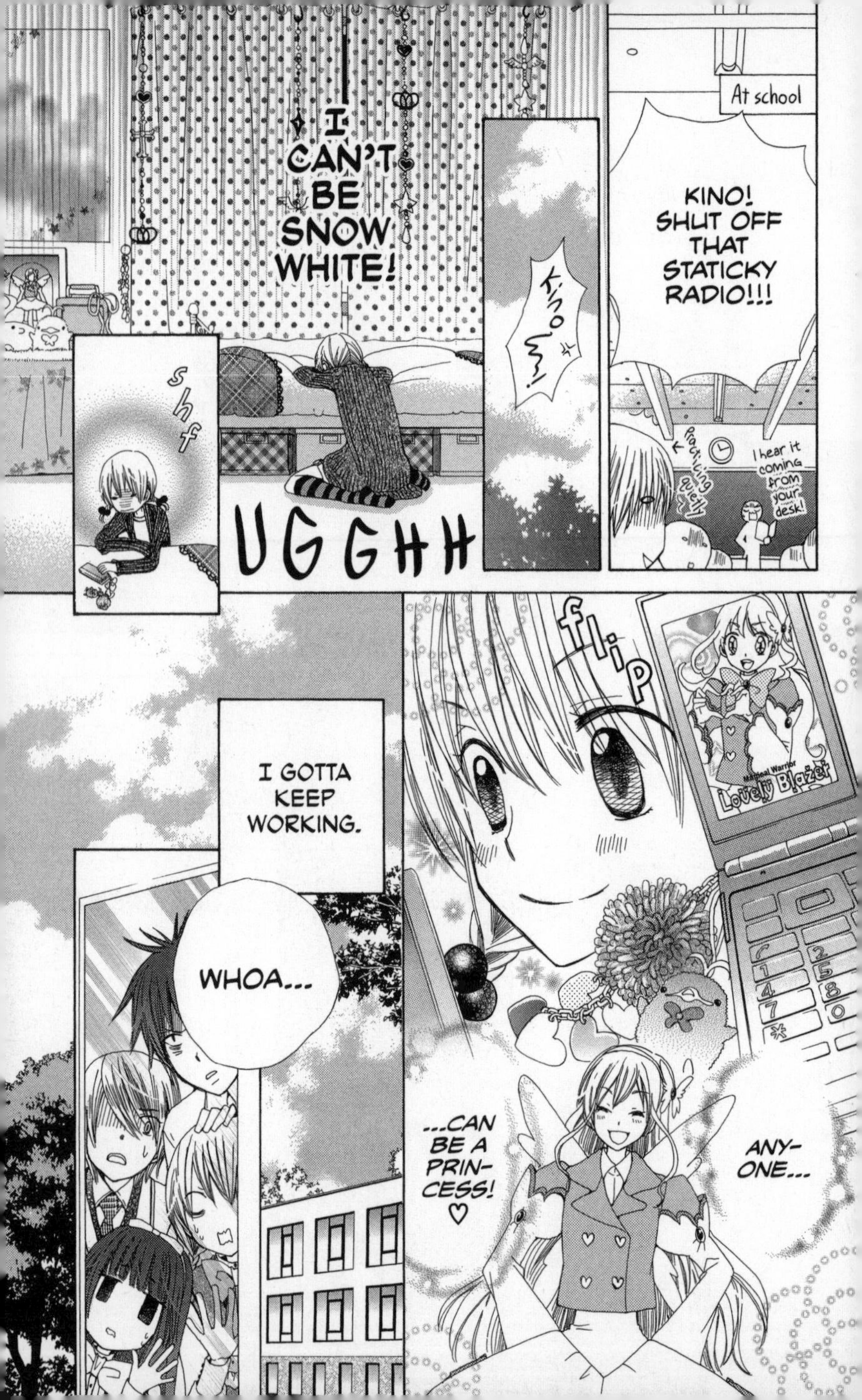
At school
KINO! SHUT OFF THAT STATICKY RADIO!!!
Practicing quietly
I hear it coming from your desk!
Kino~!
I CAN'T BE SNOW WHITE!
UGGHH
shf
flip
Magical Warrior
Lovely Blazer
ANY-ONE...
...CAN BE A PRIN-CESS! ♡
I GOTTA KEEP WORKING.
WHOA...

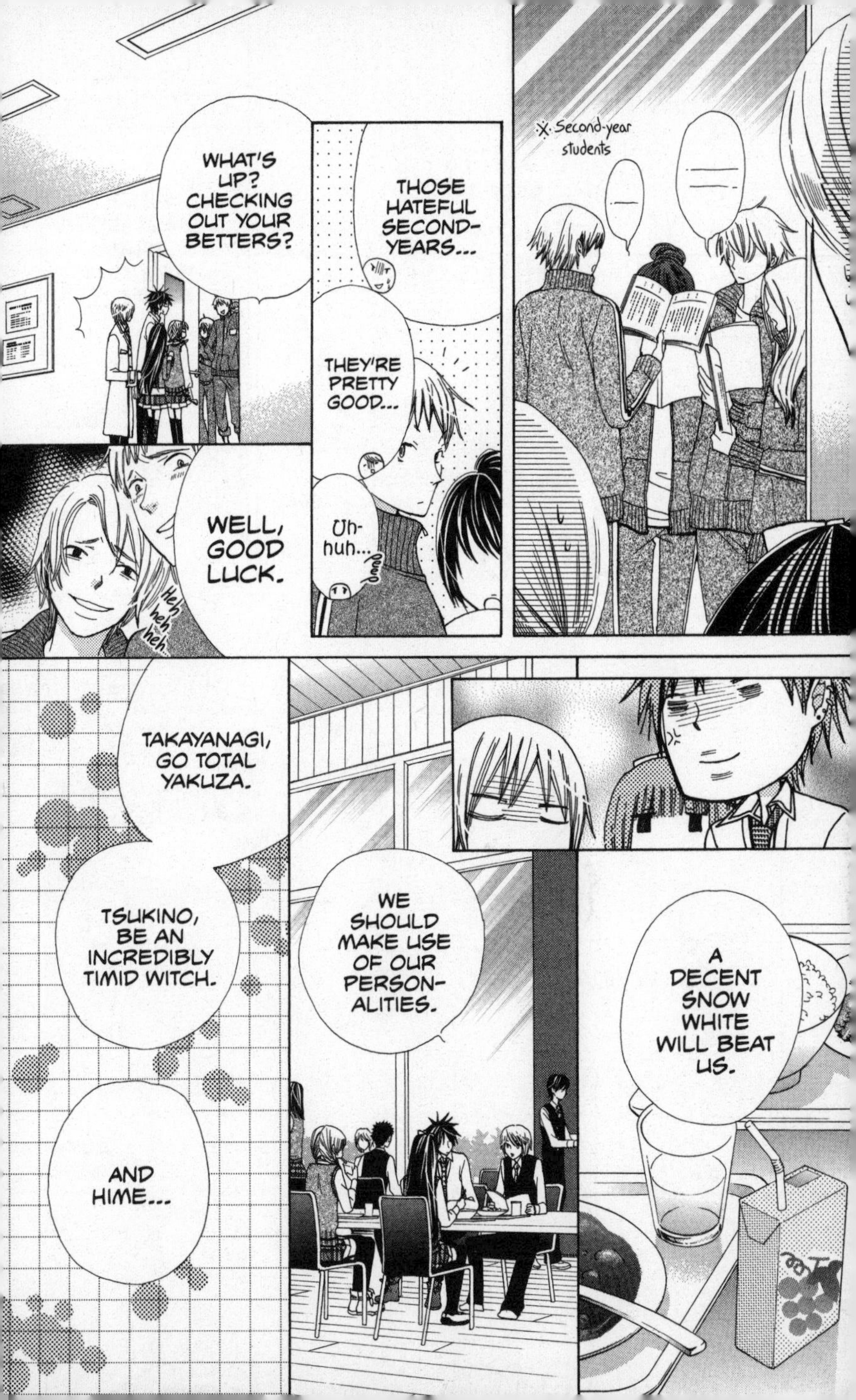
※ Second-year students
THOSE HATEFUL SECOND-YEARS...
THEY'RE PRETTY GOOD...
Uh-huh...
WHAT'S UP? CHECKING OUT YOUR BETTERS?
WELL, GOOD LUCK.
Heh heh heh.
A DECENT SNOW WHITE WILL BEAT US.
WE SHOULD MAKE USE OF OUR PERSONALITIES.
TAKAYANAGI, GO TOTAL YAKUZA.
TSUKINO, BE AN INCREDIBLY TIMID WITCH.
AND HIME...

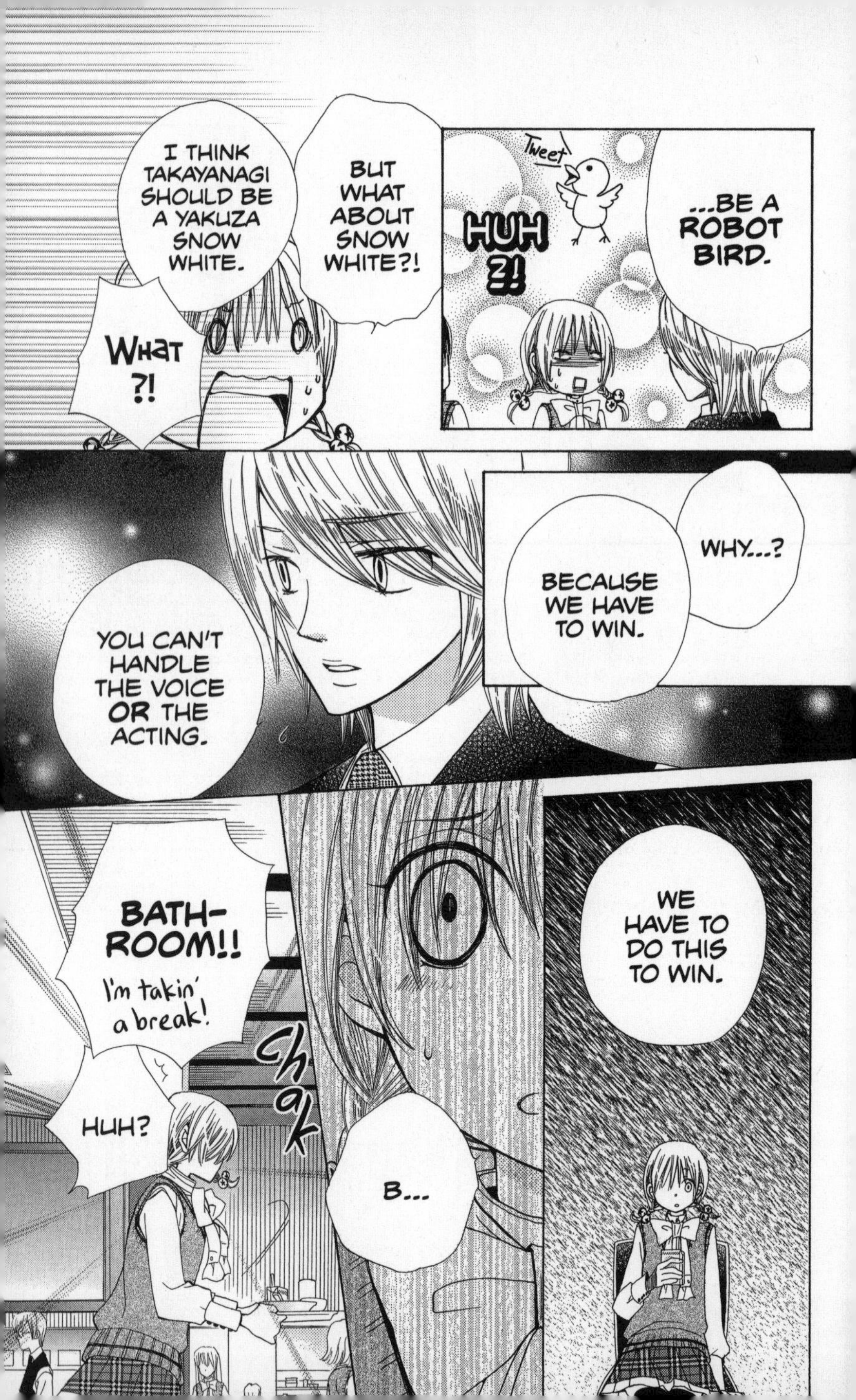
...BE A ROBOT BIRD.
Tweet
HUH?!
BUT WHAT ABOUT SNOW WHITE?!
I THINK TAKAYANAGI SHOULD BE A YAKUZA SNOW WHITE.
WHAT?!
WHY...?
BECAUSE WE HAVE TO WIN.
YOU CAN'T HANDLE THE VOICE OR THE ACTING.
WE HAVE TO DO THIS TO WIN.
B...
Chak
BATH-ROOM!!
I'm takin' a break!
HUH?

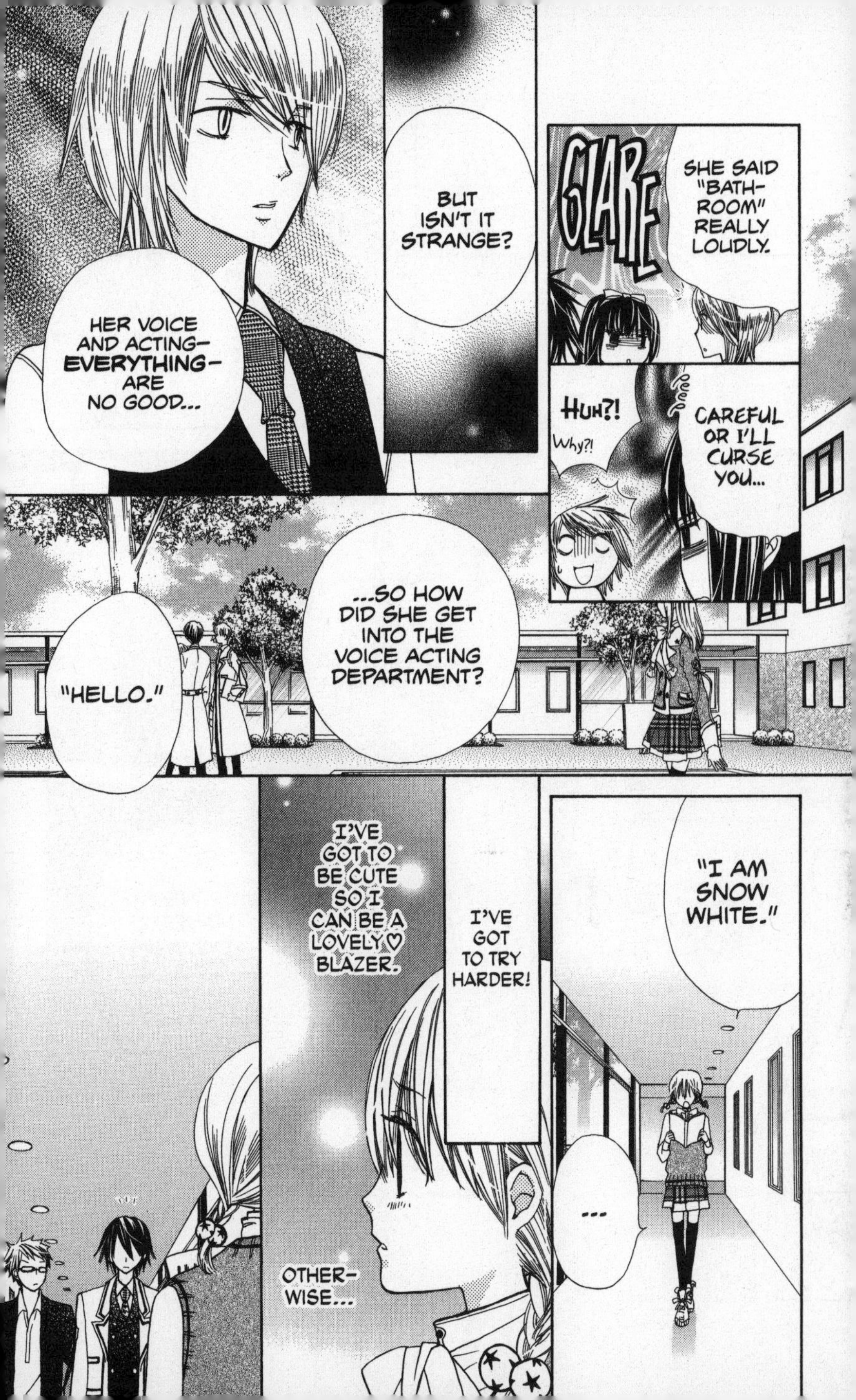
GLARE
SHE SAID "BATH-ROOM" REALLY LOUDLY.
CAREFUL OR I'LL CURSE YOU...
HUH?!
Why?!
BUT ISN'T IT STRANGE?
HER VOICE AND ACTING—EVERYTHING—ARE NO GOOD...
...SO HOW DID SHE GET INTO THE VOICE ACTING DEPARTMENT?
"HELLO."
"I AM SNOW WHITE."
...
I'VE GOT TO TRY HARDER!
I'VE GOT TO BE CUTE SO I CAN BE A LOVELY ♡ BLAZER.
OTHER-WISE...

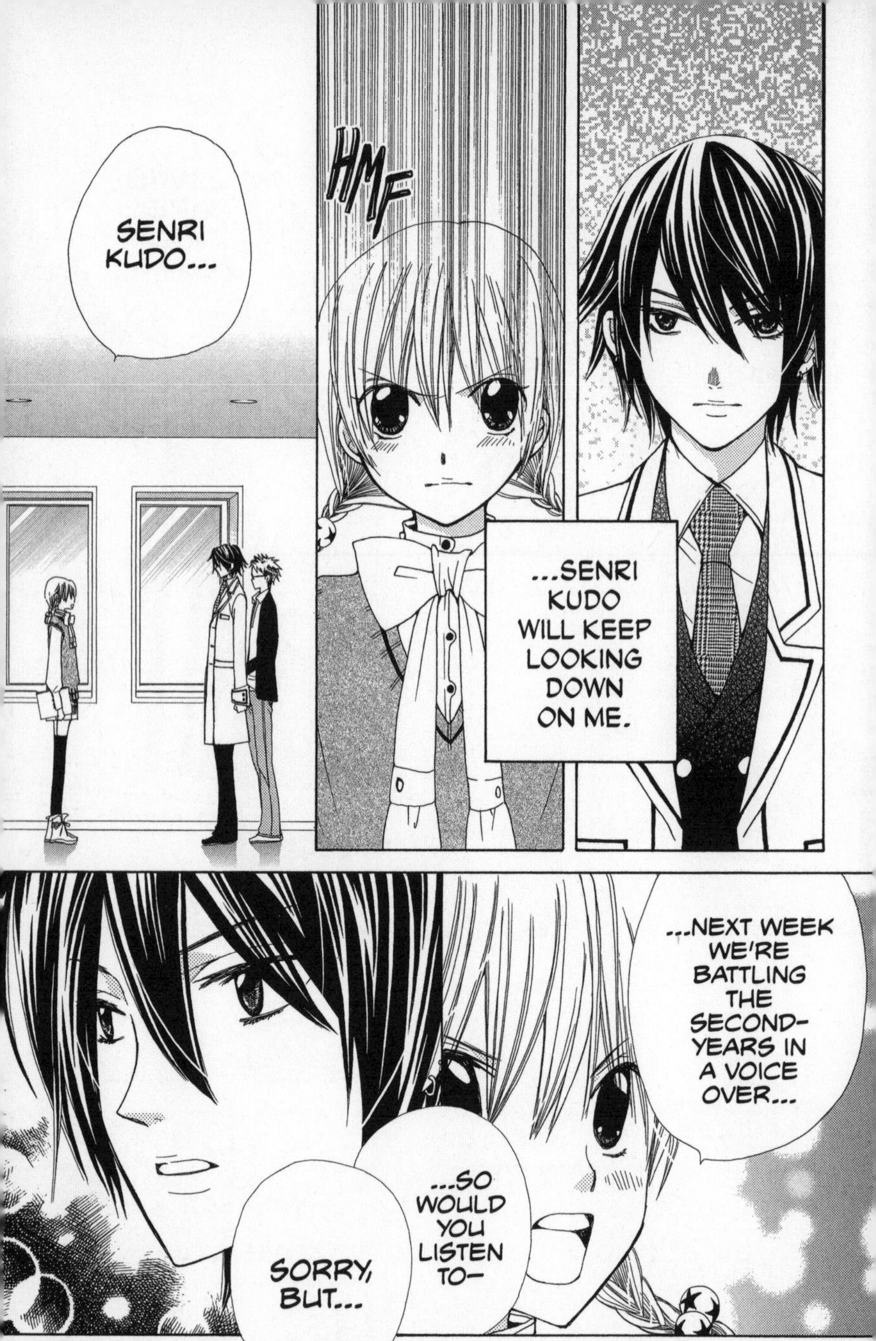
...SENRI KUDO WILL KEEP LOOKING DOWN ON ME.
HMF
SENRI KUDO...
...NEXT WEEK WE'RE BATTLING THE SECOND-YEARS IN A VOICE OVER...
...SO WOULD YOU LISTEN TO-
SORRY, BUT...

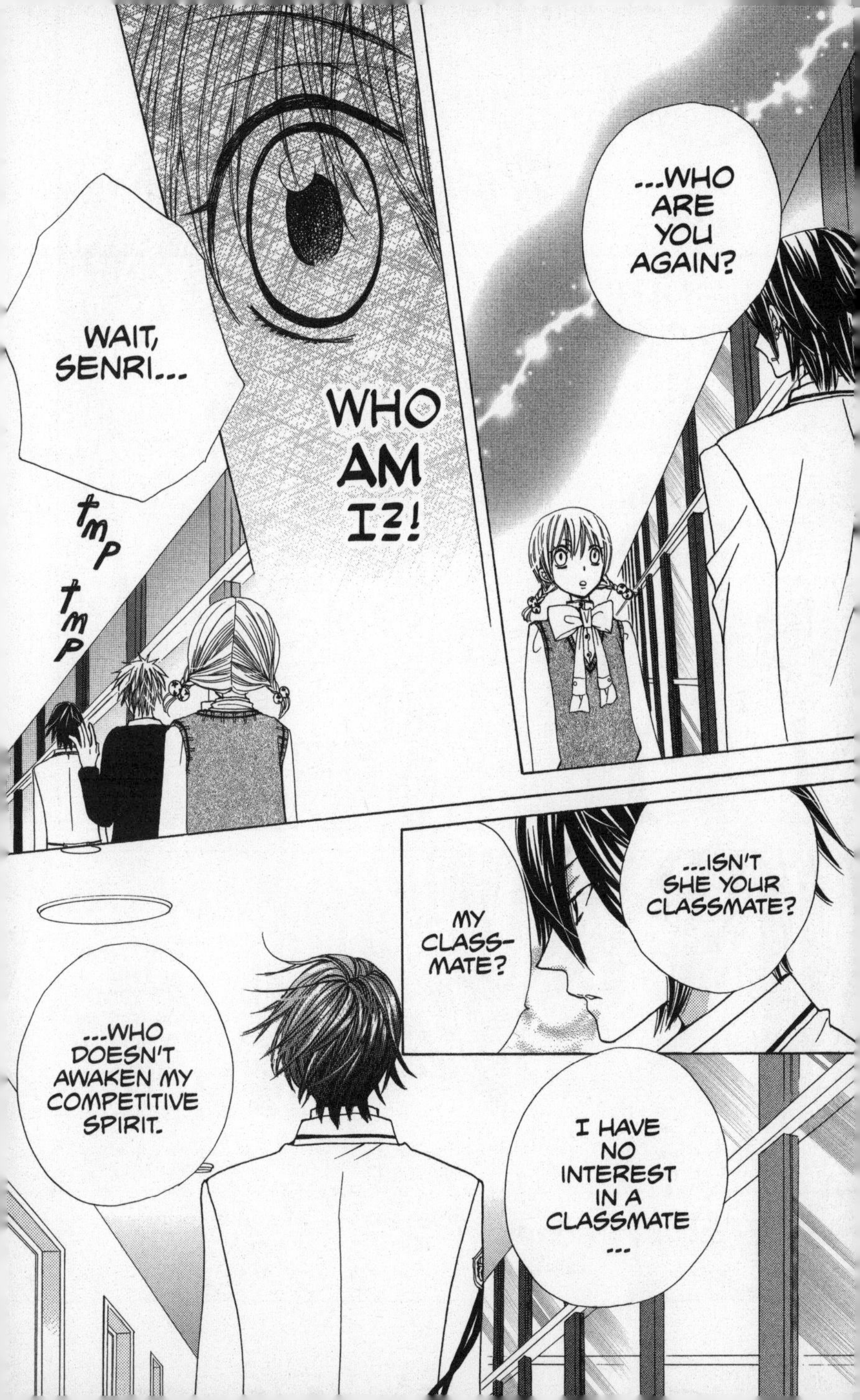
...WHO ARE YOU AGAIN?
WHO AM I?!
WAIT, SENRI...
tmp tmp
...ISN'T SHE YOUR CLASSMATE?
MY CLASSMATE?
I HAVE NO INTEREST IN A CLASSMATE ...
...WHO DOESN'T AWAKEN MY COMPETITIVE SPIRIT.

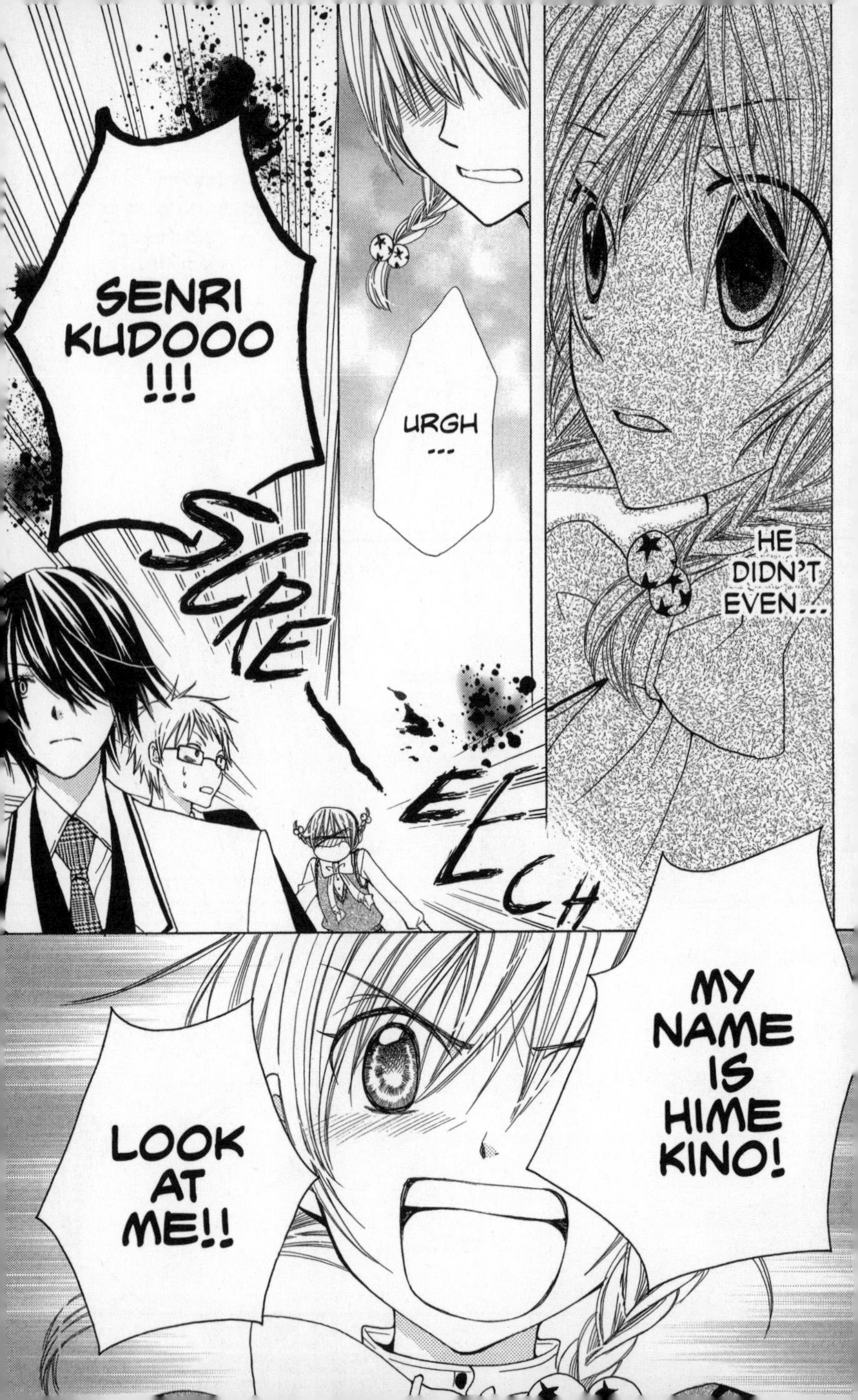
HE DIDN'T EVEN...
URGH ...
SENRI KUDOOO !!!
SCRE—EECH
MY NAME IS HIME KINO!
LOOK AT ME!!

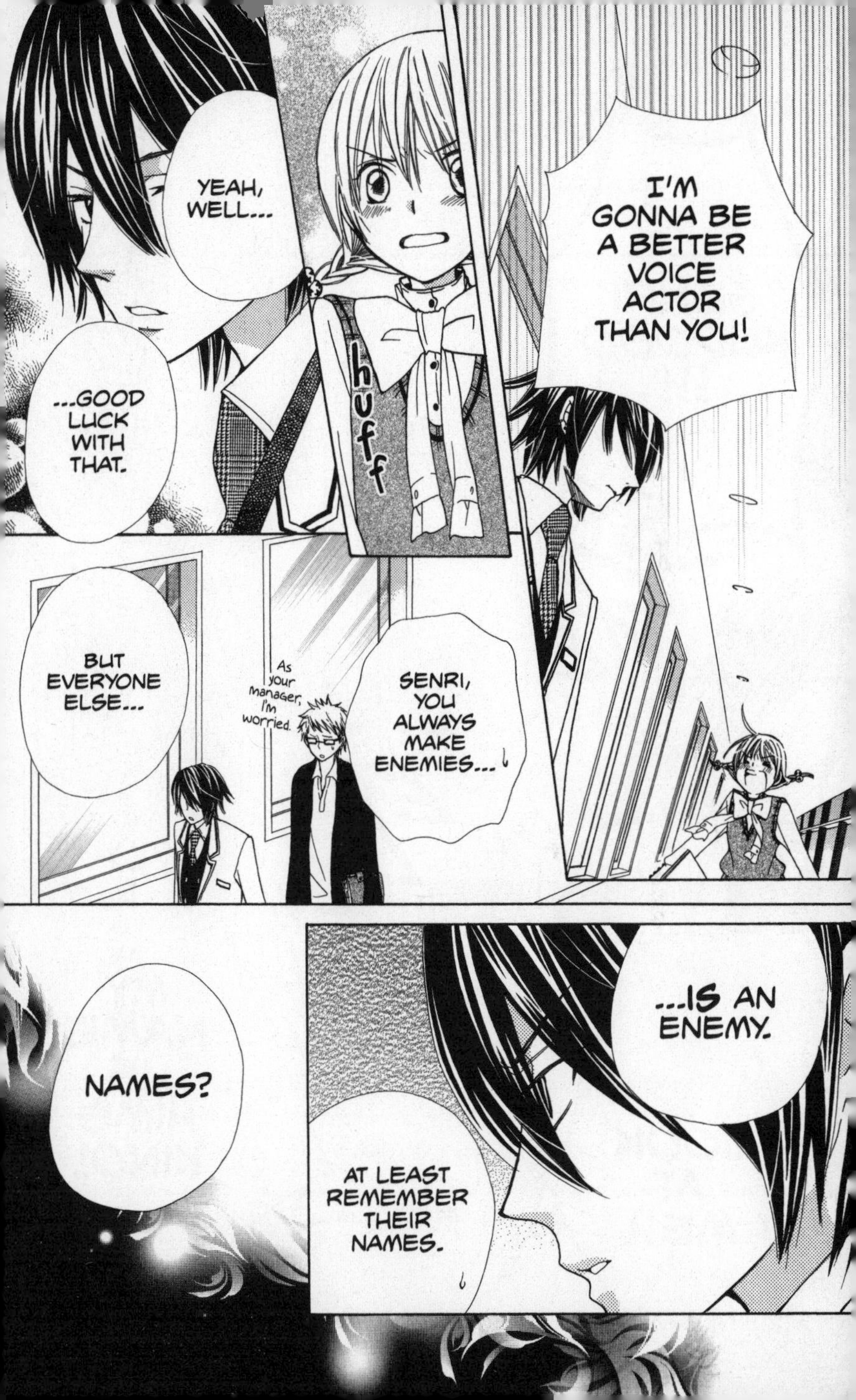
I'M GONNA BE A BETTER VOICE ACTOR THAN YOU!
huff
YEAH, WELL...
...GOOD LUCK WITH THAT.
SENRI, YOU ALWAYS MAKE ENEMIES...
As your manager, I'm worried.
BUT EVERYONE ELSE...
...IS AN ENEMY.
AT LEAST REMEMBER THEIR NAMES.
NAMES?

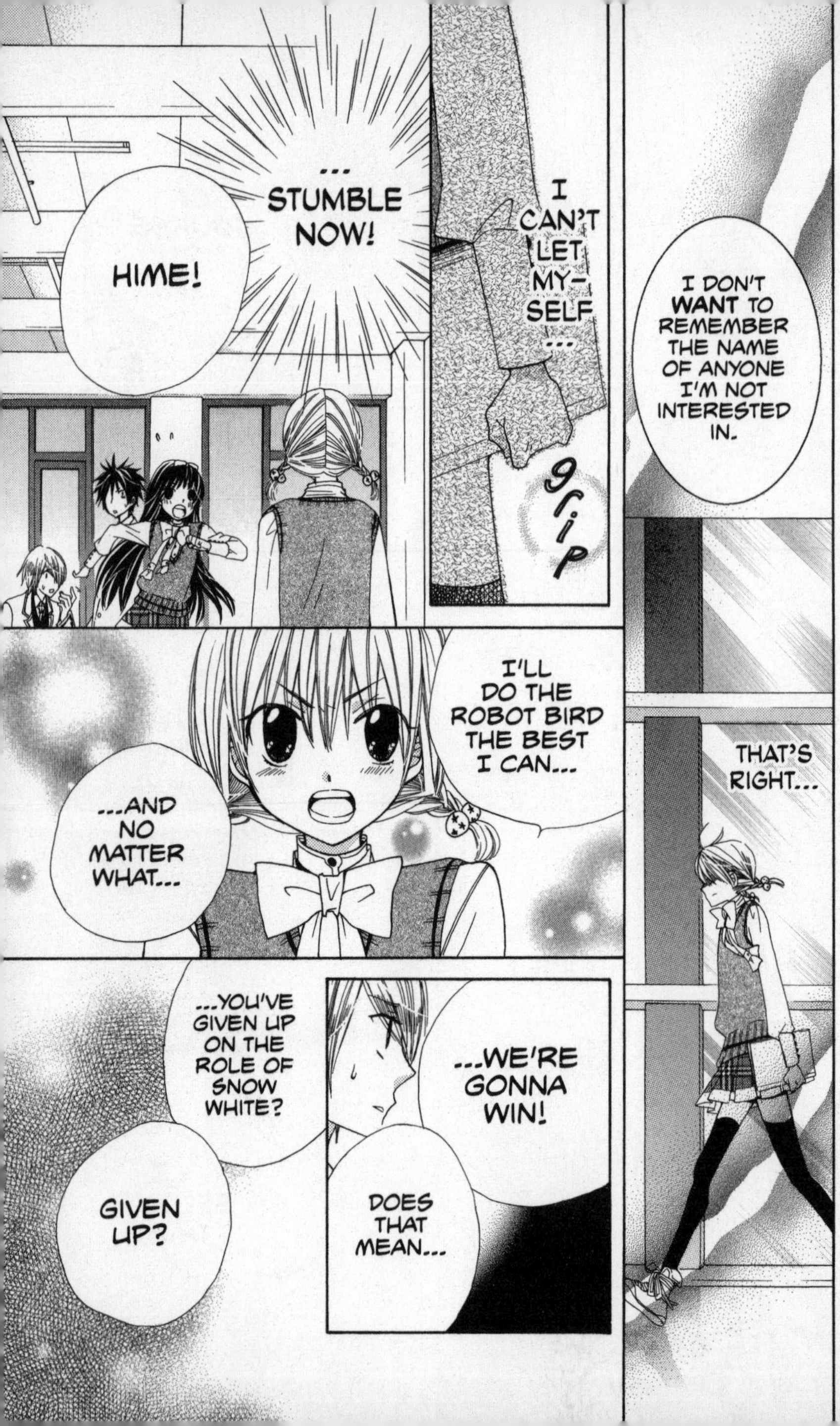
I DON'T WANT TO REMEMBER THE NAME OF ANYONE I'M NOT INTERESTED IN.
THAT'S RIGHT...
I CAN'T LET MYSELF...
grip
...STUMBLE NOW!
HIME!
I'LL DO THE ROBOT BIRD THE BEST I CAN...
...AND NO MATTER WHAT...
...WE'RE GONNA WIN!
DOES THAT MEAN...
...YOU'VE GIVEN UP ON THE ROLE OF SNOW WHITE?
GIVEN UP?

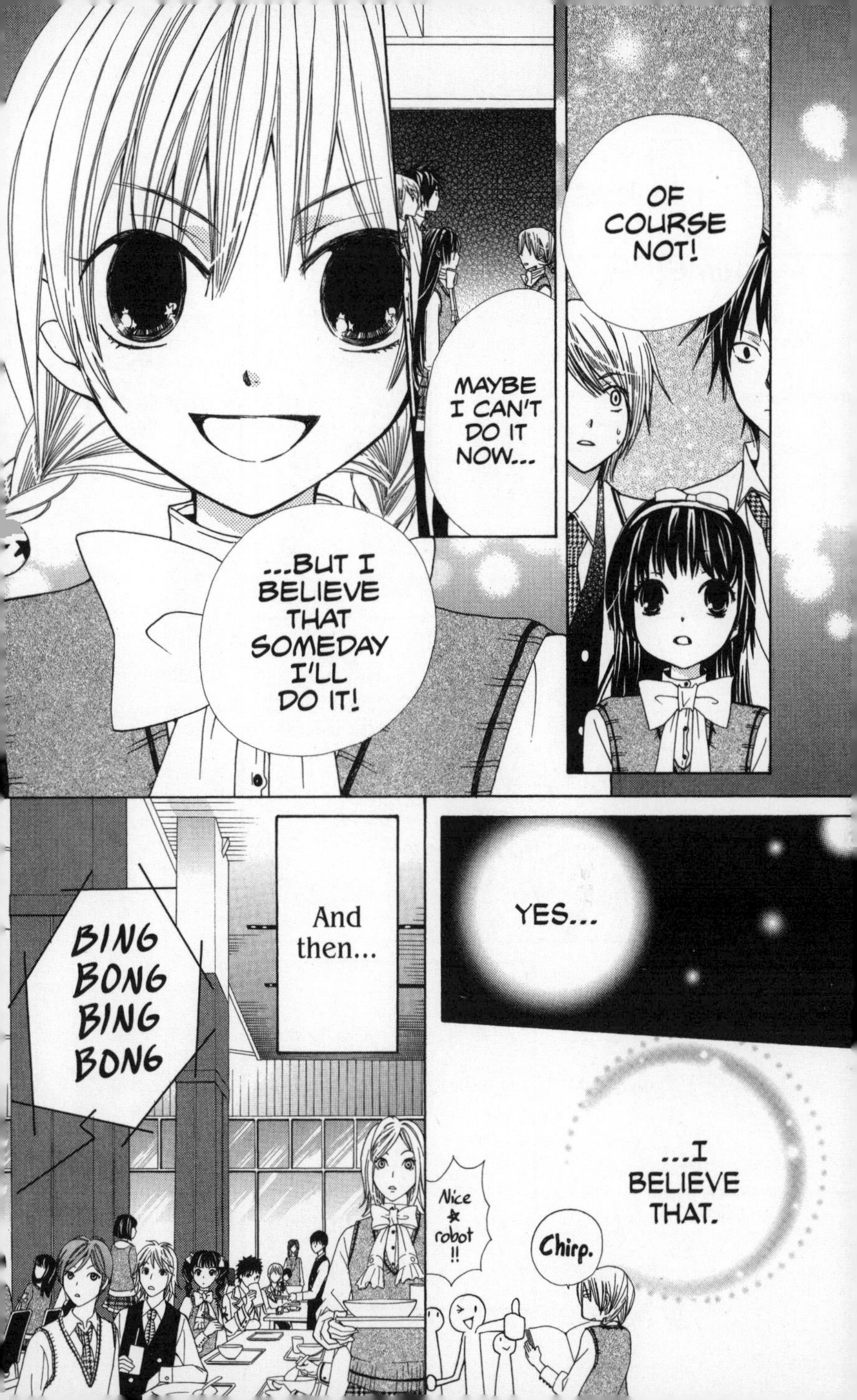

OF COURSE NOT!
MAYBE I CAN'T DO IT NOW...
...BUT I BELIEVE THAT SOMEDAY I'LL DO IT!
YES...
...I BELIEVE THAT.
Nice & robot!!
Chirp.
And then...
BING BONG BING BONG

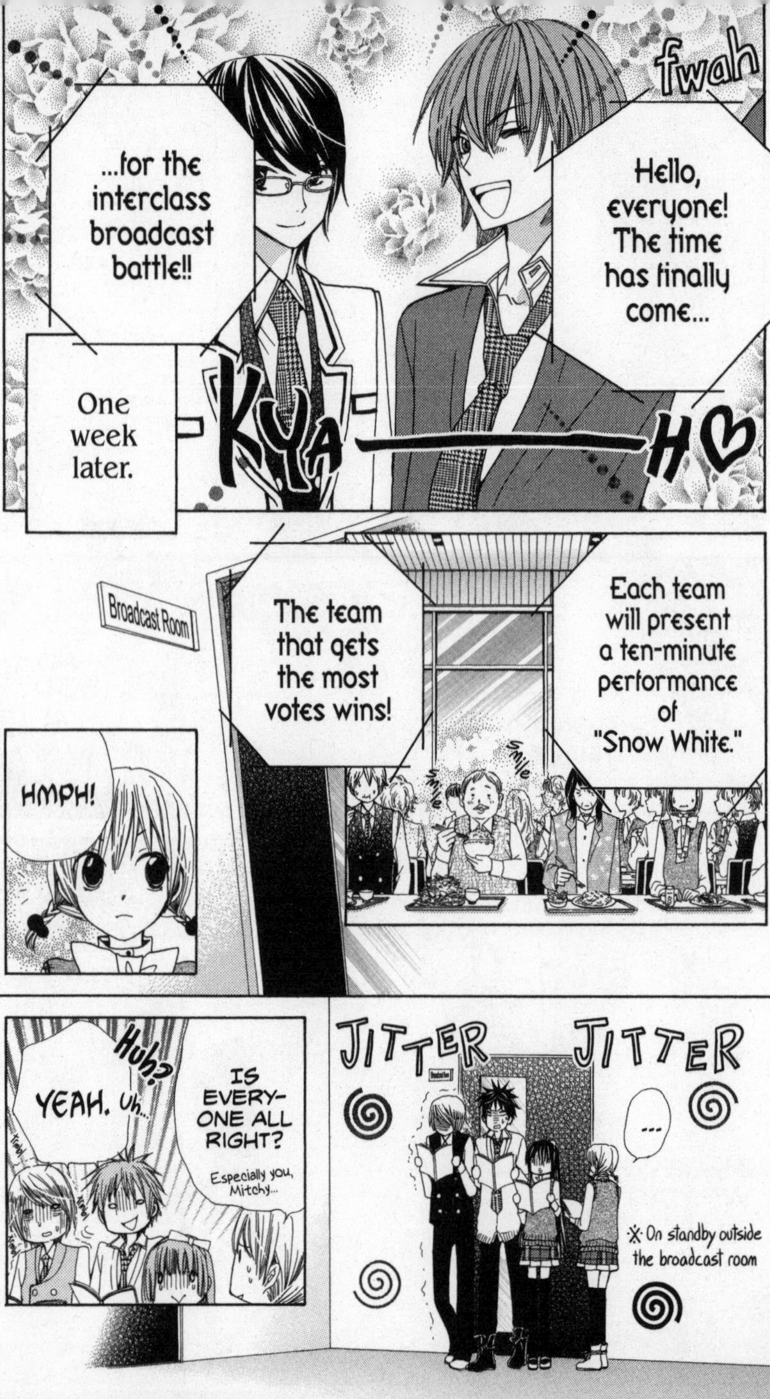
fwah
Hello, everyone! The time has finally come...
...for the interclass broadcast battle!!
KYA—H
One week later.
Each team will present a ten-minute performance of "Snow White."
The team that gets the most votes wins!
Smile
Smile
Broadcast Room
HMPH!
JITTER JITTER
...
※: On standby outside the broadcast room
IS EVERYONE ALL RIGHT?
Especially you, Mitchy...
Huh?
YEAH. Uh...

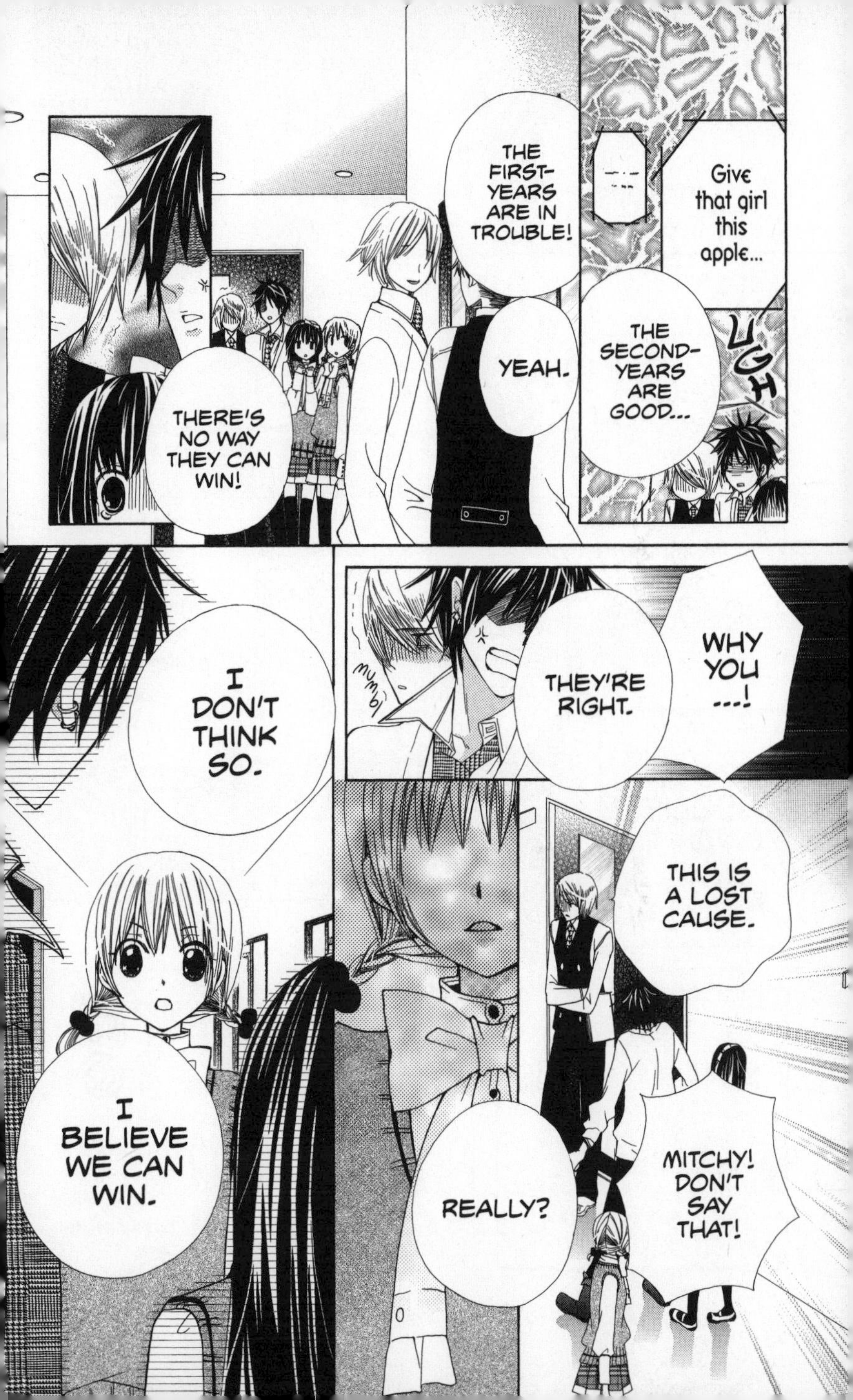
Give that girl this apple...
UGH
THE SECOND-YEARS ARE GOOD...
THE FIRST-YEARS ARE IN TROUBLE!
YEAH.
THERE'S NO WAY THEY CAN WIN!
WHY YOU ...!
THEY'RE RIGHT.
mumbl
THIS IS A LOST CAUSE.
MITCHY! DON'T SAY THAT!
REALLY?
I DON'T THINK SO.
I BELIEVE WE CAN WIN.

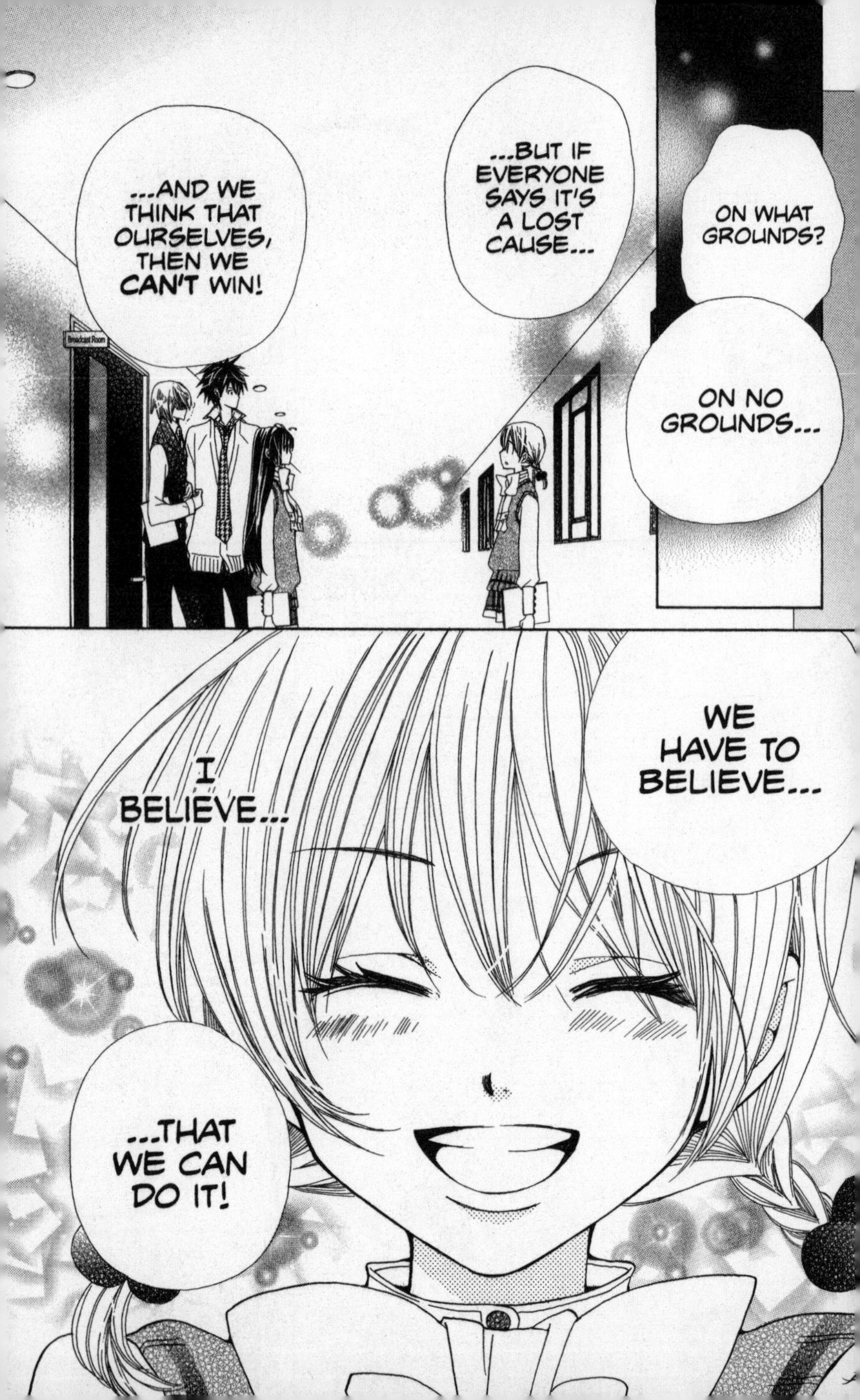
ON WHAT GROUNDS?
ON NO GROUNDS...
...BUT IF EVERYONE SAYS IT'S A LOST CAUSE...
...AND WE THINK THAT OURSELVES, THEN WE CAN'T WIN!
WE HAVE TO BELIEVE...
I BELIEVE...
...THAT WE CAN DO IT!

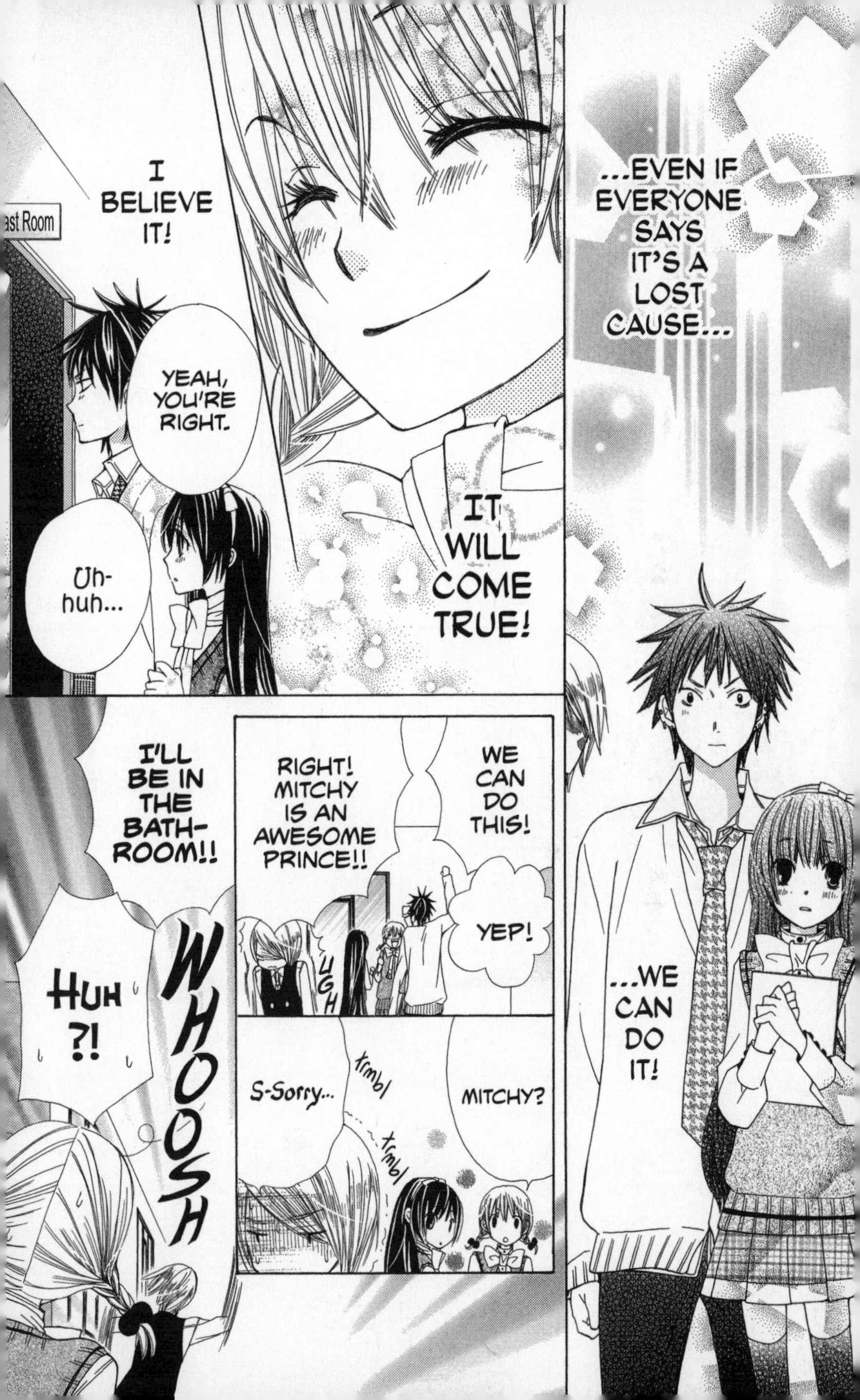
...EVEN IF EVERYONE SAYS IT'S A LOST CAUSE...
...WE CAN DO IT!
IT WILL COME TRUE!
ast Room
I BELIEVE IT!
YEAH, YOU'RE RIGHT.
Uh-huh...
WE CAN DO THIS!
RIGHT! MITCHY IS AN AWESOME PRINCE!!
YEP!
UGH
MITCHY?
xrmbl
S-Sorry...
xrmbl
I'LL BE IN THE BATHROOM!!
WHOOSH
HUH?!

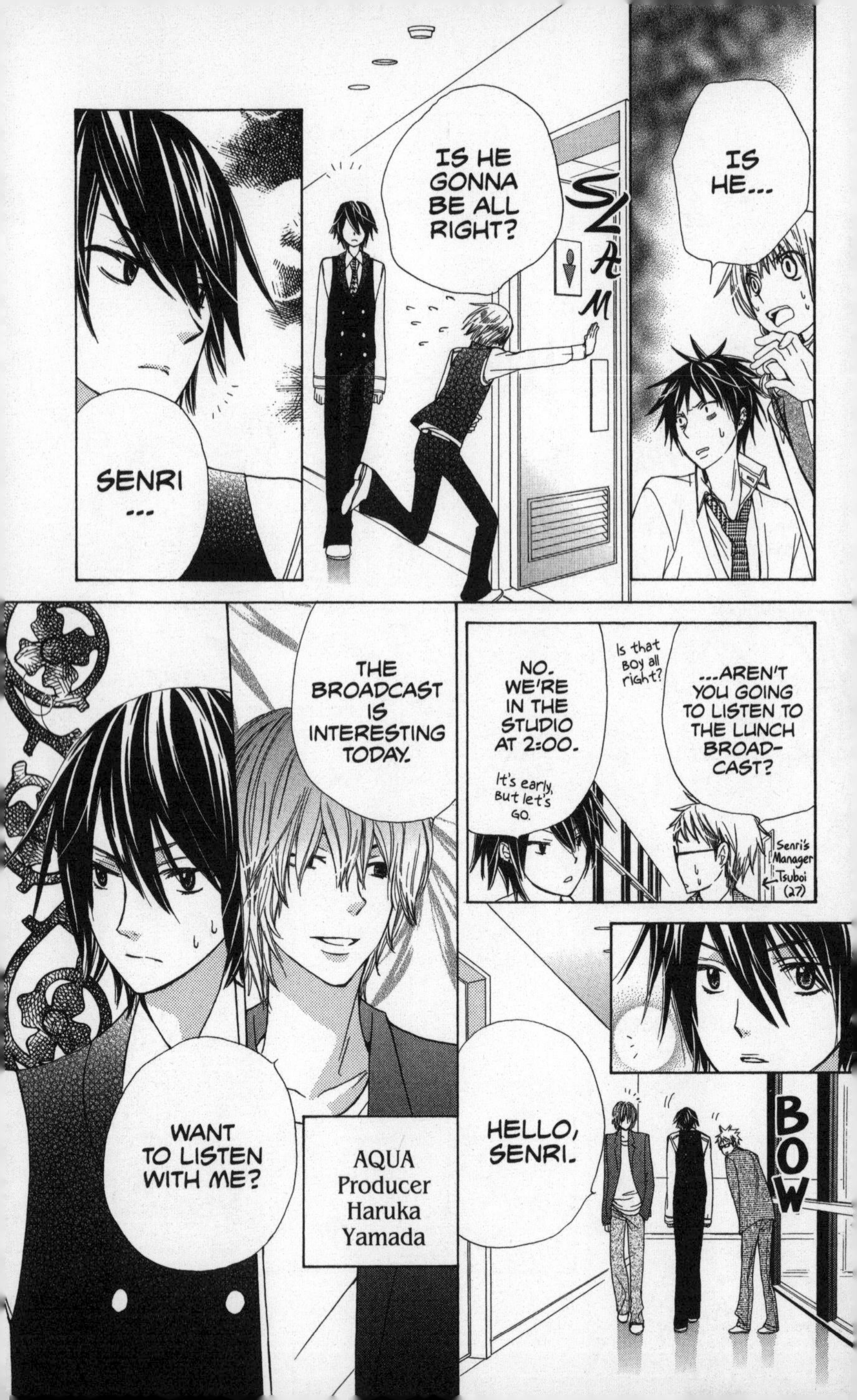
IS HE...
IS HE GONNA BE ALL RIGHT?
SLAM
SENRI ...
...AREN'T YOU GOING TO LISTEN TO THE LUNCH BROAD-CAST?
Is that boy all right?
Senri's Manager Tsuboi (27)
NO. WE'RE IN THE STUDIO AT 2:00.
It's early, but let's GO.
BOW
HELLO, SENRI.
THE BROADCAST IS INTERESTING TODAY.
AQUA Producer Haruka Yamada
WANT TO LISTEN WITH ME?

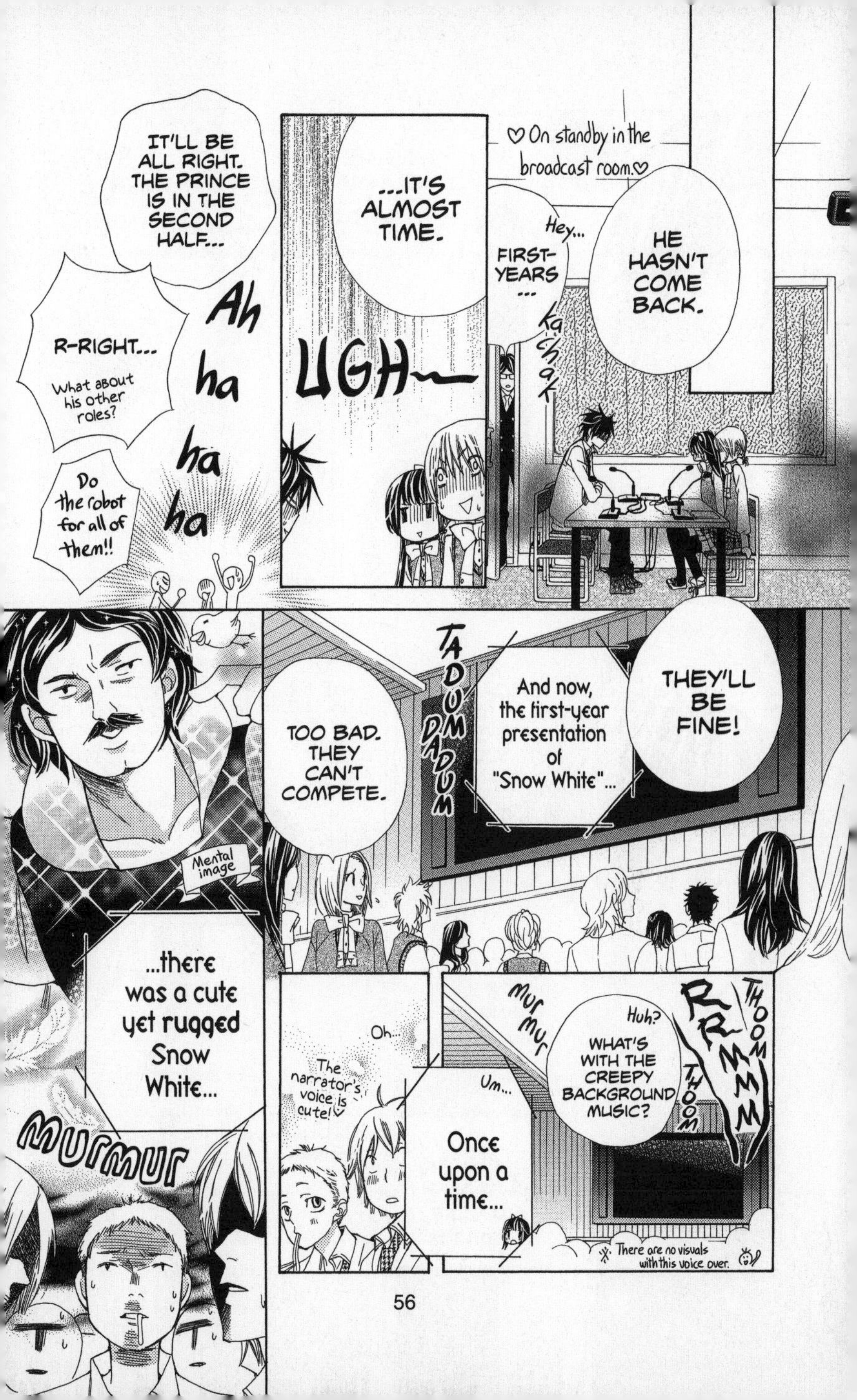
♡On standby in the broadcast room.♡
HE HASN'T COME BACK.
Hey... FIRST-YEARS...
ka chak
...IT'S ALMOST TIME.
UGH—
IT'LL BE ALL RIGHT. THE PRINCE IS IN THE SECOND HALF...
Ah ha ha ha
R-RIGHT...
What about his other roles?
Do the robot for all of them!!
THEY'LL BE FINE!
And now, the first-year presentation of "Snow White"...
TADUM DADUM
TOO BAD. THEY CAN'T COMPETE.
RRMMMM
THOOM THOOM
Huh? WHAT'S WITH THE CREEPY BACKGROUND MUSIC?
MUR MUR
※There are no visuals with this voice over.
Oh...
The narrator's voice is cute!♡
Um...
Once upon a time...
...there was a cute yet rugged Snow White...
Mental image
MURMUR

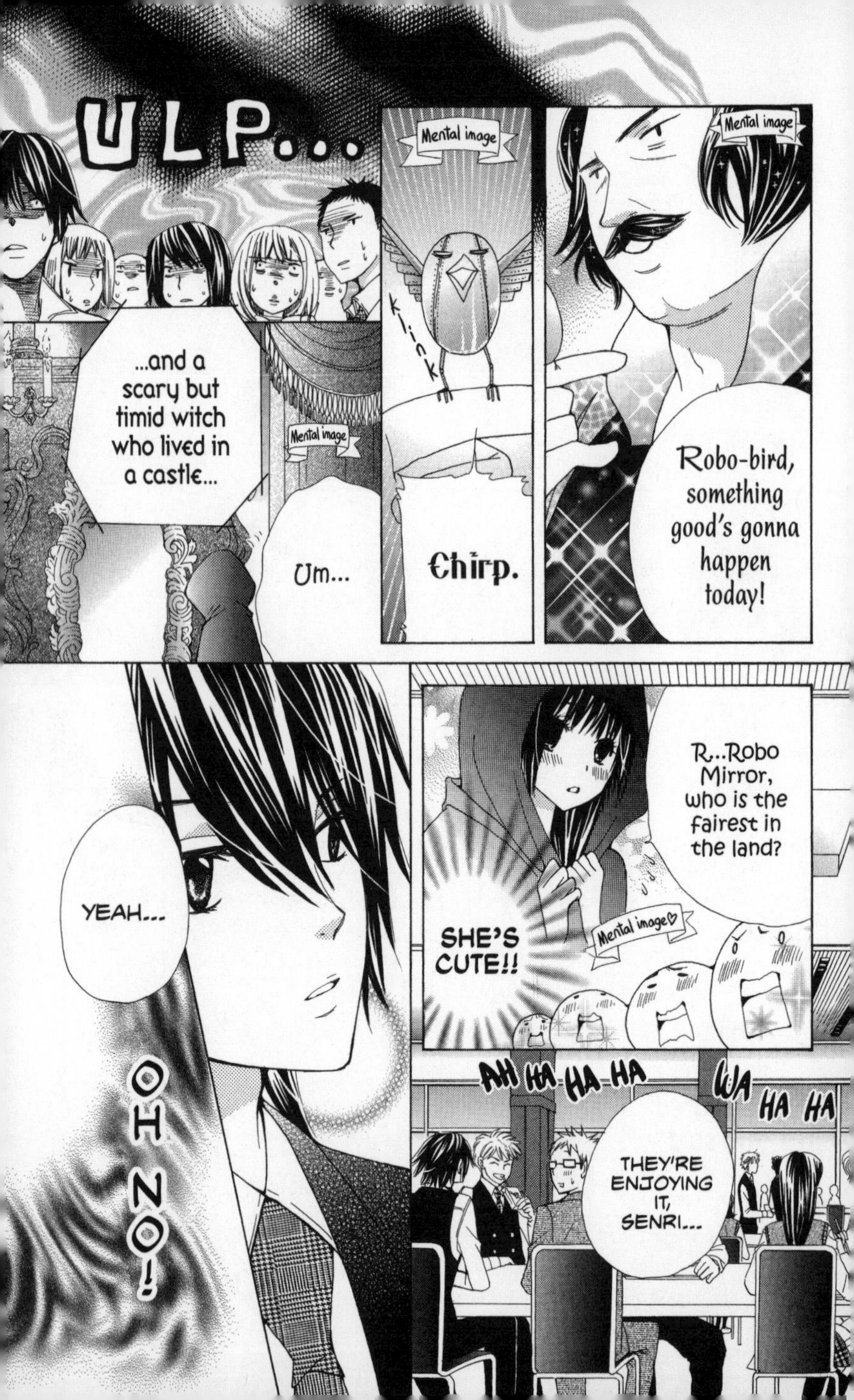
Mental image
Robo-bird, something good's gonna happen today!
Mental image
Klink
Chirp.
Mental image
...and a scary but timid witch who lived in a castle...
Um...
ULP...
R...Robo Mirror, who is the fairest in the land?
Mental image♡
SHE'S CUTE!!
AH HA HA HA
WA HA HA
THEY'RE ENJOYING IT, SENRI...
YEAH...
OH NO!

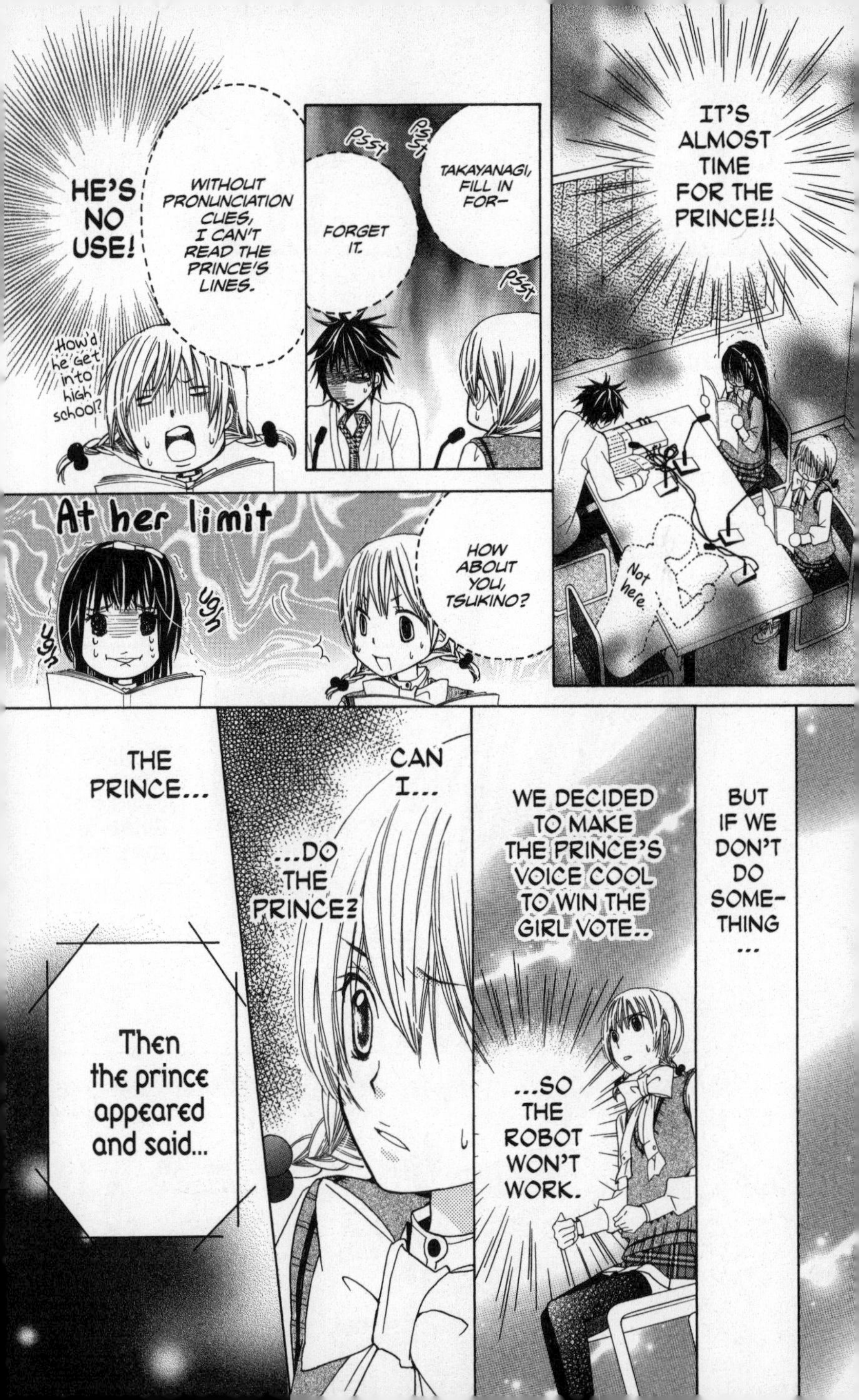
IT'S ALMOST TIME FOR THE PRINCE!!
Not here.
Psst
Psst
TAKAYANAGI, FILL IN FOR—
FORGET IT.
Psst
WITHOUT PRONUNCIATION CUES, I CAN'T READ THE PRINCE'S LINES.
HE'S NO USE!
How'd he get into high school?
HOW ABOUT YOU, TSUKINO?
ugh
ugh
At her limit
BUT IF WE DON'T DO SOME-THING...
WE DECIDED TO MAKE THE PRINCE'S VOICE COOL TO WIN THE GIRL VOTE..
...SO THE ROBOT WON'T WORK.
CAN I...
...DO THE PRINCE?
THE PRINCE...
Then the prince appeared and said...

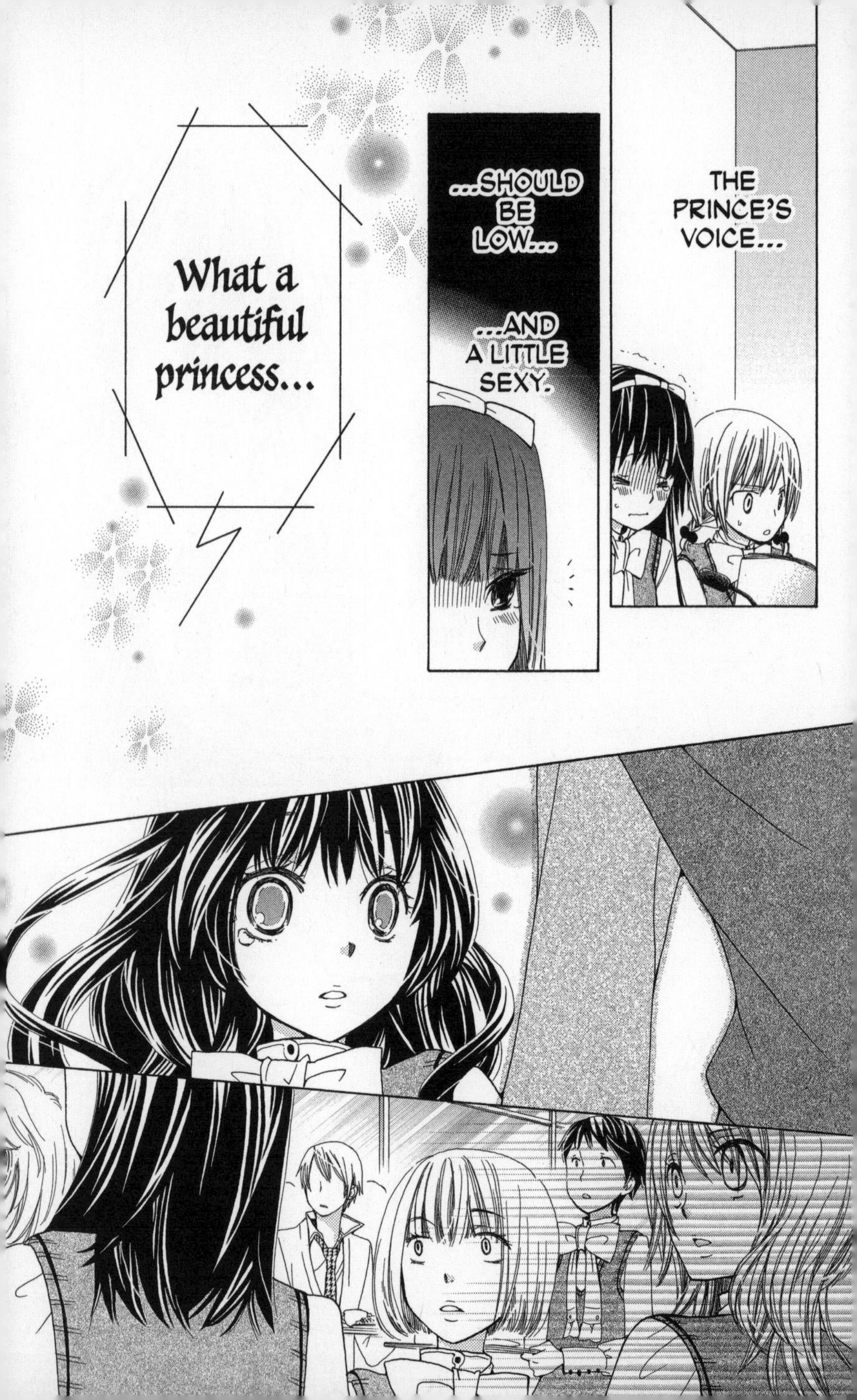
THE PRINCE'S VOICE...
...SHOULD BE LOW...
...AND A LITTLE SEXY.
What a beautiful princess...

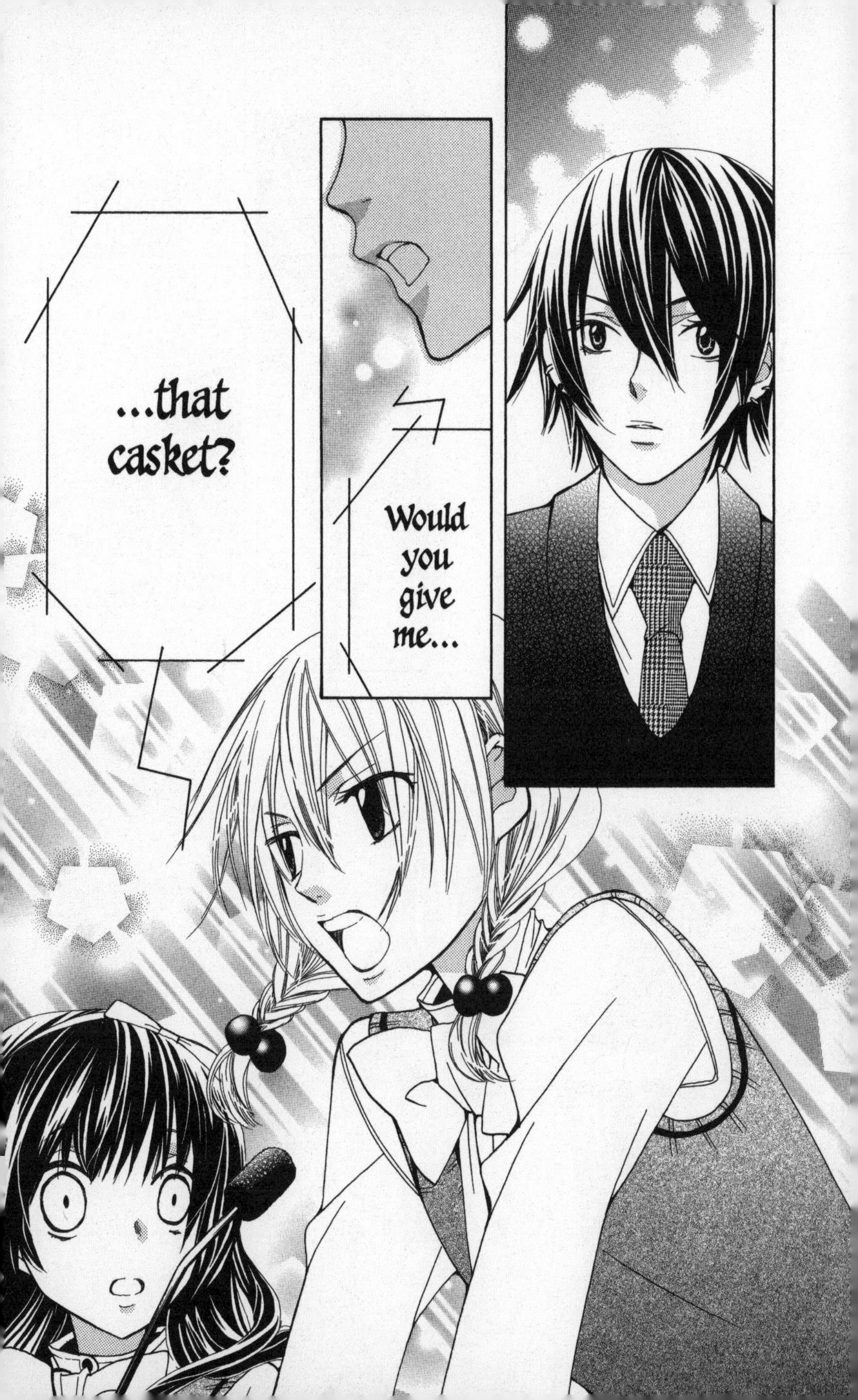
Would you give me...
...that casket?

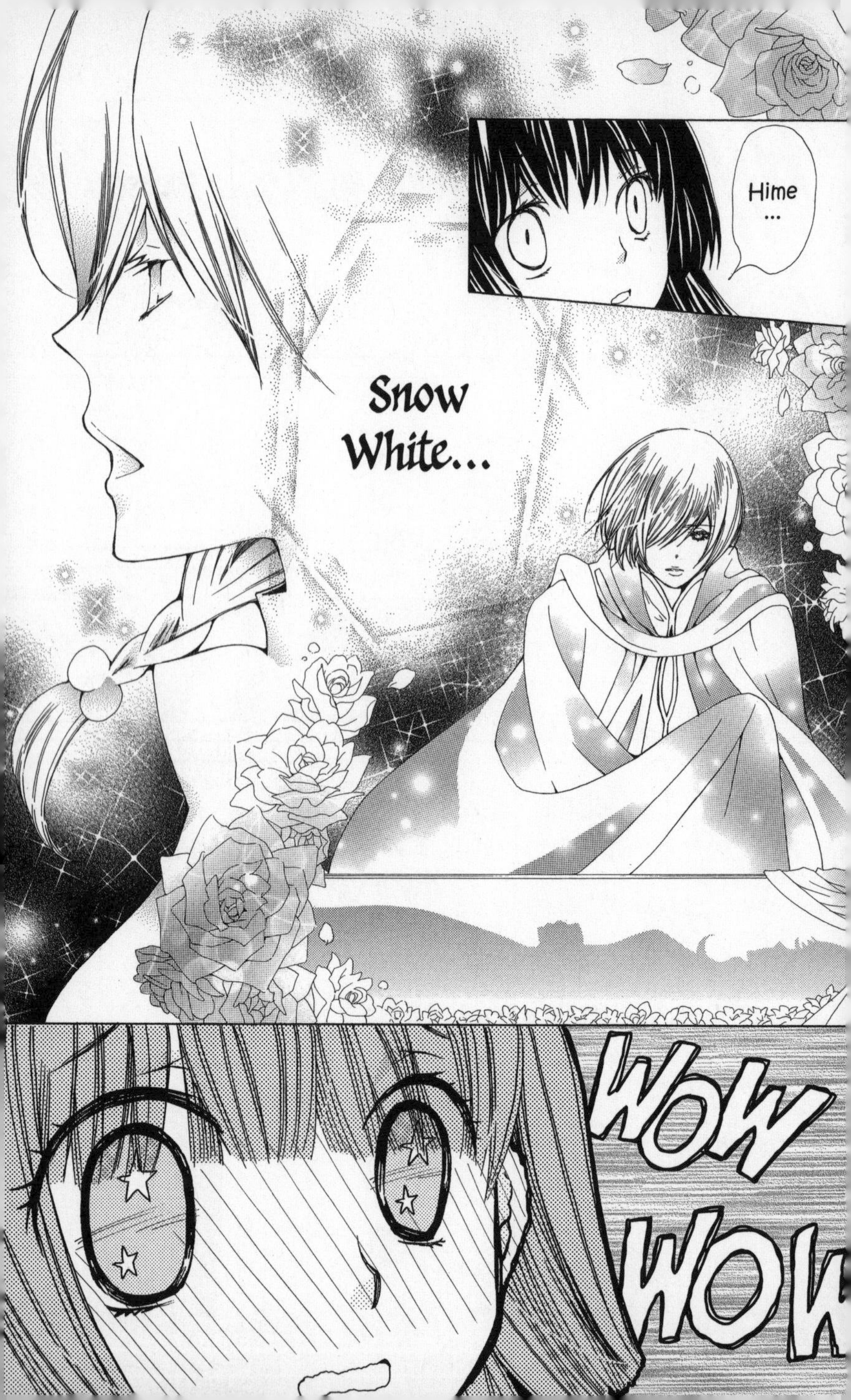
Hime ...
Snow White...
WOW WOW

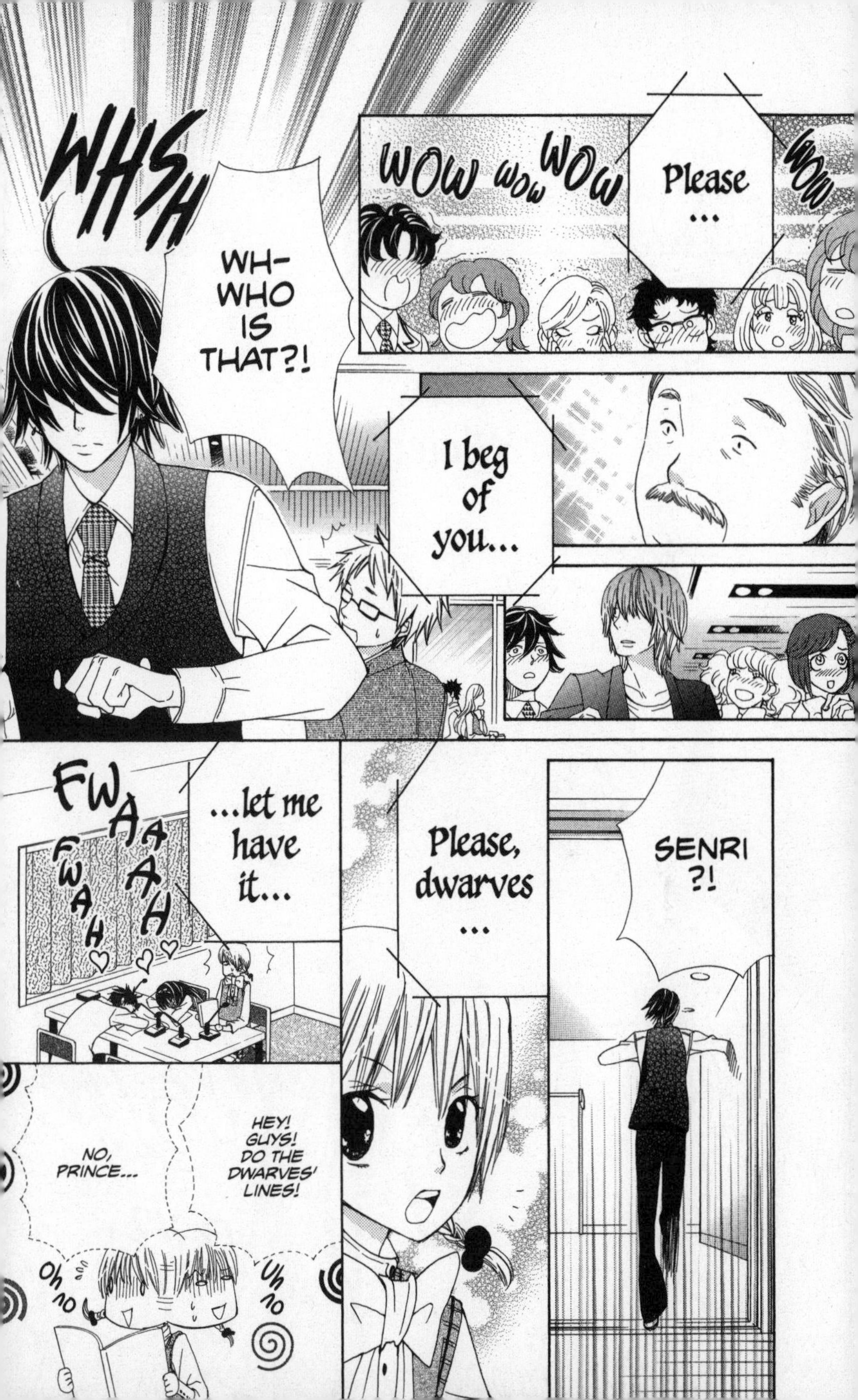
WOW
Please...
WOW WOW WOW
I beg of you...
WHSH
WH-WHO IS THAT?!
SENRI ?!
Please, dwarves...
...let me have it...
FWAAAH
FWAH
HEY! GUYS! DO THE DWARVES' LINES!
NO, PRINCE...
Uh no
Oh no

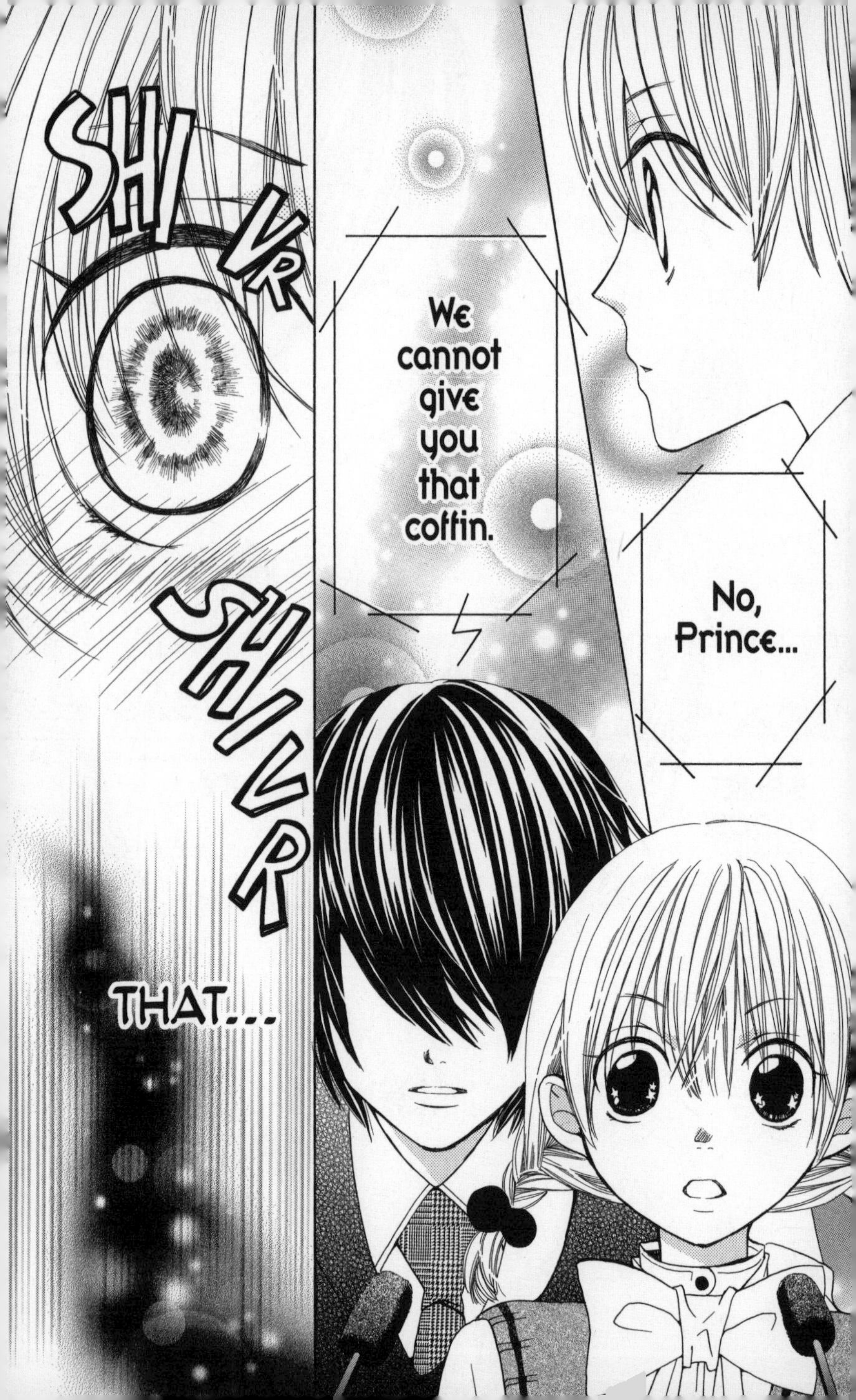
No, Prince...
We cannot give you that coffin.
SHIVR
SHIVR
THAT....

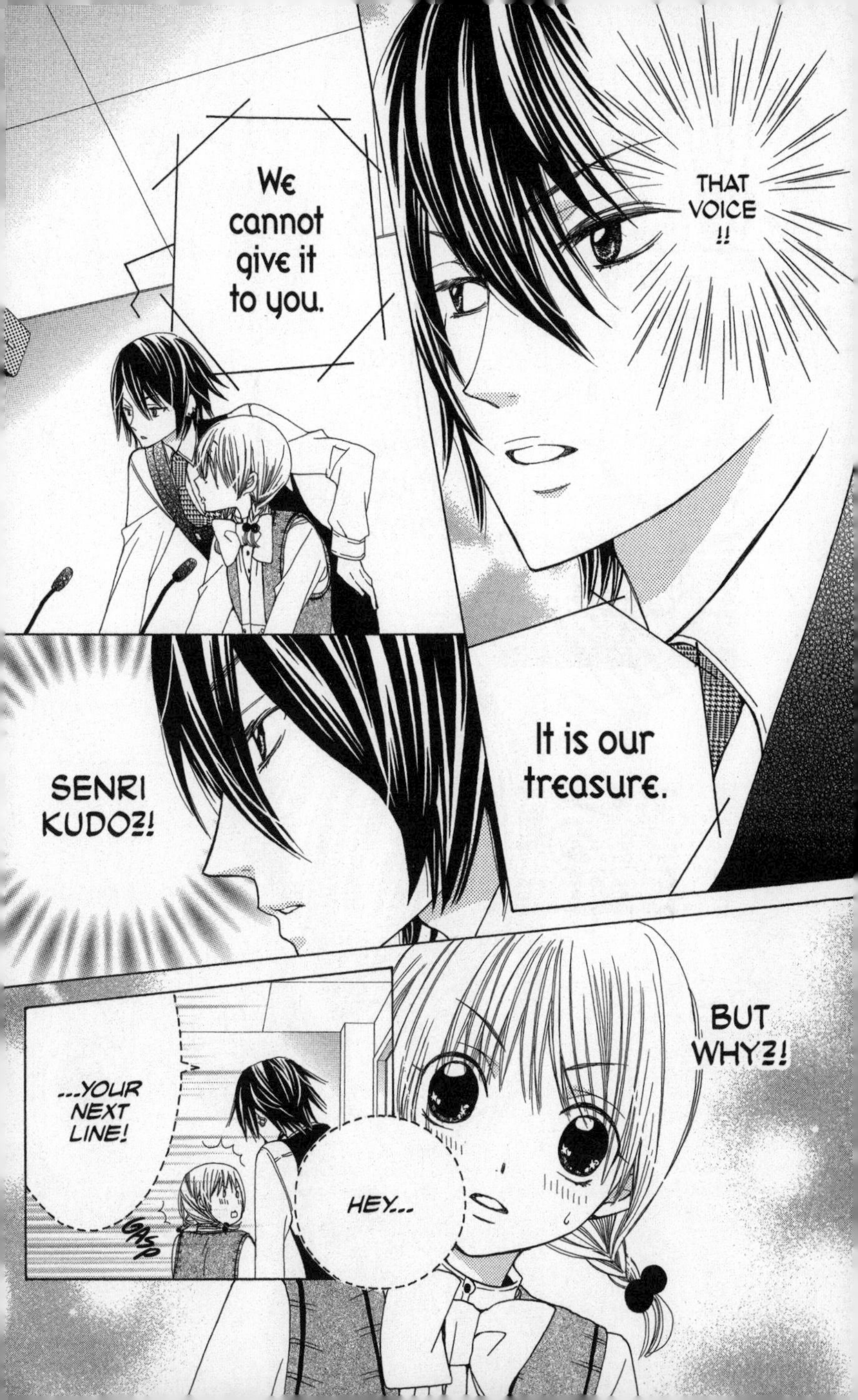
THAT VOICE !!
We cannot give it to you.
It is our treasure.
SENRI KUDO?!
BUT WHY?!
HEY...
...YOUR NEXT LINE!
GASP

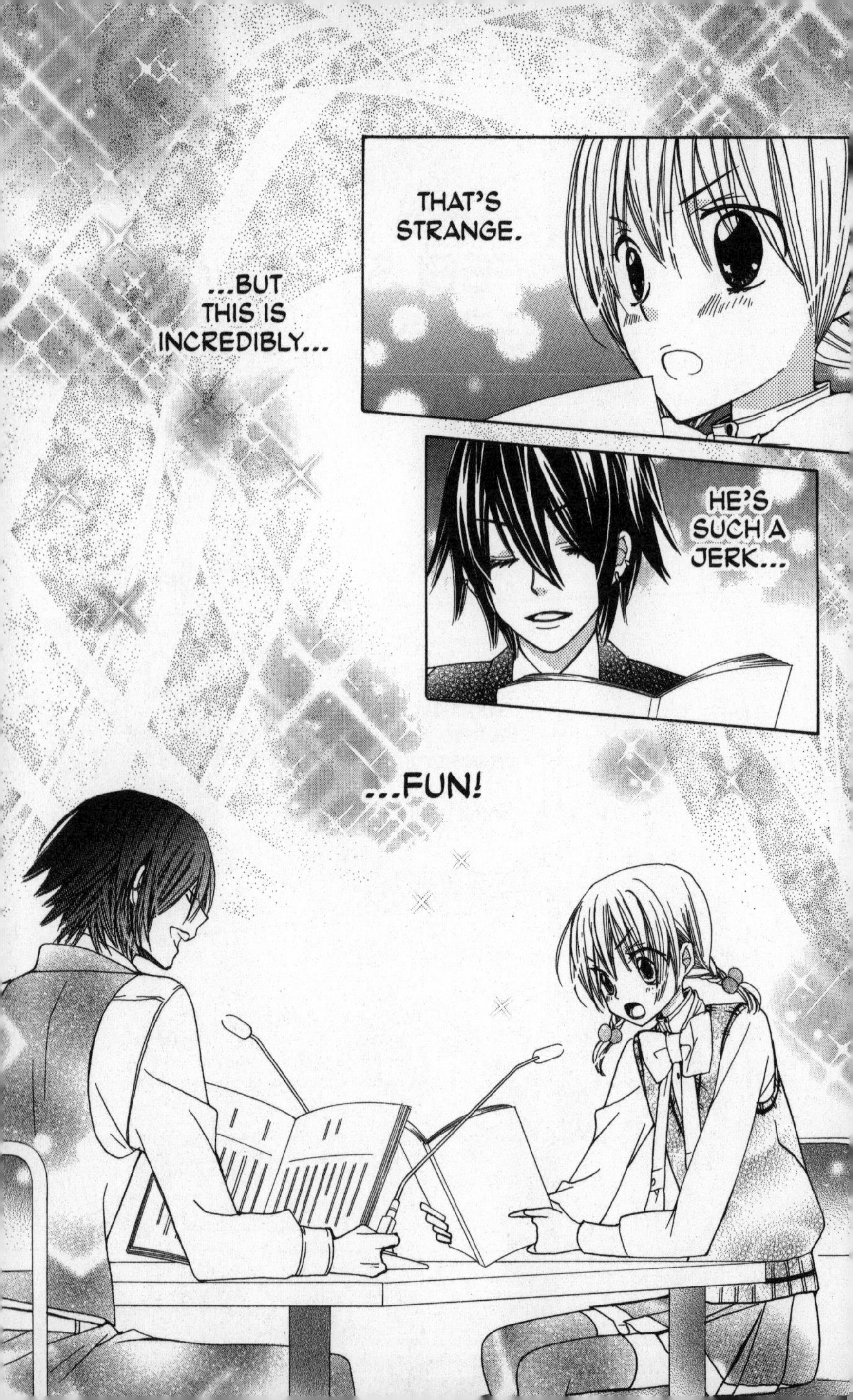
THAT'S STRANGE.
HE'S SUCH A JERK...
...BUT THIS IS INCREDIBLY...
...FUN!

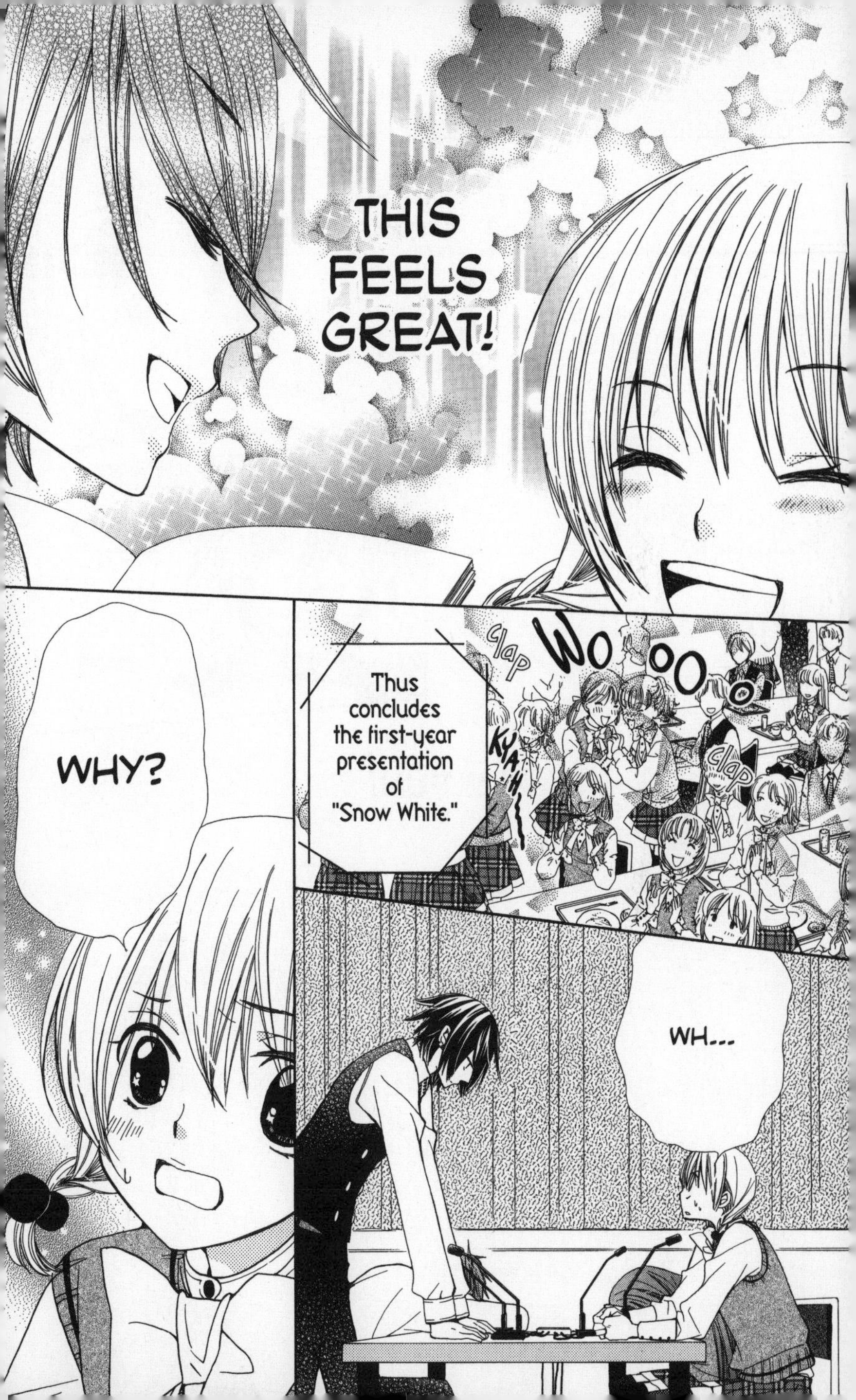
THIS FEELS GREAT!
WOOOO
clap
clap
Thus concludes the first-year presentation of "Snow White."
KYAAH!
WH...
WHY?

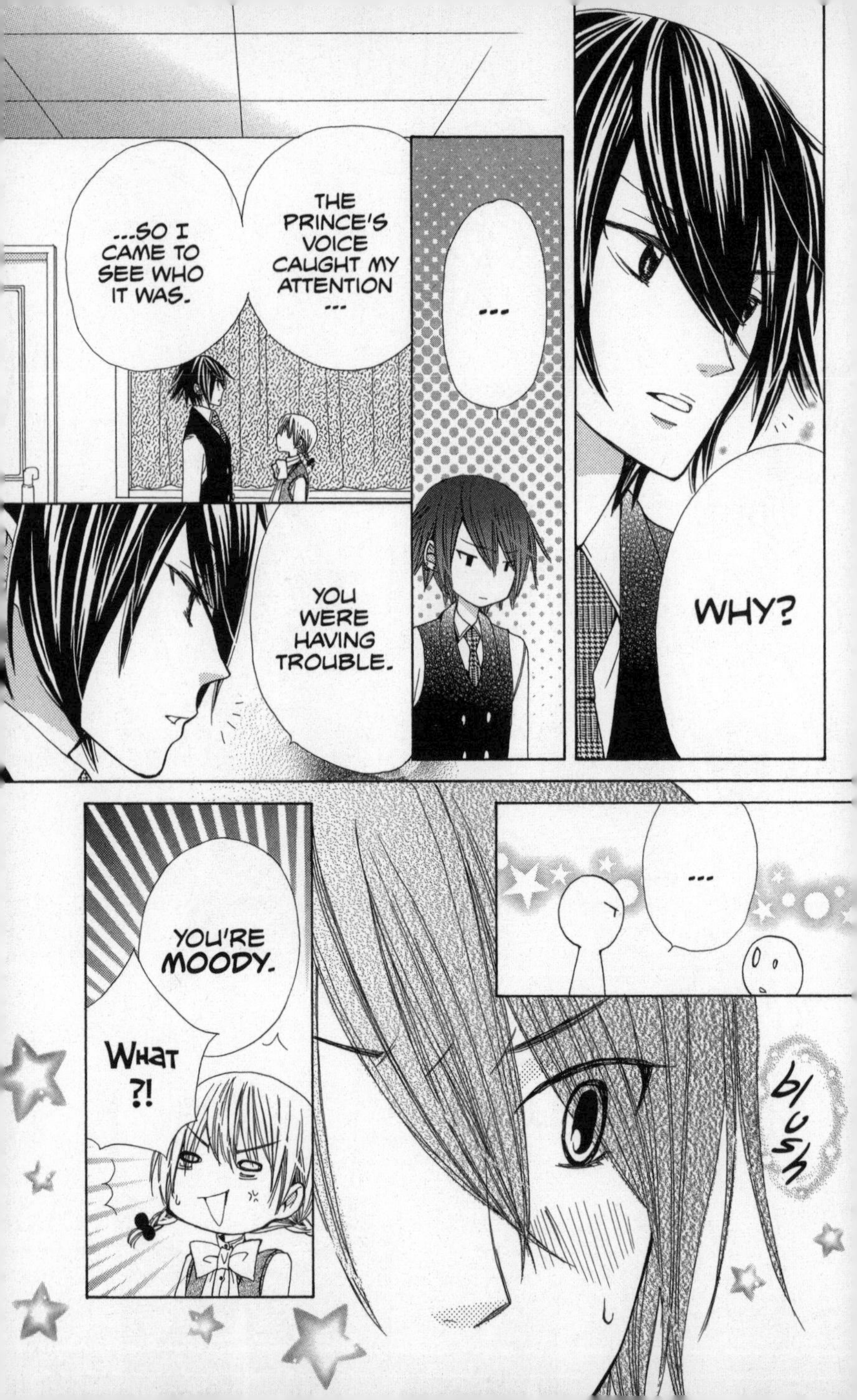
WHY?
...
THE PRINCE'S VOICE CAUGHT MY ATTENTION...
...SO I CAME TO SEE WHO IT WAS.
YOU WERE HAVING TROUBLE.
...
blush
YOU'RE MOODY.
WHAT?!

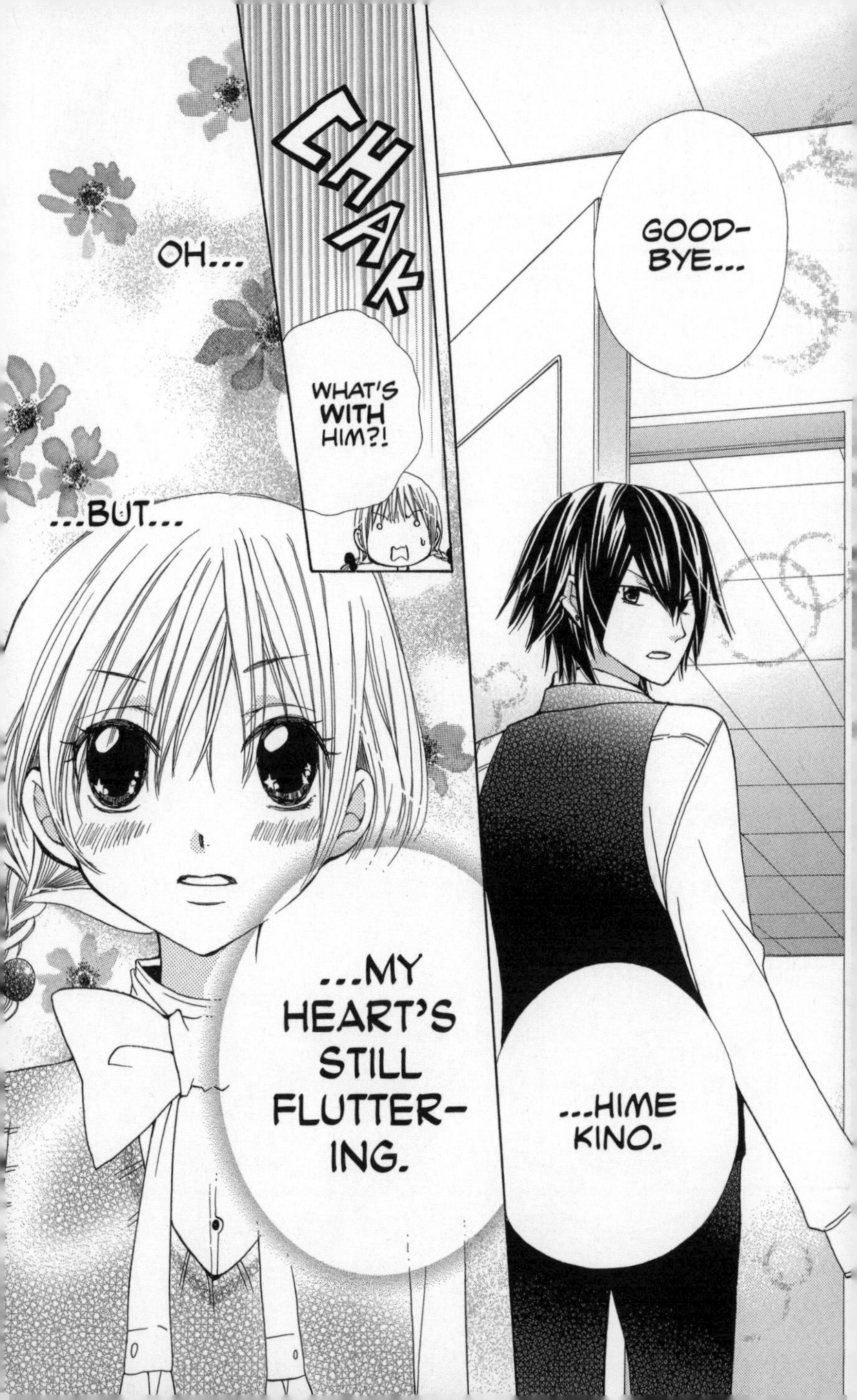
GOOD-BYE...
...HIME KINO.
CHAK
WHAT'S WITH HIM?!
OH...
...BUT...
...MY HEART'S STILL FLUTTER-ING.

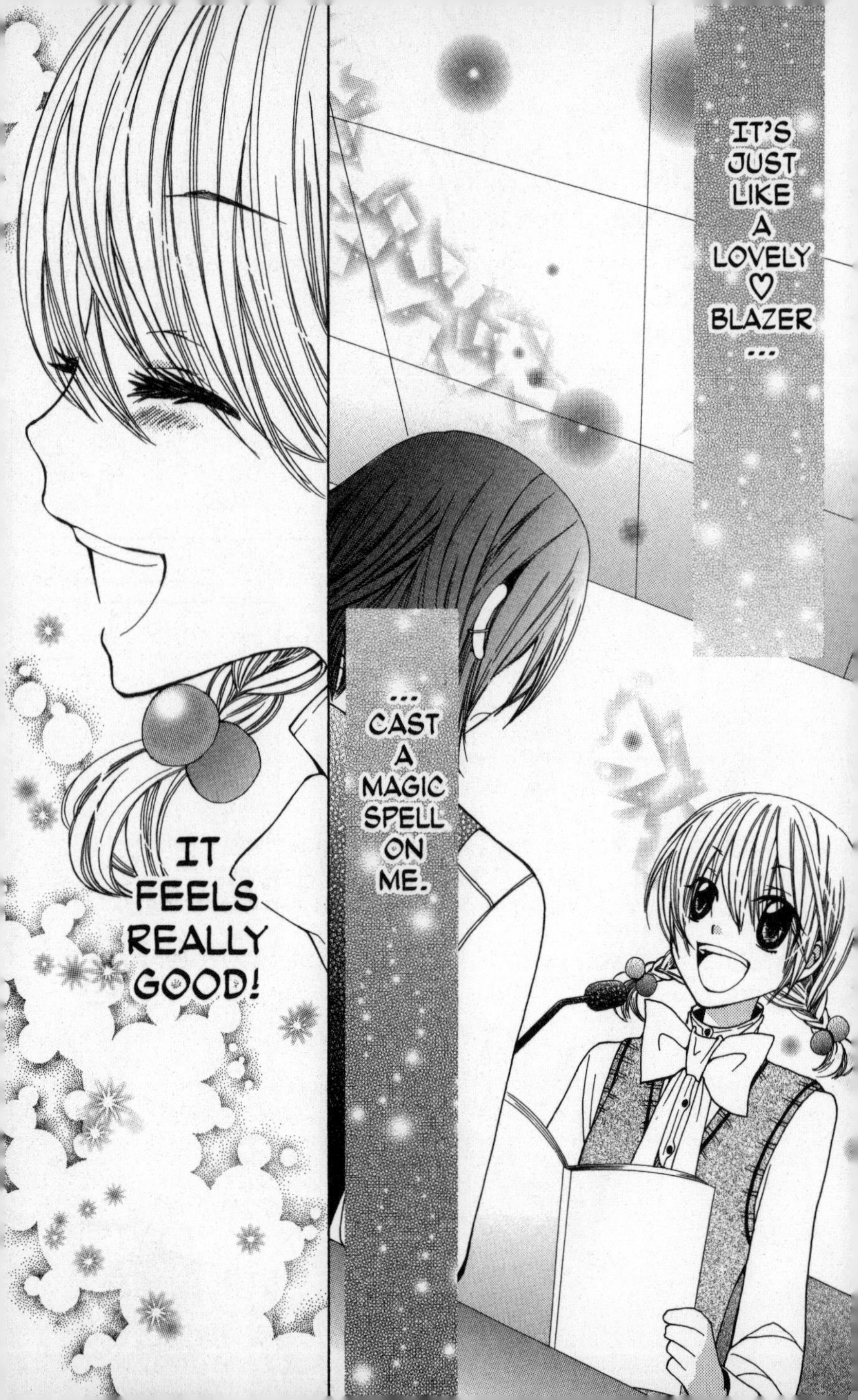
IT'S JUST LIKE A LOVELY ♡ BLAZER ...
... CAST A MAGIC SPELL ON ME.
IT FEELS REALLY GOOD!

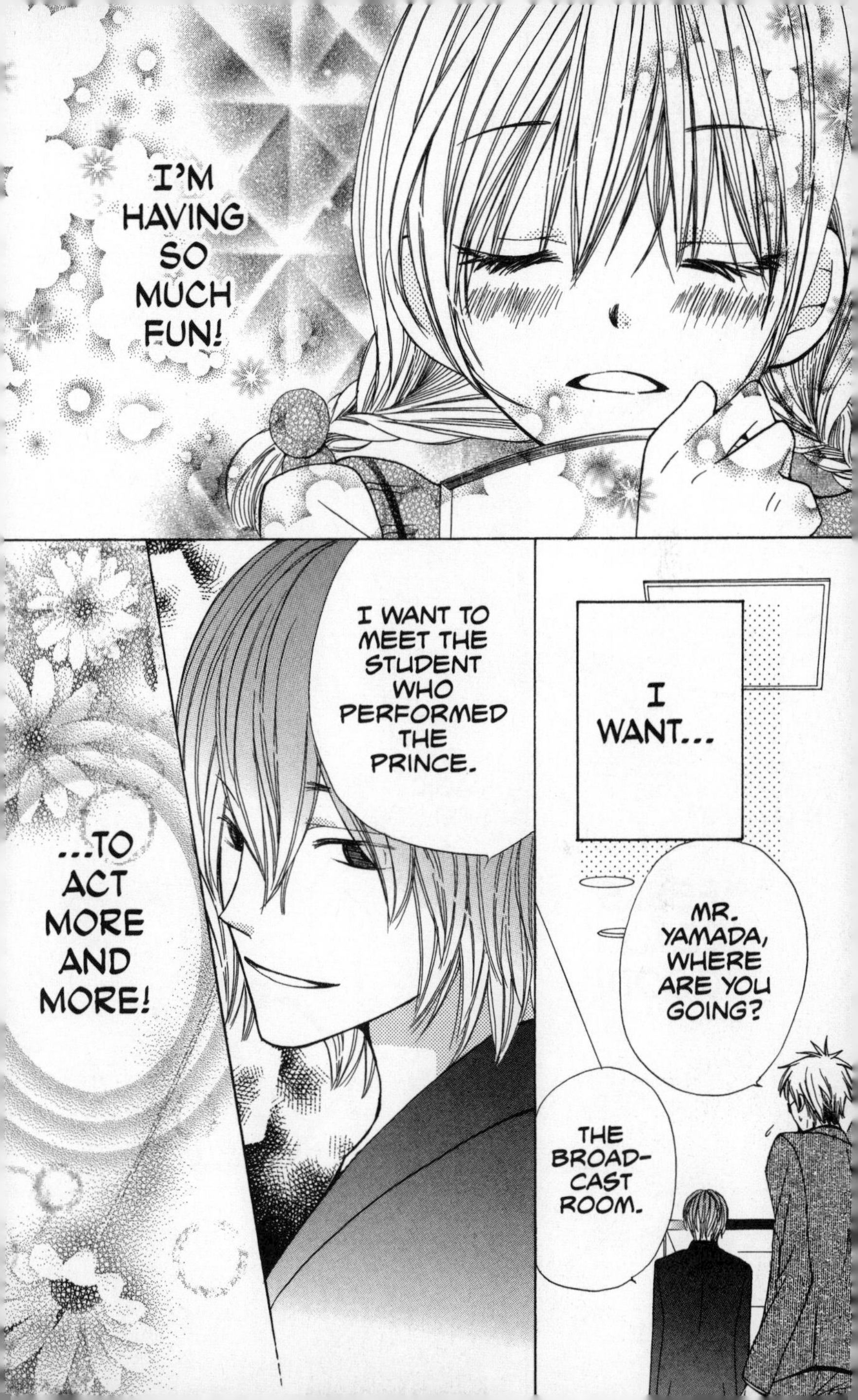
I'M HAVING SO MUCH FUN!
I WANT...
MR. YAMADA, WHERE ARE YOU GOING?
THE BROAD-CAST ROOM.
I WANT TO MEET THE STUDENT WHO PERFORMED THE PRINCE.
...TO ACT MORE AND MORE!

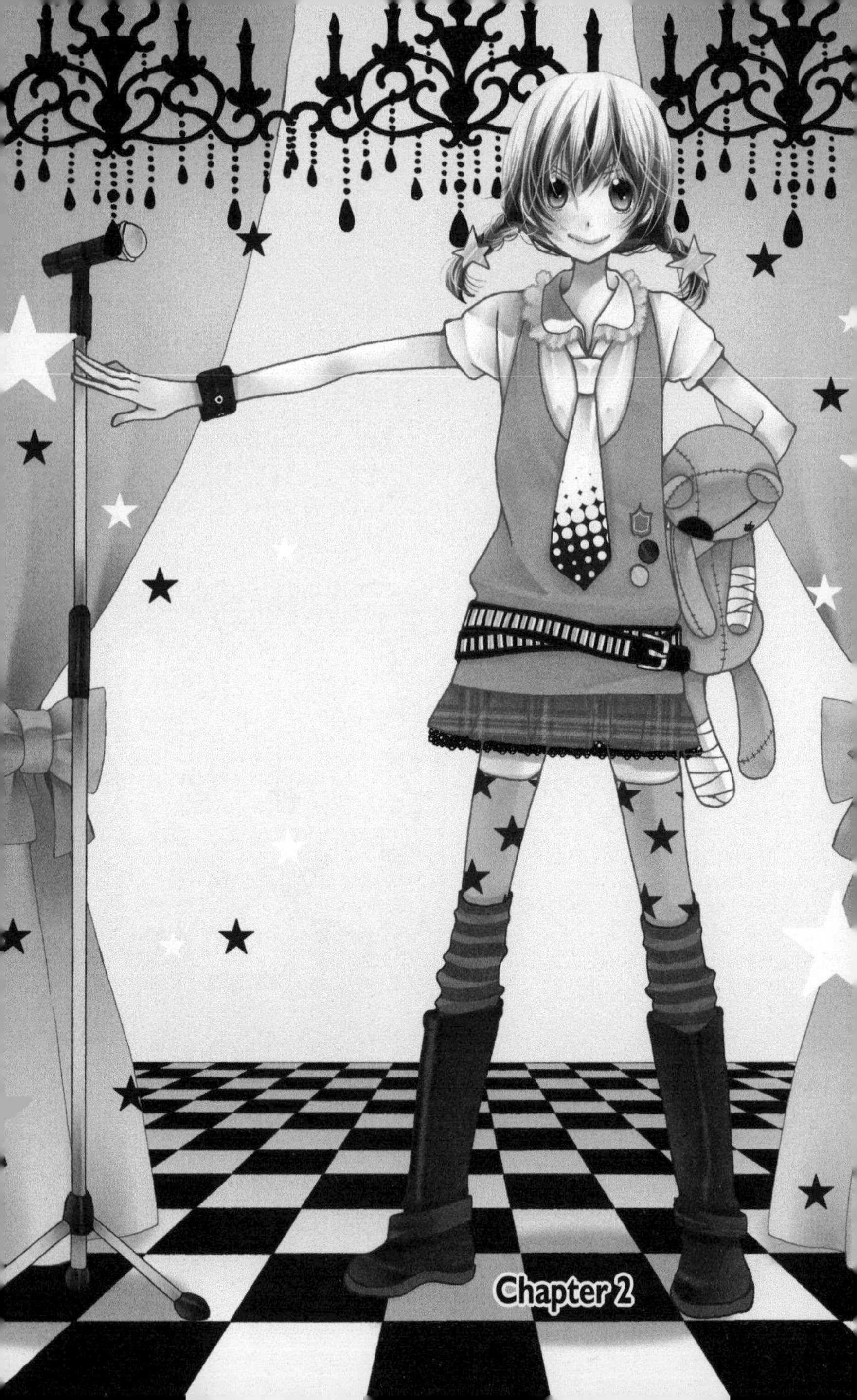
Chapter 2

Voice Over!

peep

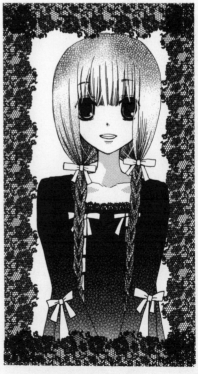

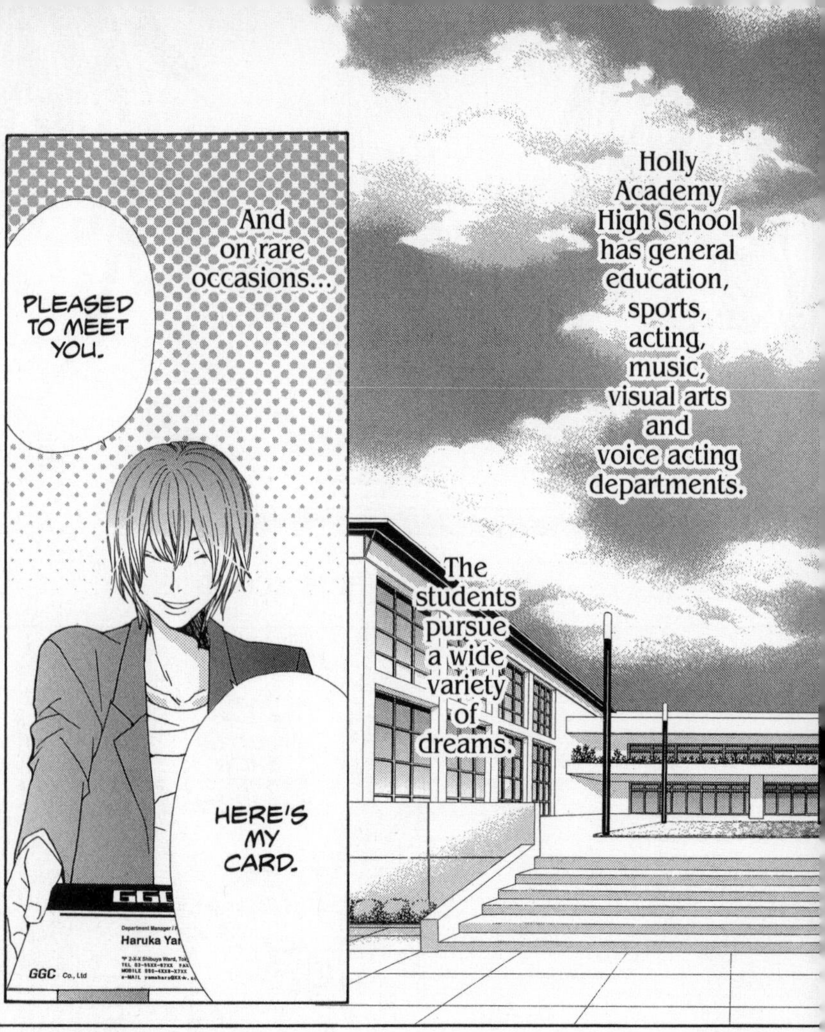
Holly Academy High School has general education, sports, acting, music, visual arts and voice acting departments.
The students pursue a wide variety of dreams.
And on rare occasions...
PLEASED TO MEET YOU.
HERE'S MY CARD.
GGC Co., Ltd

. Voice Over! ② .

I thought about various projections and came up with a cuff and ribbon on the sleeves.

Now I have to draw their summer uniforms, but I still haven't decided on anything.
I wonder what they should be like...

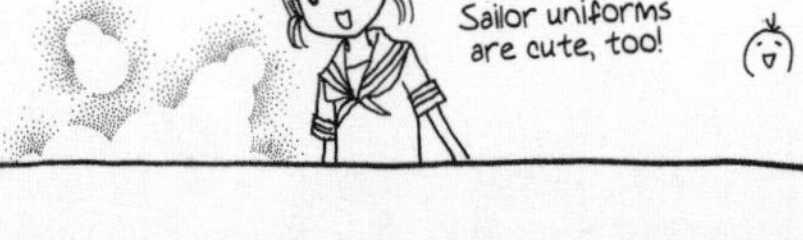
Sailor uniforms are cute, too!

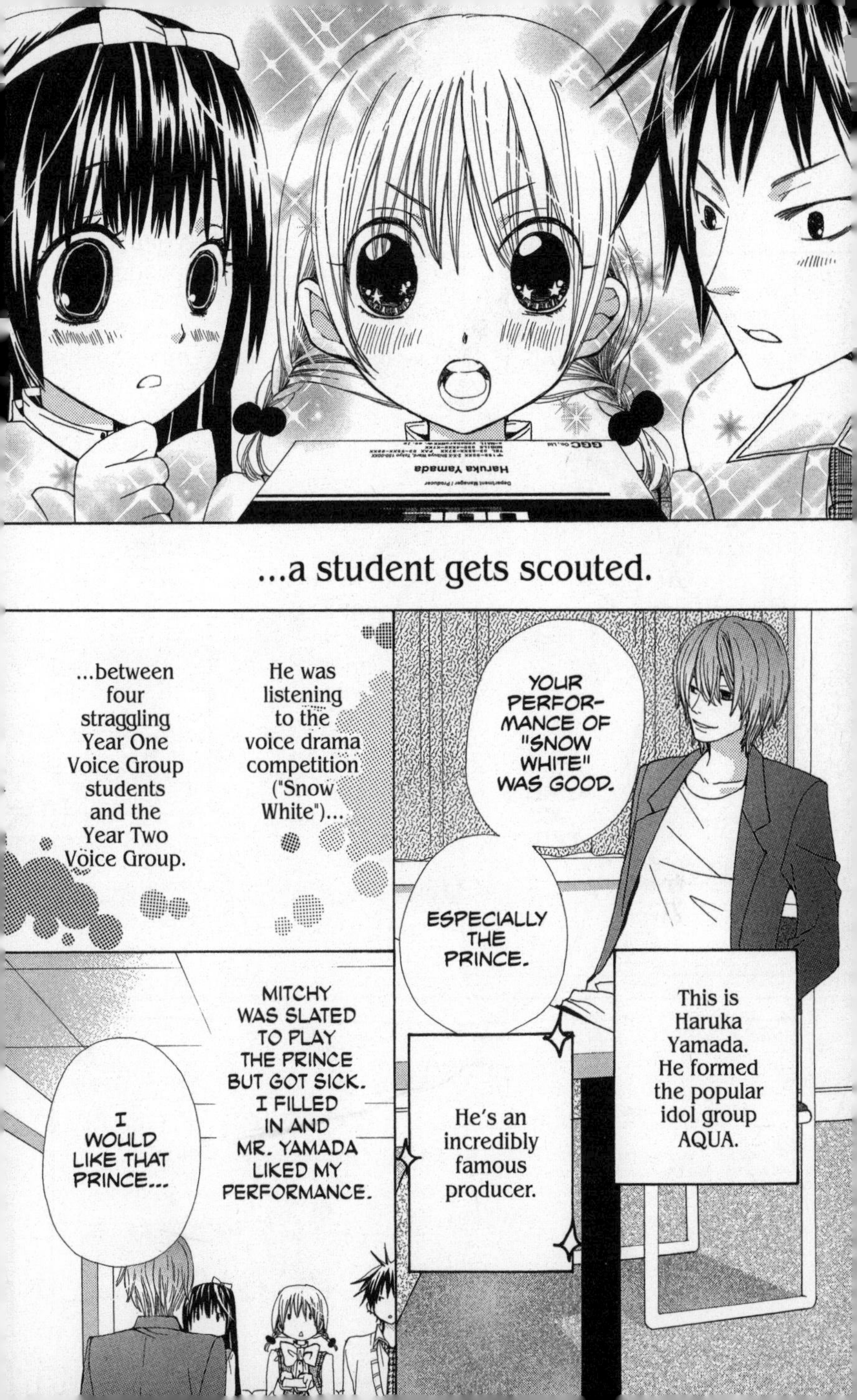
...a student gets scouted.
YOUR PERFORMANCE OF "SNOW WHITE" WAS GOOD.
ESPECIALLY THE PRINCE.
This is Haruka Yamada. He formed the popular idol group AQUA.
He's an incredibly famous producer.
He was listening to the voice drama competition ("Snow White")...
...between four straggling Year One Voice Group students and the Year Two Voice Group.
MITCHY WAS SLATED TO PLAY THE PRINCE BUT GOT SICK. I FILLED IN AND MR. YAMADA LIKED MY PERFORMANCE.
I WOULD LIKE THAT PRINCE...

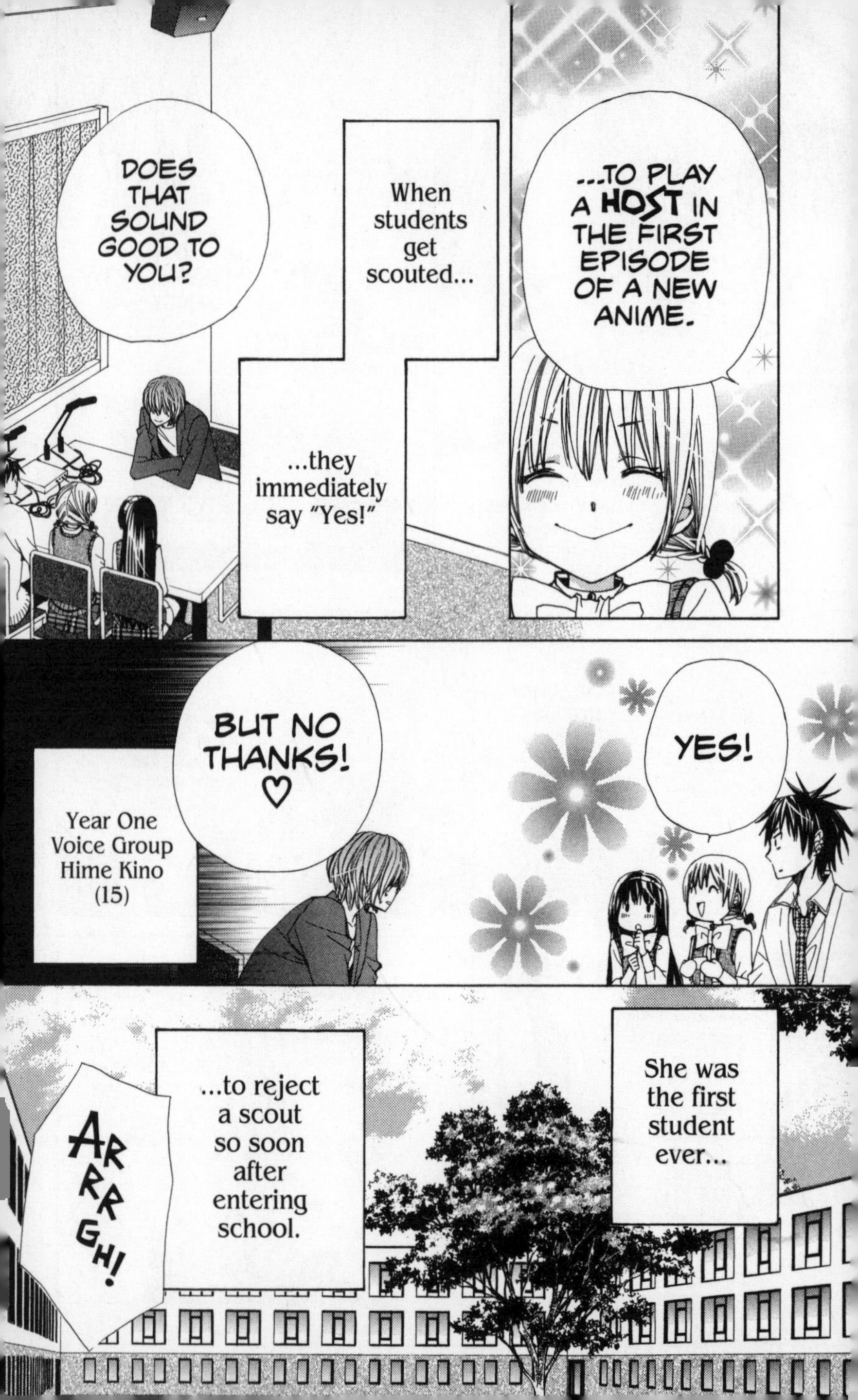
...TO PLAY A HOST IN THE FIRST EPISODE OF A NEW ANIME.
When students get scouted...
...they immediately say "Yes!"
DOES THAT SOUND GOOD TO YOU?
YES!
BUT NO THANKS! ♡
Year One Voice Group Hime Kino (15)
She was the first student ever...
...to reject a scout so soon after entering school.
ARRRGH!

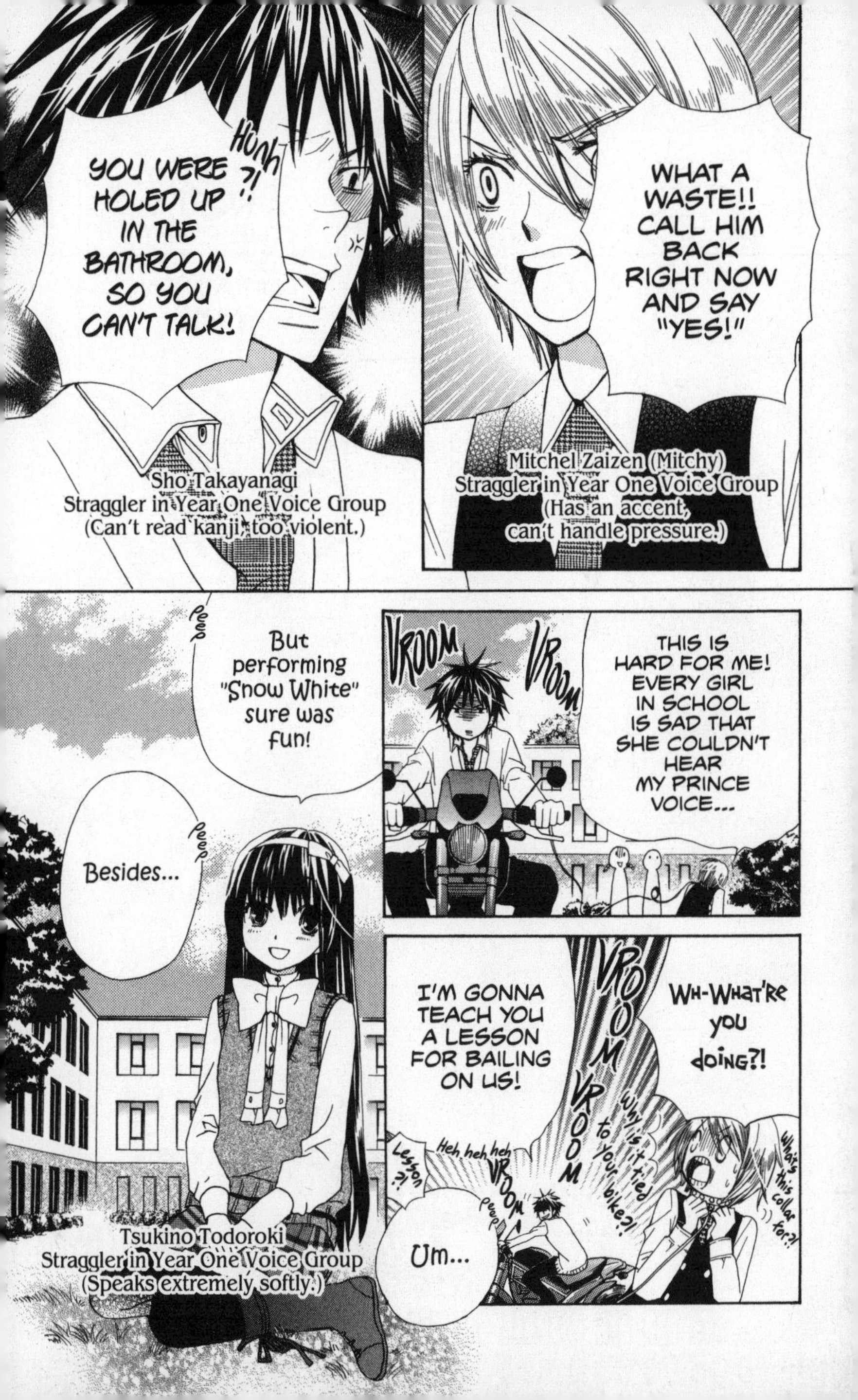
WHAT A WASTE!! CALL HIM BACK RIGHT NOW AND SAY "YES!"
Mitchel Zaizen (Mitchy)
Straggler in Year One Voice Group
(Has an accent, can't handle pressure.)
HUNH ?!
YOU WERE HOLED UP IN THE BATHROOM, SO YOU CAN'T TALK!
Sho Takayanagi
Straggler in Year One Voice Group
(Can't read kanji, too violent.)
THIS IS HARD FOR ME! EVERY GIRL IN SCHOOL IS SAD THAT SHE COULDN'T HEAR MY PRINCE VOICE...
VROOM
VROOM
Wh-What're you doing?!
What's this collar for?!
Why is it tied to your bike?!
VROOM
VROOM
I'M GONNA TEACH YOU A LESSON FOR BAILING ON US!
Heh heh heh
VROOM
Lesson?!
Peep
Um...
Peep
But performing "Snow White" sure was fun!
Peep
Besides...
Tsukino Todoroki
Straggler in Year One Voice Group
(Speaks extremely softly.)

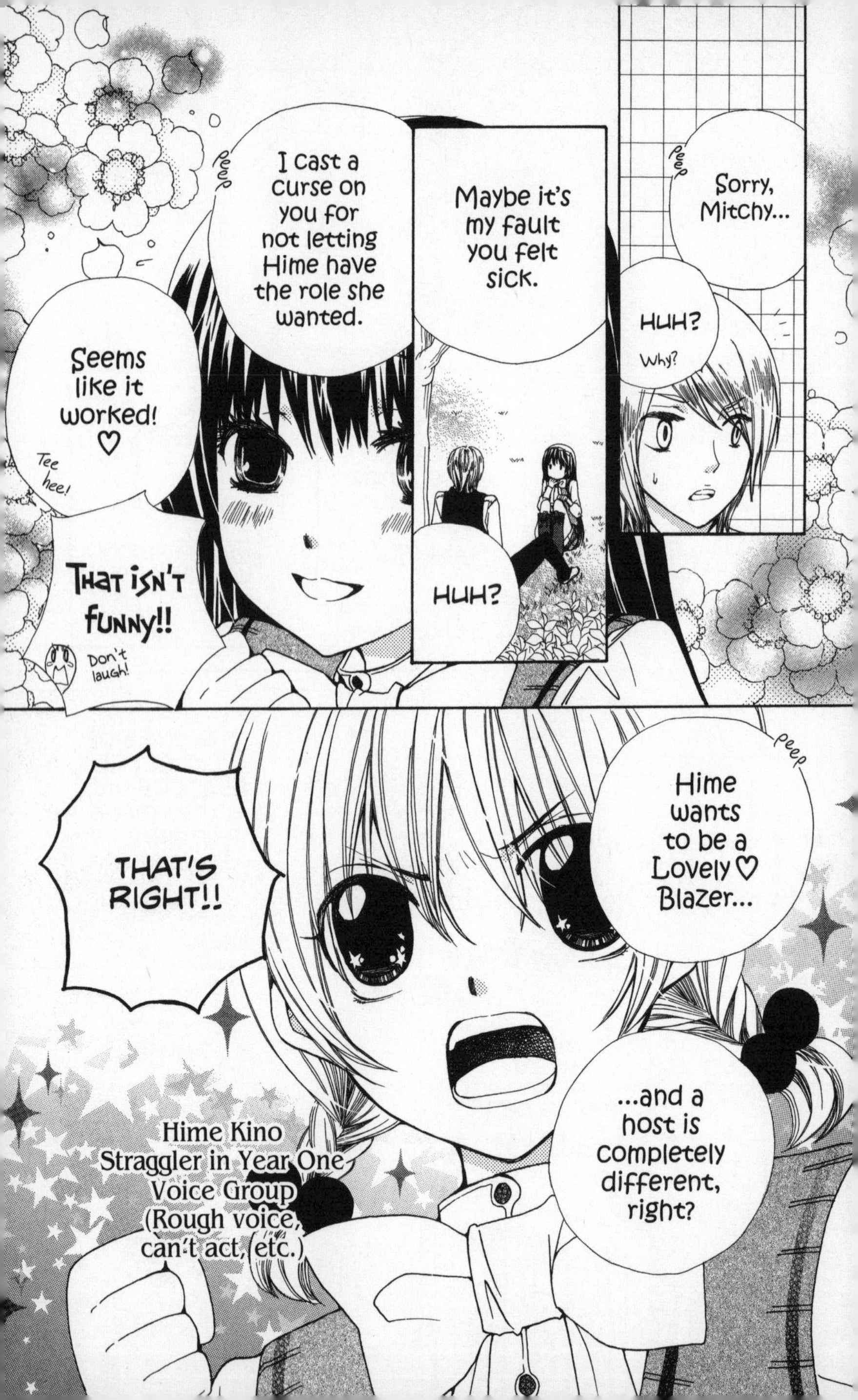
peep
Sorry, Mitchy...
HUH?
Why?
Maybe it's my fault you felt sick.
HUH?
peep
I cast a curse on you for not letting Hime have the role she wanted.
Seems like it worked! ♡
Tee hee!
THAT ISN'T FUNNY!!
Don't laugh!
peep
Hime wants to be a Lovely ♡ Blazer...
...and a host is completely different, right?
THAT'S RIGHT!!
Hime Kino
Straggler in Year One
Voice Group
(Rough voice, can't act, etc.)

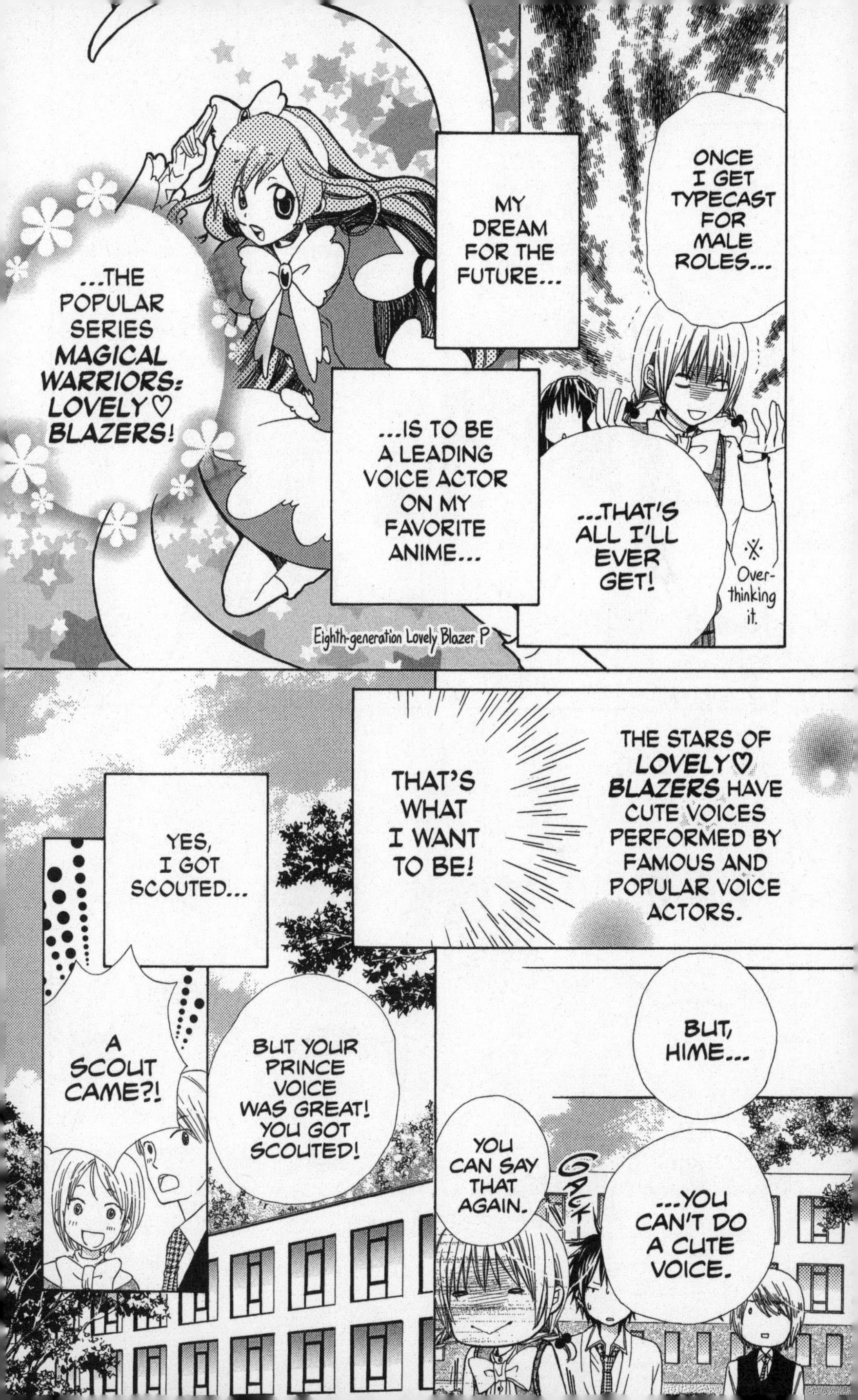
ONCE I GET TYPECAST FOR MALE ROLES...
...THAT'S ALL I'LL EVER GET!
※ Over-thinking it.
MY DREAM FOR THE FUTURE...
...IS TO BE A LEADING VOICE ACTOR ON MY FAVORITE ANIME...
...THE POPULAR SERIES MAGICAL WARRIORS: LOVELY♡ BLAZERS!
Eighth-generation Lovely Blazer P
THE STARS OF LOVELY♡ BLAZERS HAVE CUTE VOICES PERFORMED BY FAMOUS AND POPULAR VOICE ACTORS.
THAT'S WHAT I WANT TO BE!
YES, I GOT SCOUTED...
BUT, HIME...
...YOU CAN'T DO A CUTE VOICE.
GACK
YOU CAN SAY THAT AGAIN.
BUT YOUR PRINCE VOICE WAS GREAT! YOU GOT SCOUTED!
A SCOUT CAME?!

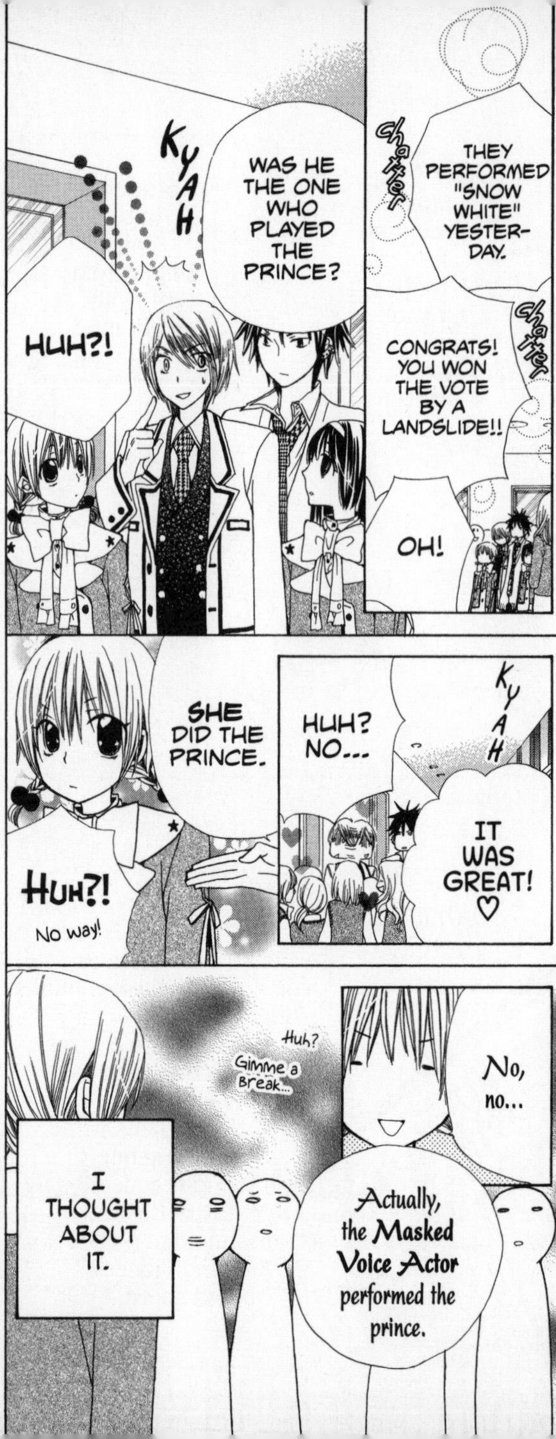
Chatter
THEY PERFORMED "SNOW WHITE" YESTERDAY.
Chatter
CONGRATS! YOU WON THE VOTE BY A LANDSLIDE!!
OH!
KYAH
WAS HE THE ONE WHO PLAYED THE PRINCE?
HUH?!
KYAH
IT WAS GREAT! ♡
HUH? NO...
SHE DID THE PRINCE.
HUH?!
No way!
No, no...
Actually, the Masked Voice Actor performed the prince.
Huh? Gimme a break...
I THOUGHT ABOUT IT.

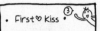

• First ♡ Kiss ③

The phrase "first ♡ kiss ☆" sounds so sweet and lovely... But! My first kiss was in kindergarten with my relative I-kun. My big sister and his big sister ordered us to.

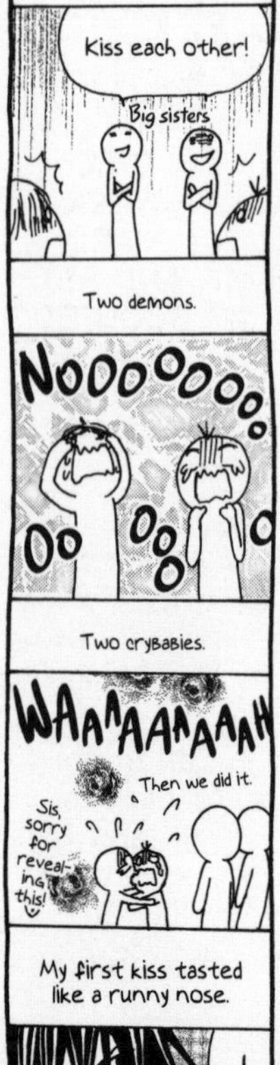
Kiss each other!
Big sisters
Two demons.
NOOOOOOOOO
OOOOO
Two crybabies.
WAAAAAAAAAH
Then we did it.
Sis, sorry for revealing this!
My first kiss tasted like a runny nose.
!

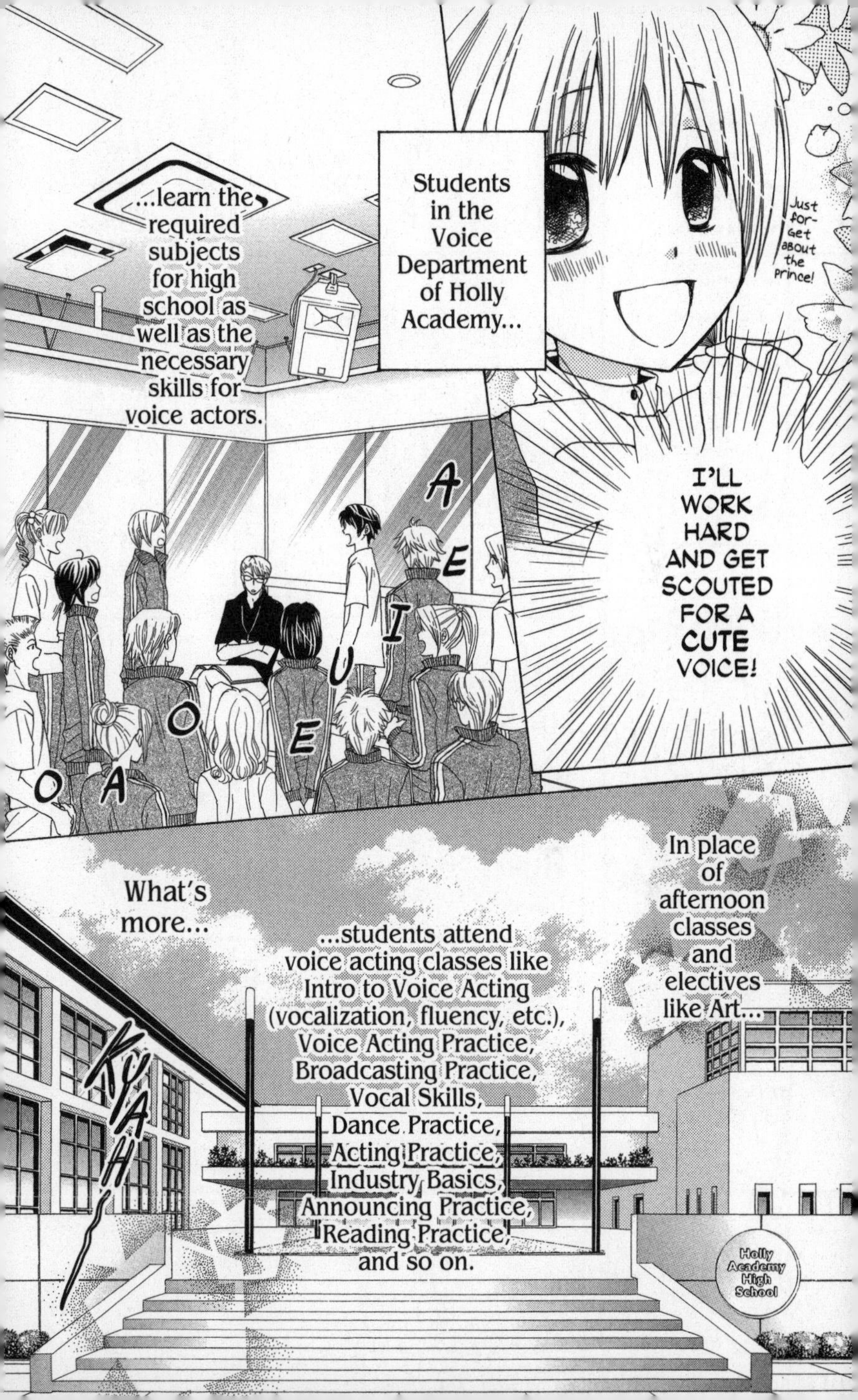
Students in the Voice Department of Holly Academy...
Just for-get about the Prince!
I'LL WORK HARD AND GET SCOUTED FOR A CUTE VOICE!
...learn the required subjects for high school as well as the necessary skills for voice actors.
A
E
I
U
E
O
A
O
In place of afternoon classes and electives like Art...
What's more...
...students attend voice acting classes like Intro to Voice Acting (vocalization, fluency, etc.), Voice Acting Practice, Broadcasting Practice, Vocal Skills, Dance Practice, Acting Practice, Industry Basics, Announcing Practice, Reading Practice, and so on.
Holly Academy High School
KYAAH!

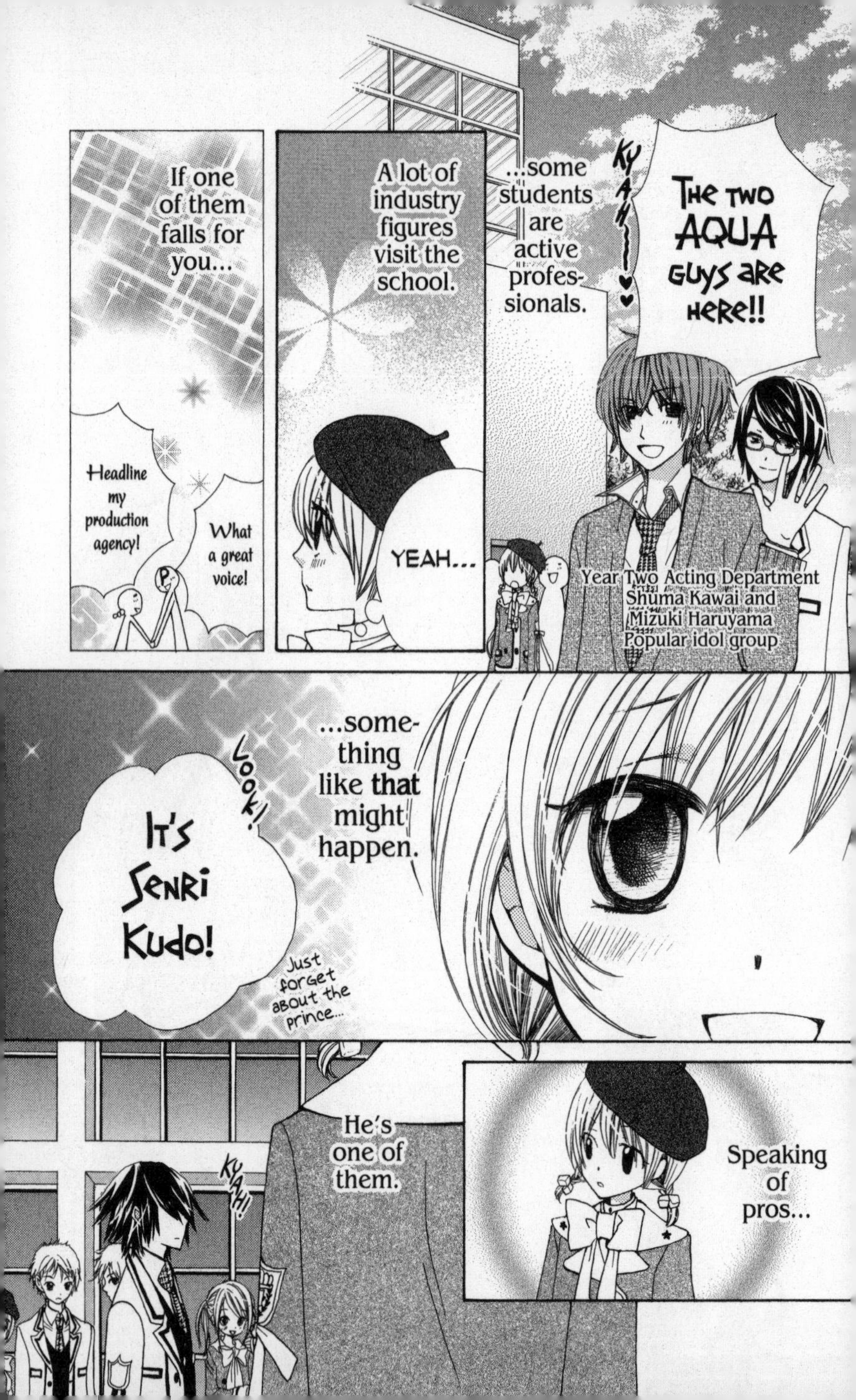

KYAH!!
THE TWO AQUA GUYS ARE HERE!!
...some students are active profes-sionals.
Year Two Acting Department Shuma Kawai and Mizuki Haruyama Popular idol group
A lot of industry figures visit the school.
YEAH...
If one of them falls for you...
Headline my production agency!
What a great voice!
...some-thing like that might happen.
LOOK!
IT'S SENRI KUDO!
Just forget about the prince...
Speaking of pros...
He's one of them.
KYAH!

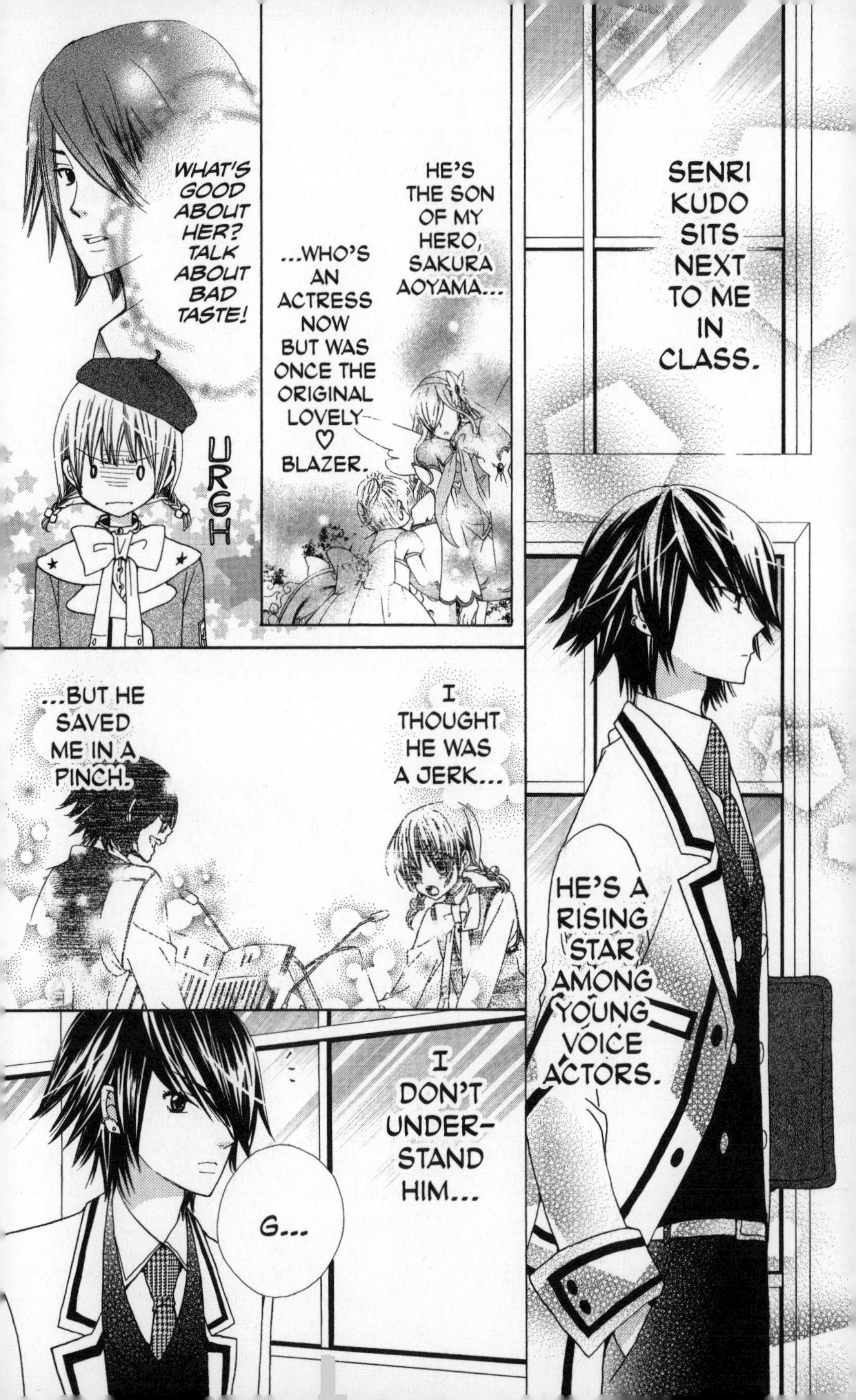
SENRI KUDO SITS NEXT TO ME IN CLASS.
HE'S A RISING STAR AMONG YOUNG VOICE ACTORS.
HE'S THE SON OF MY HERO, SAKURA AOYAMA...
...WHO'S AN ACTRESS NOW BUT WAS ONCE THE ORIGINAL LOVELY ♡ BLAZER.
WHAT'S GOOD ABOUT HER? TALK ABOUT BAD TASTE!
URGH
I THOUGHT HE WAS A JERK...
...BUT HE SAVED ME IN A PINCH.
I DON'T UNDER-STAND HIM...
G...

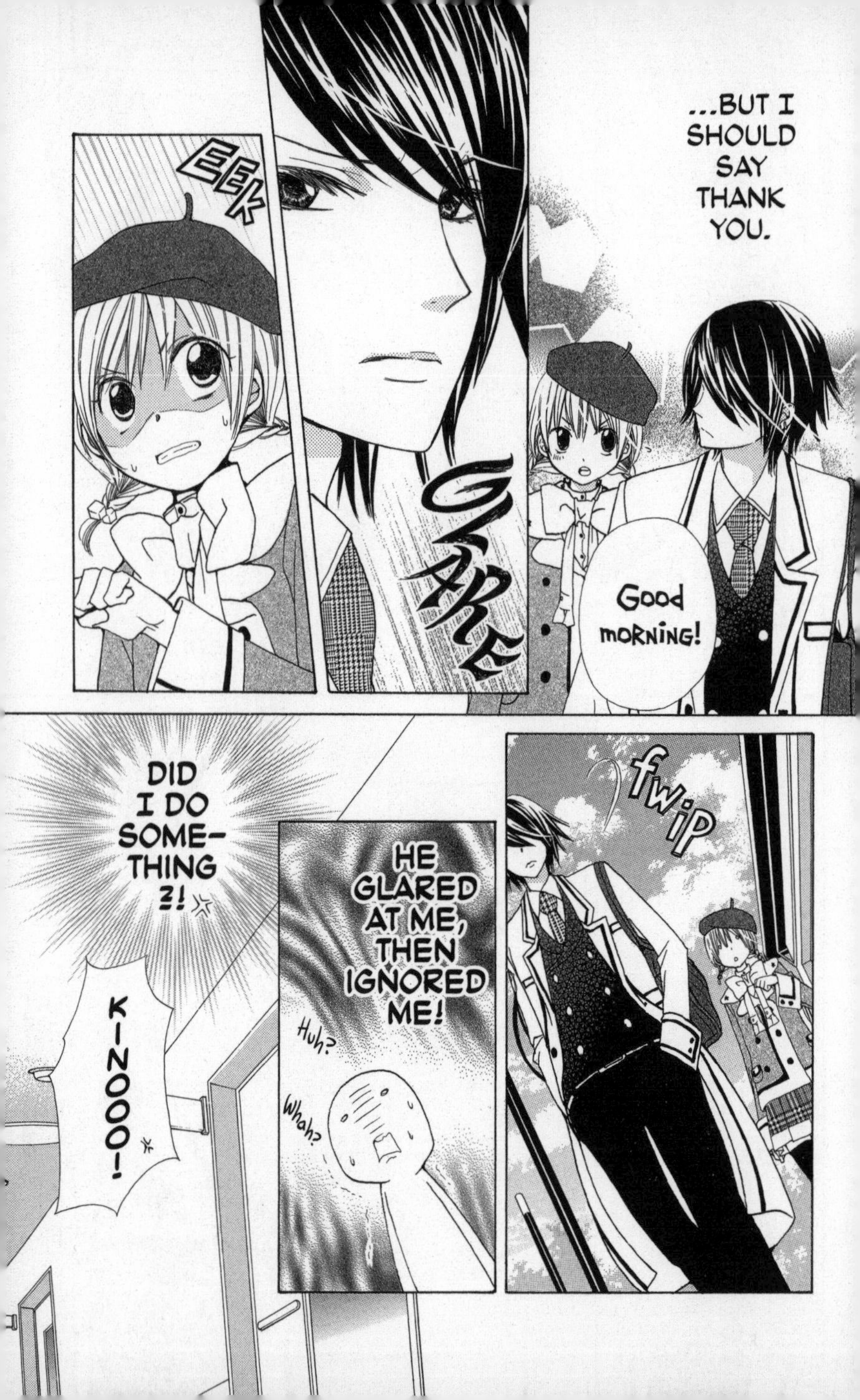
...BUT I SHOULD SAY THANK YOU.
Good morning!
GLARE
EEK
fwip
HE GLARED AT ME, THEN IGNORED ME!
Huh?
Whah?
DID I DO SOME-THING?!
KINOOOO!

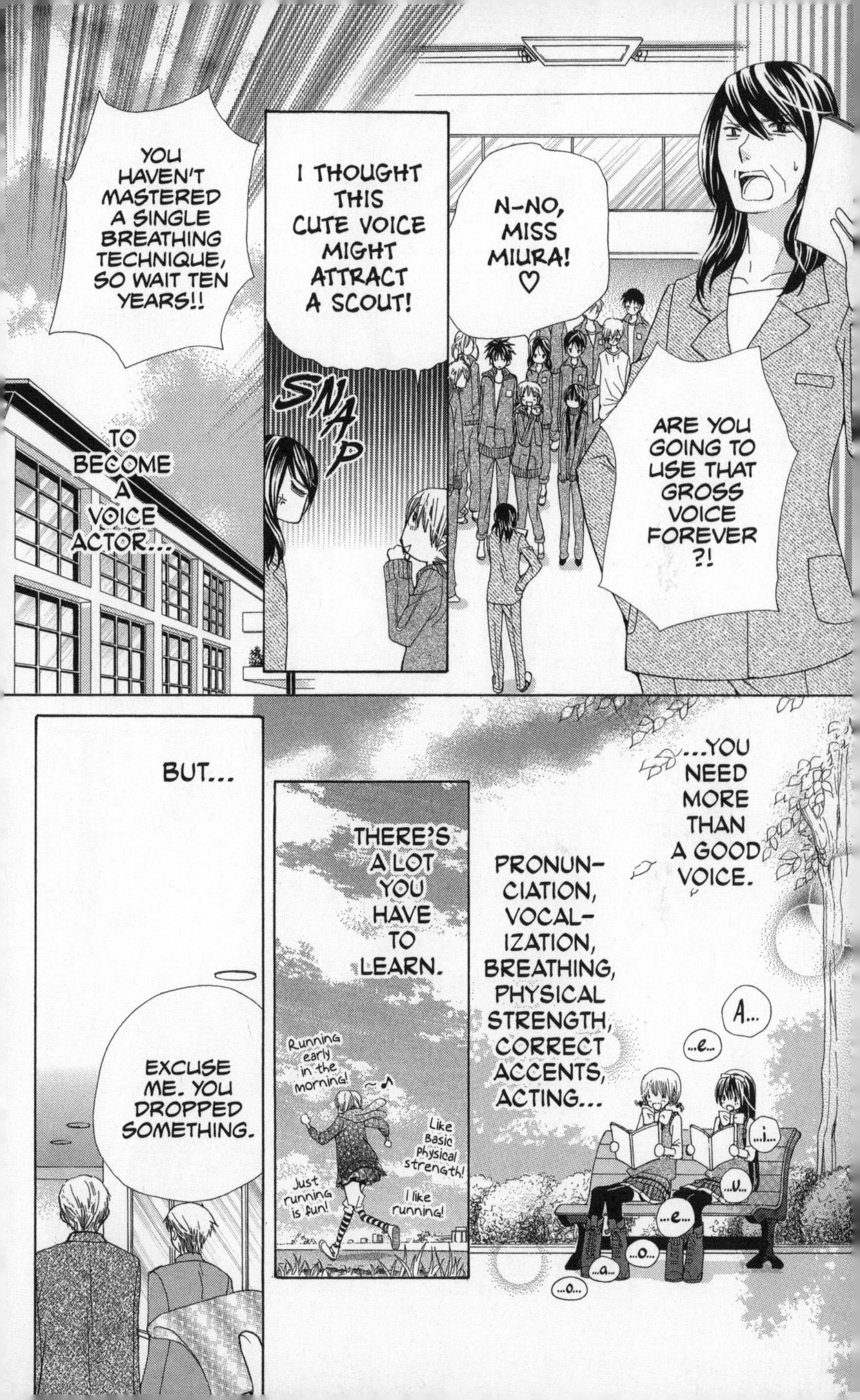
ARE YOU GOING TO USE THAT GROSS VOICE FOREVER?!
N-NO, MISS MIURA! ♡
I THOUGHT THIS CUTE VOICE MIGHT ATTRACT A SCOUT!
SNAP
YOU HAVEN'T MASTERED A SINGLE BREATHING TECHNIQUE, SO WAIT TEN YEARS!!
TO BECOME A VOICE ACTOR...
...YOU NEED MORE THAN A GOOD VOICE.
PRONUN-CIATION, VOCAL-IZATION, BREATHING, PHYSICAL STRENGTH, CORRECT ACCENTS, ACTING...
A...
...e...
...i...
...u...
...e...
...o...
...a...
...o...
THERE'S A LOT YOU HAVE TO LEARN.
Running early in the morning!
~♪
Like Basic Physical strength!
Just running is fun!
I like running!
BUT...
EXCUSE ME. YOU DROPPED SOMETHING.

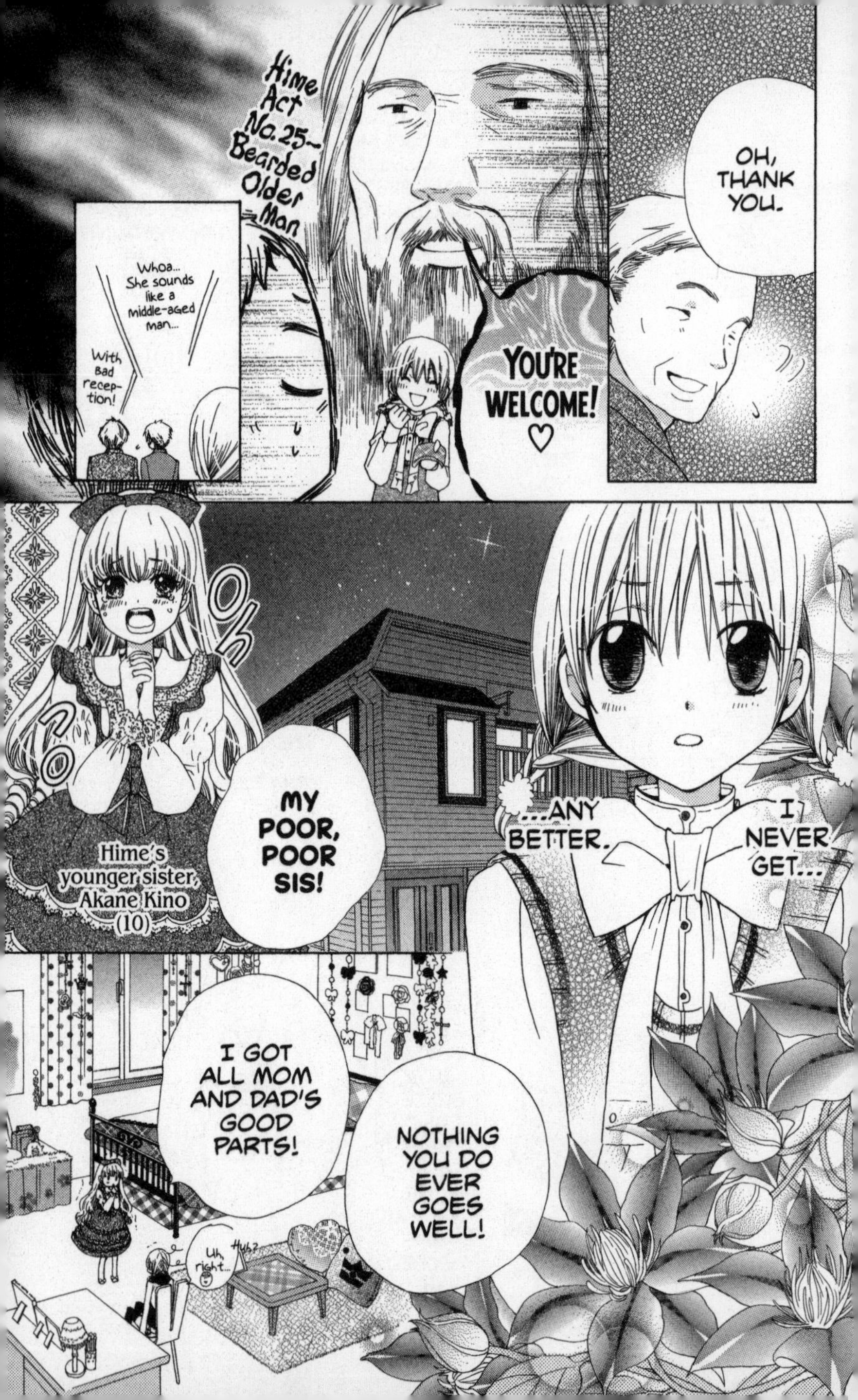
OH, THANK YOU.
YOU'RE WELCOME! ♡
Hime Act No. 25~ Bearded Older Man
Whoa... She sounds like a middle-aged man...
With bad reception!
I NEVER GET...
...ANY BETTER.
Oh
MY POOR, POOR SIS!
Hime's younger sister, Akane Kino (10)
NOTHING YOU DO EVER GOES WELL!
I GOT ALL MOM AND DAD'S GOOD PARTS!
Huh?
Uh, right...

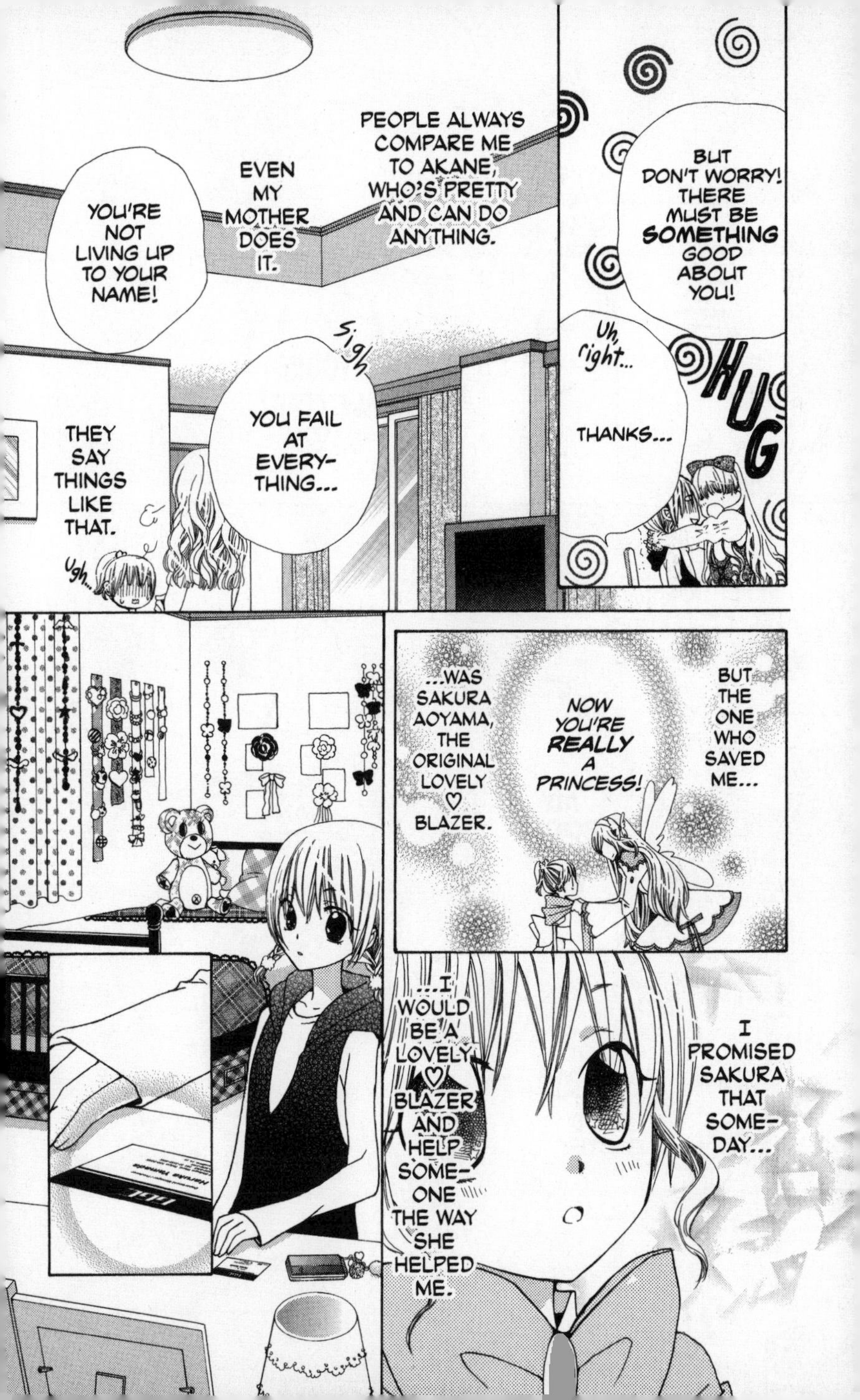
BUT DON'T WORRY! THERE MUST BE SOMETHING GOOD ABOUT YOU!
HUG
Uh, right...
THANKS...
PEOPLE ALWAYS COMPARE ME TO AKANE, WHO'S PRETTY AND CAN DO ANYTHING.
EVEN MY MOTHER DOES IT.
YOU'RE NOT LIVING UP TO YOUR NAME!
Sigh
YOU FAIL AT EVERY-THING...
THEY SAY THINGS LIKE THAT.
Ugh...
BUT THE ONE WHO SAVED ME...
NOW YOU'RE REALLY A PRINCESS!
...WAS SAKURA AOYAMA, THE ORIGINAL LOVELY ♡ BLAZER.
I PROMISED SAKURA THAT SOME-DAY...
...I WOULD BE A LOVELY ♡ BLAZER AND HELP SOME-ONE THE WAY SHE HELPED ME.

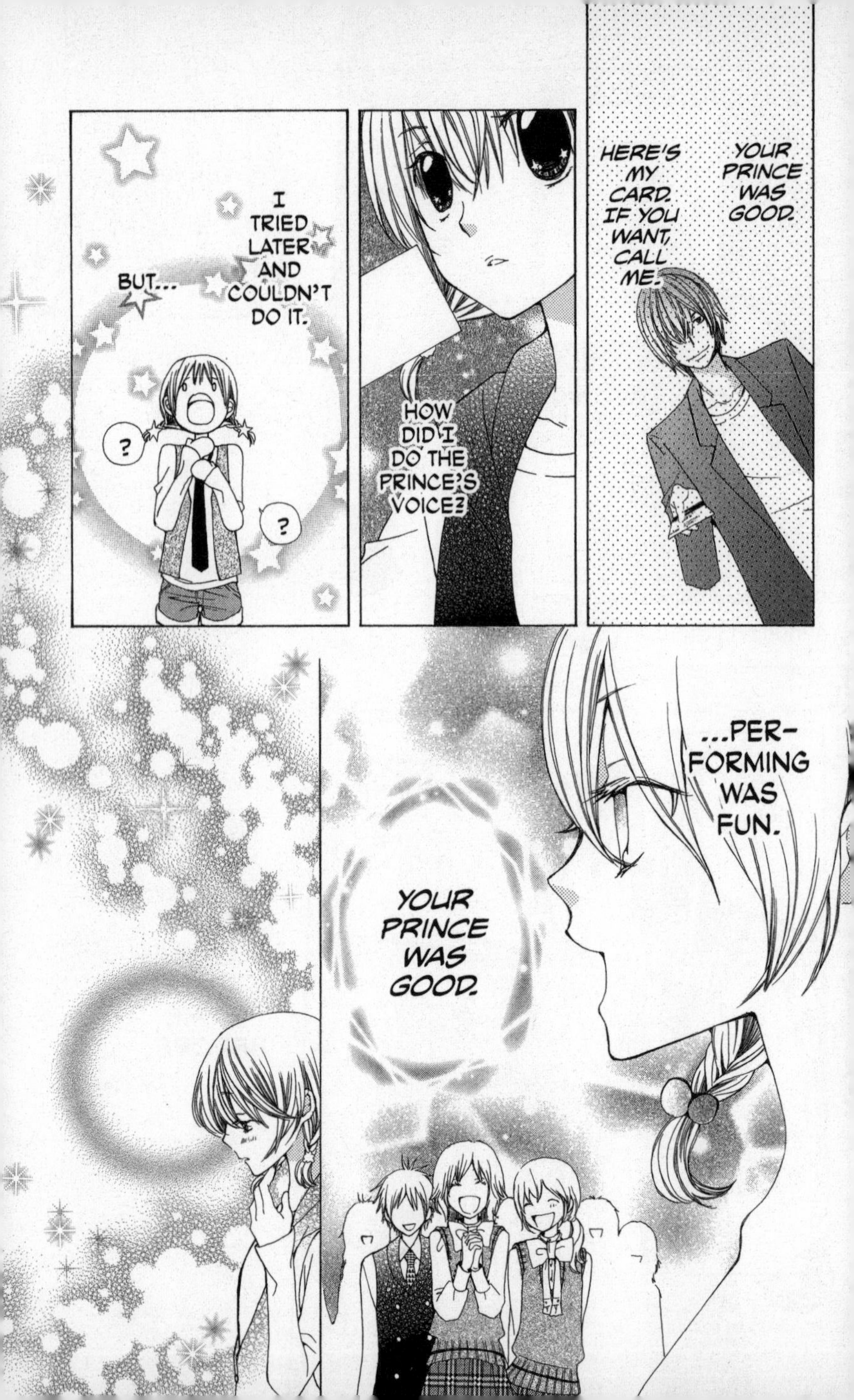
YOUR PRINCE WAS GOOD.
HERE'S MY CARD. IF YOU WANT, CALL ME.
HOW DID I DO THE PRINCE'S VOICE?
I TRIED LATER AND COULDN'T DO IT.
BUT...
?
?
...PER-FORMING WAS FUN.
YOUR PRINCE WAS GOOD.

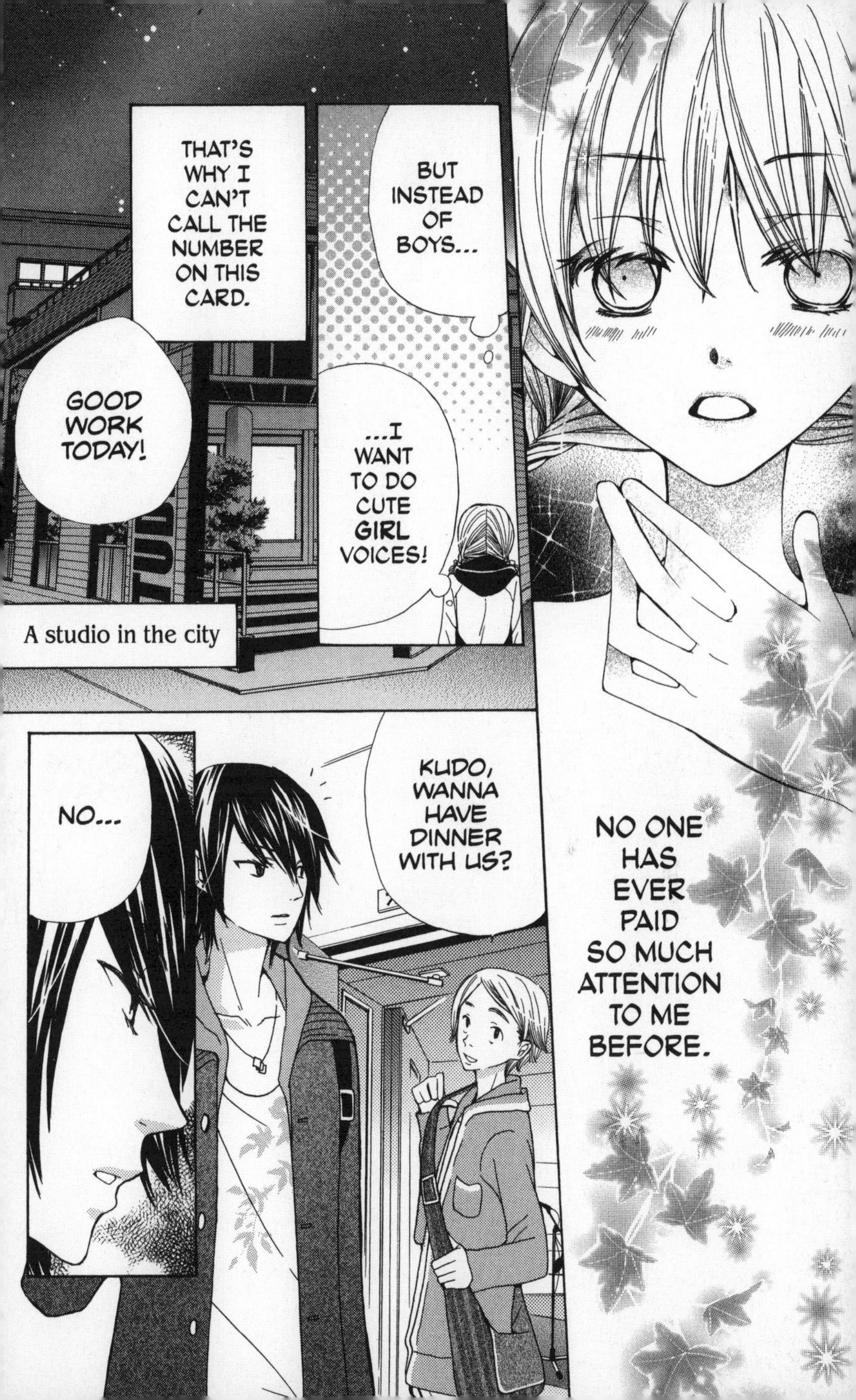
NO ONE HAS EVER PAID SO MUCH ATTENTION TO ME BEFORE.
BUT INSTEAD OF BOYS...
THAT'S WHY I CAN'T CALL THE NUMBER ON THIS CARD.
...I WANT TO DO CUTE GIRL VOICES!
GOOD WORK TODAY!
A studio in the city
KUDO, WANNA HAVE DINNER WITH US?
NO...

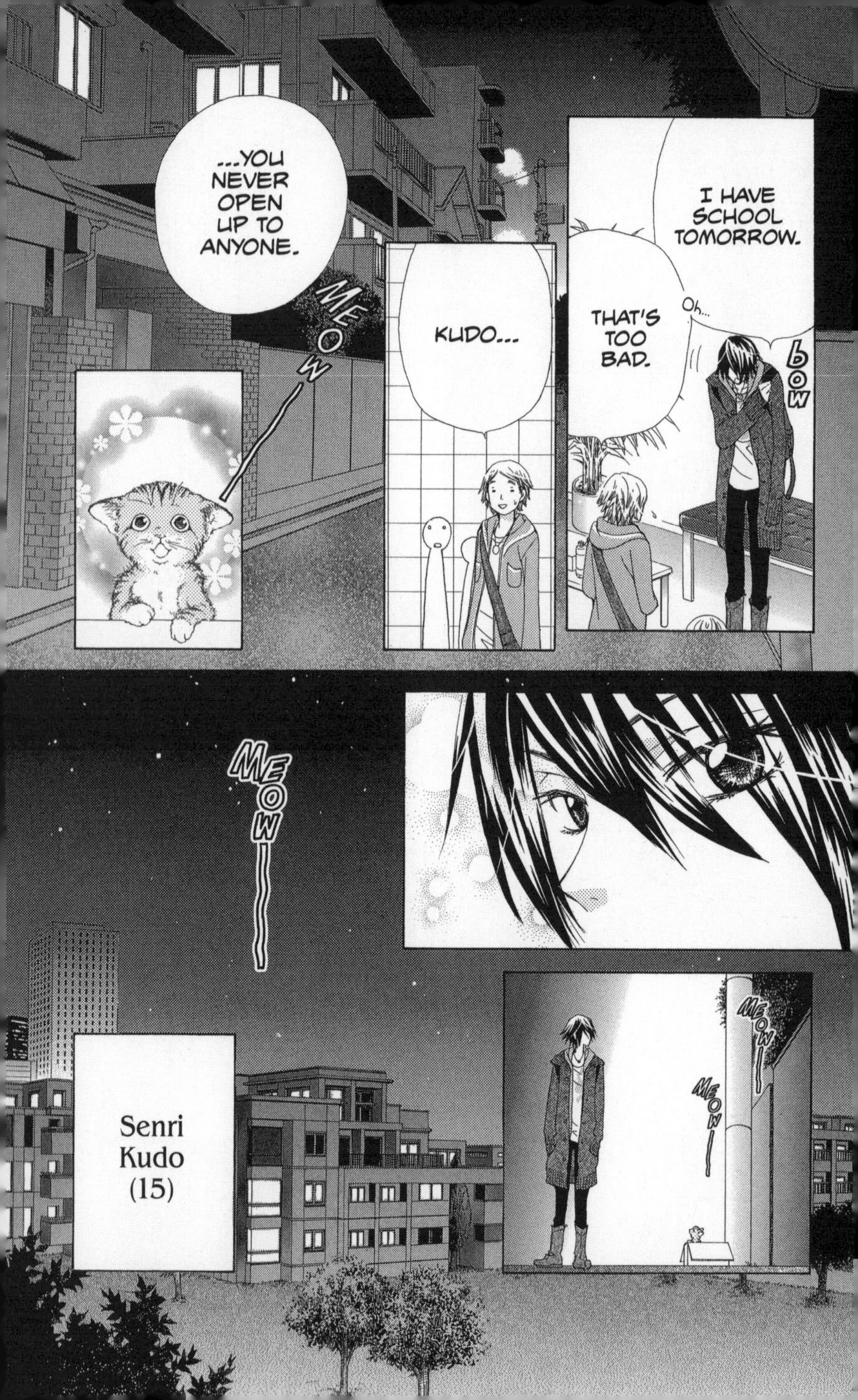
I HAVE SCHOOL TOMORROW.
BOW
Oh...
THAT'S TOO BAD.
KUDO...
...YOU NEVER OPEN UP TO ANYONE.
MEOW
MEOW
MEOW
MEOW
Senri Kudo (15)

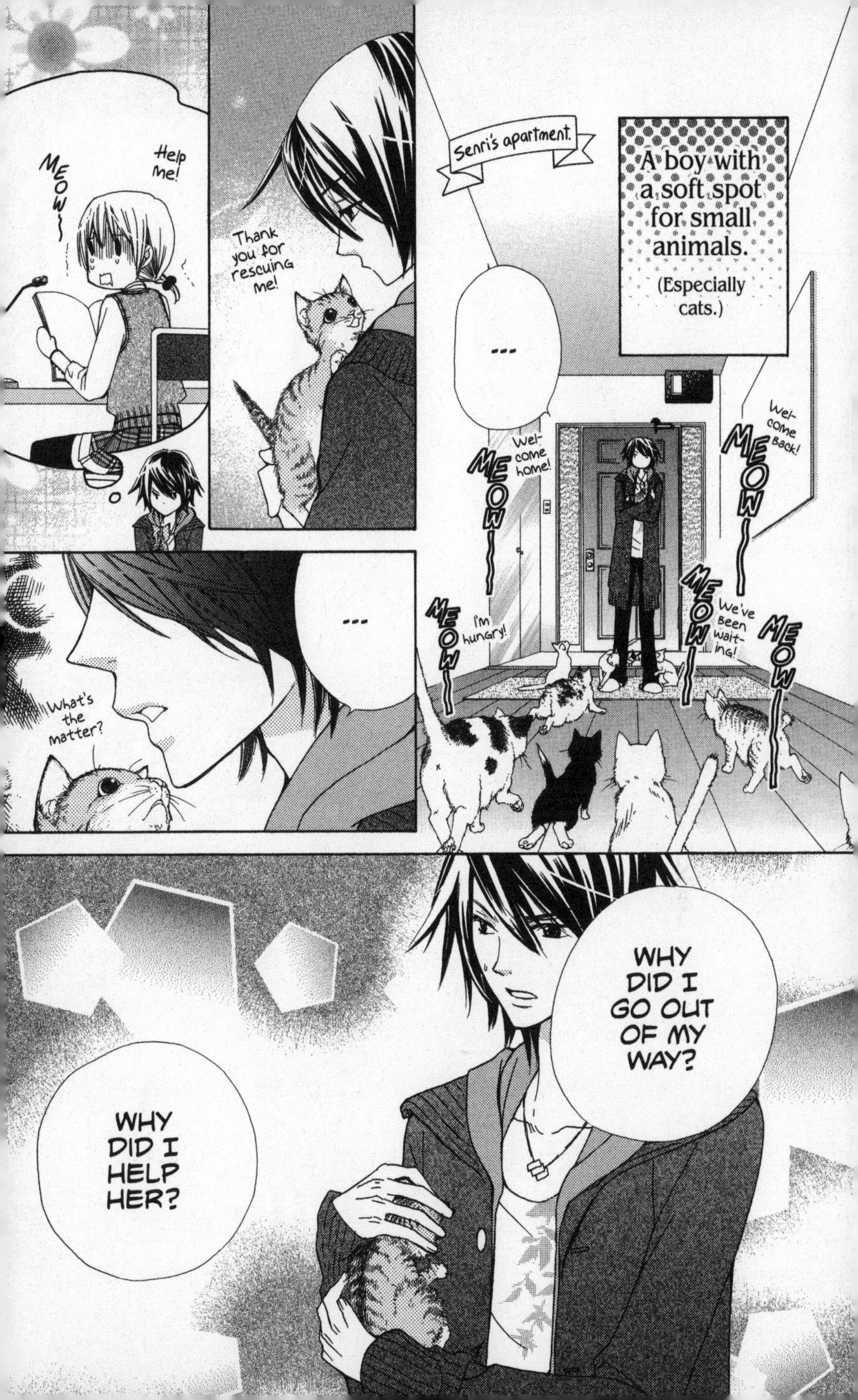
A boy with a soft spot for small animals.
(Especially cats.)
Senri's apartment.
...
Wel-come back!
MEOW~
Wel-come home!
MEOW~
MEOW~
MEOW~
We've been wait-ing!
I'm hungry!
MEOW~
Thank you for rescuing me!
Help me!
MEOW~
...
What's the matter?
WHY DID I GO OUT OF MY WAY?
WHY DID I HELP HER?

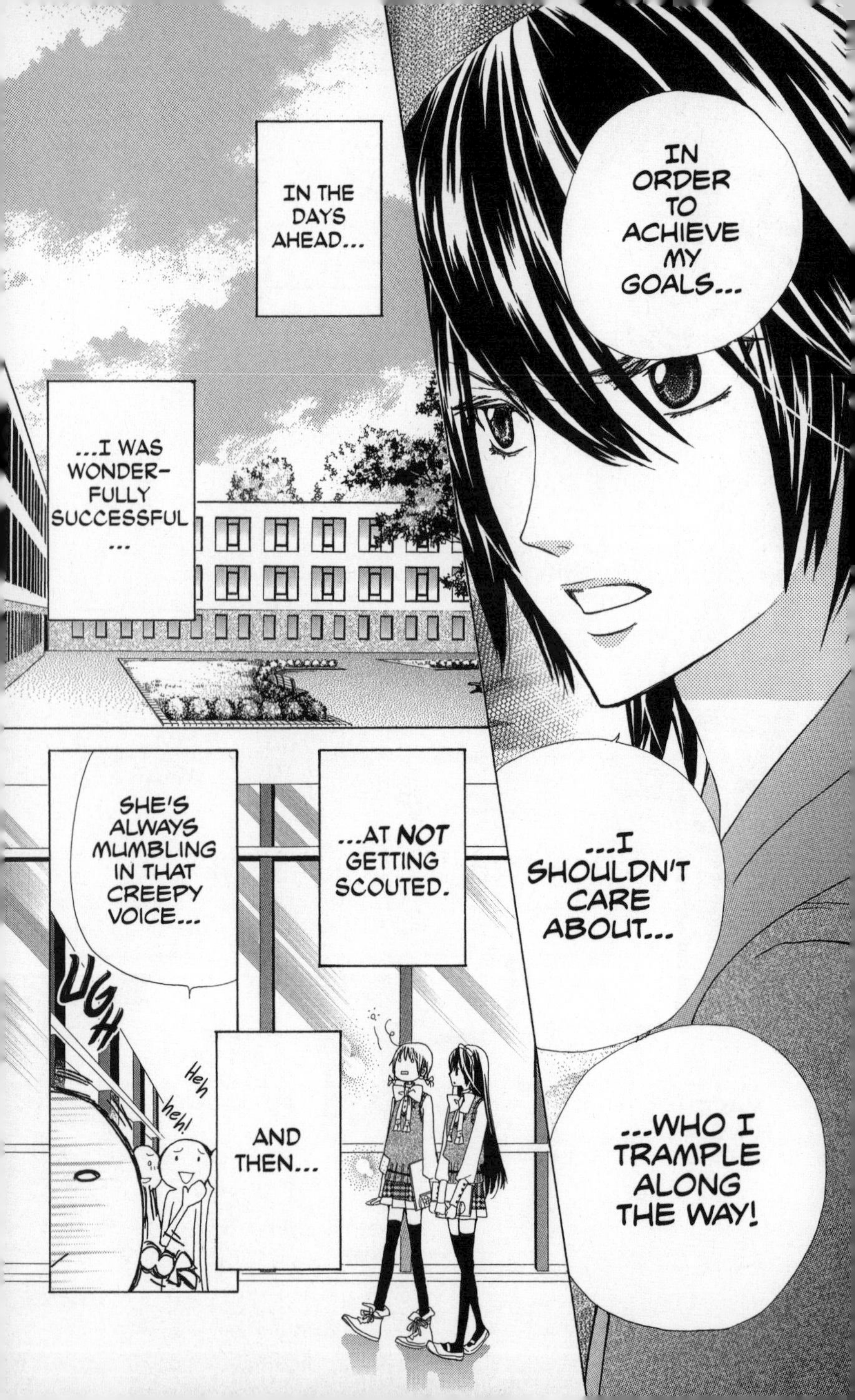

IN ORDER TO ACHIEVE MY GOALS...
...I SHOULDN'T CARE ABOUT...
...WHO I TRAMPLE ALONG THE WAY!
IN THE DAYS AHEAD...
...I WAS WONDER-FULLY SUCCESSFUL...
...AT NOT GETTING SCOUTED.
AND THEN...
SHE'S ALWAYS MUMBLING IN THAT CREEPY VOICE...
UGH
Heh heh!

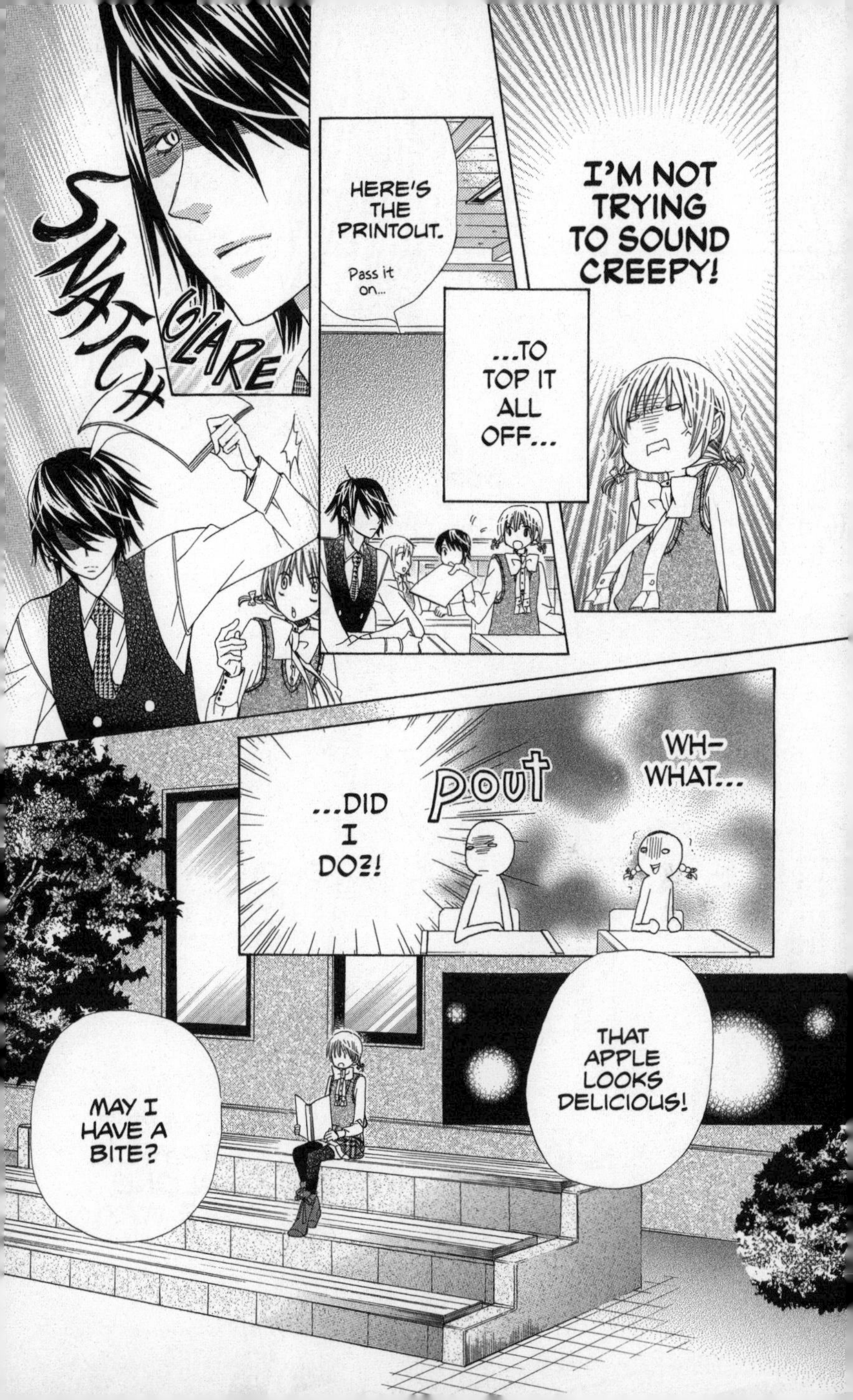
I'M NOT TRYING TO SOUND CREEPY!
HERE'S THE PRINTOUT.
Pass it on...
...TO TOP IT ALL OFF...
GLARE
SNATCH
WH- WHAT...
Pout
...DID I DO?!
THAT APPLE LOOKS DELICIOUS!
MAY I HAVE A BITE?

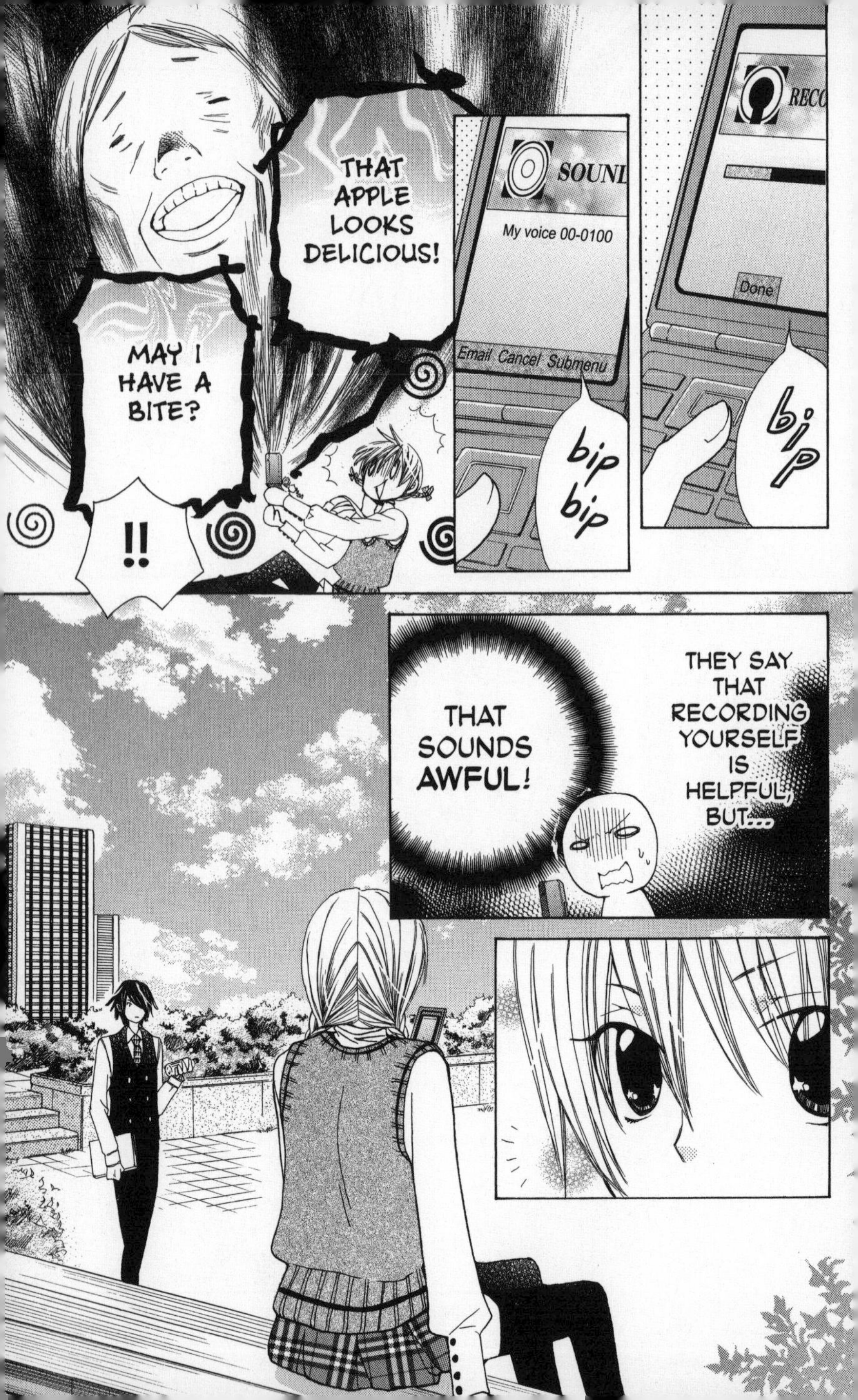
RECO
Done
bip
SOUN
My voice 00-0100
Email Cancel Submenu
bip bip
THAT APPLE LOOKS DELICIOUS!
MAY I HAVE A BITE?
!!
THEY SAY THAT RECORDING YOURSELF IS HELPFUL, BUT...
THAT SOUNDS AWFUL!

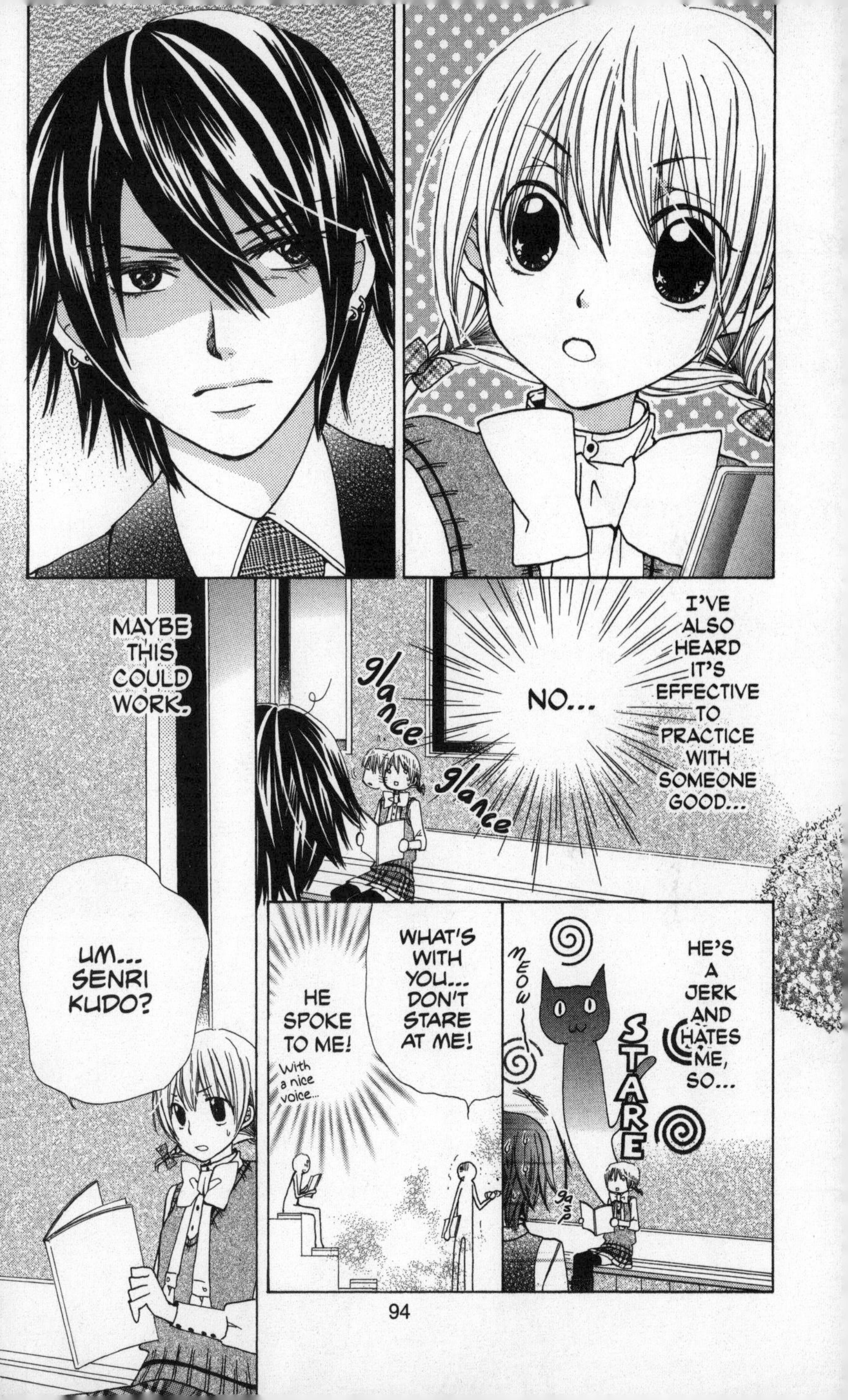
I'VE ALSO HEARD IT'S EFFECTIVE TO PRACTICE WITH SOMEONE GOOD...
NO...
glance
glance
MAYBE THIS COULD WORK.
HE'S A JERK AND HATES ME, SO...
MEOW
STARE
gasp
WHAT'S WITH YOU... DON'T STARE AT ME!
HE SPOKE TO ME!
With a nice voice...
UM... SENRI KUDO?

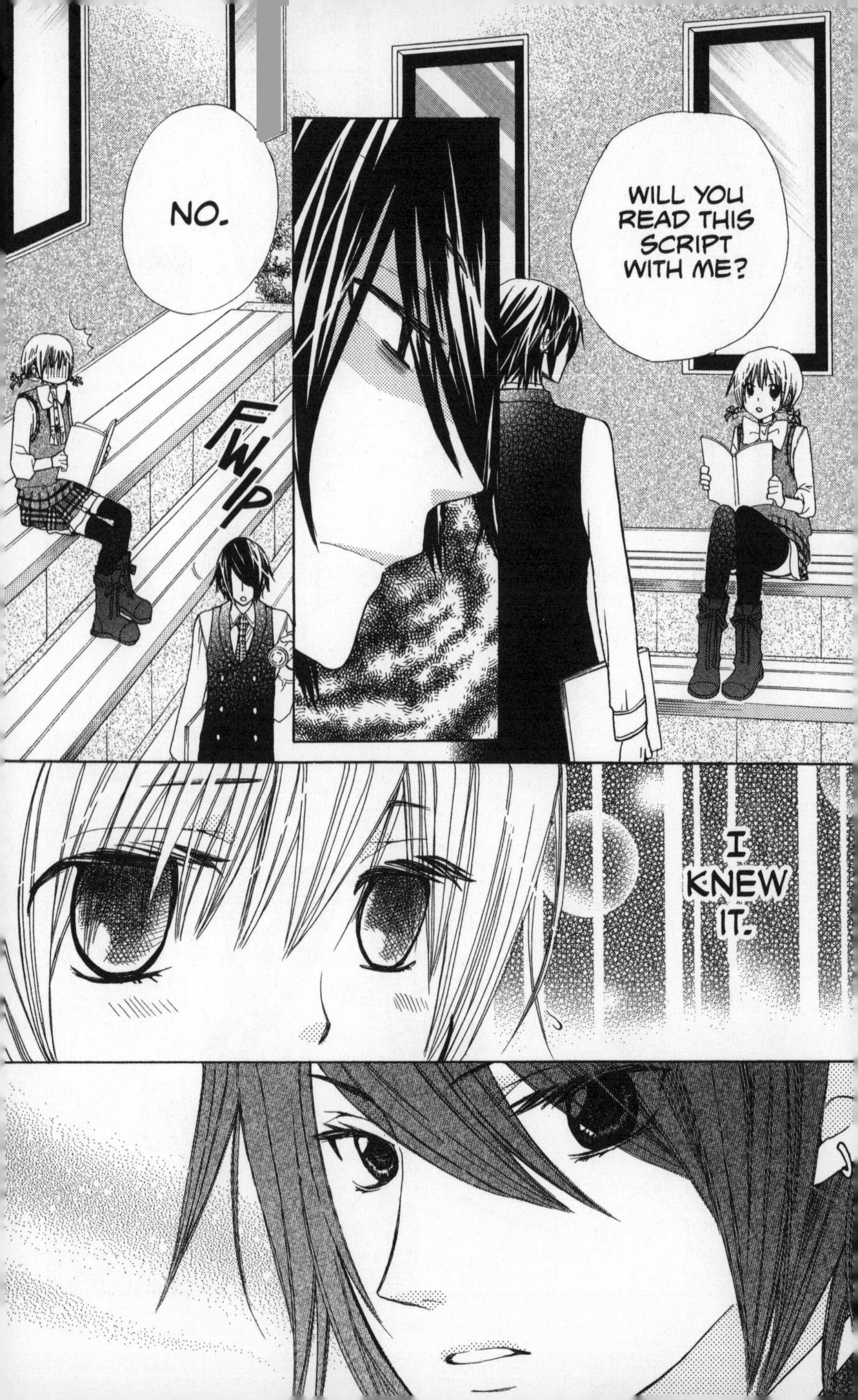
WILL YOU READ THIS SCRIPT WITH ME?
NO.
FWIP
I KNEW IT.

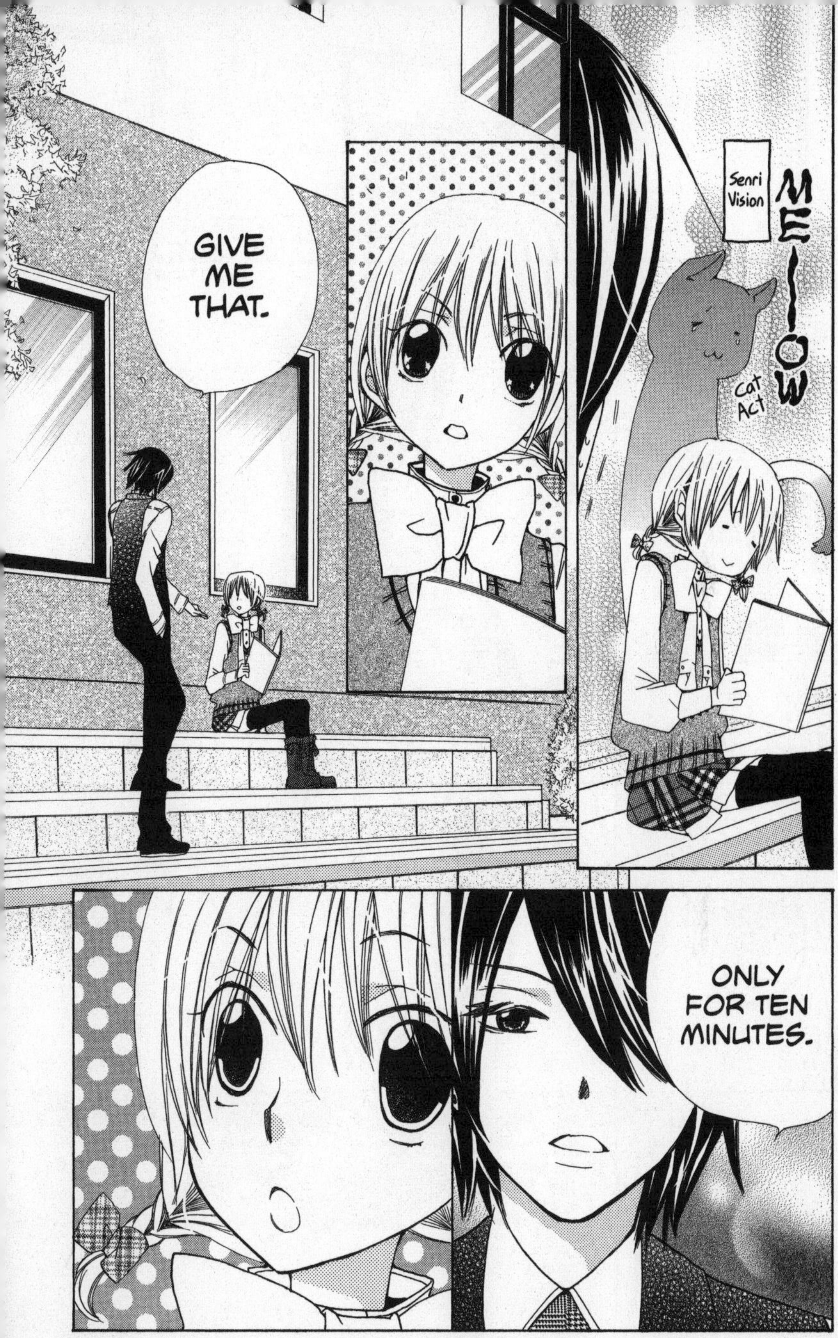
Senri Vision
MEOW
Cat Act
GIVE ME THAT.
ONLY FOR TEN MINUTES.

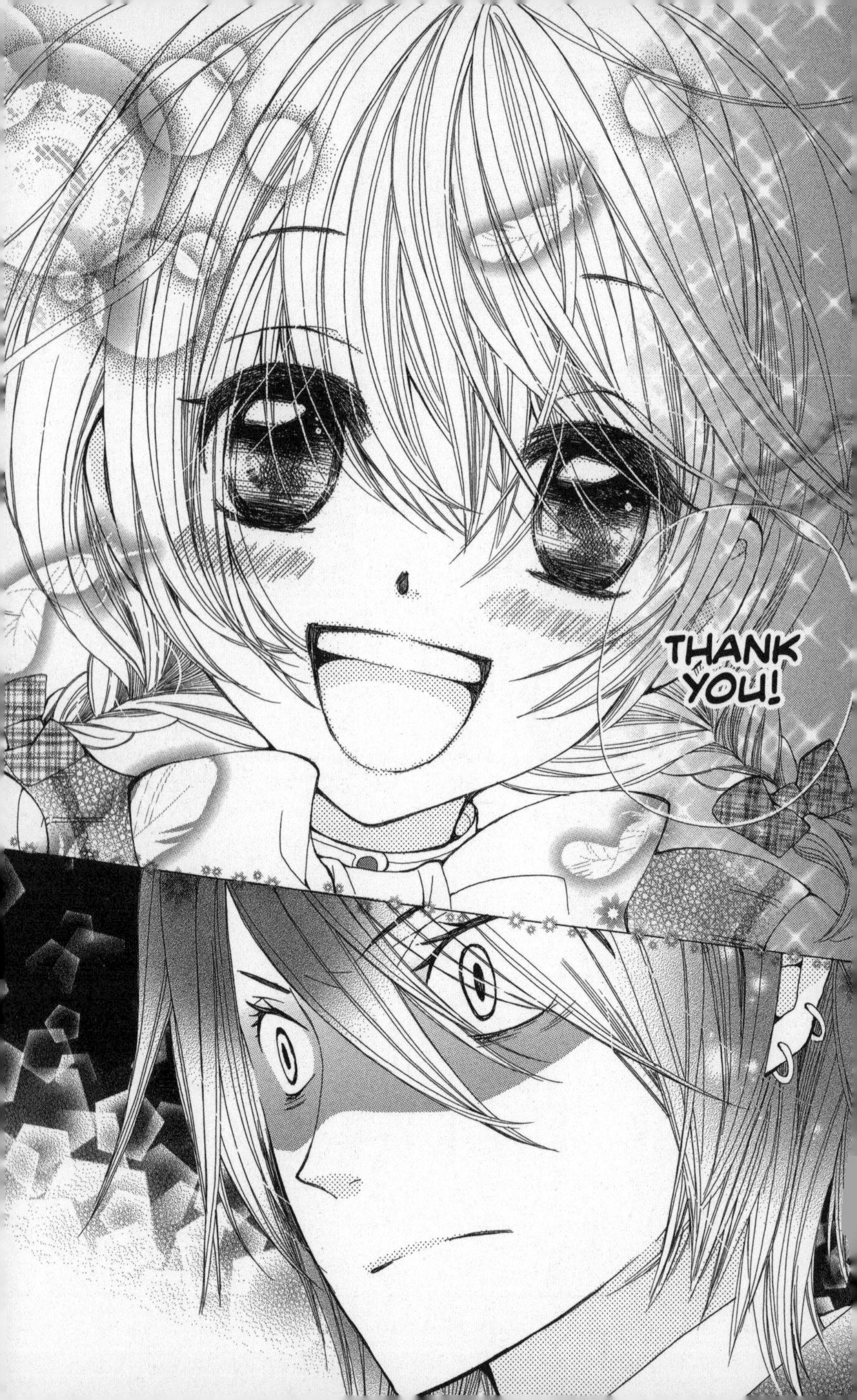
THANK YOU!

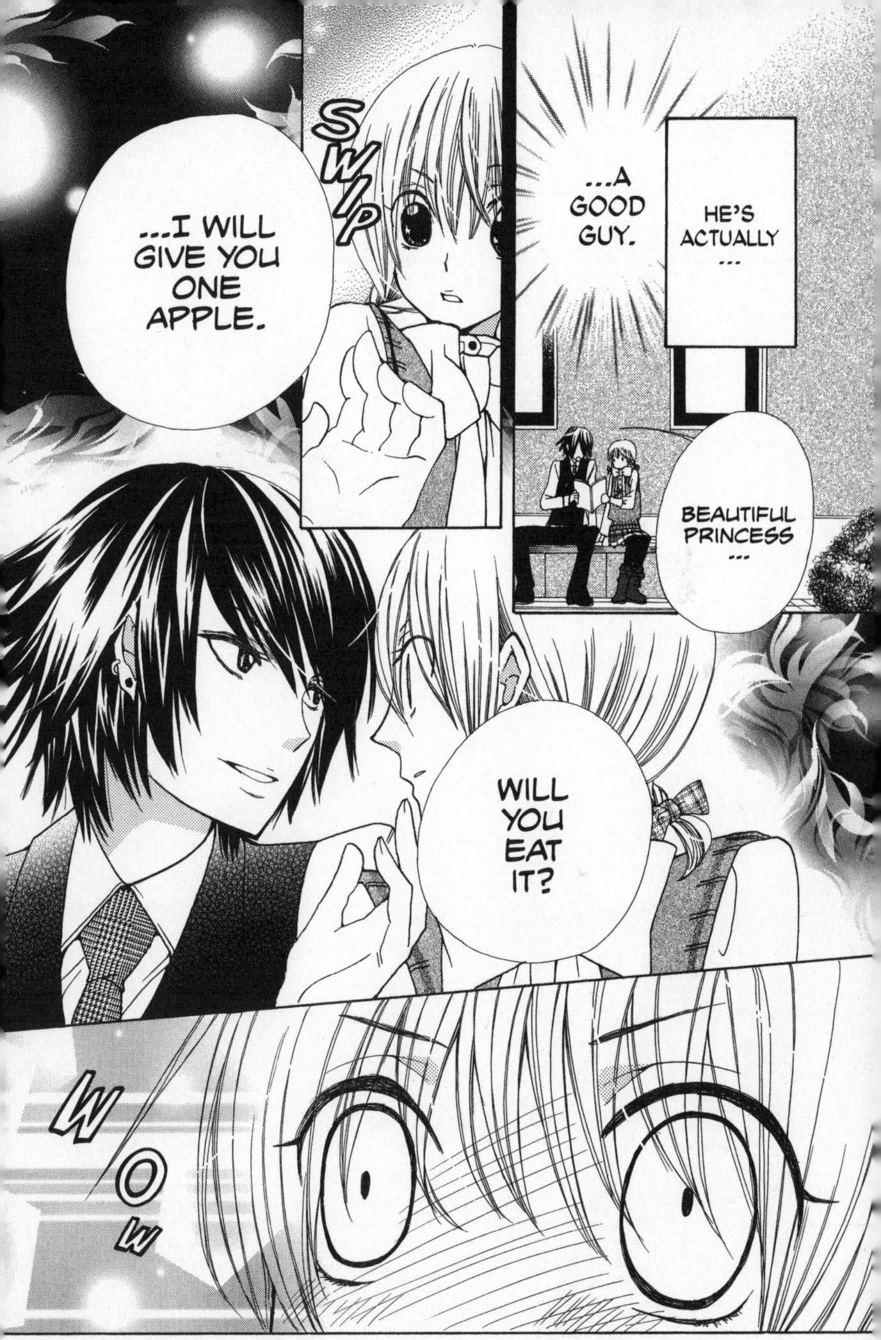
HE'S ACTUALLY ...
...A GOOD GUY.
SWIP
BEAUTIFUL PRINCESS ...
...I WILL GIVE YOU ONE APPLE.
WILL YOU EAT IT?
WOW

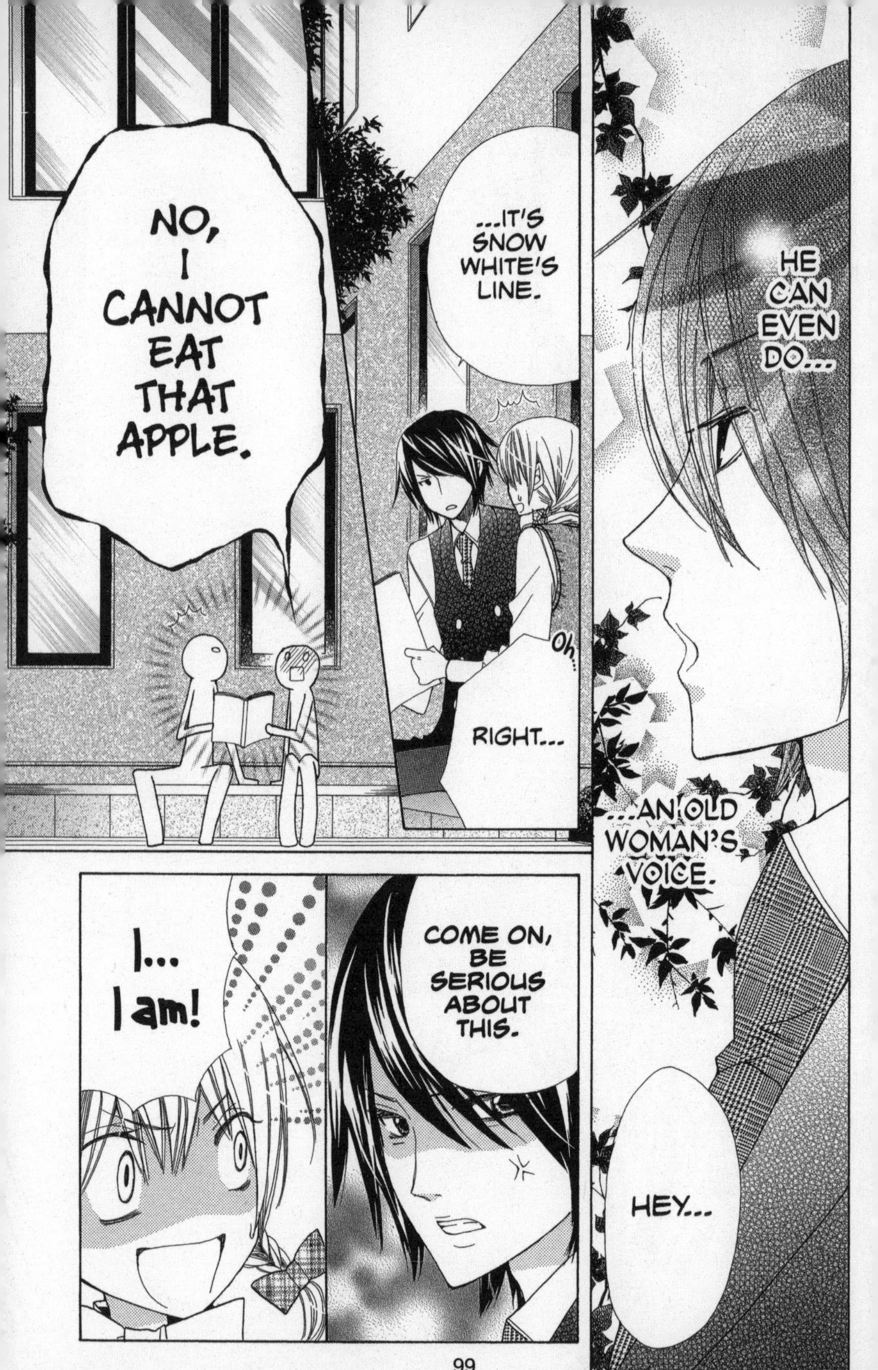
HE CAN EVEN DO...
...AN OLD WOMAN'S VOICE.
HEY...
NO, I CANNOT EAT THAT APPLE.
...IT'S SNOW WHITE'S LINE.
Oh...
RIGHT...
COME ON, BE SERIOUS ABOUT THIS.
I... I am!

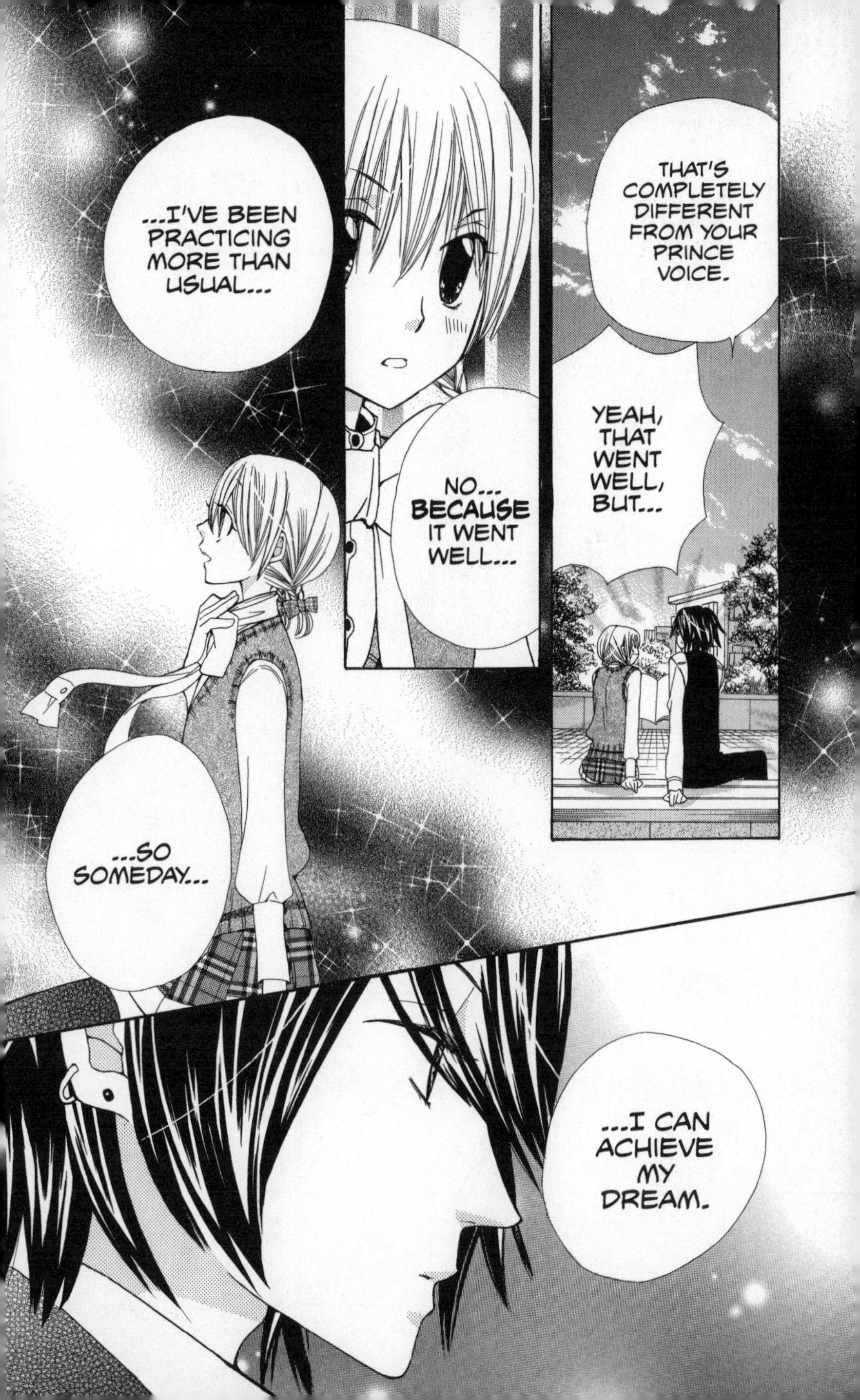
THAT'S COMPLETELY DIFFERENT FROM YOUR PRINCE VOICE.
YEAH, THAT WENT WELL, BUT...
NO... BECAUSE IT WENT WELL...
...I'VE BEEN PRACTICING MORE THAN USUAL...
...SO SOMEDAY...
...I CAN ACHIEVE MY DREAM.

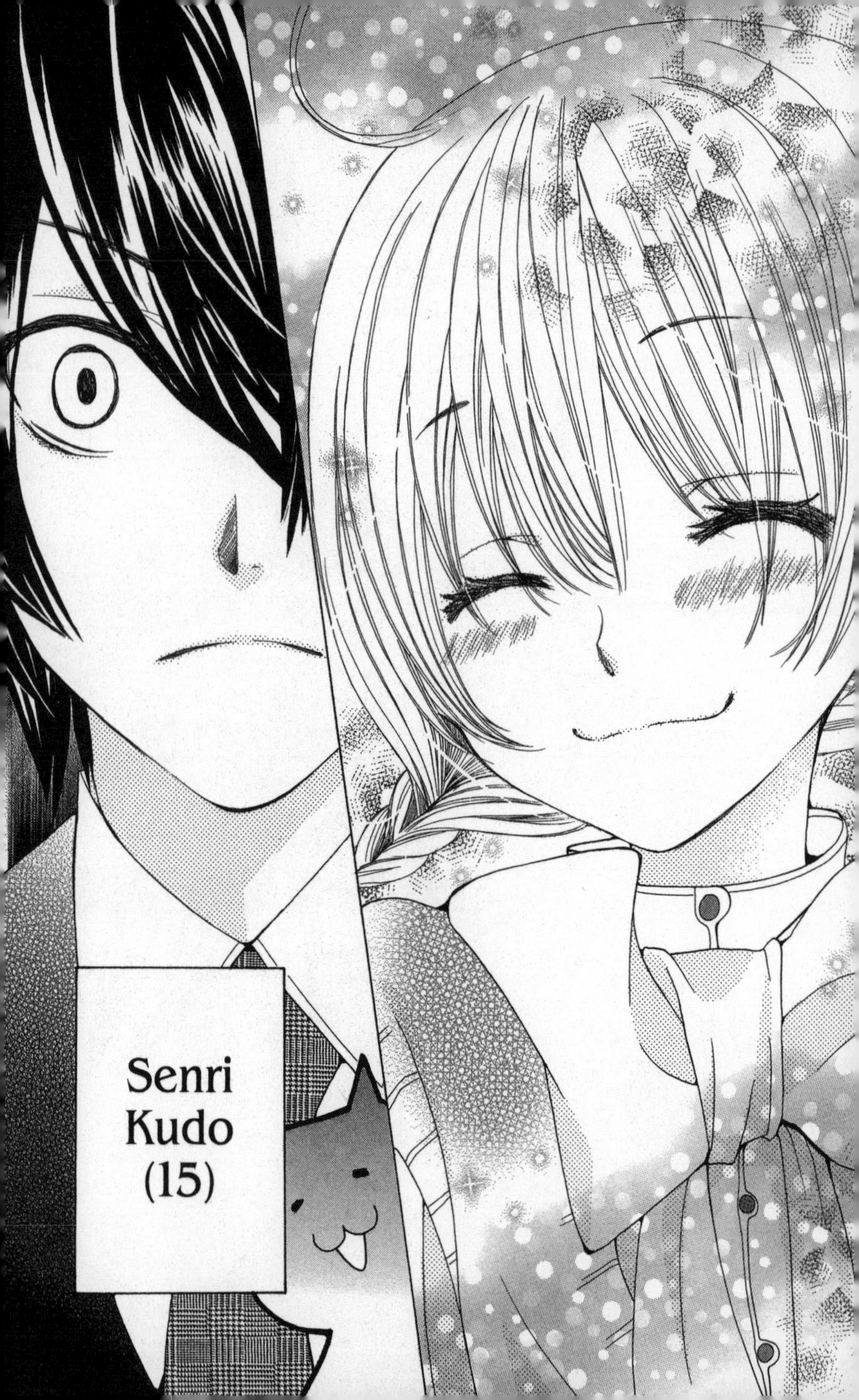
Senri Kudo (15)

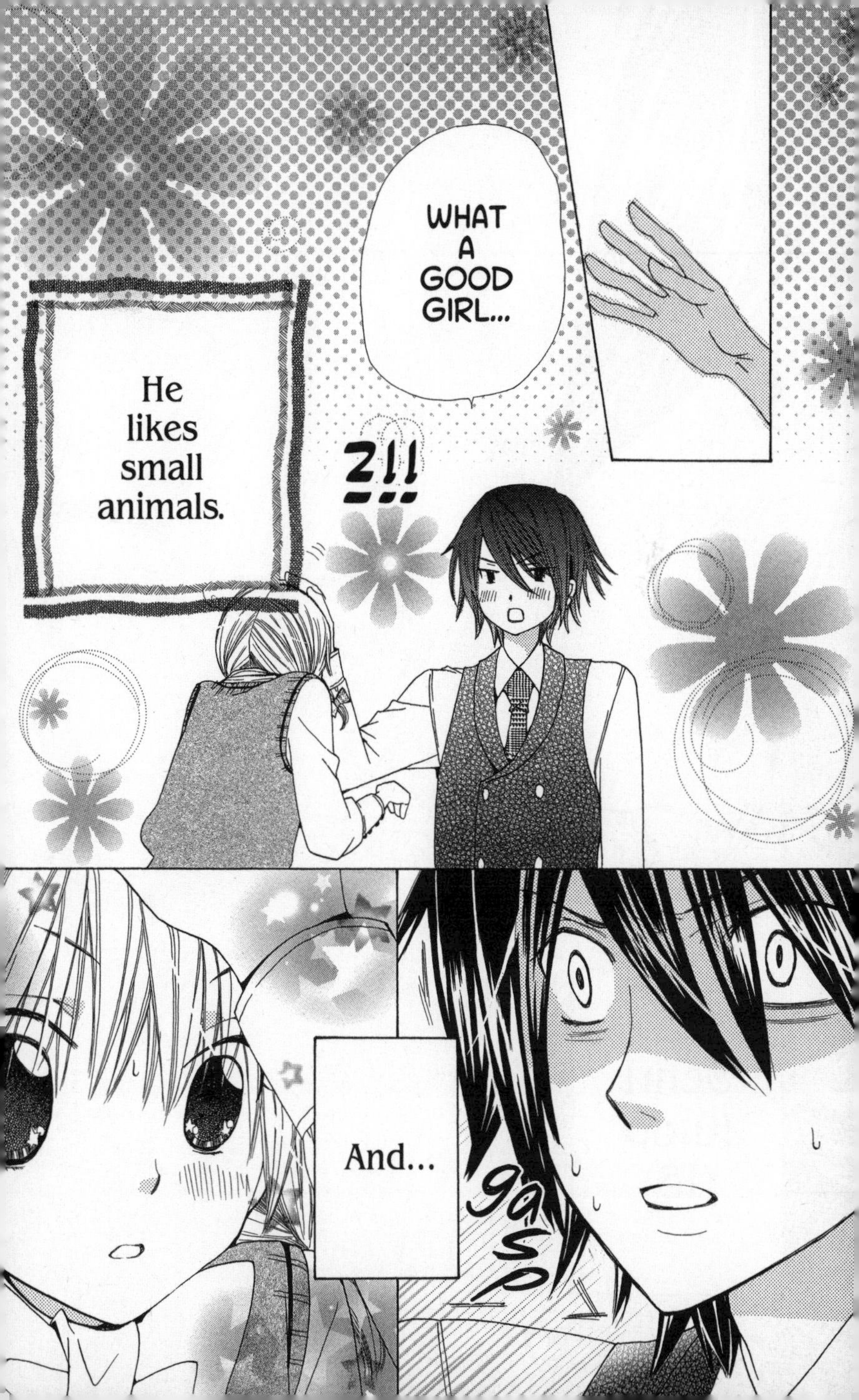
WHAT A GOOD GIRL...
Z!!
He likes small animals.
GASP
And...

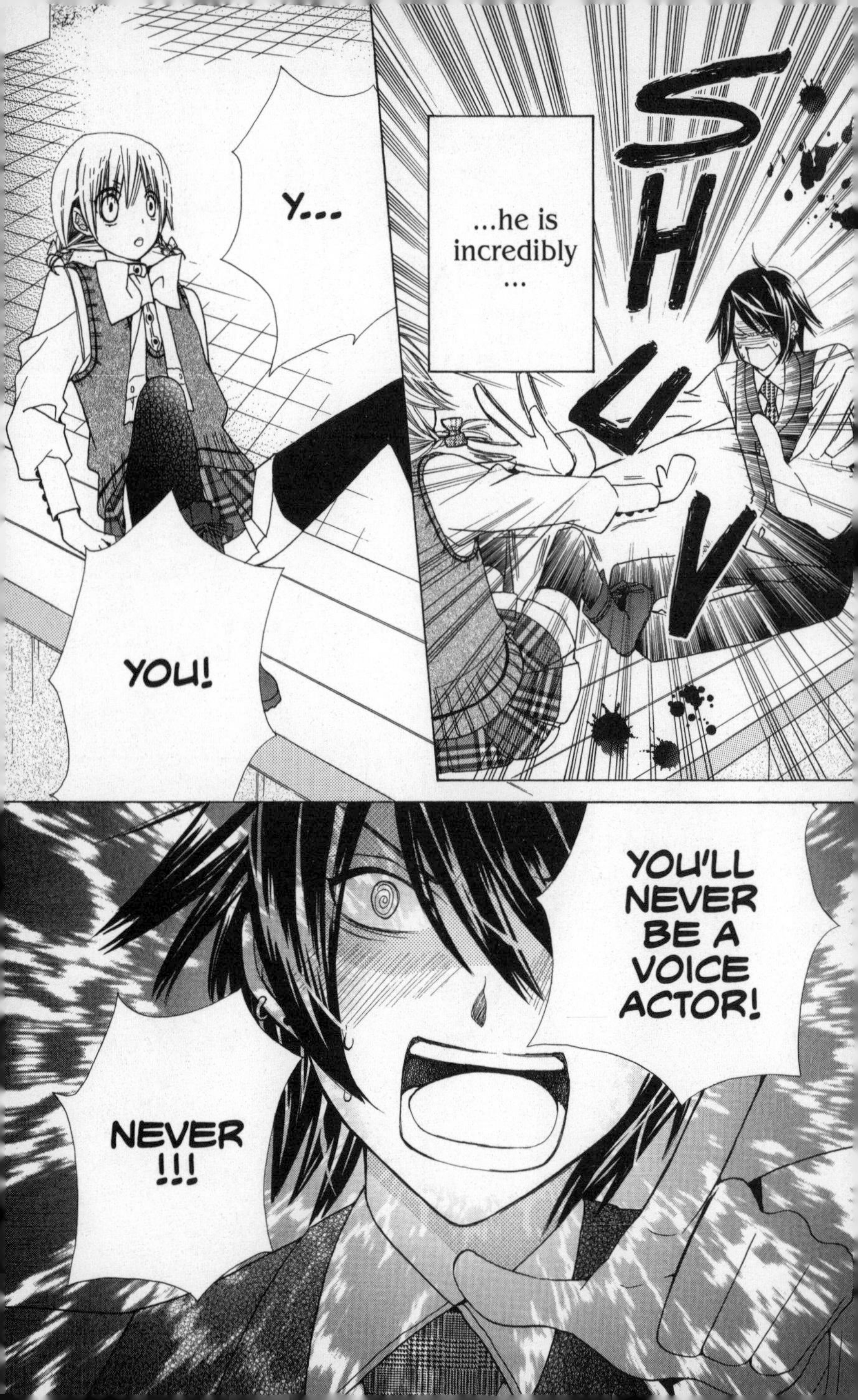
...he is incredibly ...
SHUV
Y...
YOU!
YOU'LL NEVER BE A VOICE ACTOR!
NEVER !!!

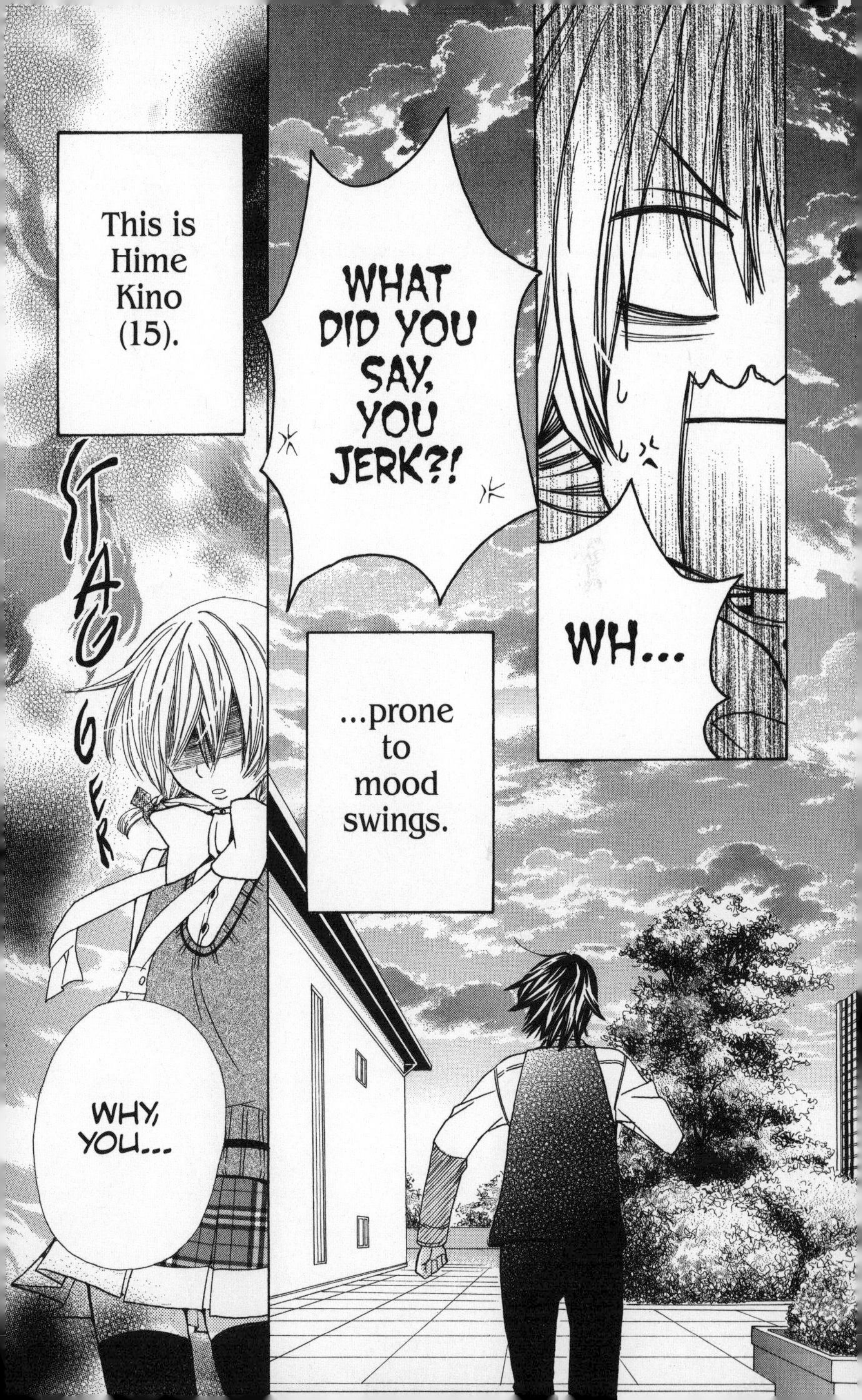
WH...
WHAT DID YOU SAY, YOU JERK?!
...prone to mood swings.
This is Hime Kino (15).
STAGGER
WHY, YOU...

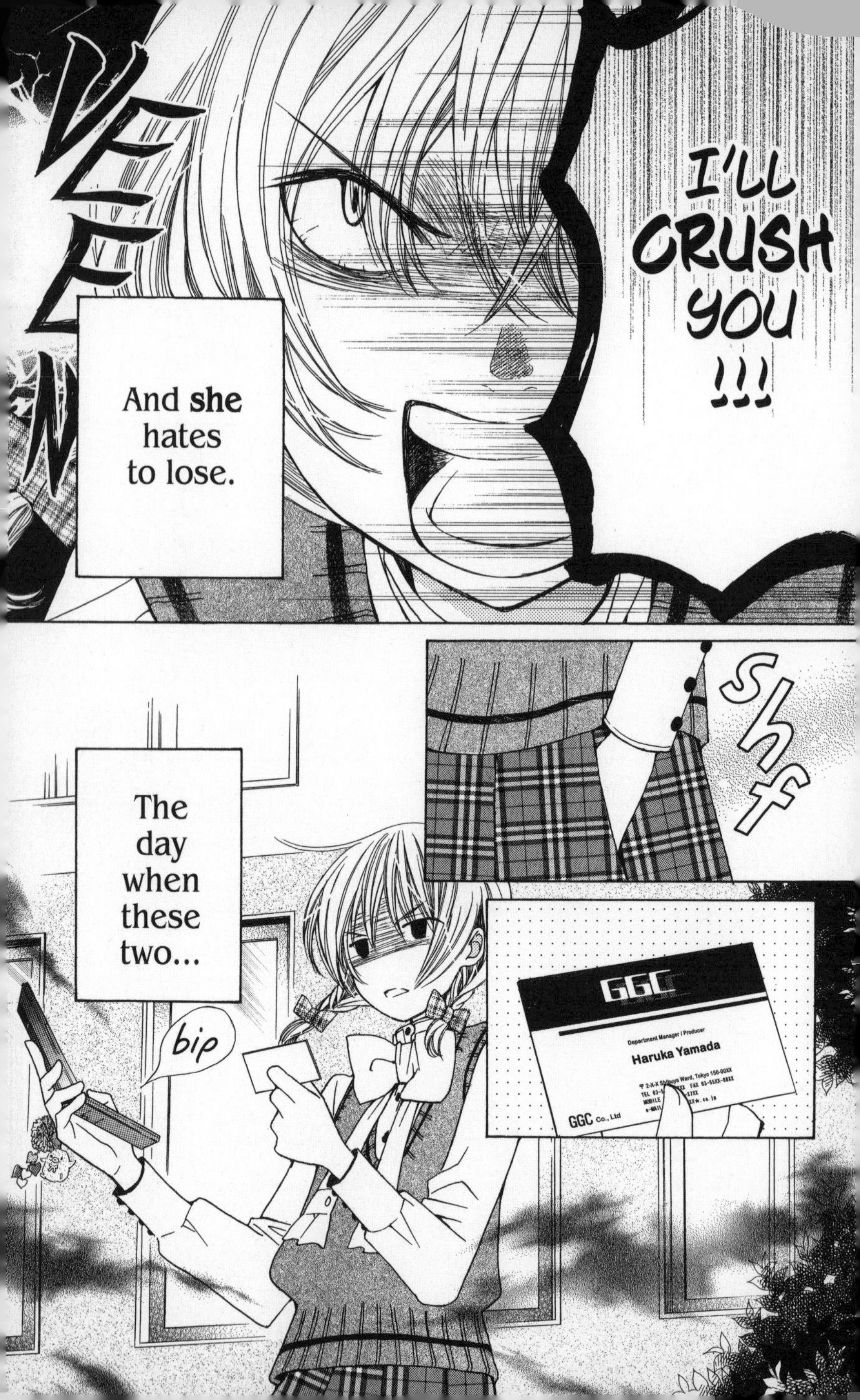
I'LL CRUSH YOU!!!
And she hates to lose.
VEEEN
shf
GGC
Department Manager / Producer
Haruka Yamada
GGC Co., Ltd
The day when these two...
bip

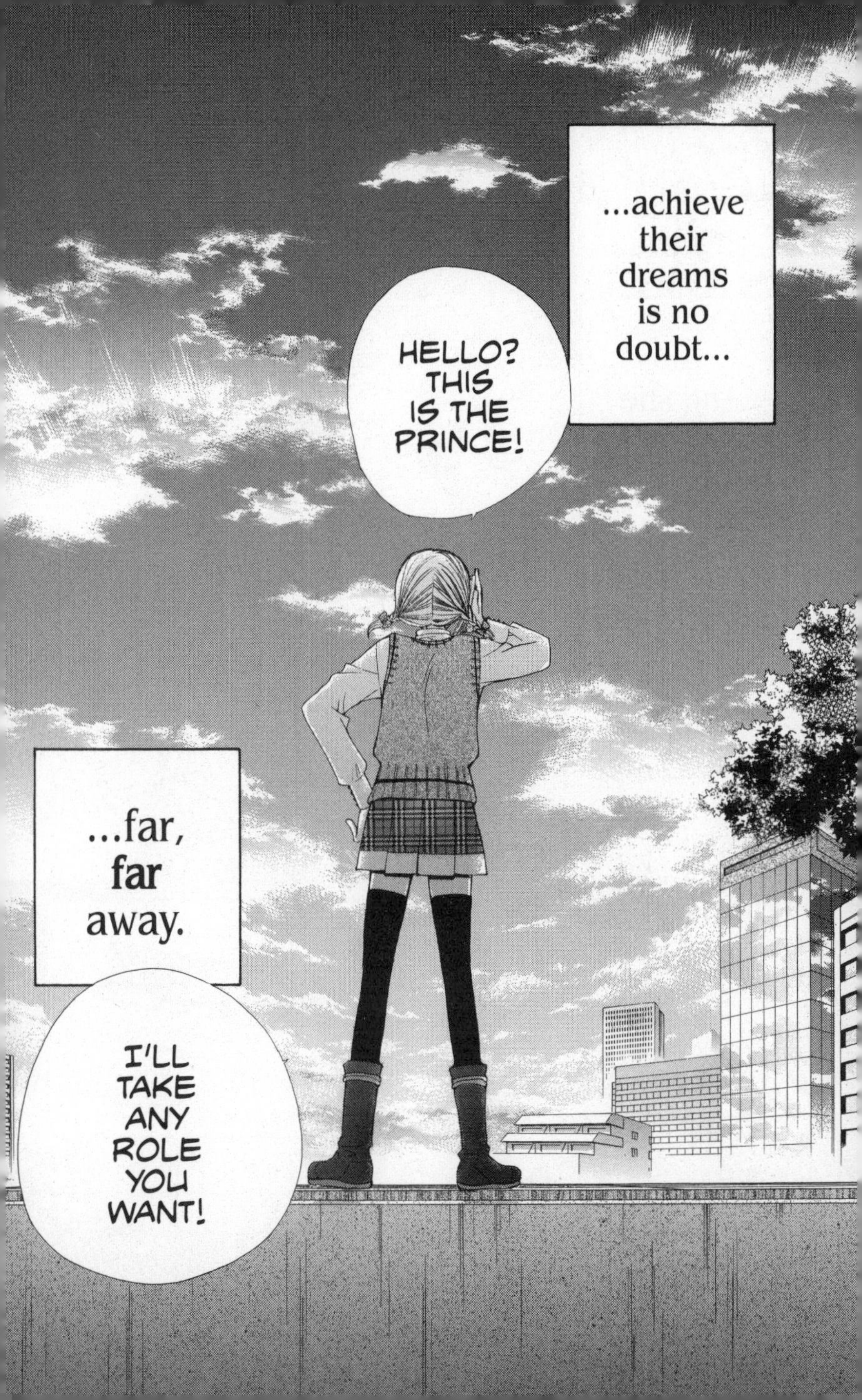
...achieve their dreams is no doubt...
HELLO? THIS IS THE PRINCE!
...far, **far** away.
I'LL TAKE ANY ROLE YOU WANT!

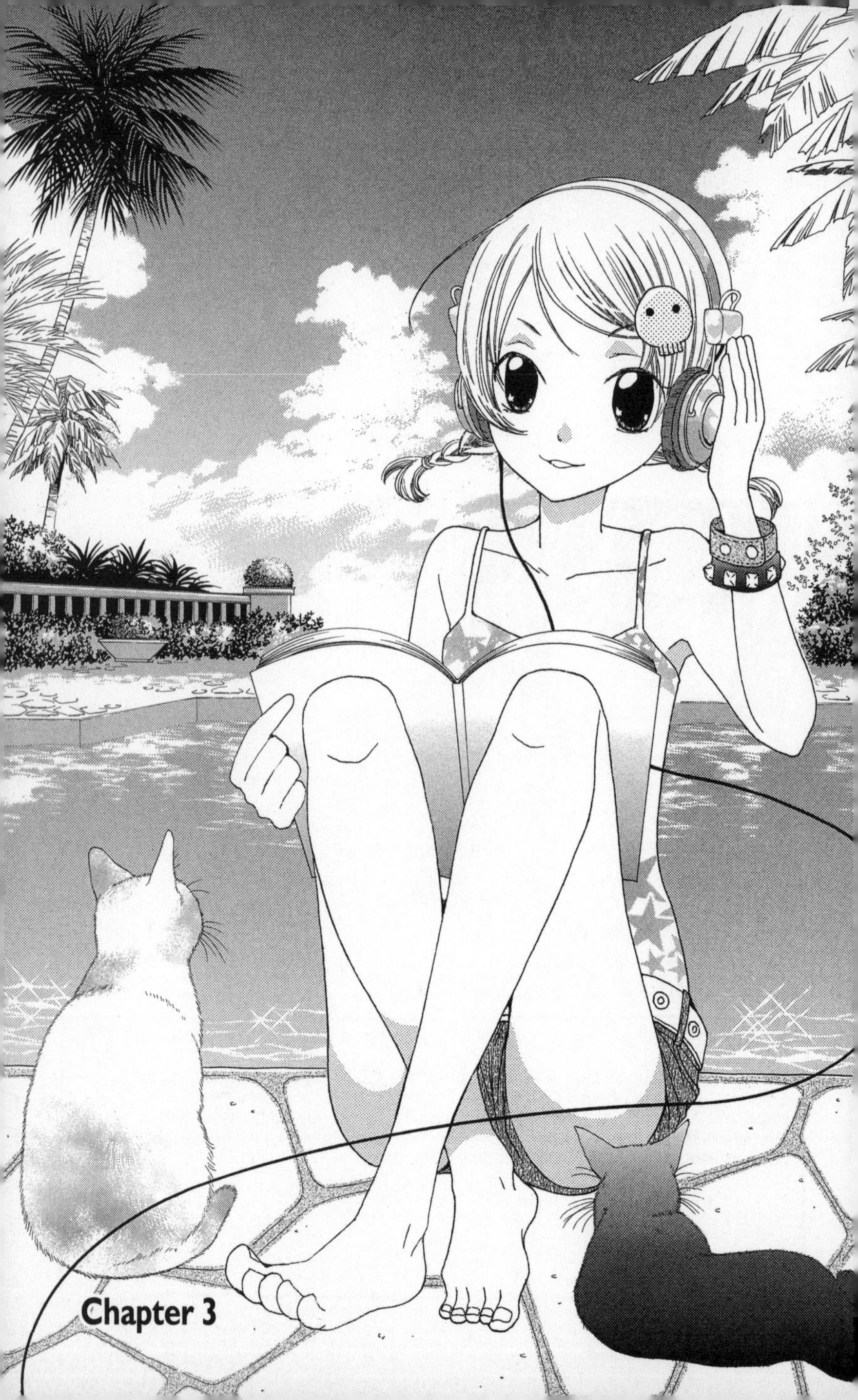
Chapter 3

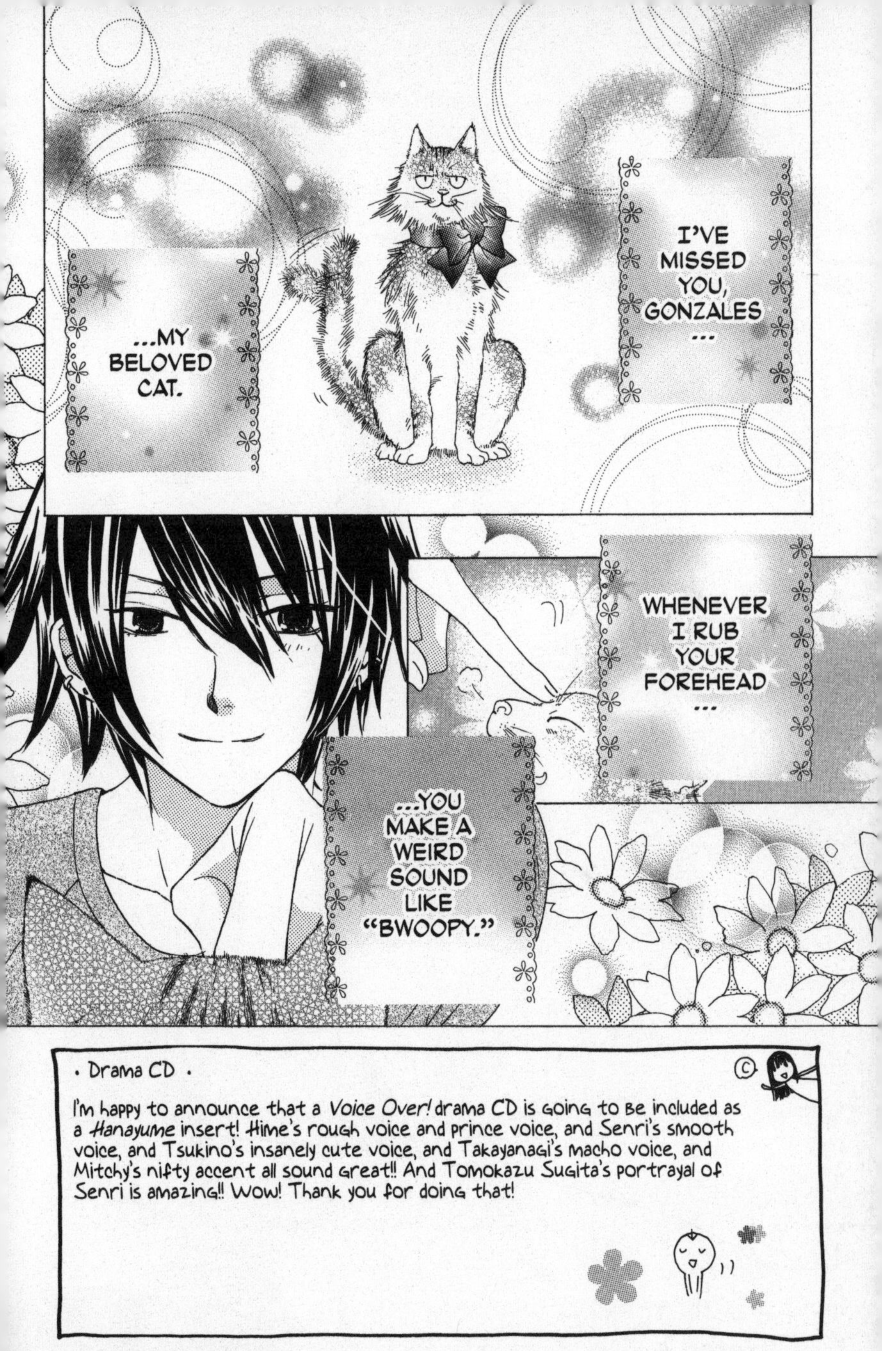
I'VE MISSED YOU, GONZALES...
...MY BELOVED CAT.
WHENEVER I RUB YOUR FOREHEAD...
...YOU MAKE A WEIRD SOUND LIKE "BWOOPY."

• Drama CD •

I'm happy to announce that a *Voice Over!* drama CD is going to be included as a *Hanayume* insert! Hime's rough voice and prince voice, and Senri's smooth voice, and Tsukino's insanely cute voice, and Takayanagi's macho voice, and Mitchy's nifty accent all sound great!! And Tomokazu Sugita's portrayal of Senri is amazing!! Wow! Thank you for doing that!

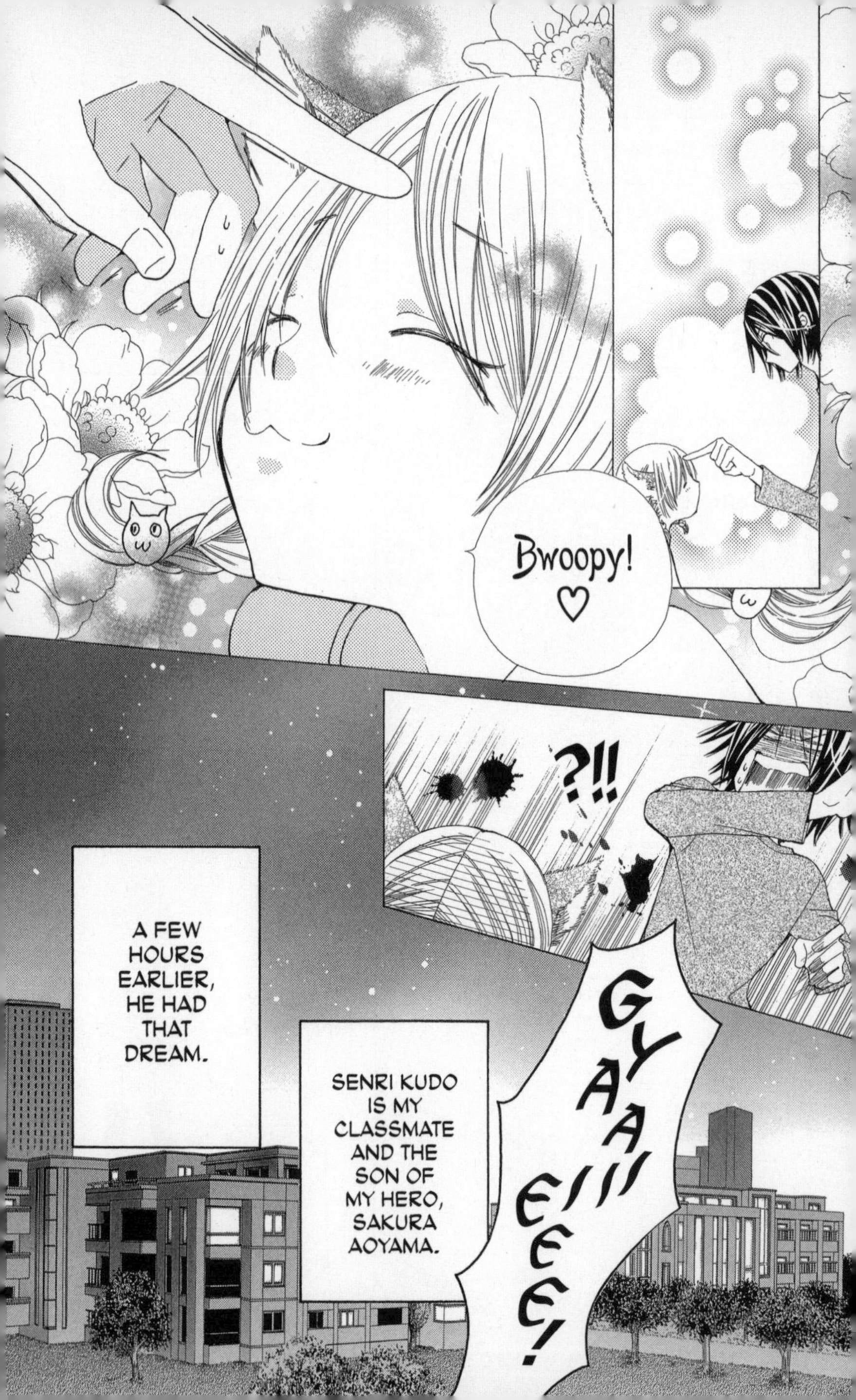
Bwoopy! ♡
?!!
GYAAIIIIEEEE!
A FEW HOURS EARLIER, HE HAD THAT DREAM.
SENRI KUDO IS MY CLASSMATE AND THE SON OF MY HERO, SAKURA AOYAMA.

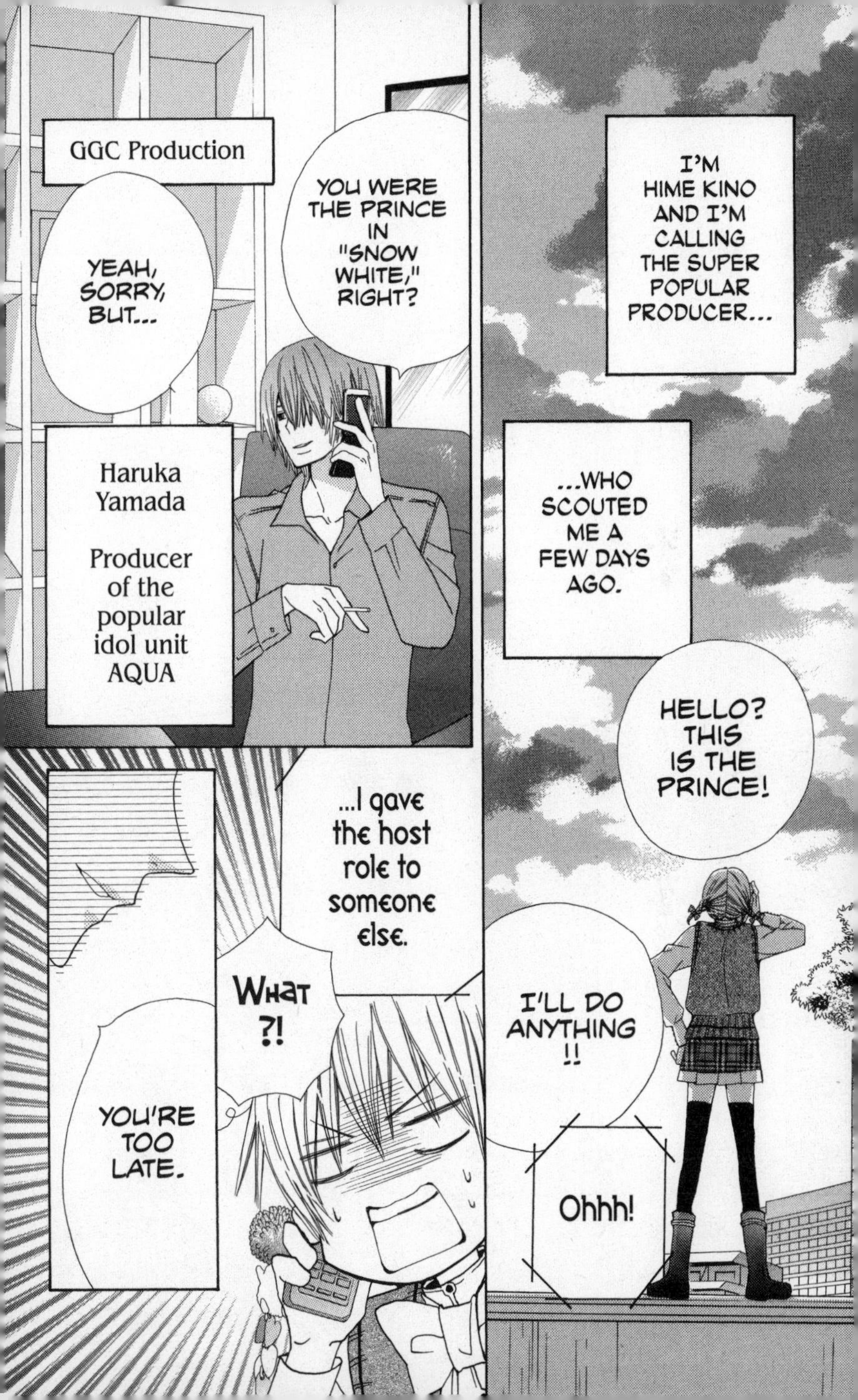
I'M HIME KINO AND I'M CALLING THE SUPER POPULAR PRODUCER...
...WHO SCOUTED ME A FEW DAYS AGO.
HELLO? THIS IS THE PRINCE!
I'LL DO ANYTHING !!
Ohhh!
GGC Production
YOU WERE THE PRINCE IN "SNOW WHITE," RIGHT?
YEAH, SORRY, BUT...
Haruka Yamada
Producer of the popular idol unit AQUA
...I gave the host role to someone else.
WHAT ?!
YOU'RE TOO LATE.

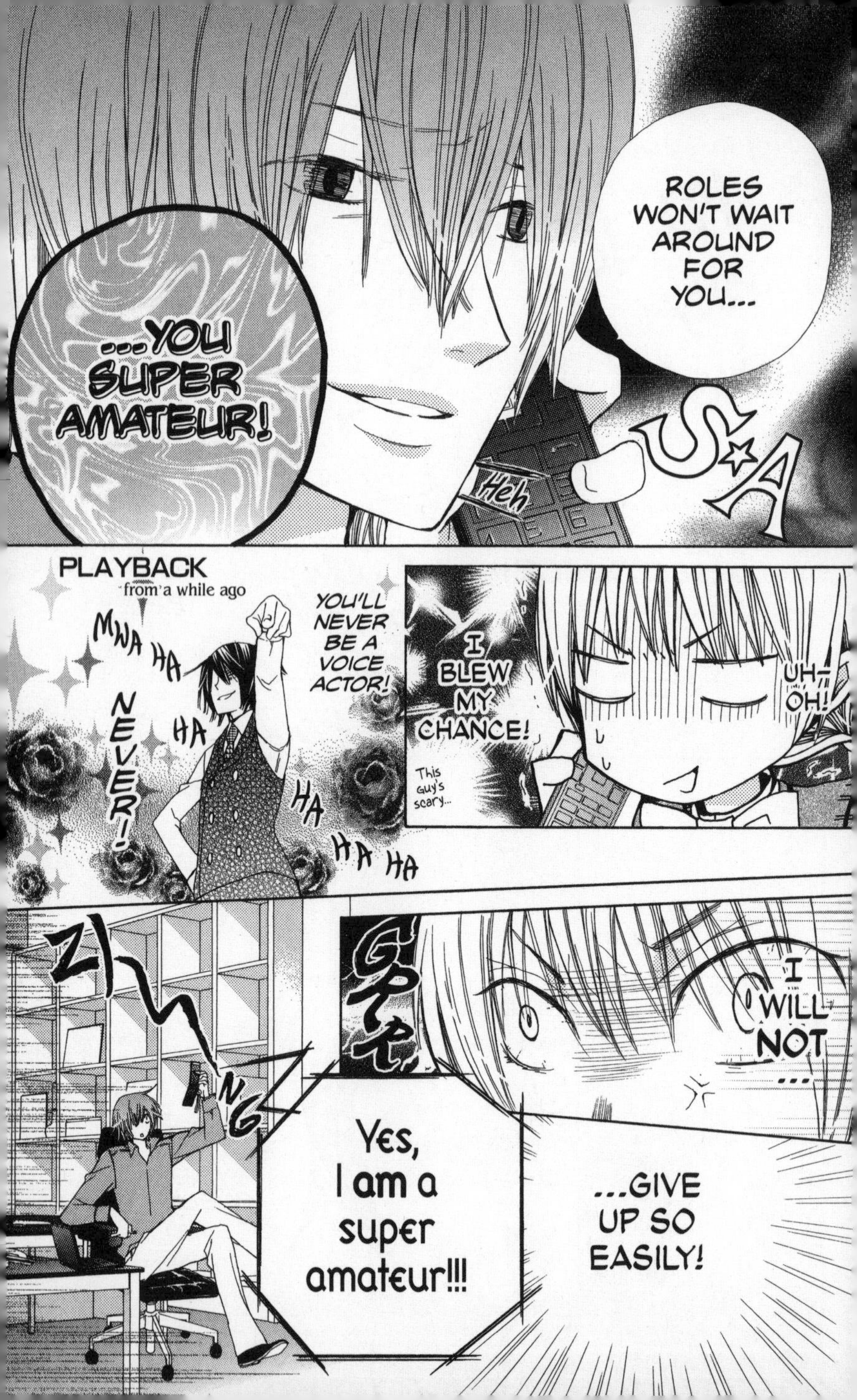
ROLES WON'T WAIT AROUND FOR YOU...
Heh
S☆A
...YOU SUPER AMATEUR!
UH-OH!
I BLEW MY CHANCE!
This guy's scary...
PLAYBACK from a while ago
YOU'LL NEVER BE A VOICE ACTOR!
MWA HA HA HA HA HA HA
NEVER!
I WILL NOT...
...GIVE UP SO EASILY!
Yes, I am a super amateur!!!
ZING

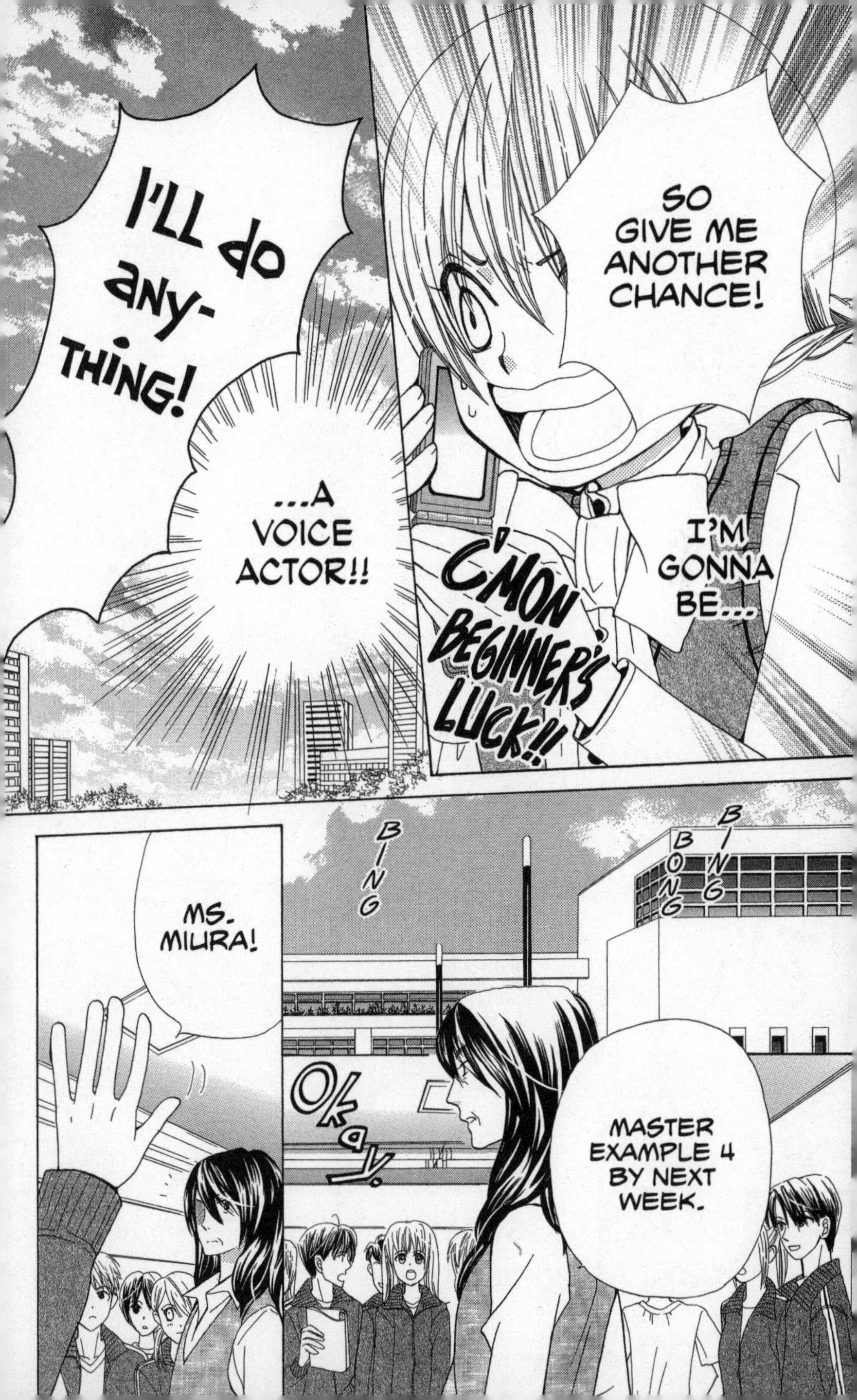
SO GIVE ME ANOTHER CHANCE!
I'M GONNA BE...
C'MON BEGINNER'S LUCK!!
...A VOICE ACTOR!!
I'LL do any-THING!
BING BONG
BING
BING
MASTER EXAMPLE 4 BY NEXT WEEK.
Okay.
MS. MIURA!

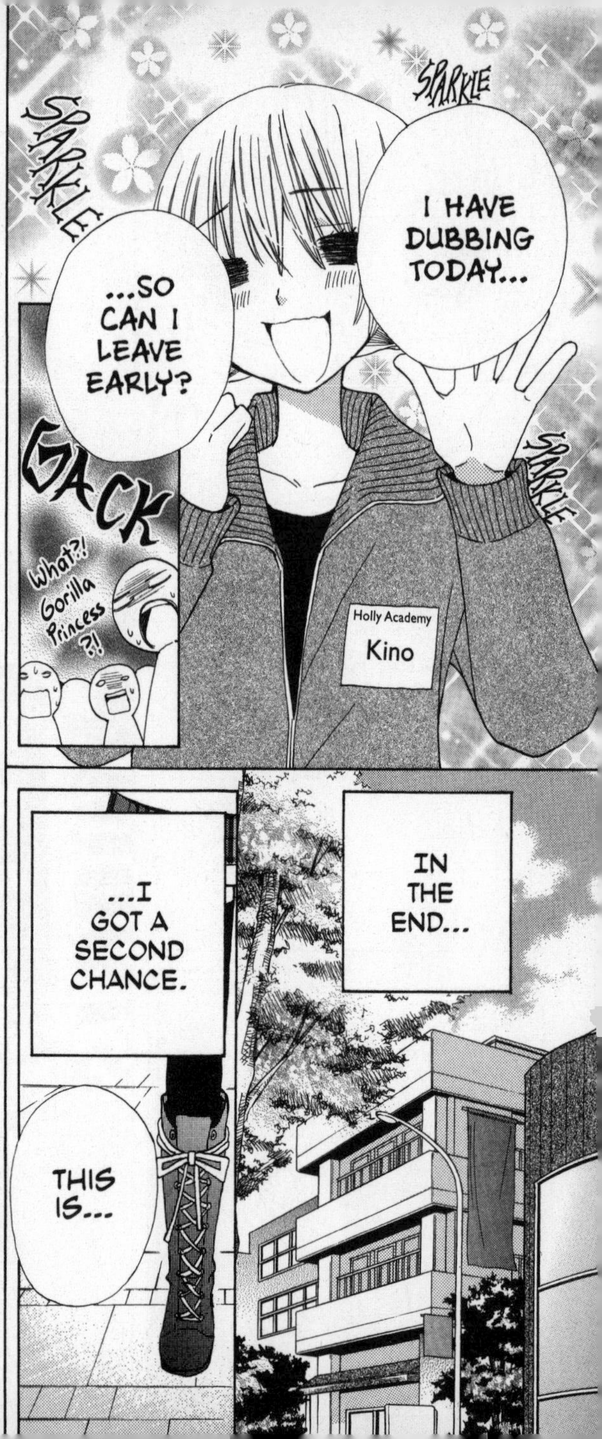
SPARKLE
SPARKLE
I HAVE DUBBING TODAY...
...SO CAN I LEAVE EARLY?
SPARKLE
Holly Academy
Kino
GACK
What?! Gorilla Princess ?!
IN THE END...
...I GOT A SECOND CHANCE.
THIS IS...

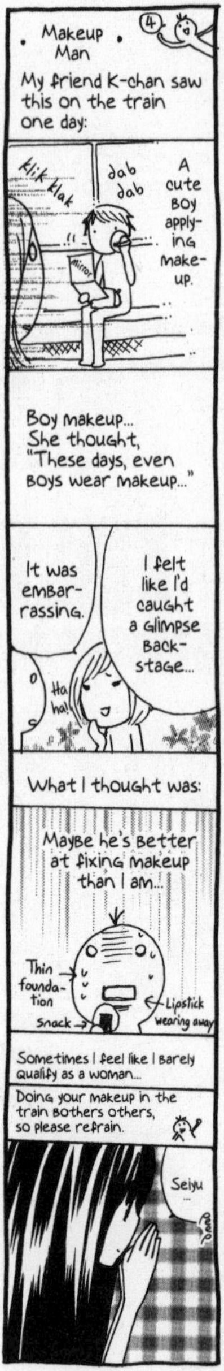
Makeup Man ④
My friend K-chan saw this on the train one day:
klik klak
dab dab
A cute boy applying make-up.
mirror
Boy makeup... She thought, "These days, even boys wear makeup..."
I felt like I'd caught a glimpse backstage...
It was embarrassing.
Ha ha!
What I thought was:
Maybe he's better at fixing makeup than I am...
Thin foundation
Lipstick wearing away
Snack
Sometimes I feel like I barely qualify as a woman...
Doing your makeup in the train bothers others, so please refrain.
Seiyu ...

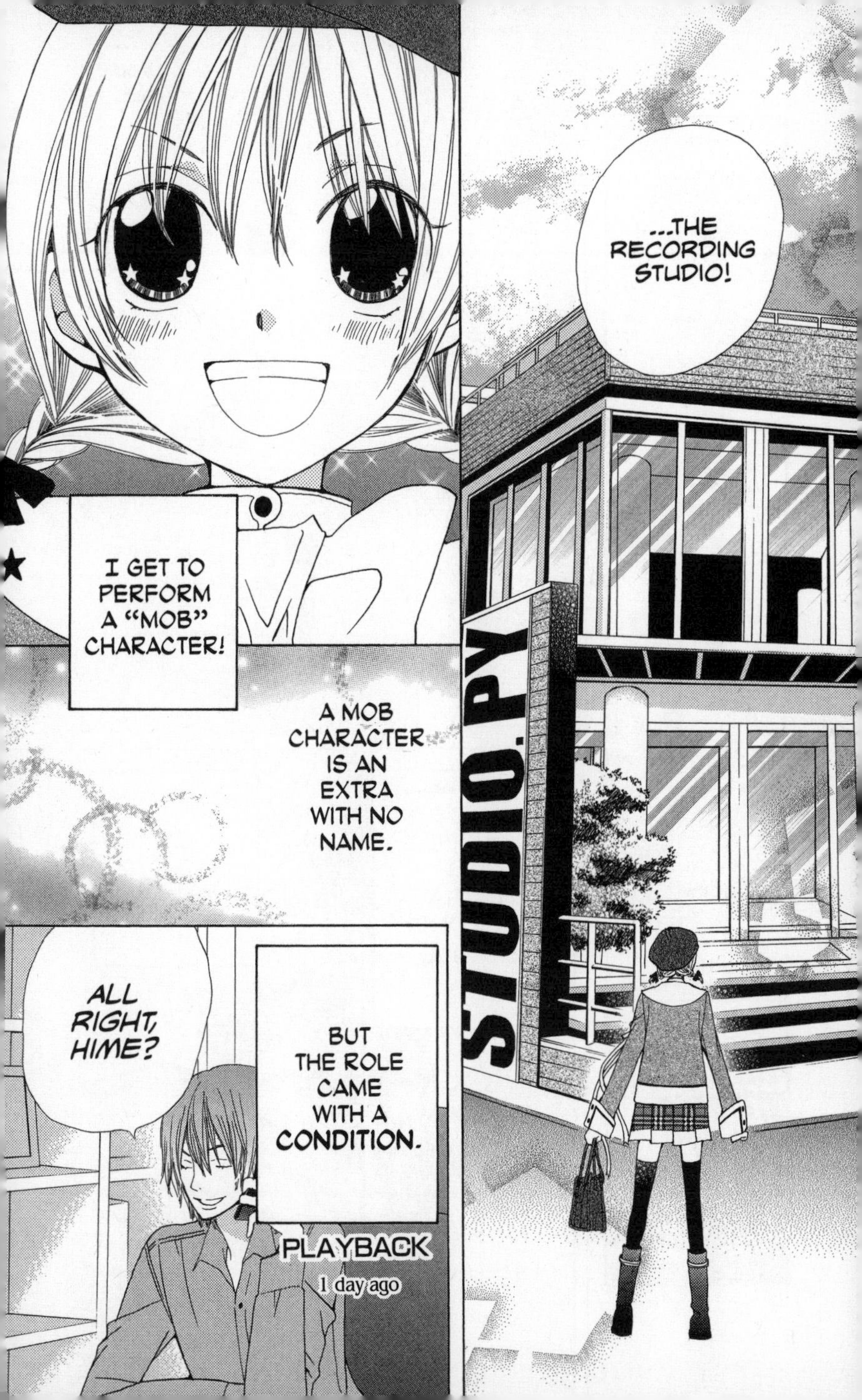
...THE RECORDING STUDIO!
STUDIO. PY
I GET TO PERFORM A "MOB" CHARACTER!
A MOB CHARACTER IS AN EXTRA WITH NO NAME.
BUT THE ROLE CAME WITH A CONDITION.
ALL RIGHT, HIME?
PLAYBACK
1 day ago

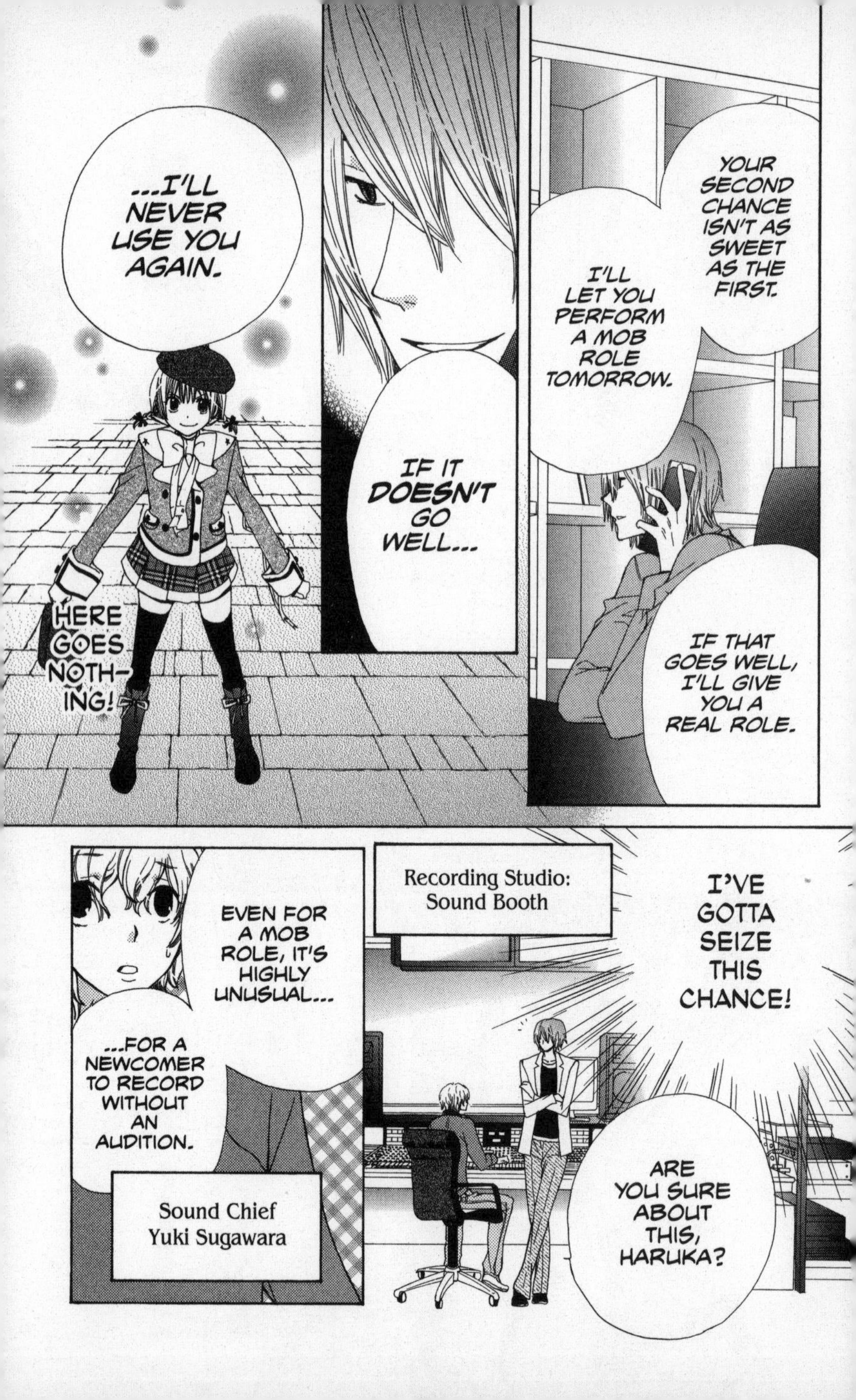
YOUR SECOND CHANCE ISN'T AS SWEET AS THE FIRST.
I'LL LET YOU PERFORM A MOB ROLE TOMORROW.
IF THAT GOES WELL, I'LL GIVE YOU A REAL ROLE.
IF IT DOESN'T GO WELL...
...I'LL NEVER USE YOU AGAIN.
HERE GOES NOTHING!
Recording Studio: Sound Booth
I'VE GOTTA SEIZE THIS CHANCE!
ARE YOU SURE ABOUT THIS, HARUKA?
EVEN FOR A MOB ROLE, IT'S HIGHLY UNUSUAL...
...FOR A NEWCOMER TO RECORD WITHOUT AN AUDITION.
Sound Chief Yuki Sugawara

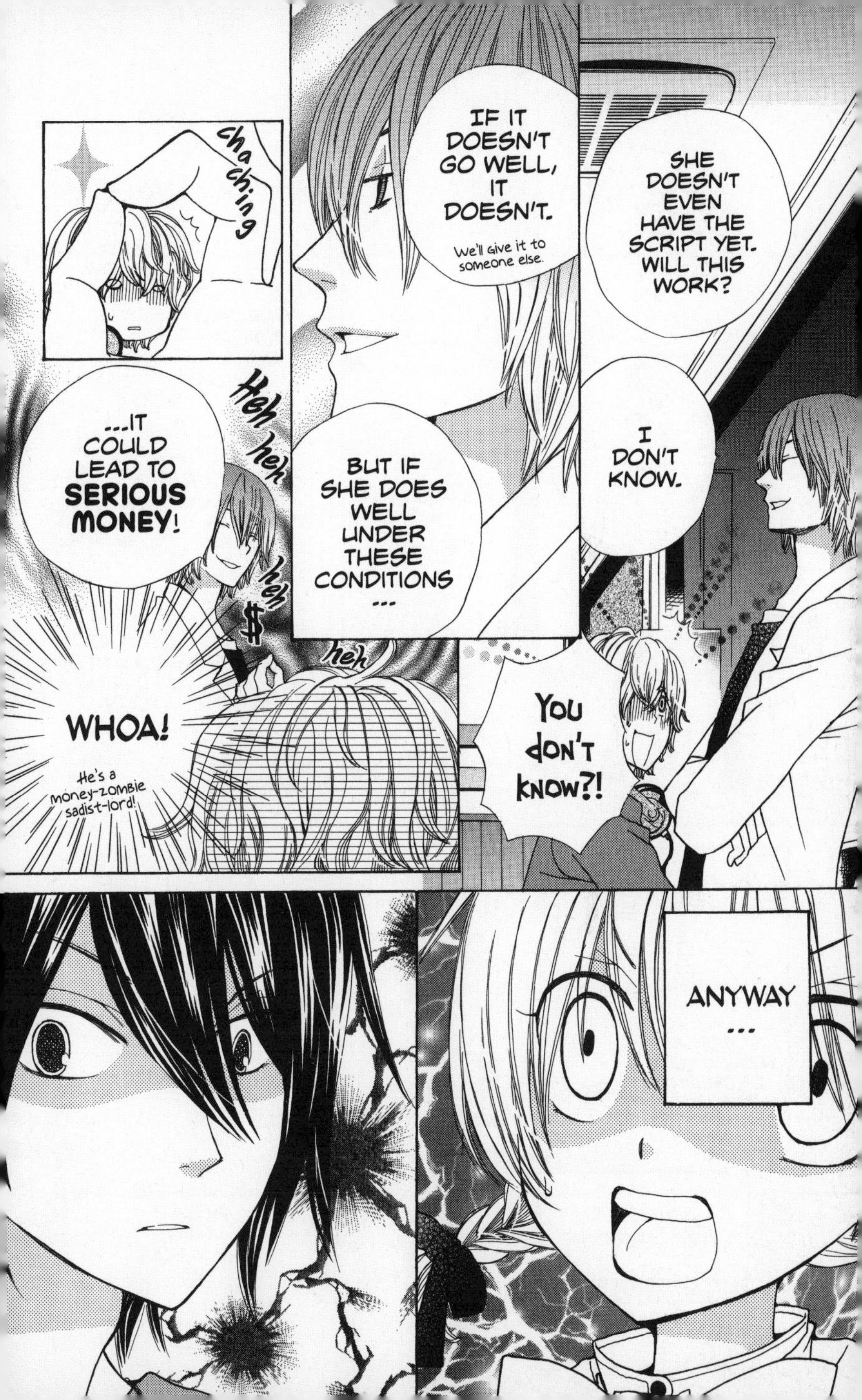
SHE DOESN'T EVEN HAVE THE SCRIPT YET. WILL THIS WORK?
I DON'T KNOW.
YOU DON'T KNOW?!
IF IT DOESN'T GO WELL, IT DOESN'T.
We'll give it to someone else.
BUT IF SHE DOES WELL UNDER THESE CONDITIONS...
cha ching
...IT COULD LEAD TO SERIOUS MONEY!
Heh heh heh heh
$
WHOA!
He's a money-zombie sadist-lord!
ANYWAY...

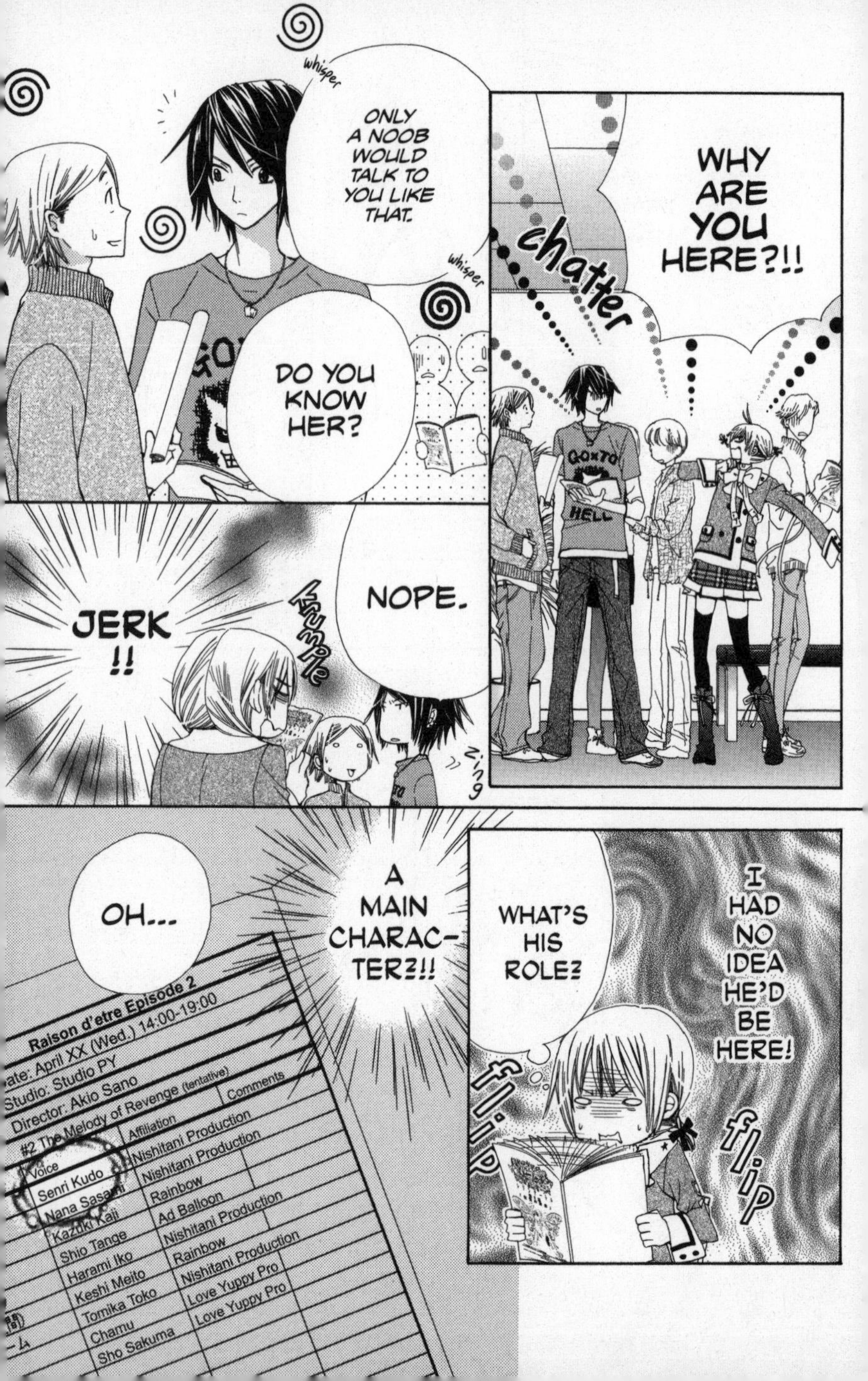
WHY ARE YOU HERE?!!
chatter
whisper
ONLY A NOOB WOULD TALK TO YOU LIKE THAT.
whisper
DO YOU KNOW HER?
NOPE.
krumple
JERK!!
zing
I HAD NO IDEA HE'D BE HERE!
WHAT'S HIS ROLE?
flip
flip
A MAIN CHARAC-TER?!!
OH...
Raison d'etre Episode 2
ate: April XX (Wed.) 14:00-19:00
Studio: Studio PY
Director: Akio Sano
#2 The Melody of Revenge (tentative)
Voice
Affiliation
Comments
Senri Kudo
Nishitani Production
Nana Sasami
Nishitani Production
Kazuki Kai
Rainbow
Shio Tange
Ad Balloon
Harami Iko
Nishitani Production
Keshi Meito
Rainbow
Tomika Toko
Nishitani Production
Chamu
Love Yuppy Pro
Sho Sakuma
Love Yuppy Pro

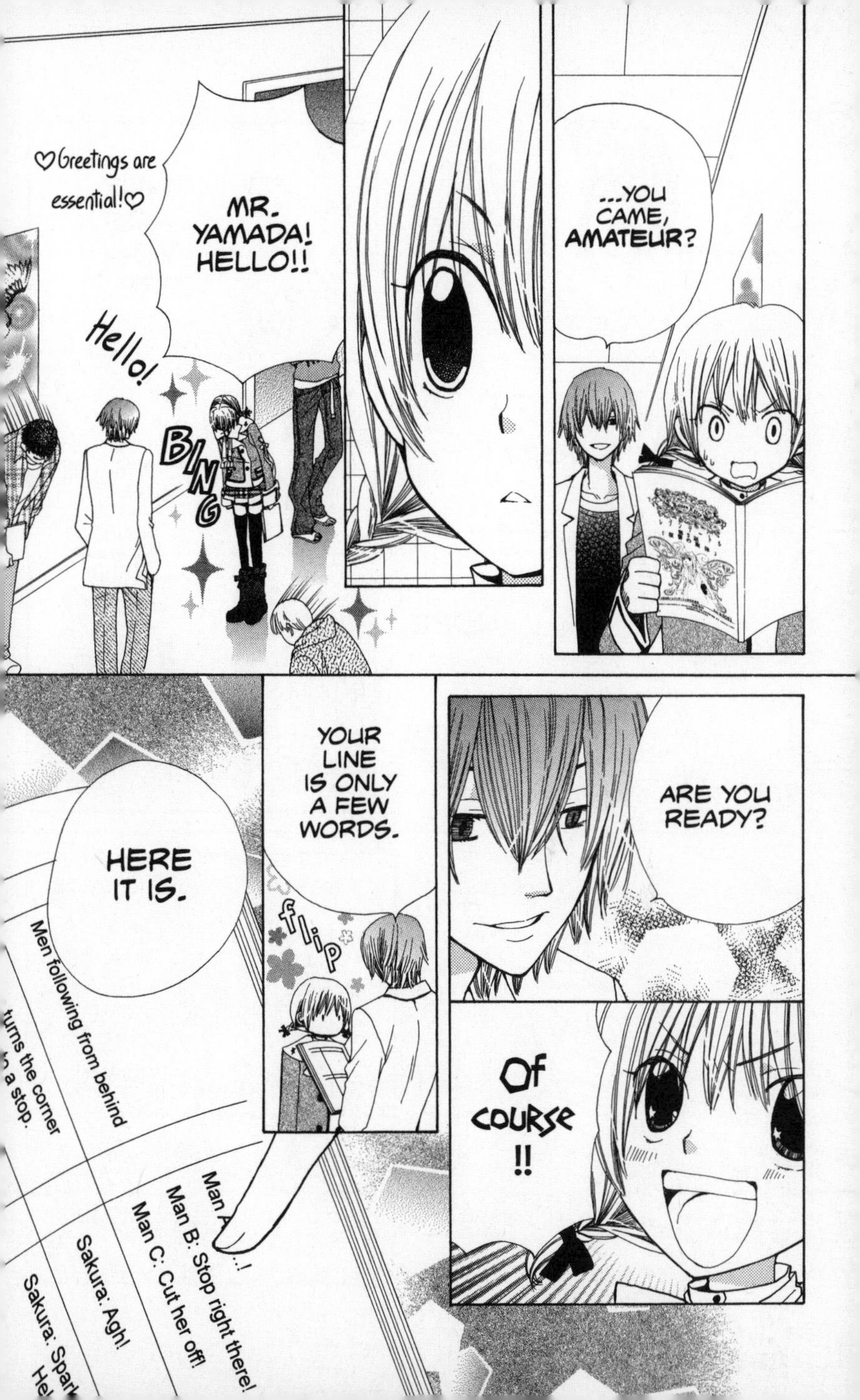
...YOU CAME, AMATEUR?
MR. YAMADA! HELLO!!
Hello!
BING
♡Greetings are essential!♡
ARE YOU READY?
Of course!!
YOUR LINE IS ONLY A FEW WORDS.
flip
HERE IT IS.
Men following from behind
turns the corner
Man B: Stop right there!
Man C: Cut her off!
Sakura: Agh!

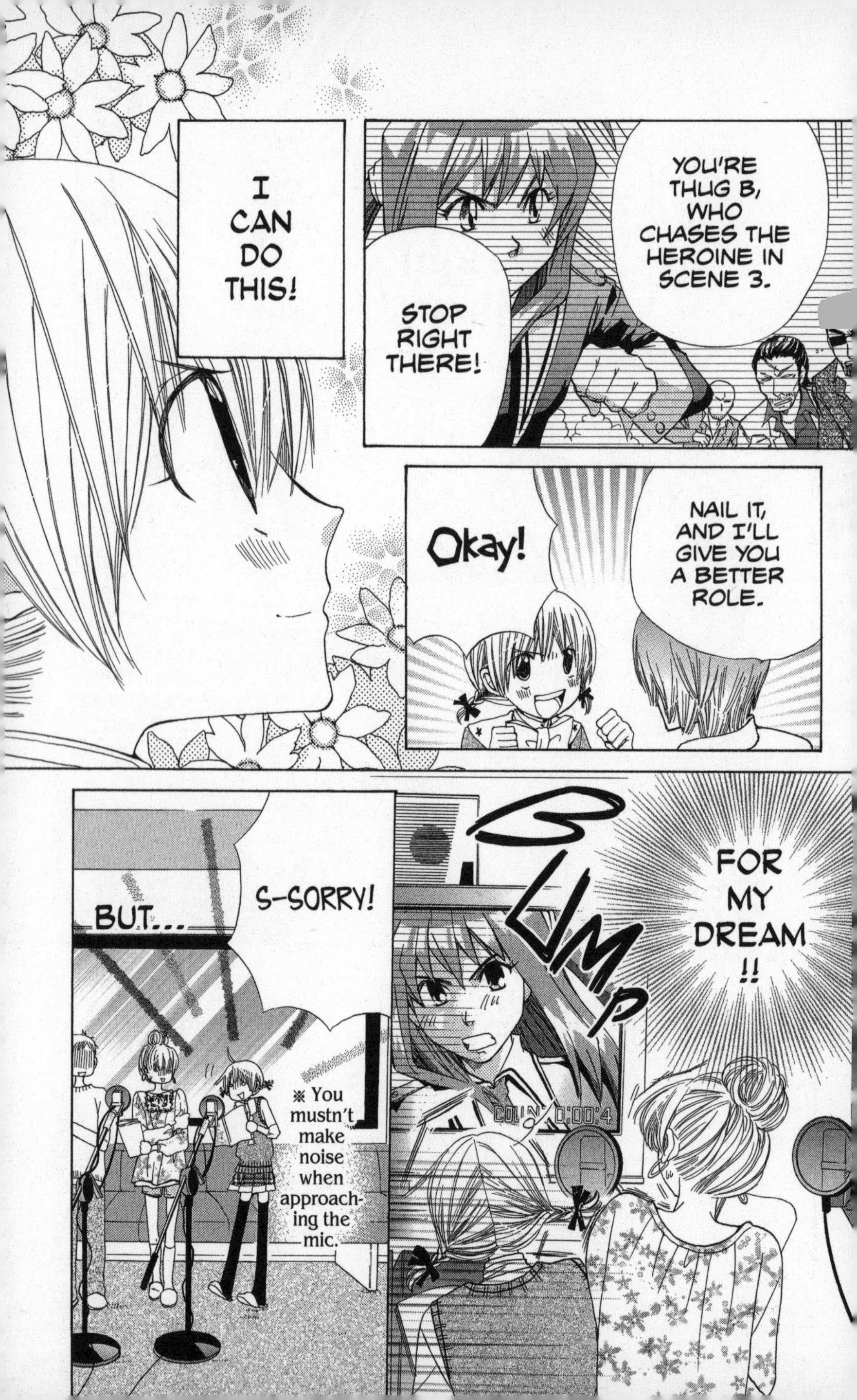
YOU'RE THUG B, WHO CHASES THE HEROINE IN SCENE 3.
STOP RIGHT THERE!
NAIL IT, AND I'LL GIVE YOU A BETTER ROLE.
Okay!
I CAN DO THIS!
FOR MY DREAM!!
SLUMP
S-SORRY!
BUT...
※ You mustn't make noise when approaching the mic.

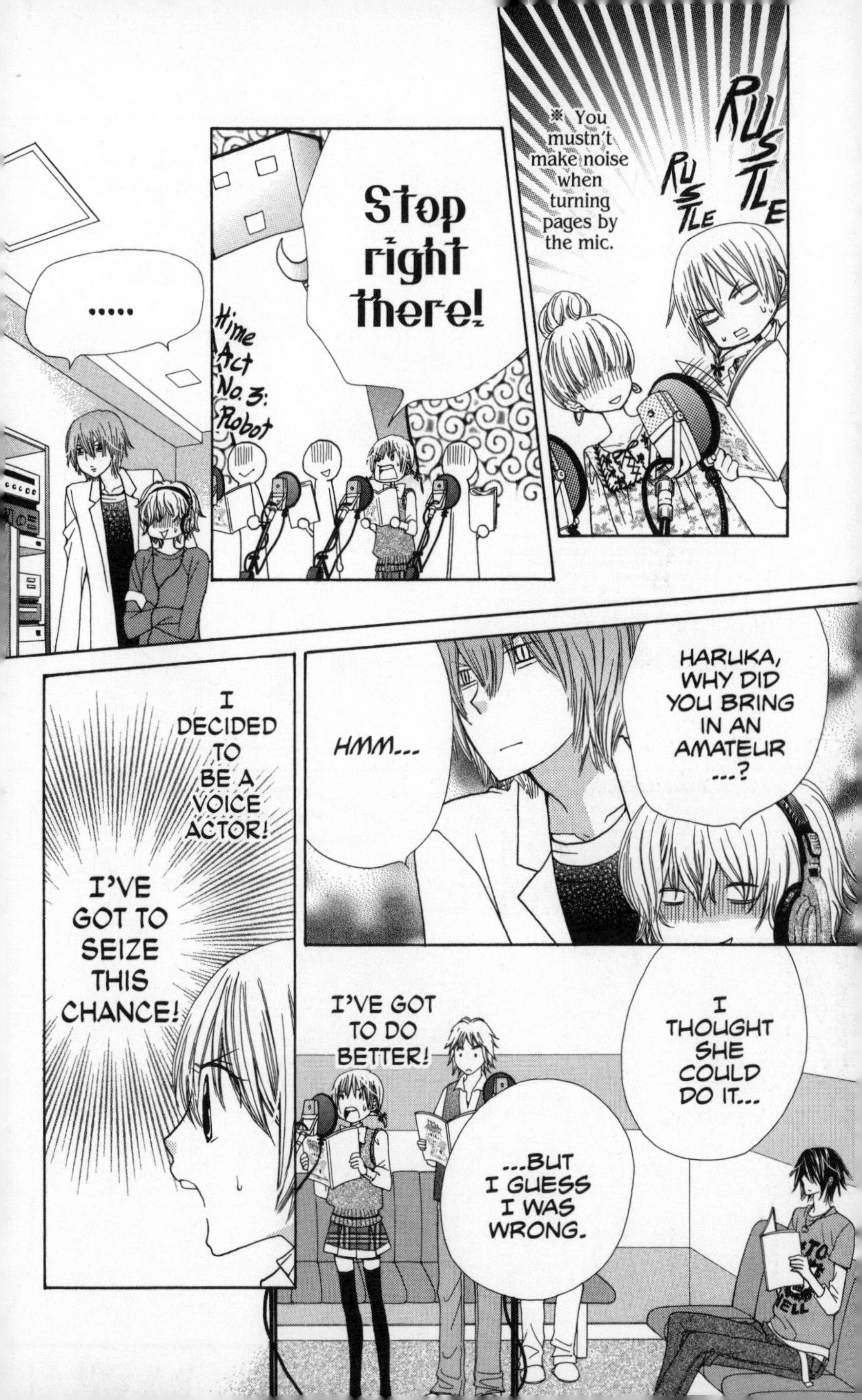
RUSTLE
RUSTLE
※ You mustn't make noise when turning pages by the mic.
Stop right there!
Hime Act No. 3: Robot
.....
HARUKA, WHY DID YOU BRING IN AN AMATEUR ...?
HMM...
I THOUGHT SHE COULD DO IT...
...BUT I GUESS I WAS WRONG.
I'VE GOT TO DO BETTER!
I DECIDED TO BE A VOICE ACTOR!
I'VE GOT TO SEIZE THIS CHANCE!

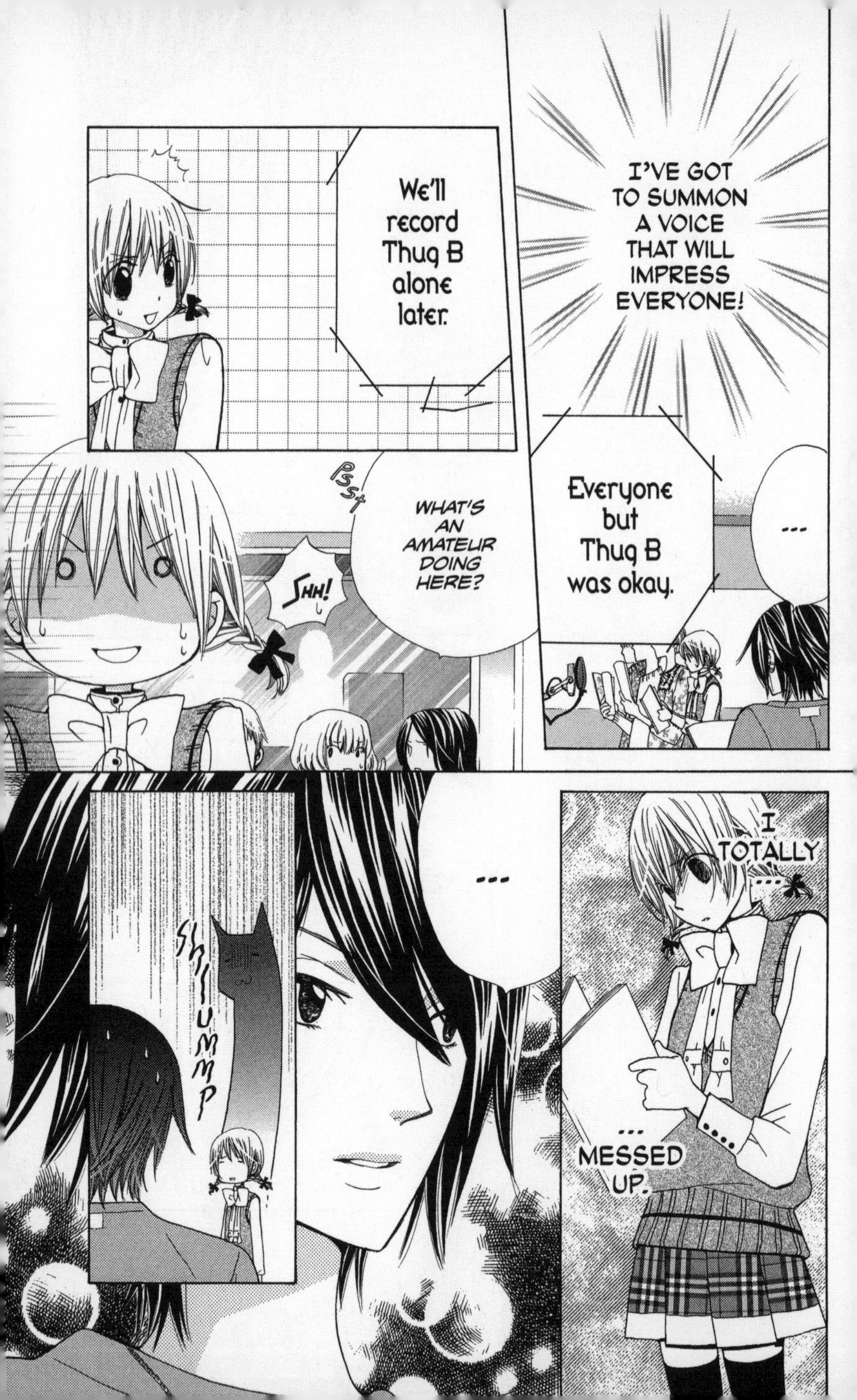
I'VE GOT TO SUMMON A VOICE THAT WILL IMPRESS EVERYONE!
...
Everyone but Thug B was okay.
We'll record Thug B alone later.
Psst
WHAT'S AN AMATEUR DOING HERE?
SHH!
I TOTALLY ...
... MESSED UP.
...
SHHUMMP

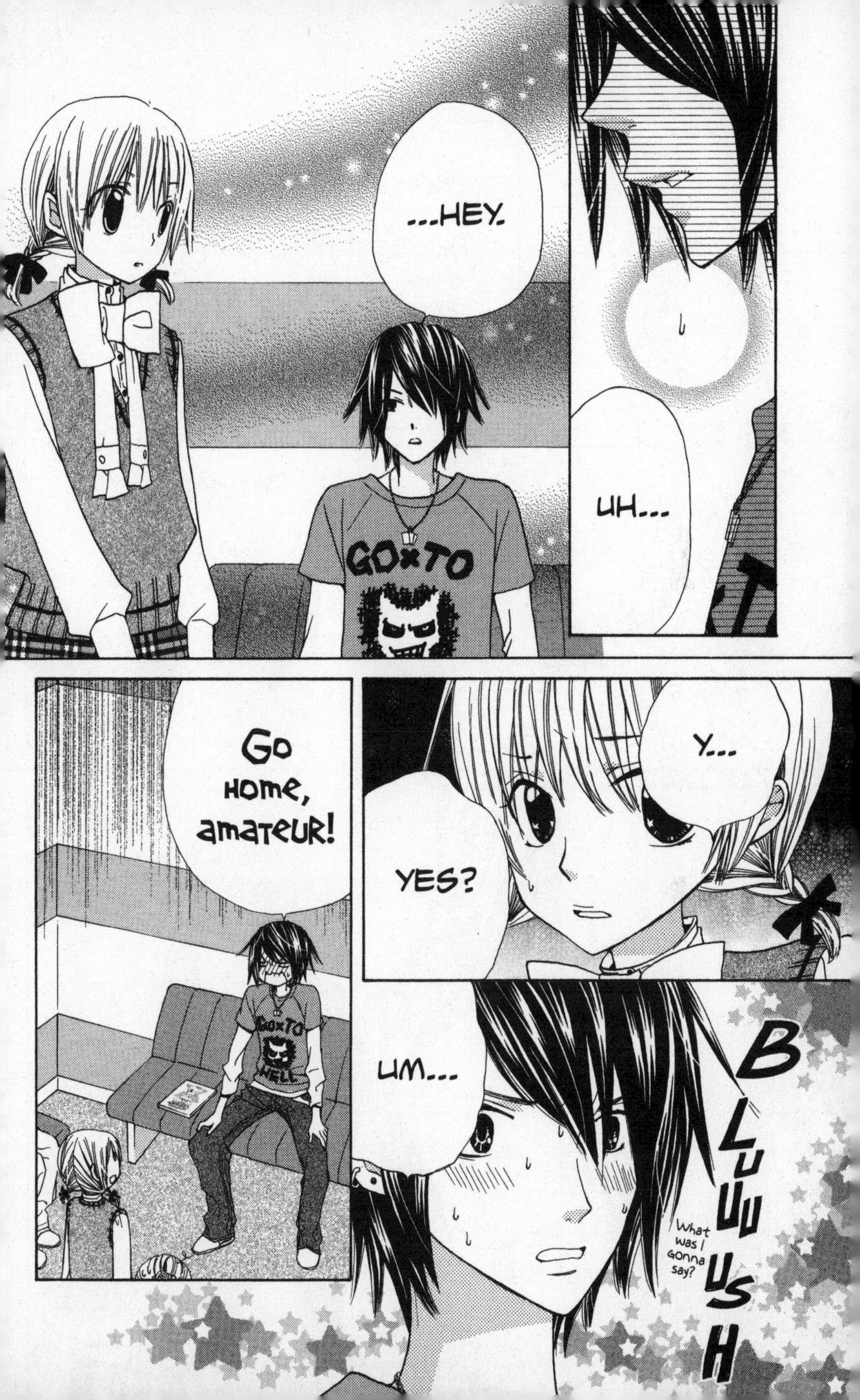
UH...
...HEY.
GO×TO
Y...
YES?
UM...
BLUUUUSH
What was I gonna say?
Go home, amateur!
GO×TO HELL

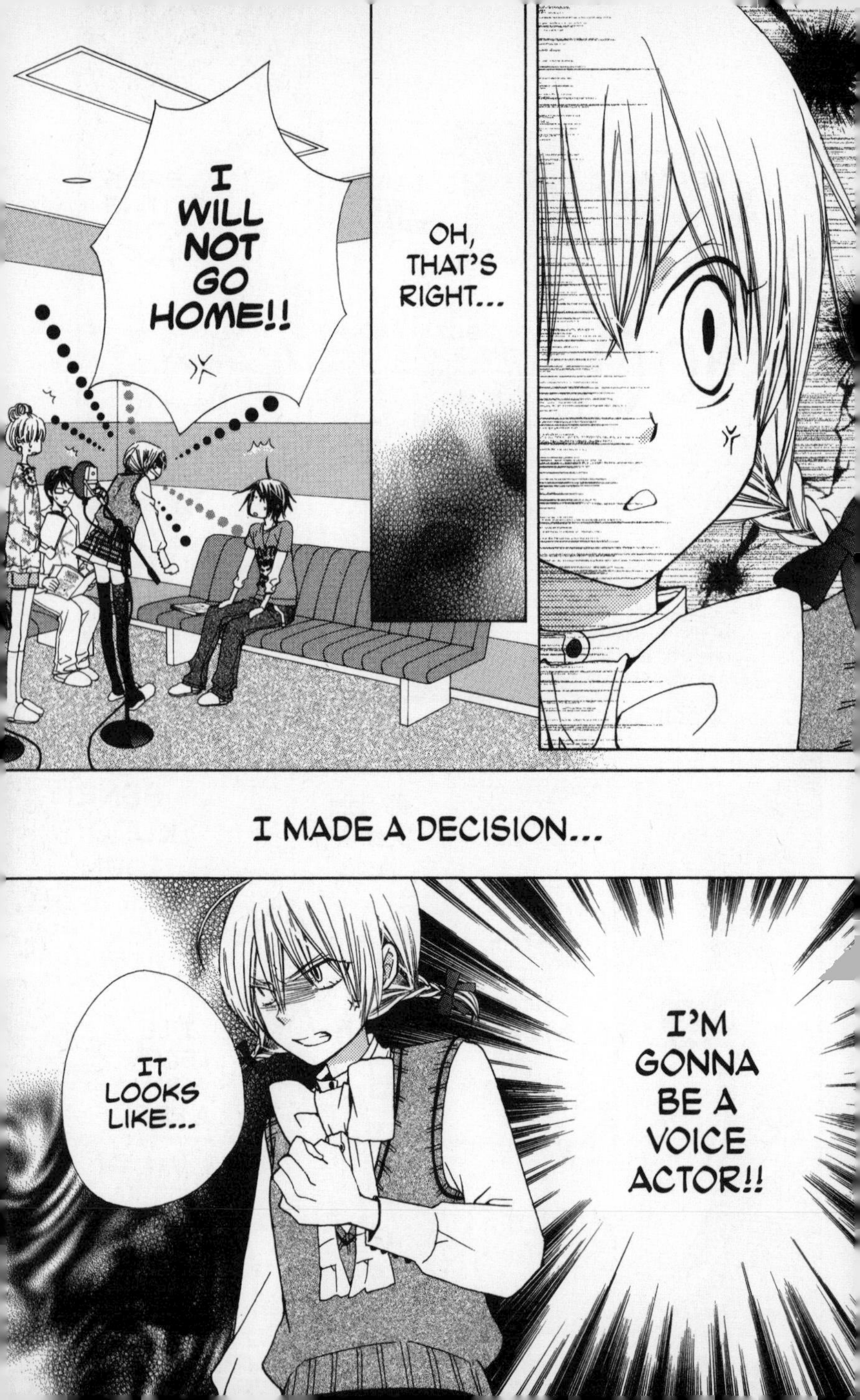
OH, THAT'S RIGHT...
I WILL NOT GO HOME!!
I MADE A DECISION...
IT LOOKS LIKE...
I'M GONNA BE A VOICE ACTOR!!

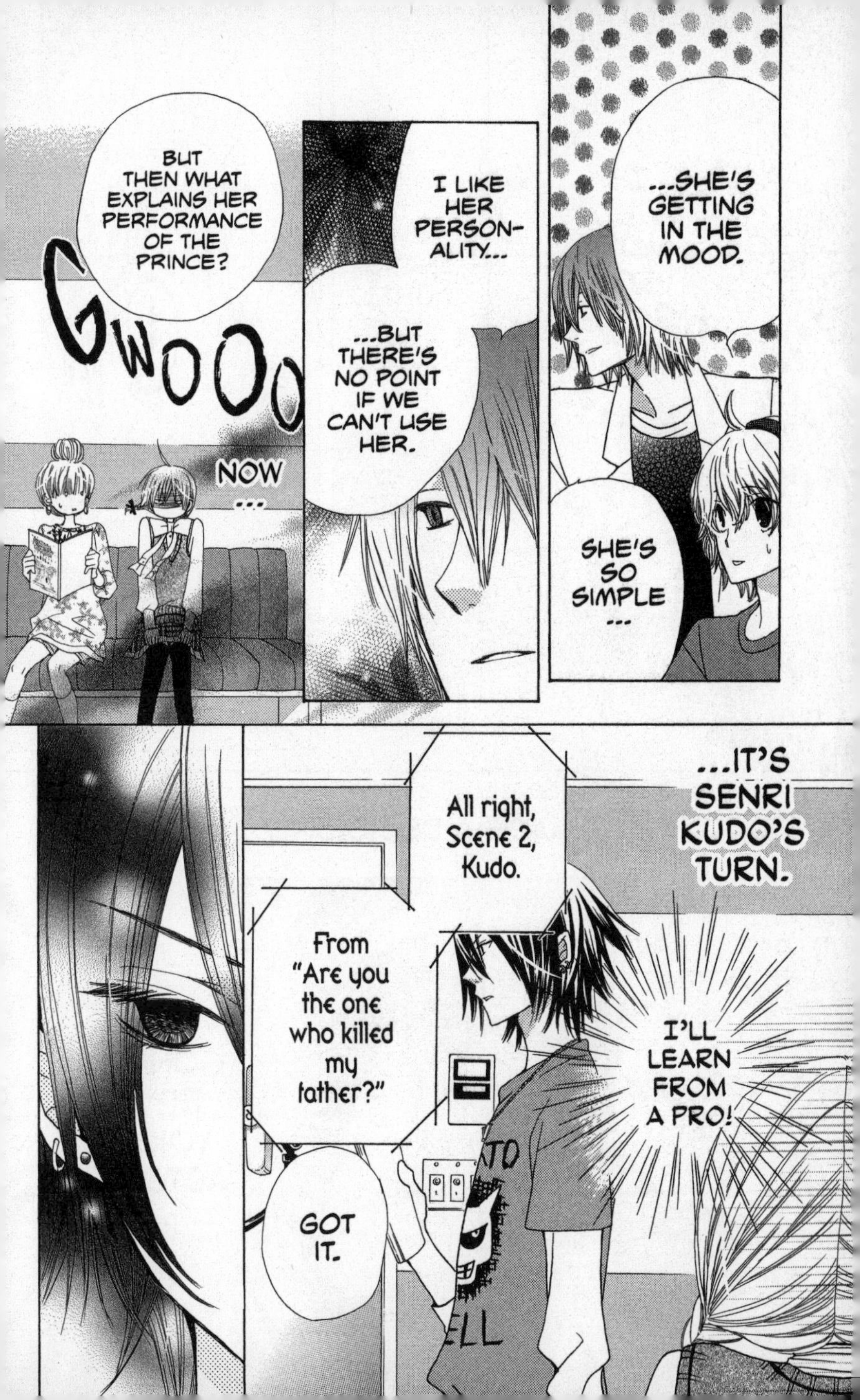
...SHE'S GETTING IN THE MOOD.
SHE'S SO SIMPLE...
I LIKE HER PERSONALITY...
...BUT THERE'S NO POINT IF WE CAN'T USE HER.
BUT THEN WHAT EXPLAINS HER PERFORMANCE OF THE PRINCE?
GWOOOO
NOW...
...IT'S SENRI KUDO'S TURN.
All right, Scene 2, Kudo.
From "Are you the one who killed my father?"
I'LL LEARN FROM A PRO!
GOT IT.

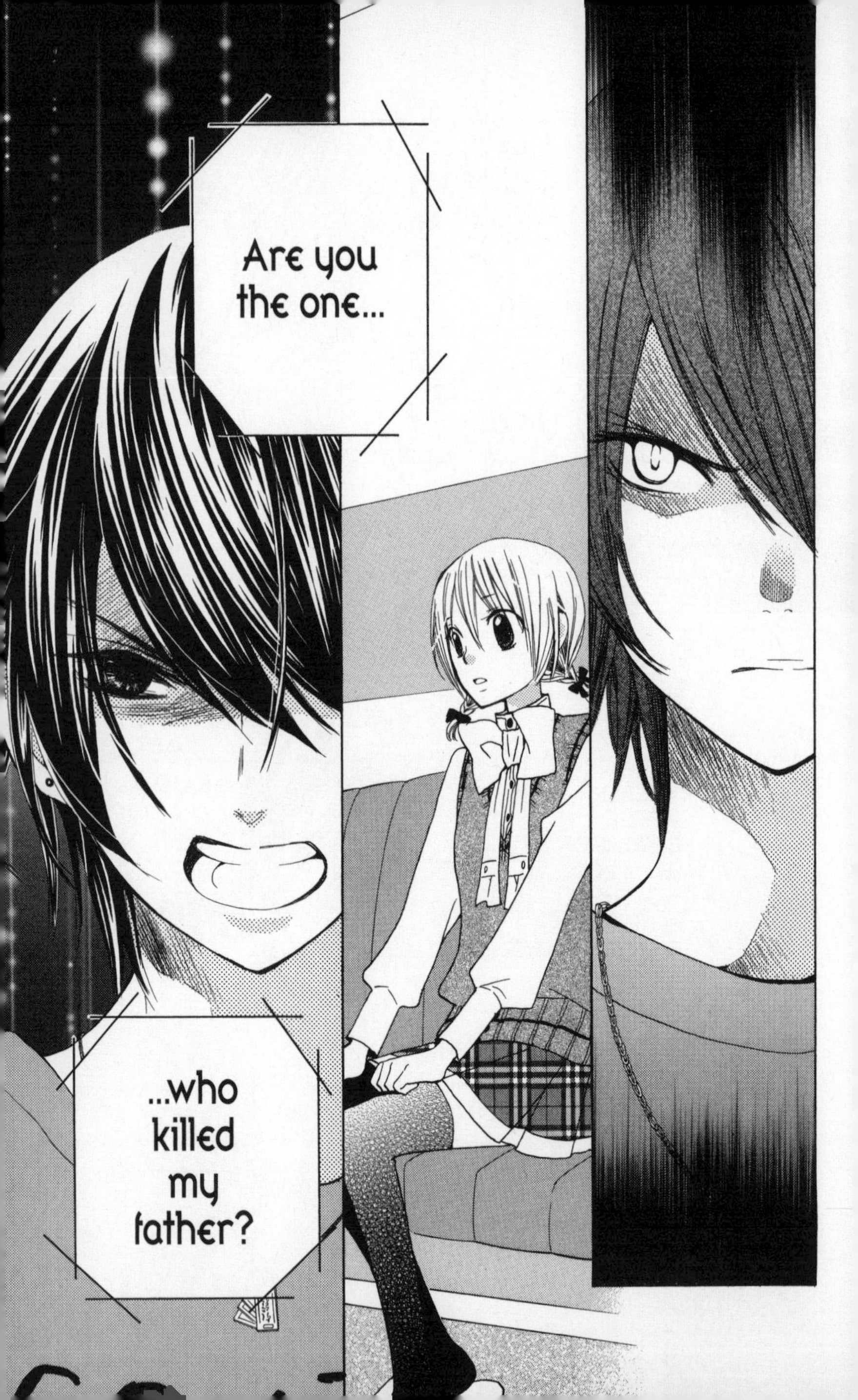
Are you the one...
...who killed my father?

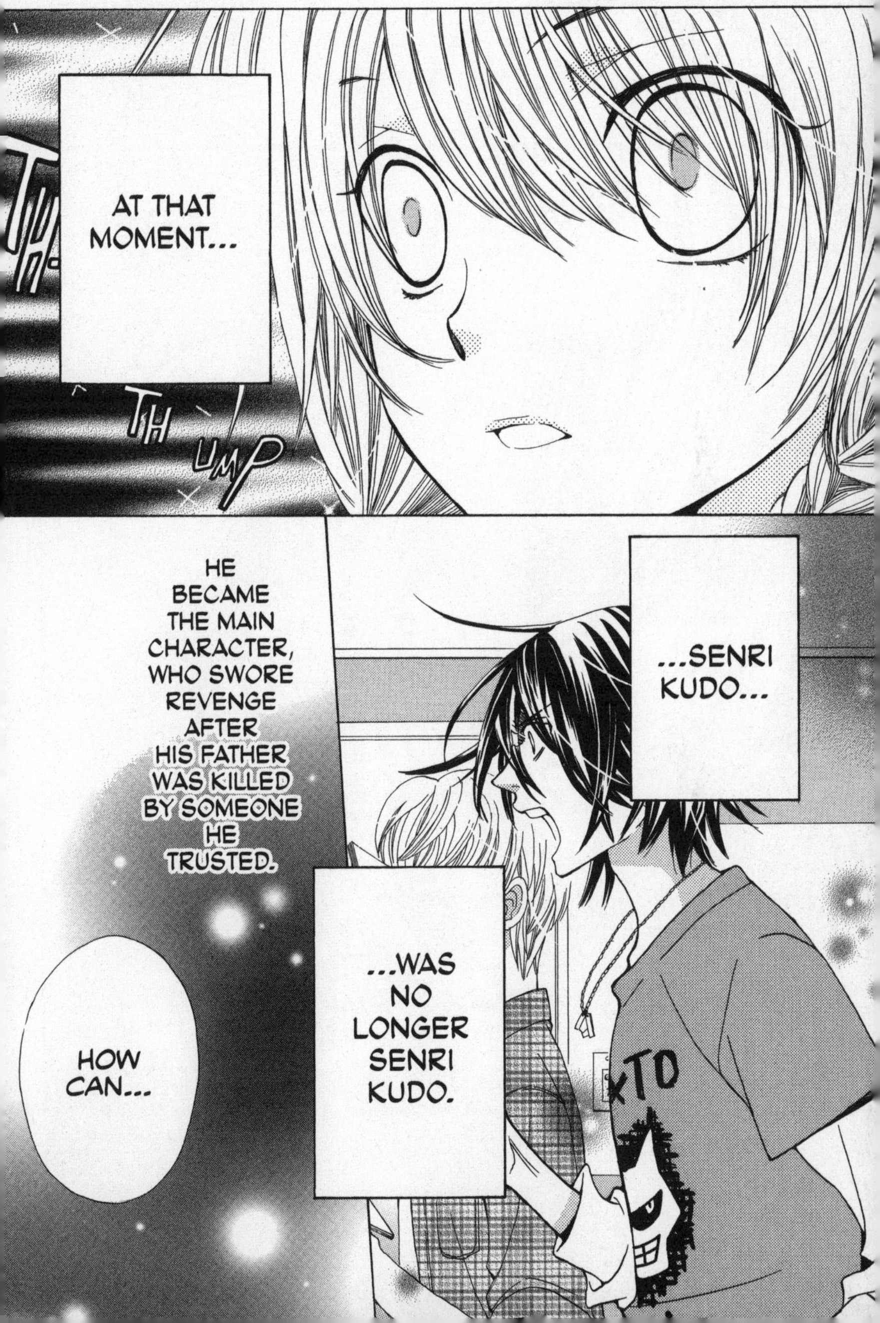
AT THAT MOMENT...
TH- THUMP
...SENRI KUDO...
...WAS NO LONGER SENRI KUDO.
HE BECAME THE MAIN CHARACTER, WHO SWORE REVENGE AFTER HIS FATHER WAS KILLED BY SOMEONE HE TRUSTED.
HOW CAN...

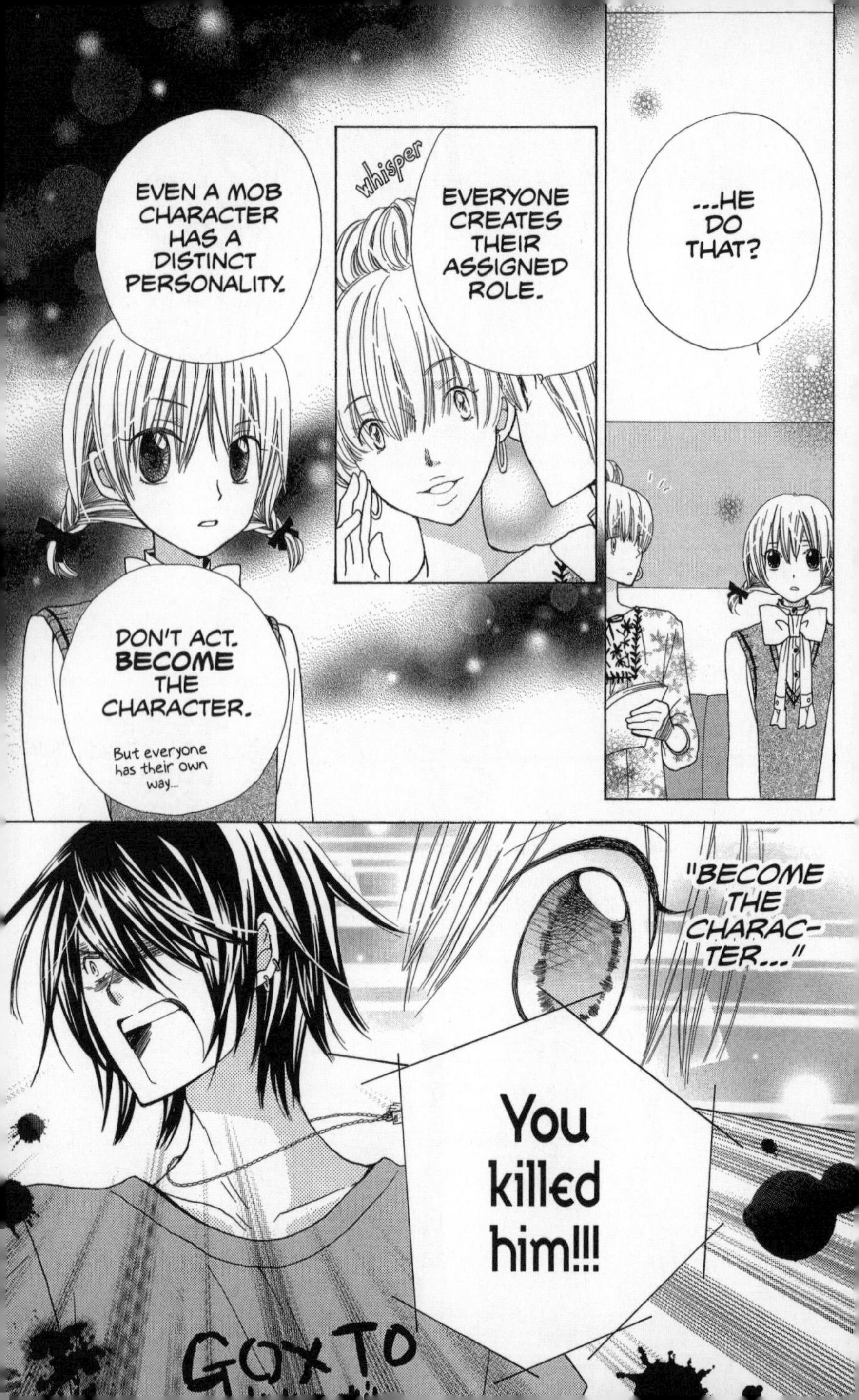
...HE DO THAT?
whisper
EVERYONE CREATES THEIR ASSIGNED ROLE.
EVEN A MOB CHARACTER HAS A DISTINCT PERSONALITY.
DON'T ACT. **BECOME** THE CHARACTER.
But everyone has their own way...
"BECOME THE CHARAC-TER..."
You killed him!!!

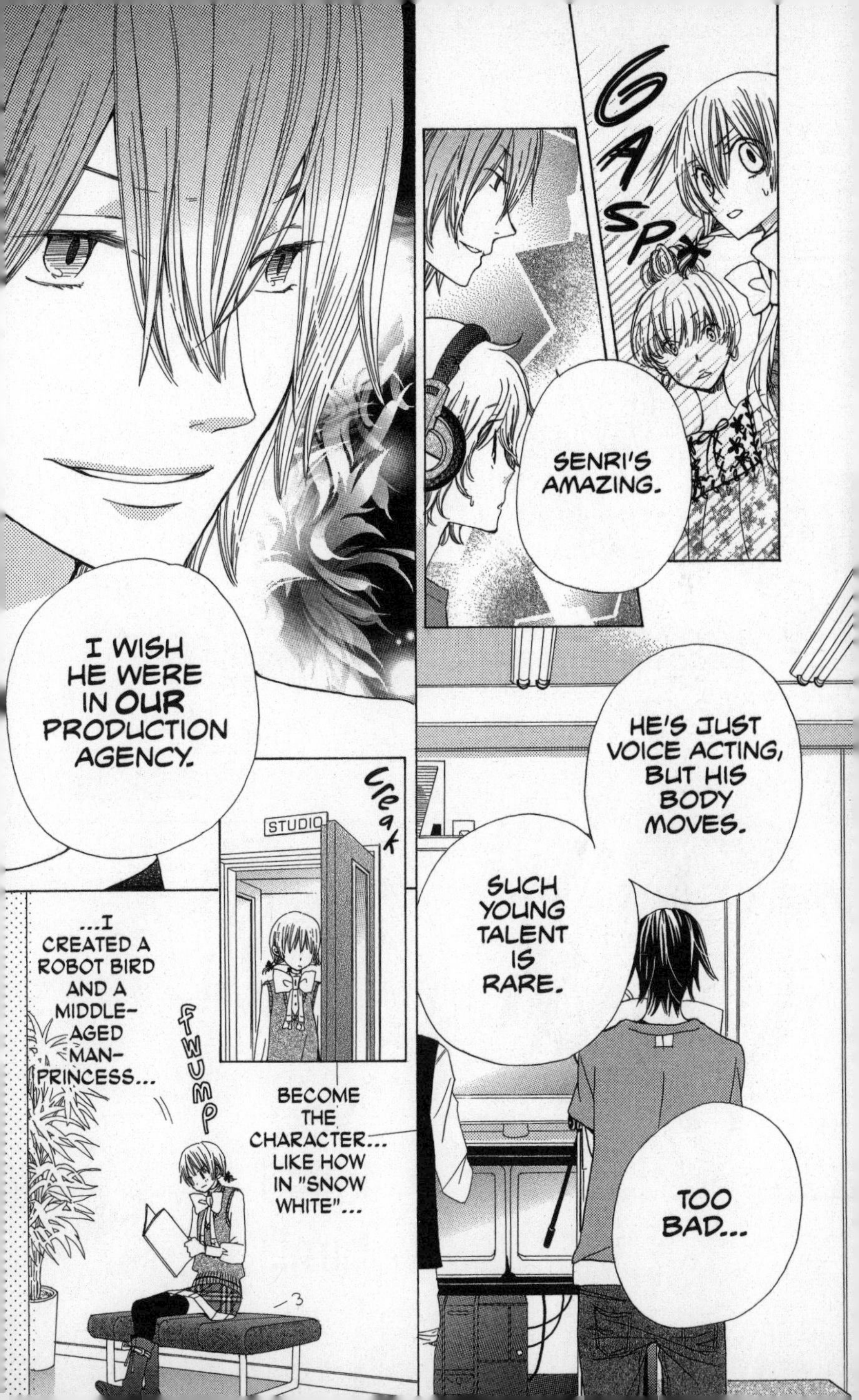
GASP
SENRI'S AMAZING.
I WISH HE WERE IN OUR PRODUCTION AGENCY.
HE'S JUST VOICE ACTING, BUT HIS BODY MOVES.
SUCH YOUNG TALENT IS RARE.
TOO BAD...
STUDIO
creak
...I CREATED A ROBOT BIRD AND A MIDDLE-AGED MAN-PRINCESS...
FWUMP
BECOME THE CHARACTER... LIKE HOW IN "SNOW WHITE"...

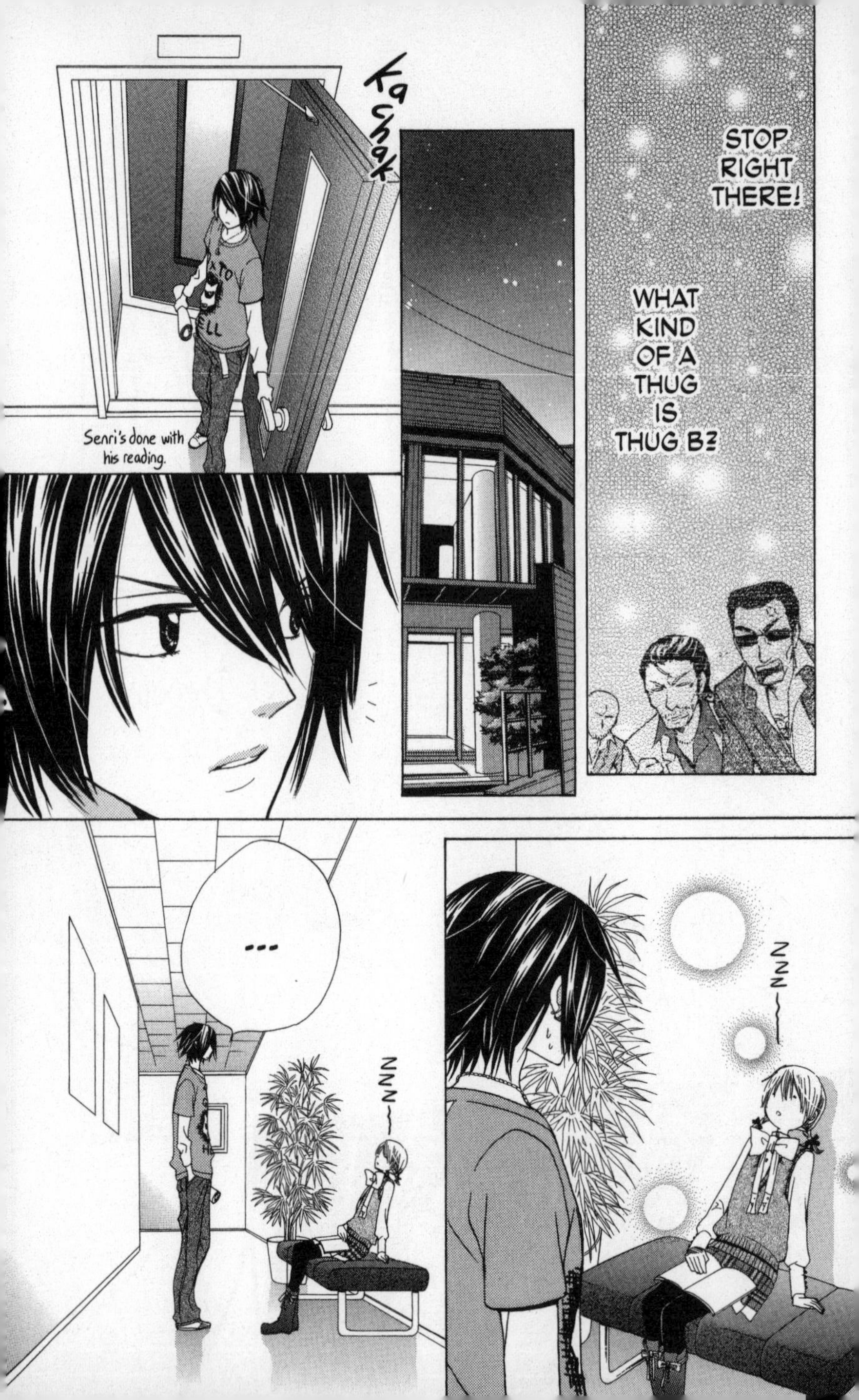
STOP RIGHT THERE!
WHAT KIND OF A THUG IS THUG B?
Kachak
Senri's done with his reading.
Zzz~
...
Zzz~

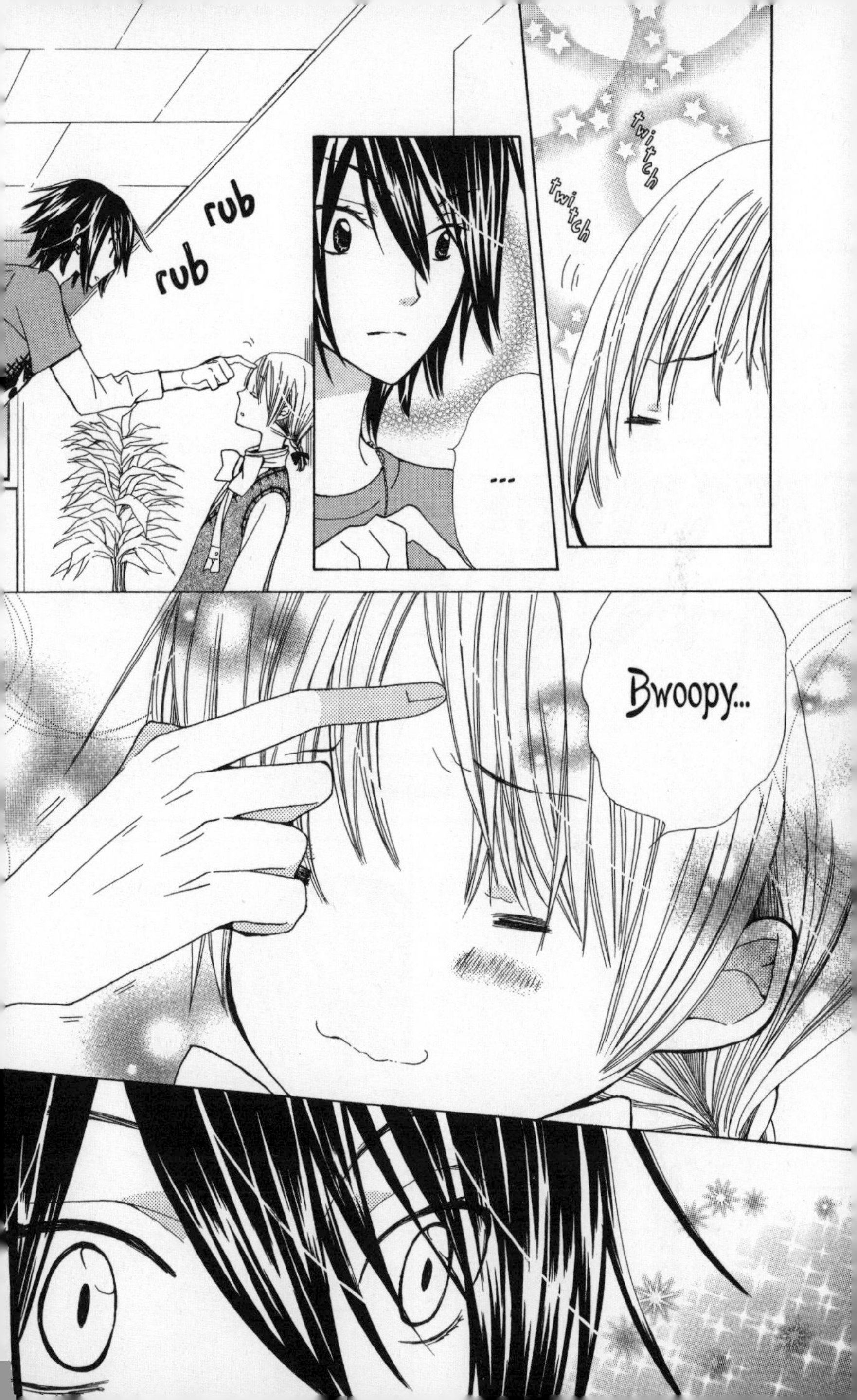
twitch
twitch
...
rub
rub
Bwoopy...

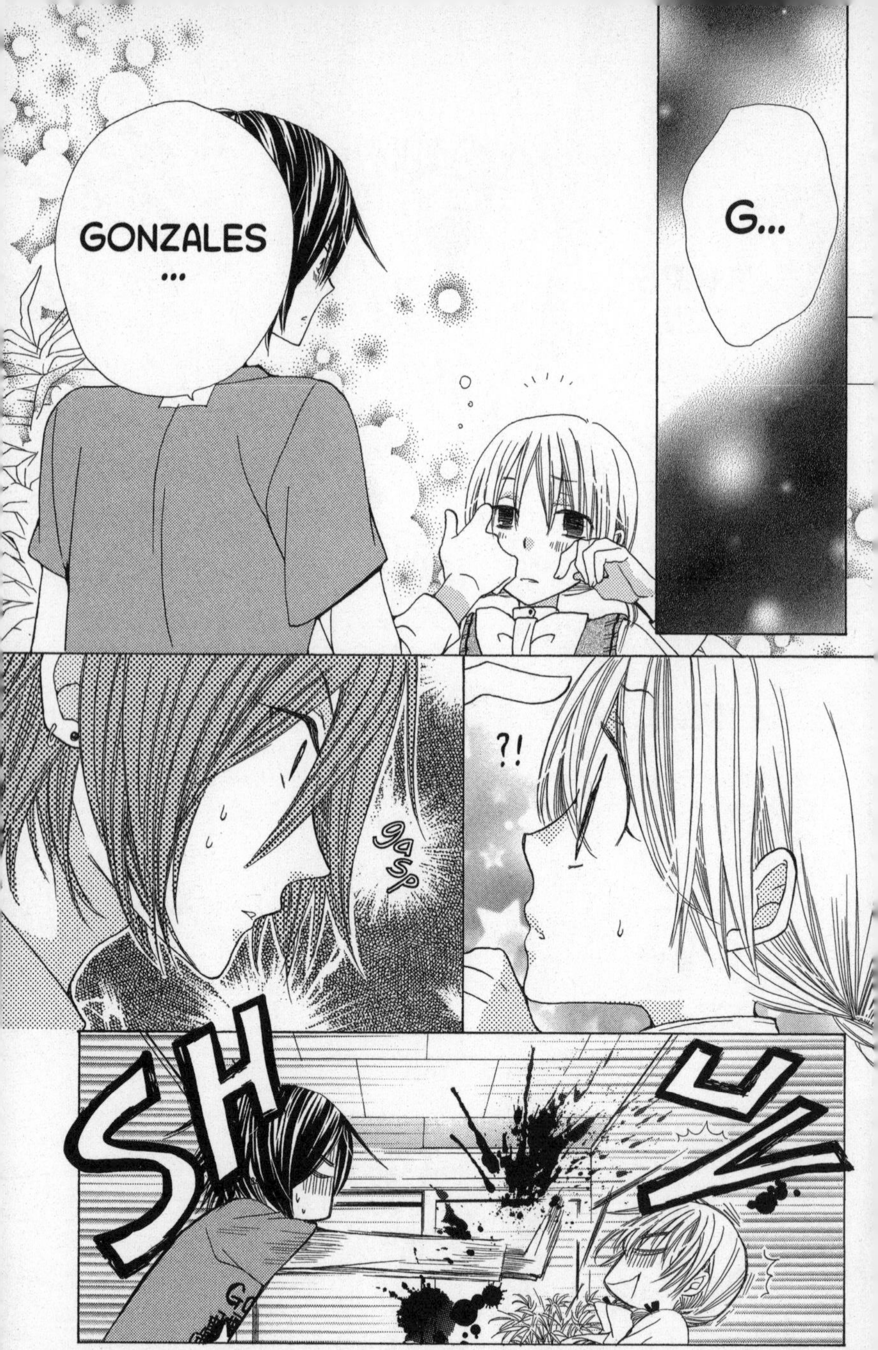
G...
GONZALES ...
?!
gasp
SH

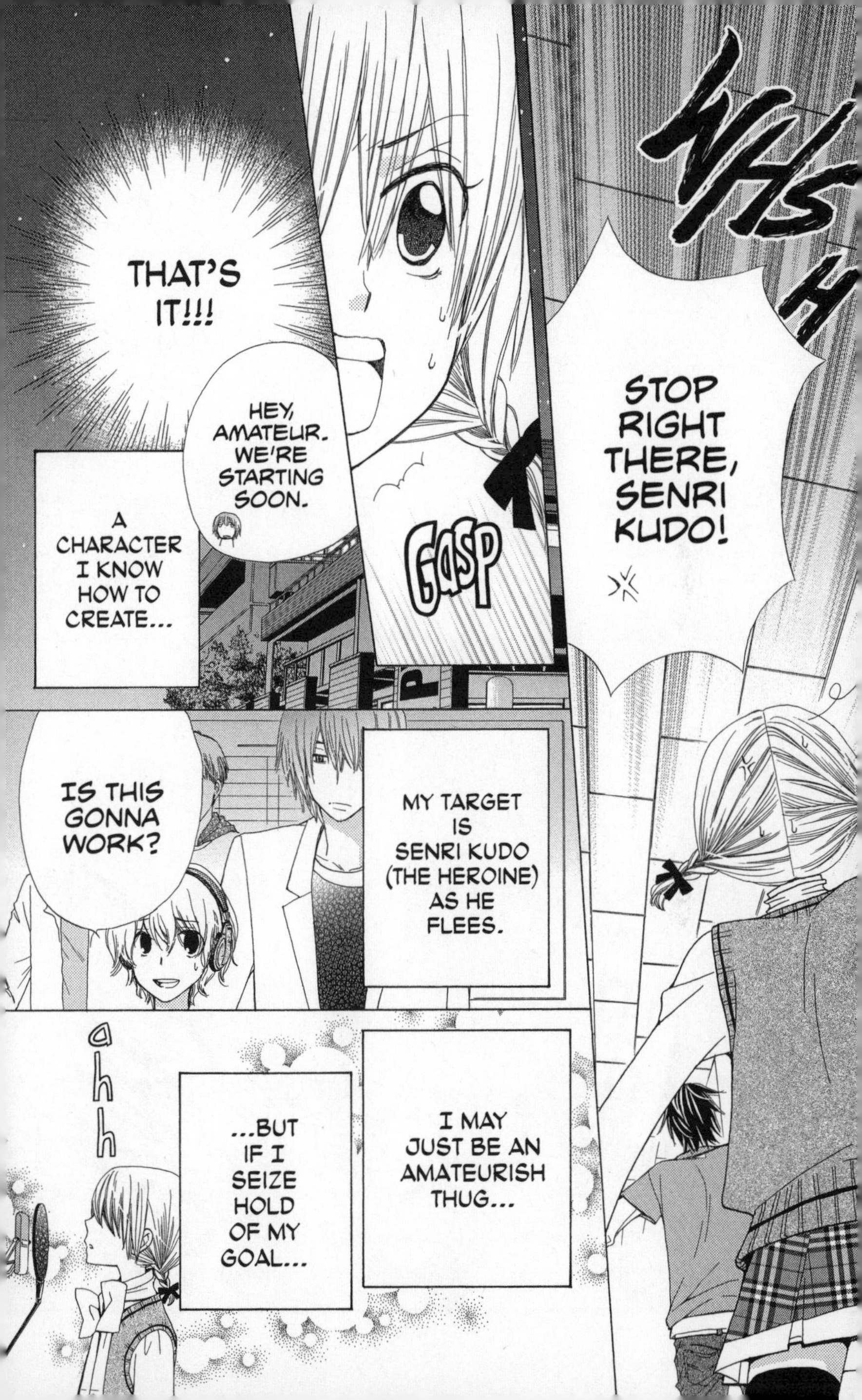
WHSH
STOP RIGHT THERE, SENRI KUDO!
GASP
HEY, AMATEUR. WE'RE STARTING SOON.
THAT'S IT!!!
A CHARACTER I KNOW HOW TO CREATE...
MY TARGET IS SENRI KUDO (THE HEROINE) AS HE FLEES.
IS THIS GONNA WORK?
I MAY JUST BE AN AMATEURISH THUG...
...BUT IF I SEIZE HOLD OF MY GOAL...
ahh

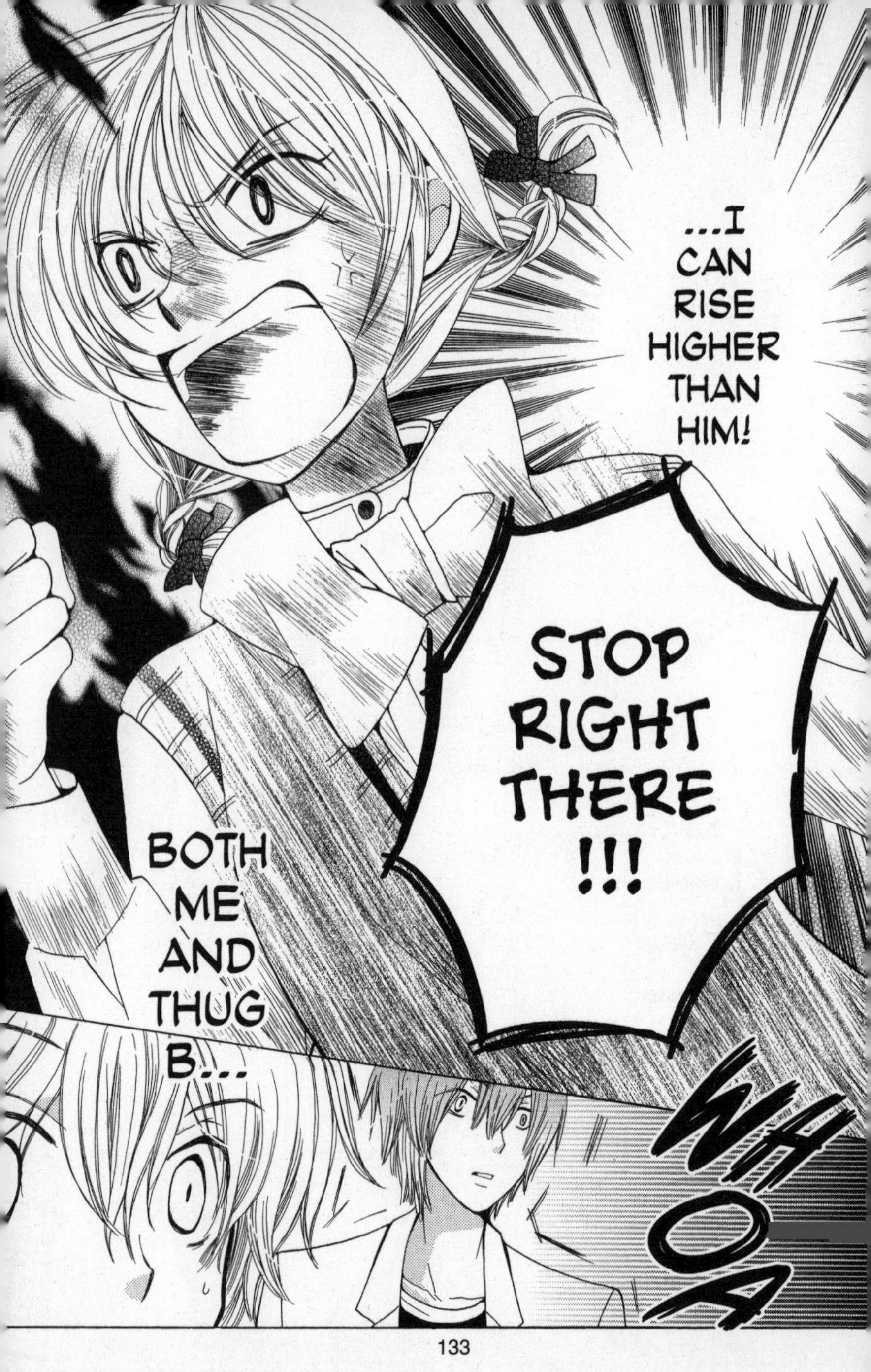
...I CAN RISE HIGHER THAN HIM!
STOP RIGHT THERE!!!
BOTH ME AND THUG B...
WHOA

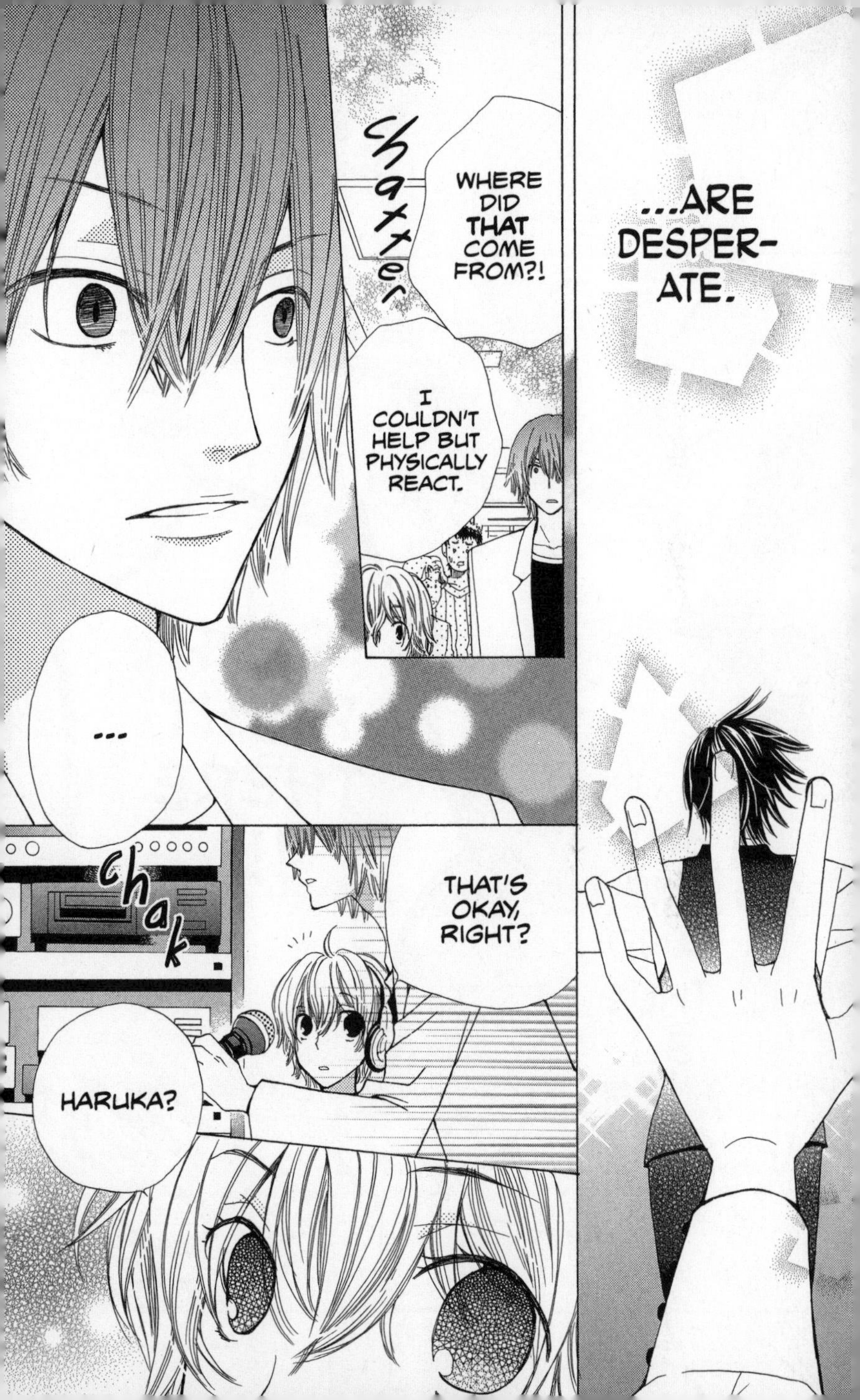

...ARE DESPER-ATE.
WHERE DID THAT COME FROM?!
chatter
I COULDN'T HELP BUT PHYSICALLY REACT.
...
THAT'S OKAY, RIGHT?
chak
HARUKA?

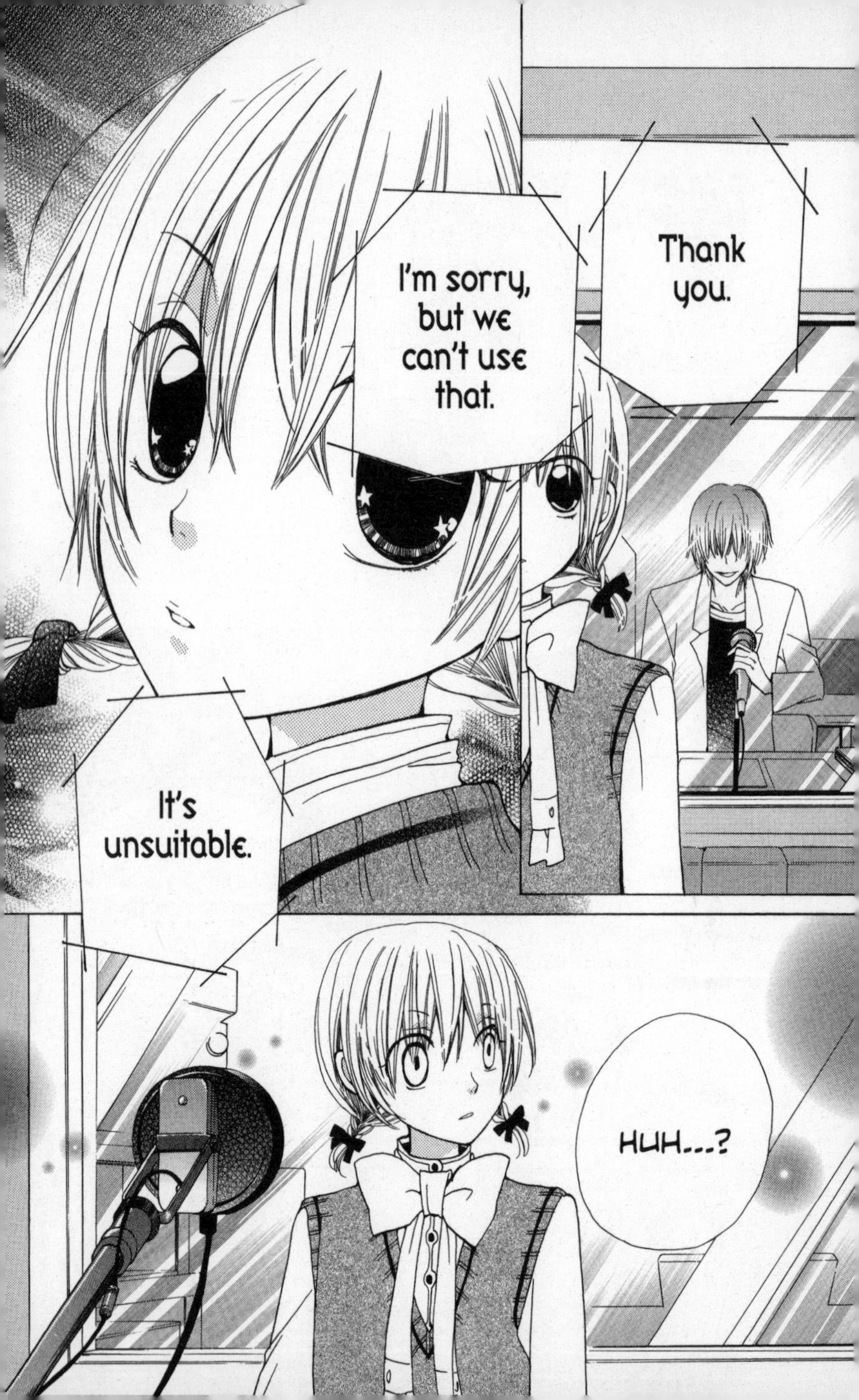
Thank you.
I'm sorry, but we can't use that.
It's unsuitable.
HUH...?

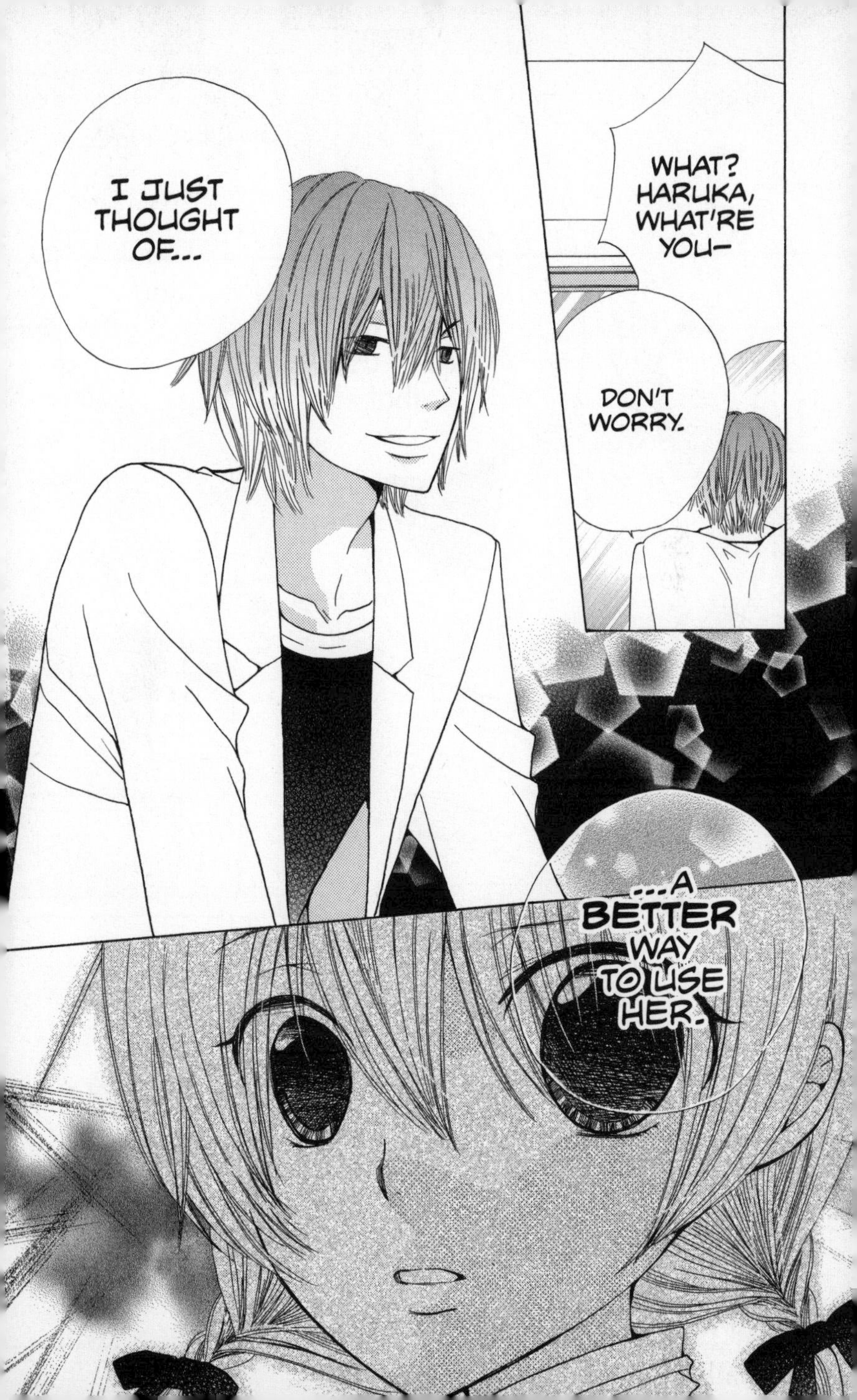
WHAT? HARUKA, WHAT'RE YOU-
DON'T WORRY.
I JUST THOUGHT OF...
...A BETTER WAY TO USE HER.

Chapter 4

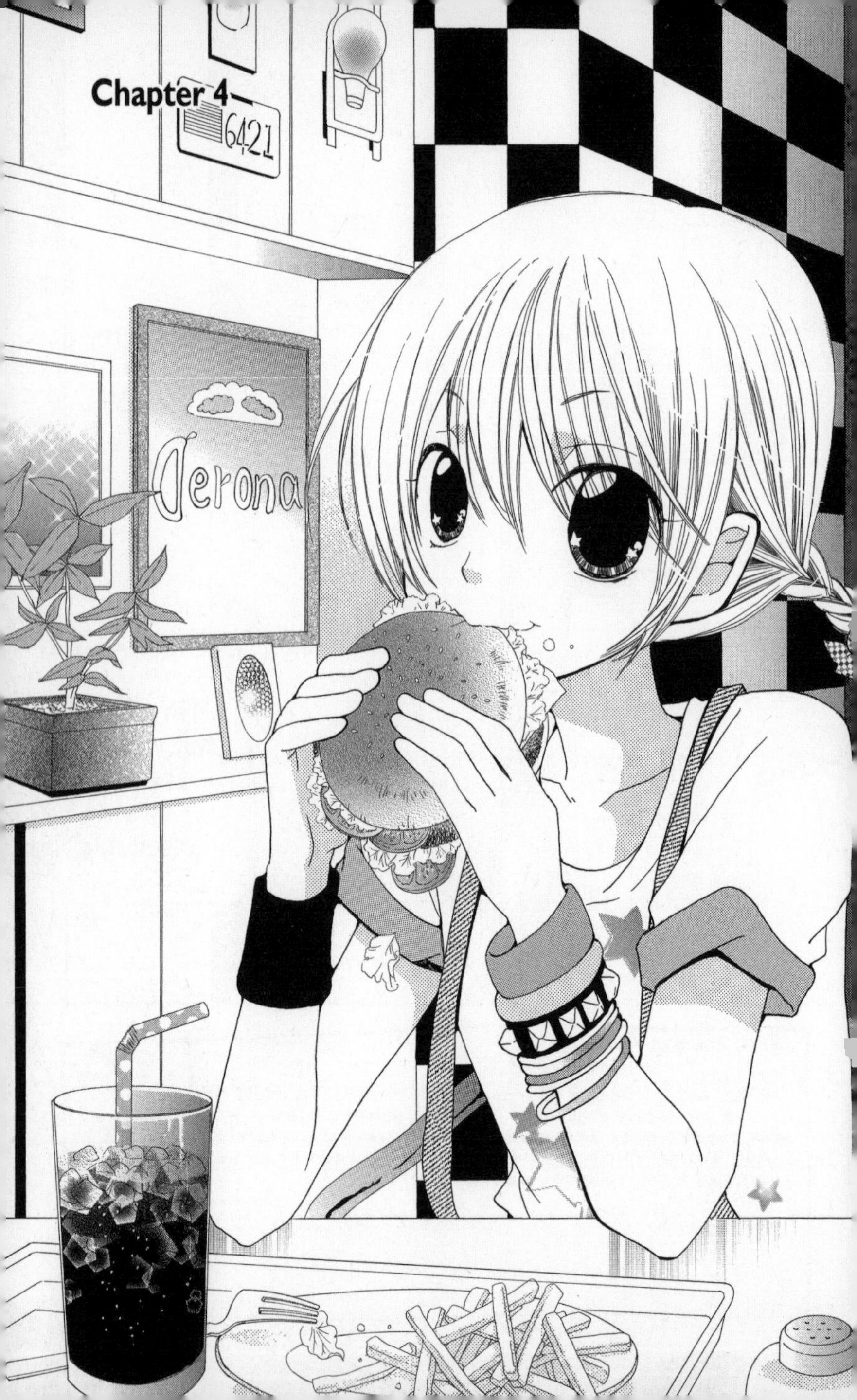

6421
Verona

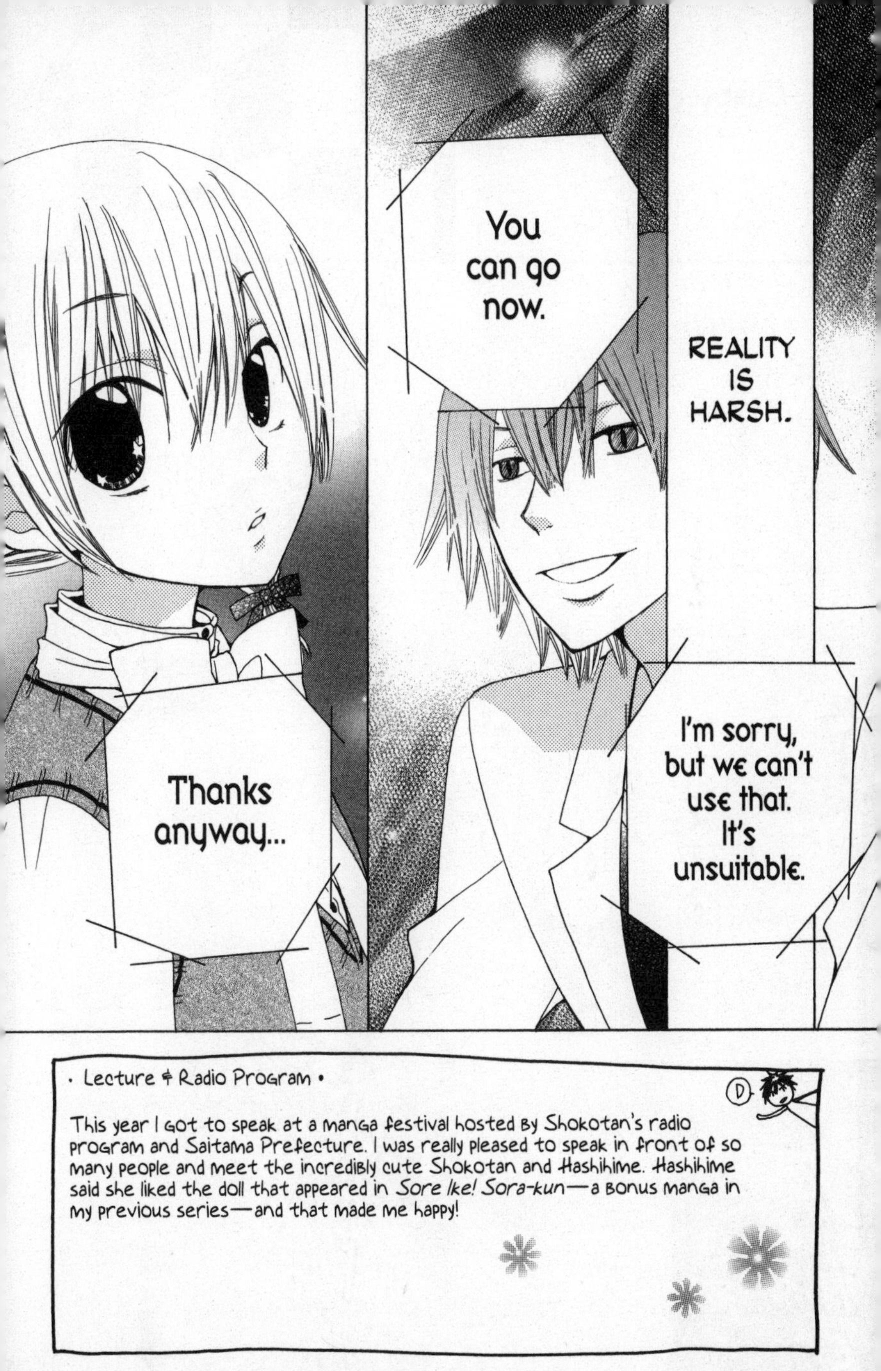
REALITY IS HARSH.
I'm sorry, but we can't use that. It's unsuitable.
You can go now.
Thanks anyway...

• Lecture & Radio Program •

This year I got to speak at a manga festival hosted by Shokotan's radio program and Saitama Prefecture. I was really pleased to speak in front of so many people and meet the incredibly cute Shokotan and Hashihime. Hashihime said she liked the doll that appeared in *Sore Ike! Sora-kun*—a bonus manga in my previous series—and that made me happy!

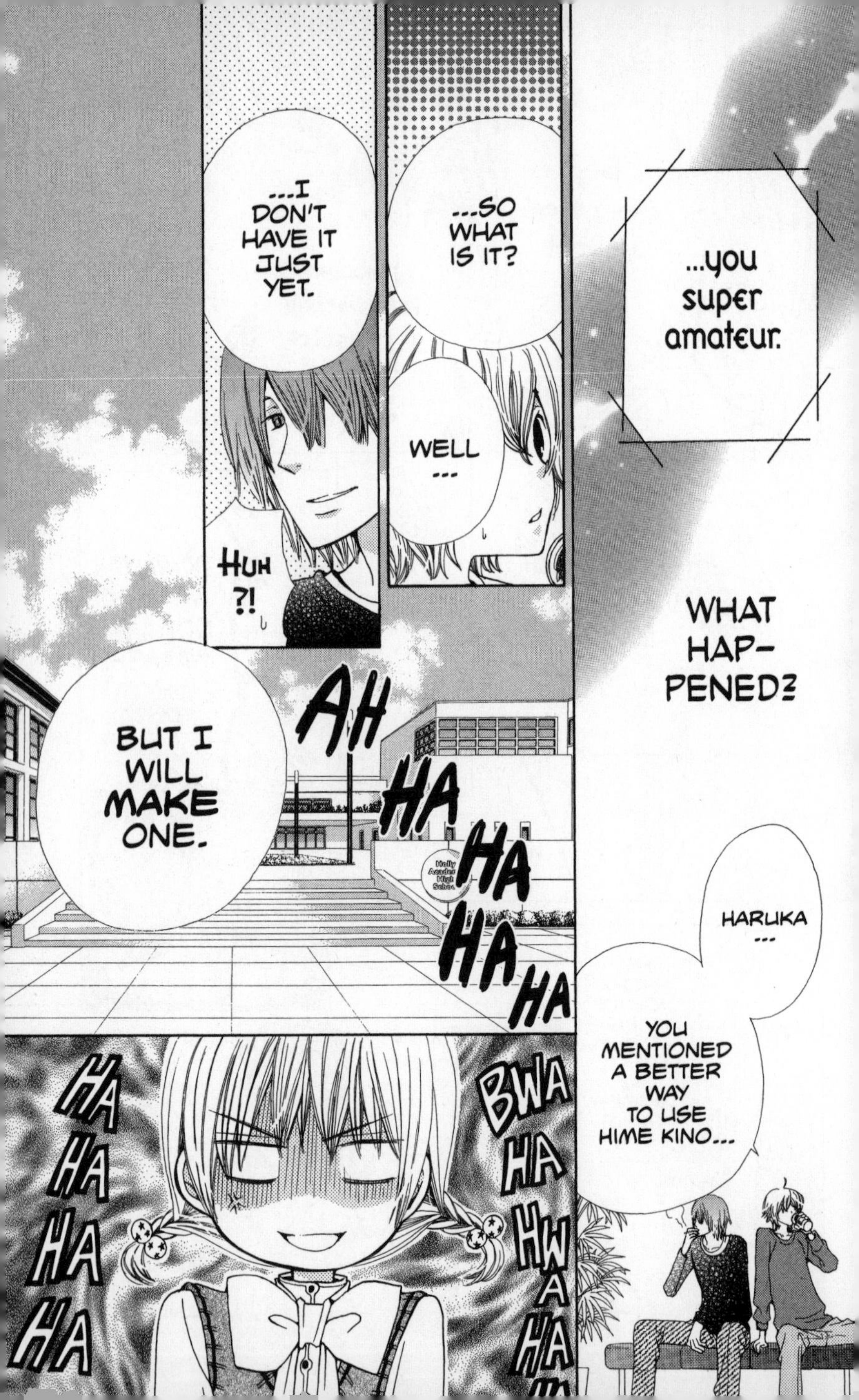
...you super amateur.
WHAT HAPPENED?
HARUKA...
YOU MENTIONED A BETTER WAY TO USE HIME KINO...
...SO WHAT IS IT?
WELL...
...I DON'T HAVE IT JUST YET.
HUH ?!
BUT I WILL MAKE ONE.
AH HA HA HA HA
BWA HA HA HWA HA HA
HA HA HA HA HA HA

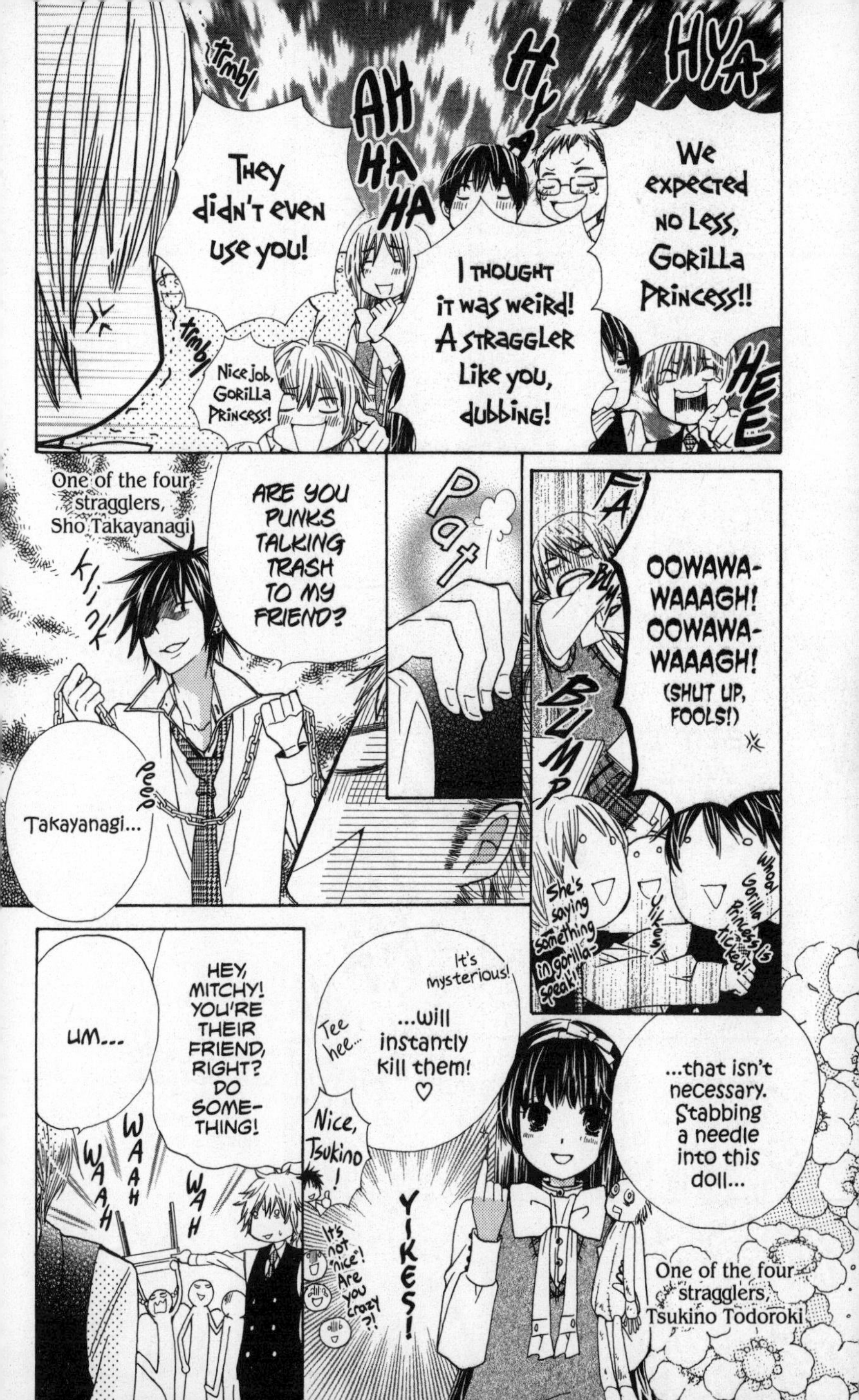
HYA
We expected no less, Gorilla Princess!!
HYA HYA
AH HA HA HA
I thought it was weird! A straggler like you, dubbing!
HEE HEE
They didn't even use you!
trmbl
Nice job, Gorilla Princess!
trmbl
FA
BUMP BUMP BUMP
OOWAWA-WAAAGH! OOWAWA-WAAAGH! (SHUT UP, FOOLS!)
Whoa! Gorilla Princess is ticked!
Yikes!
She's saying something in gorilla-speak!
Pat
One of the four stragglers, Sho Takayanagi
ARE YOU PUNKS TALKING TRASH TO MY FRIEND?
klink
Peep
Takayanagi...
...that isn't necessary. Stabbing a needle into this doll...
...will instantly kill them! ♡
It's mysterious!
Tee hee...
Nice, Tsukino!
YIKES!
It's not "nice"! Are you crazy?!
One of the four stragglers, Tsukino Todoroki
HEY, MITCHY! YOU'RE THEIR FRIEND, RIGHT? DO SOMETHING!
um...
WAAH WAAH WAAH WAAH

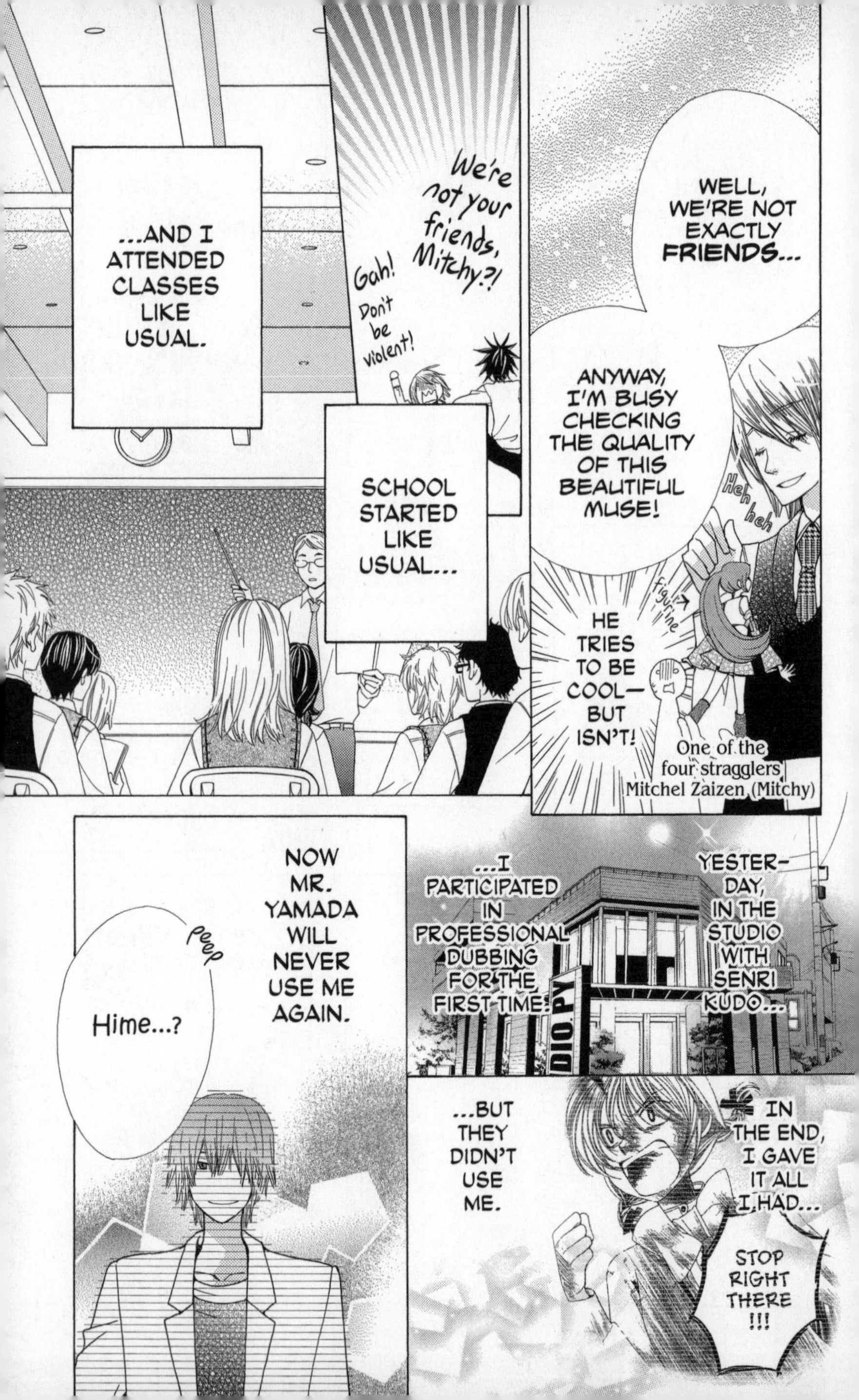

SCHOOL STARTED LIKE USUAL...
...AND I ATTENDED CLASSES LIKE USUAL.
WELL, WE'RE NOT EXACTLY FRIENDS...
ANYWAY, I'M BUSY CHECKING THE QUALITY OF THIS BEAUTIFUL MUSE!
Heh heh
figurine→
HE TRIES TO BE COOL—BUT ISN'T!
One of the four stragglers Mitchel Zaizen (Mitchy)
We're not your friends, Mitchy?!
Gah! Don't be violent!
YESTERDAY, IN THE STUDIO WITH SENRI KUDO...
...I PARTICIPATED IN PROFESSIONAL DUBBING FOR THE FIRST TIME.
DIO PY
IN THE END, I GAVE IT ALL I HAD...
...BUT THEY DIDN'T USE ME.
STOP RIGHT THERE!!!
NOW MR. YAMADA WILL NEVER USE ME AGAIN.
Peep
Hime...?

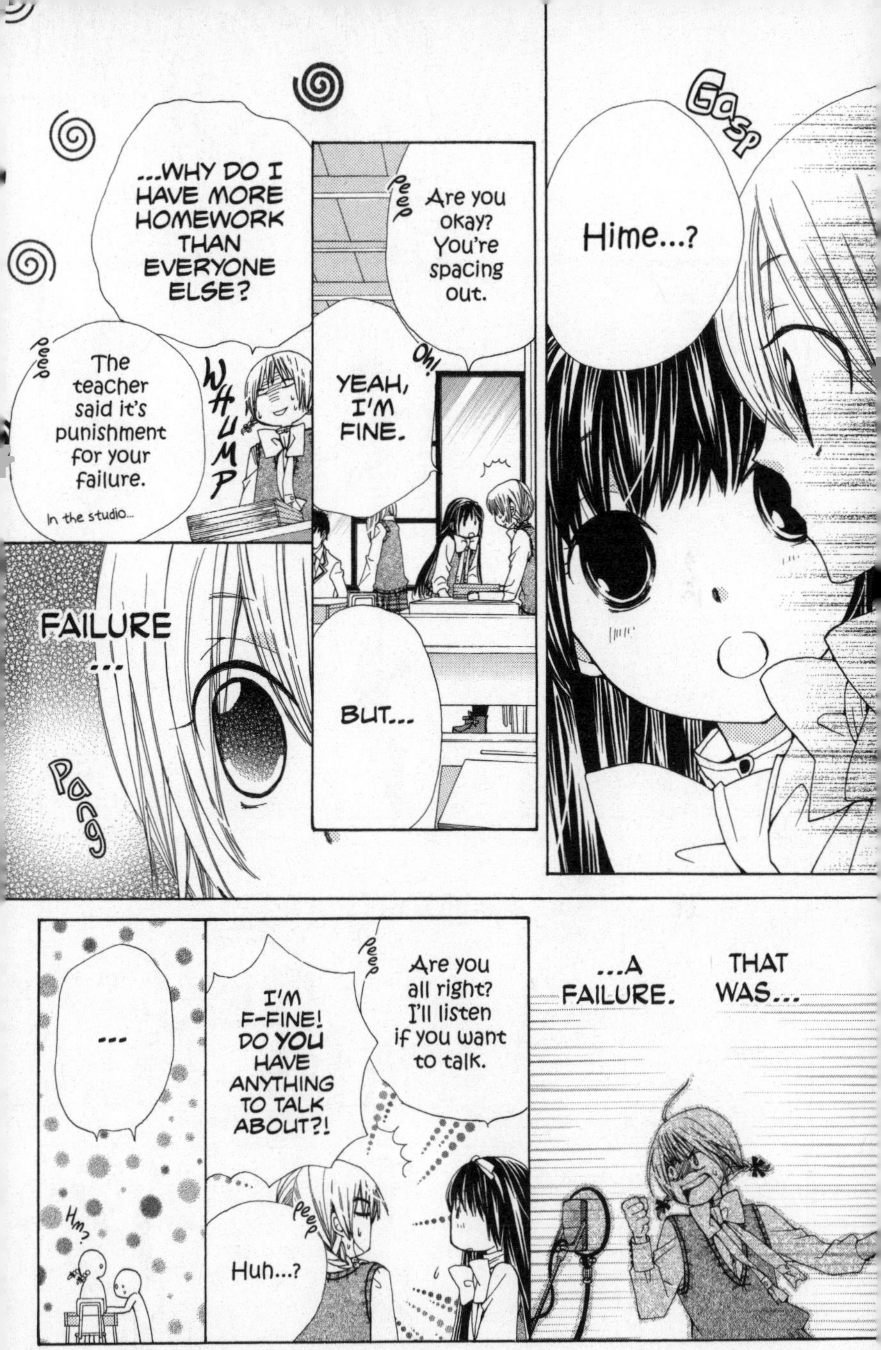
Gasp
Hime...?
Peep
Are you okay? You're spacing out.
Oh!
YEAH, I'M FINE.
BUT...
...WHY DO I HAVE MORE HOMEWORK THAN EVERYONE ELSE?
Peep
The teacher said it's punishment for your failure.
WHUMP
In the studio...
FAILURE...
Pang
THAT WAS...
...A FAILURE.
Peep
Are you all right? I'll listen if you want to talk.
I'M F-FINE! DO YOU HAVE ANYTHING TO TALK ABOUT?!
Peep
Huh...?
...
Hm?

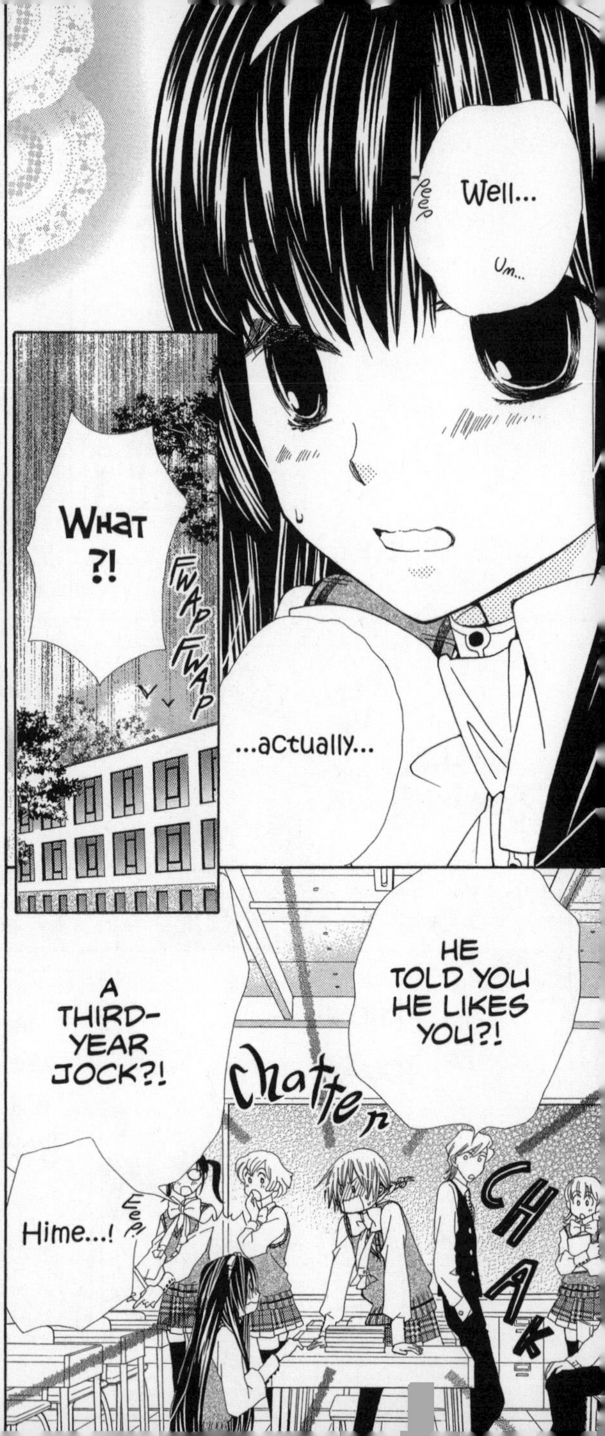
peep
Well...
Um...
...actually...
WHAT?!
FWAP FWAP
HE TOLD YOU HE LIKES YOU?!
Chatter
CHAK
A THIRD-YEAR JOCK?!
Eep!
Hime...!

• Toodachi Collection • ⑤

My assistants and I play the video game *Toodachi Collection* on the DS together. We make all kinds of characters and make them friends and lovers and so on. A character that looks just like me goes around confessing her feelings to everyone but always gets turned down!

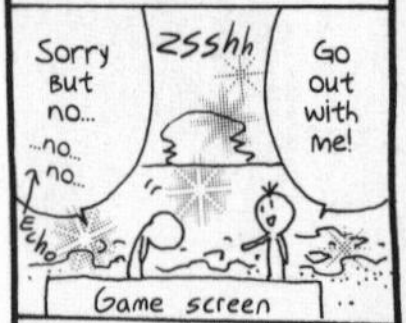
Go out with me!
zsshh
Sorry but no...
...no... no...
Echo
Game screen

Every time, I'm hurt a little more.

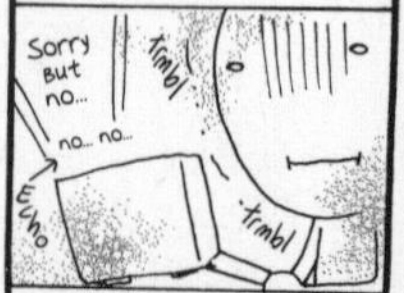
Sorry but no...
no... no...
Echo
trmbl
trmbl

Recently again, she took a liking to a guy with a lovey-dovey girlfriend and said she wants to tell him. (She's sure to fail.)

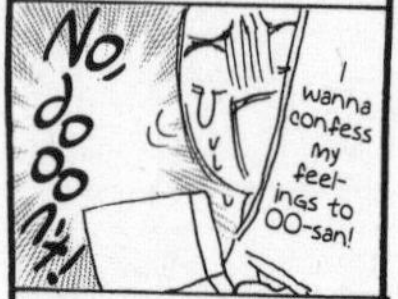
I wanna confess my feelings to OO-san!
No, dooon't!

She got turned down.

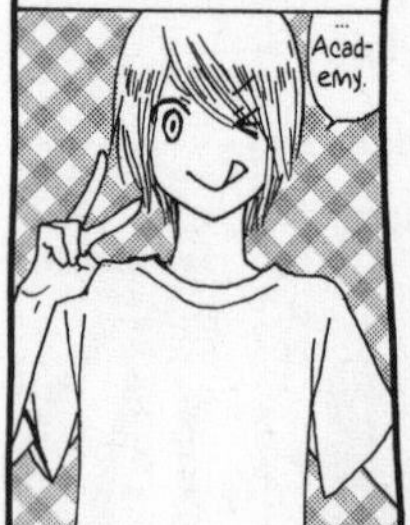
...Academy.

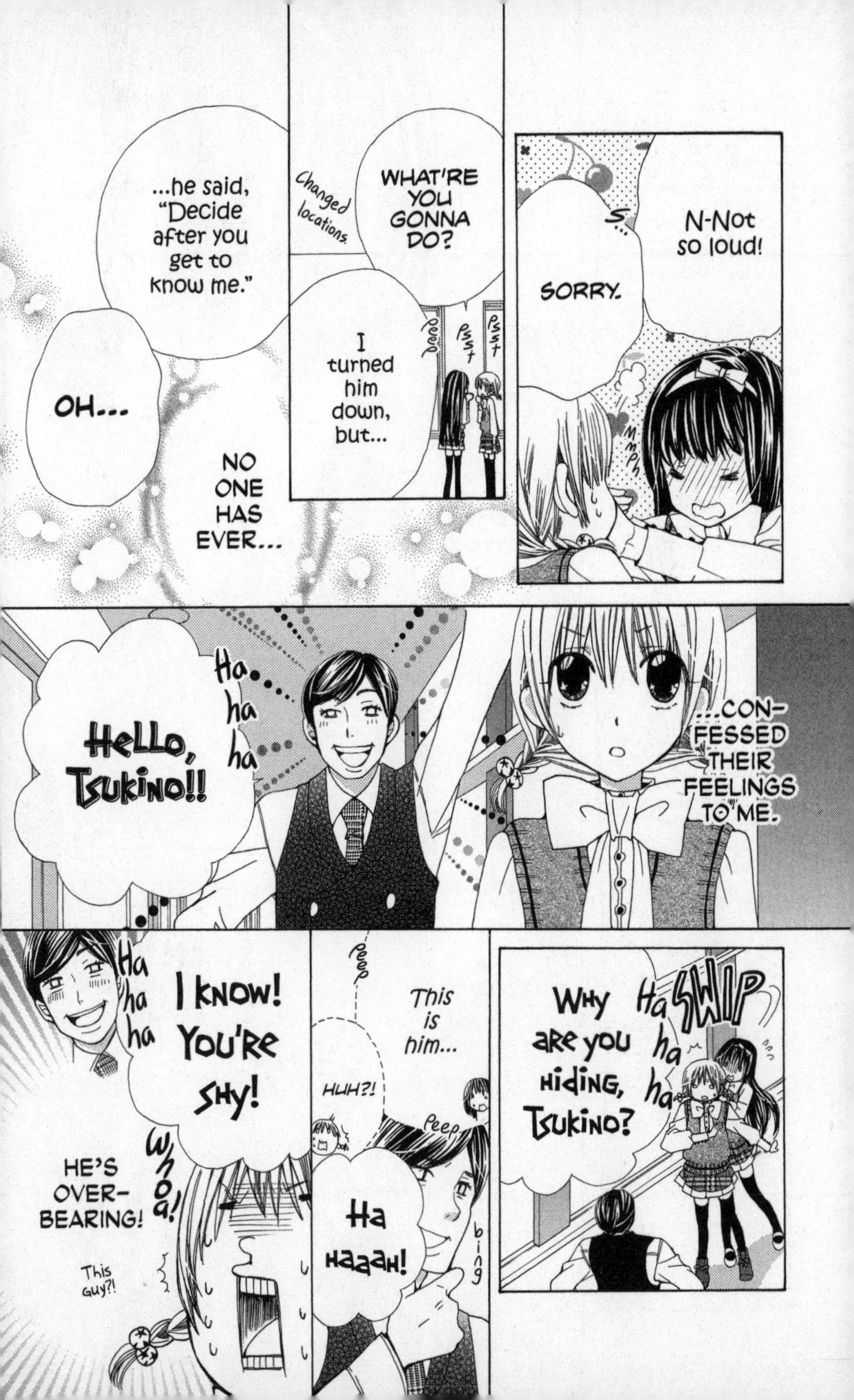
N-Not so loud!
S...
SORRY.
Mmph
WHAT'RE YOU GONNA DO?
Changed locations
I turned him down, but...
Psst
Psst
Peep
...he said, "Decide after you get to know me."
OH...
NO ONE HAS EVER...
...CON-FESSED THEIR FEELINGS TO ME.
Ha ha ha
HELLO, TSUKINO!!
SWIP
Ha ha ha
Why are you hiding, Tsukino?
Peep
This is him...
HUH?!
Peep
Ha haaah!
bing
Ha ha ha
I KNOW! YOU'RE SHY!
Whoa!
HE'S OVER-BEARING!
This guy?!

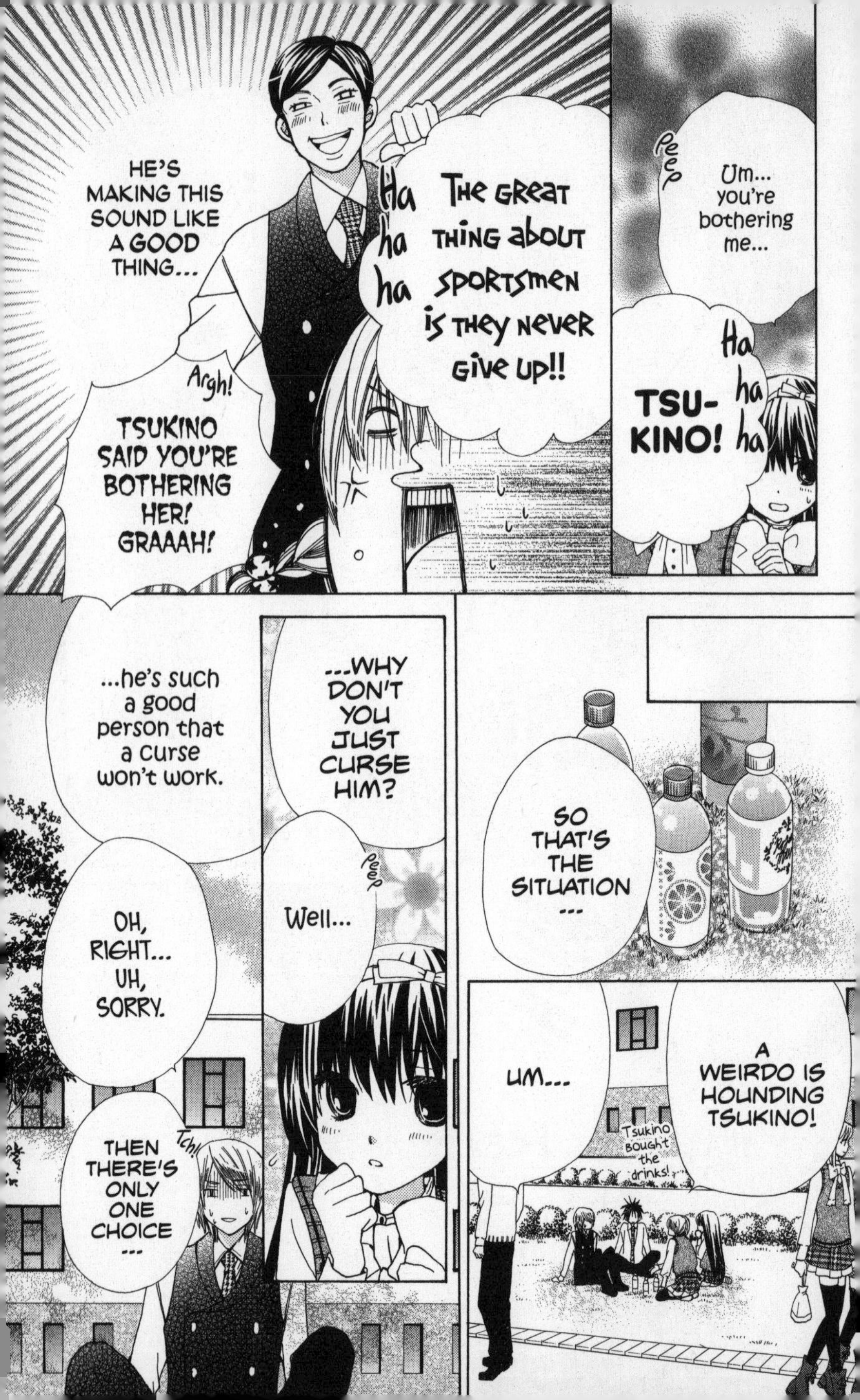
Peep
Um... you're bothering me...
Ha ha ha
TSU-KINO!
Ha ha ha
The great thing about sportsmen is they never give up!!
HE'S MAKING THIS SOUND LIKE A GOOD THING...
Argh!
TSUKINO SAID YOU'RE BOTHERING HER! GRAAAH!
SO THAT'S THE SITUATION ...
A WEIRDO IS HOUNDING TSUKINO!
Tsukino bought the drinks!
UM...
...WHY DON'T YOU JUST CURSE HIM?
Peep
Well...
...he's such a good person that a curse won't work.
OH, RIGHT... UH, SORRY.
Tch!
THEN THERE'S ONLY ONE CHOICE ...

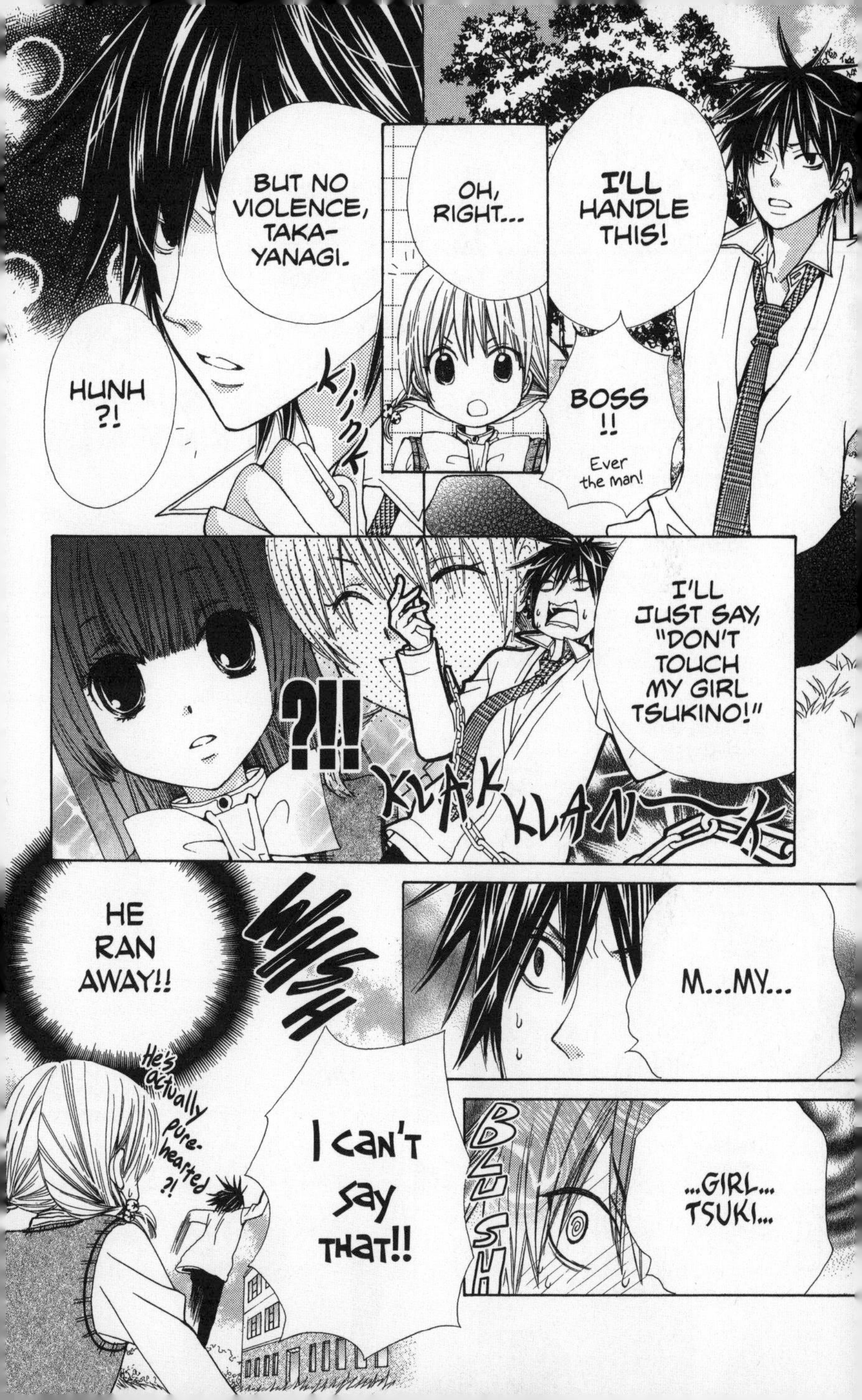
I'LL HANDLE THIS!
BOSS!!
Ever the man!
OH, RIGHT...
BUT NO VIOLENCE, TAKA-YANAGI.
HUNH?!
KLINK
I'LL JUST SAY, "DON'T TOUCH MY GIRL TSUKINO!"
?!!
KLAK KLAK KLAN—K
M...MY...
...GIRL... TSUKI...
BLUSH
I can't say THAT!!
WHSH
HE RAN AWAY!!
He's actually pure-hearted?!

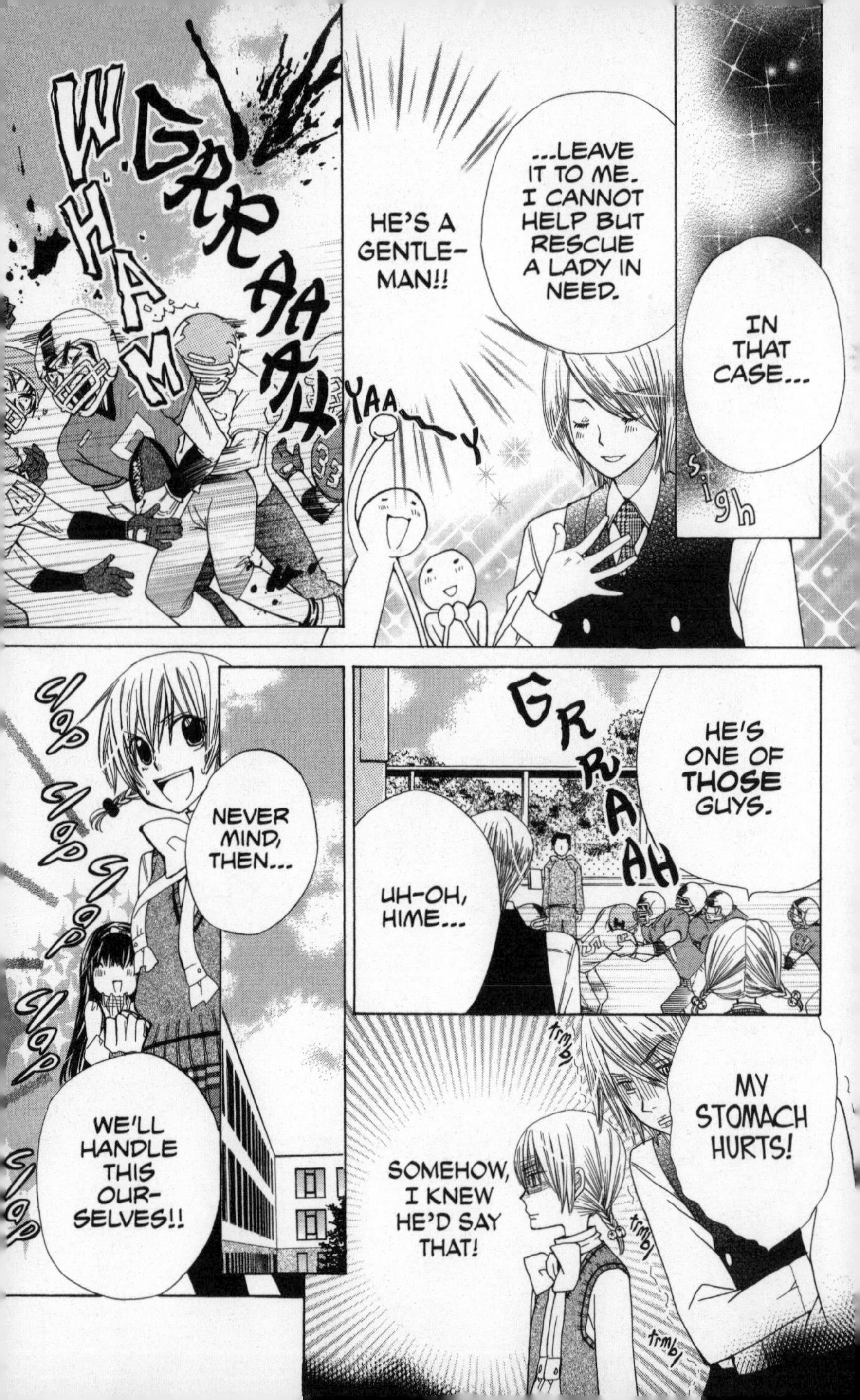
IN THAT CASE...
sigh
...LEAVE IT TO ME. I CANNOT HELP BUT RESCUE A LADY IN NEED.
HE'S A GENTLEMAN!!
YAA~~Y
WHAM
GRRAAAAH
HE'S ONE OF THOSE GUYS.
GRRAAH
UH-OH, HIME...
MY STOMACH HURTS!
trmbl
trmbl
trmbl
SOMEHOW, I KNEW HE'D SAY THAT!
NEVER MIND, THEN...
WE'LL HANDLE THIS OURSELVES!!
clap clap clap clap clap clap
clap

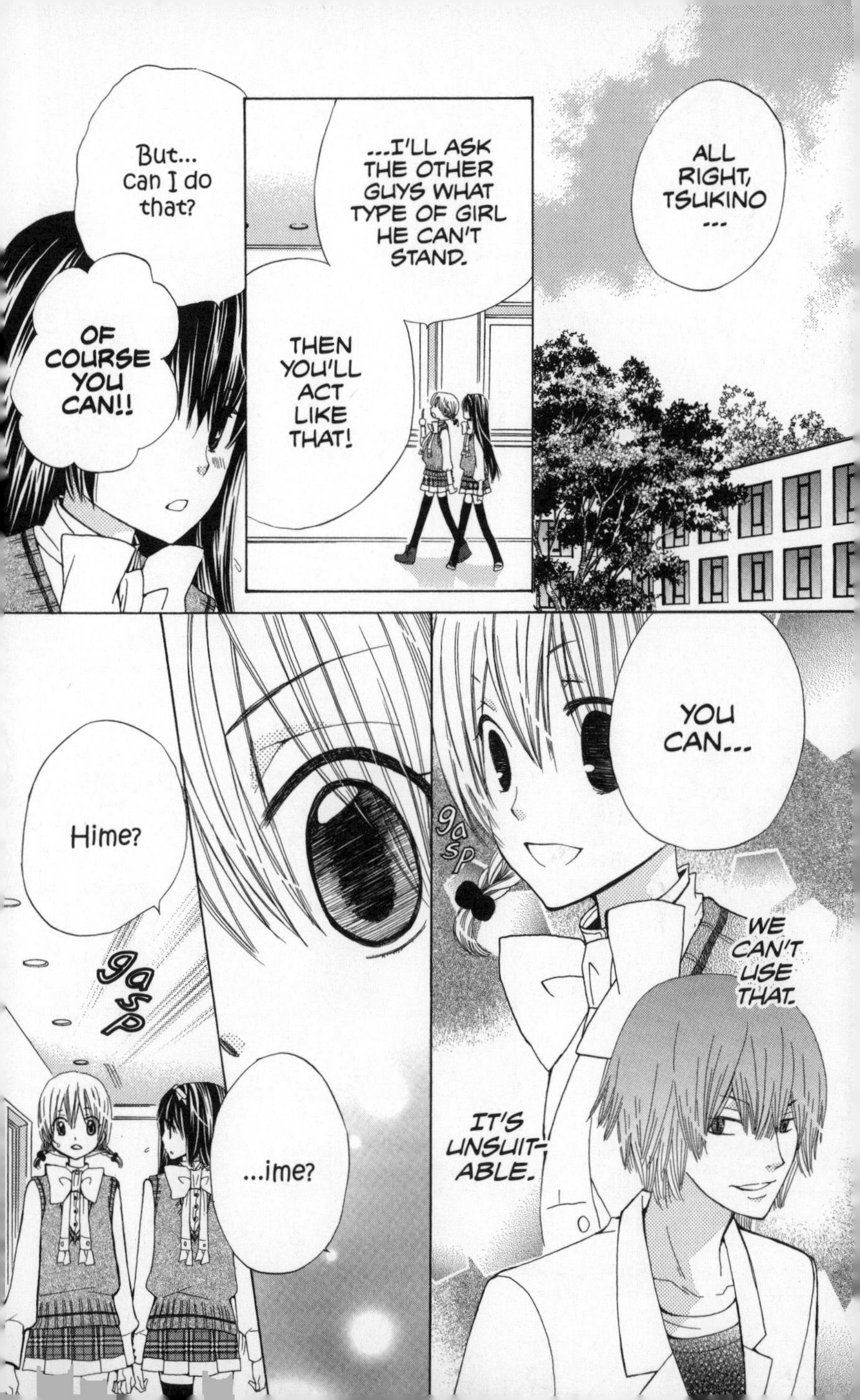
ALL RIGHT, TSUKINO ...
...I'LL ASK THE OTHER GUYS WHAT TYPE OF GIRL HE CAN'T STAND.
THEN YOU'LL ACT LIKE THAT!
But... can I do that?
OF COURSE YOU CAN!!
YOU CAN...
gasp
WE CAN'T USE THAT.
IT'S UNSUIT-ABLE.
Hime?
gasp
...ime?

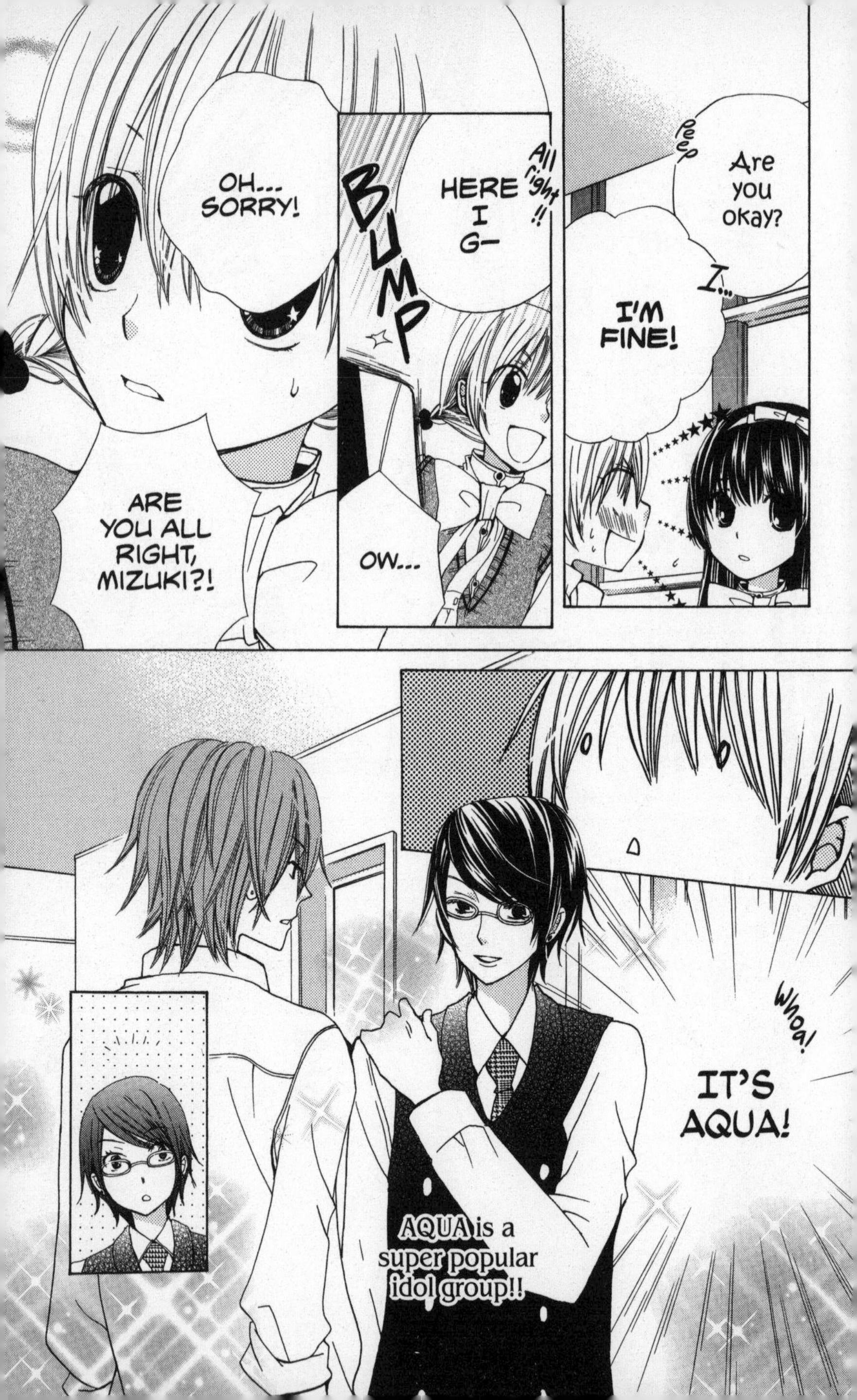
Peep
Are you okay?
I...
I'M FINE!
All right!!
HERE I G—
BUMP
OW...
OH... SORRY!
ARE YOU ALL RIGHT, MIZUKI?!
Whoa!
IT'S AQUA!
AQUA is a super popular idol group!!

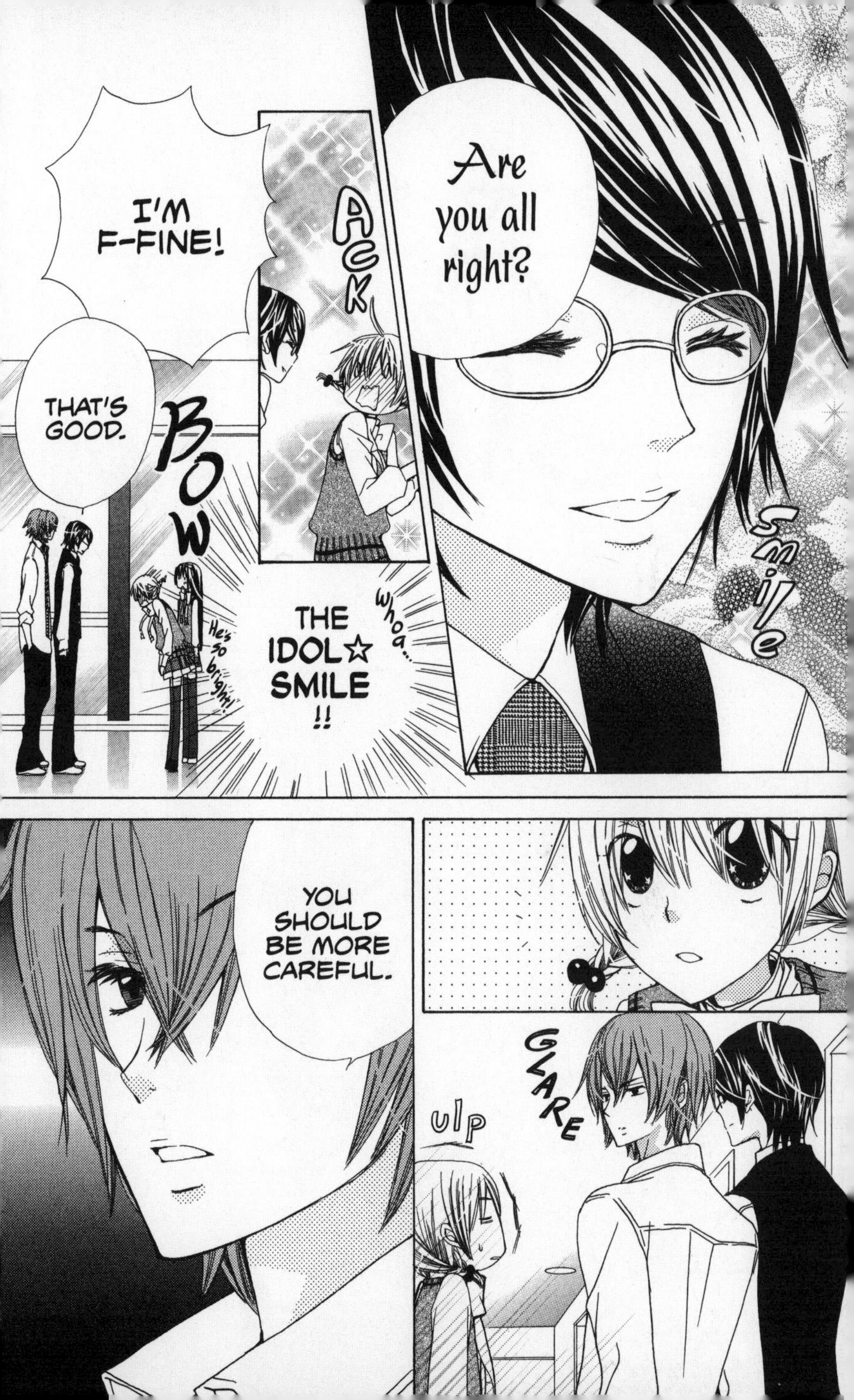
Are you all right?
Smile
ACK
I'M F-FINE!
THE IDOL☆ SMILE !!
whoa...
THAT'S GOOD.
BOW
He's so bright!
GLARE
ulp
YOU SHOULD BE MORE CAREFUL.

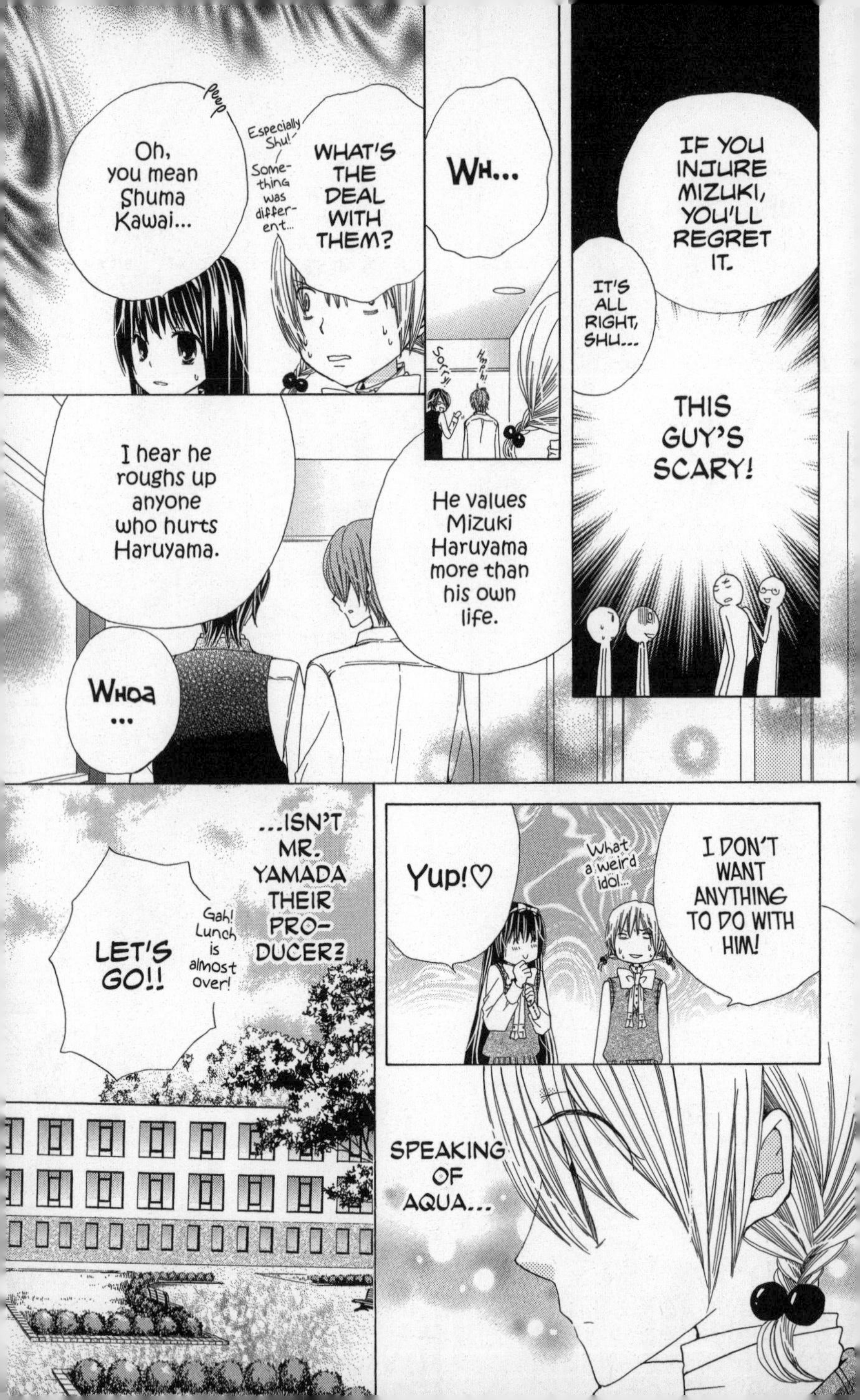

IF YOU INJURE MIZUKI, YOU'LL REGRET IT.
IT'S ALL RIGHT, SHU...
THIS GUY'S SCARY!
WH...
Sorry!
Hmph!
WHAT'S THE DEAL WITH THEM?
Especially Shu! Something was different...
peep
Oh, you mean Shuma Kawai...
He values Mizuki Haruyama more than his own life.
I hear he roughs up anyone who hurts Haruyama.
Whoa...
I DON'T WANT ANYTHING TO DO WITH HIM!
What a weird idol...
Yup!♡
SPEAKING OF AQUA...
...ISN'T MR. YAMADA THEIR PRODUCER?
LET'S GO!!
Gah! Lunch is almost over!

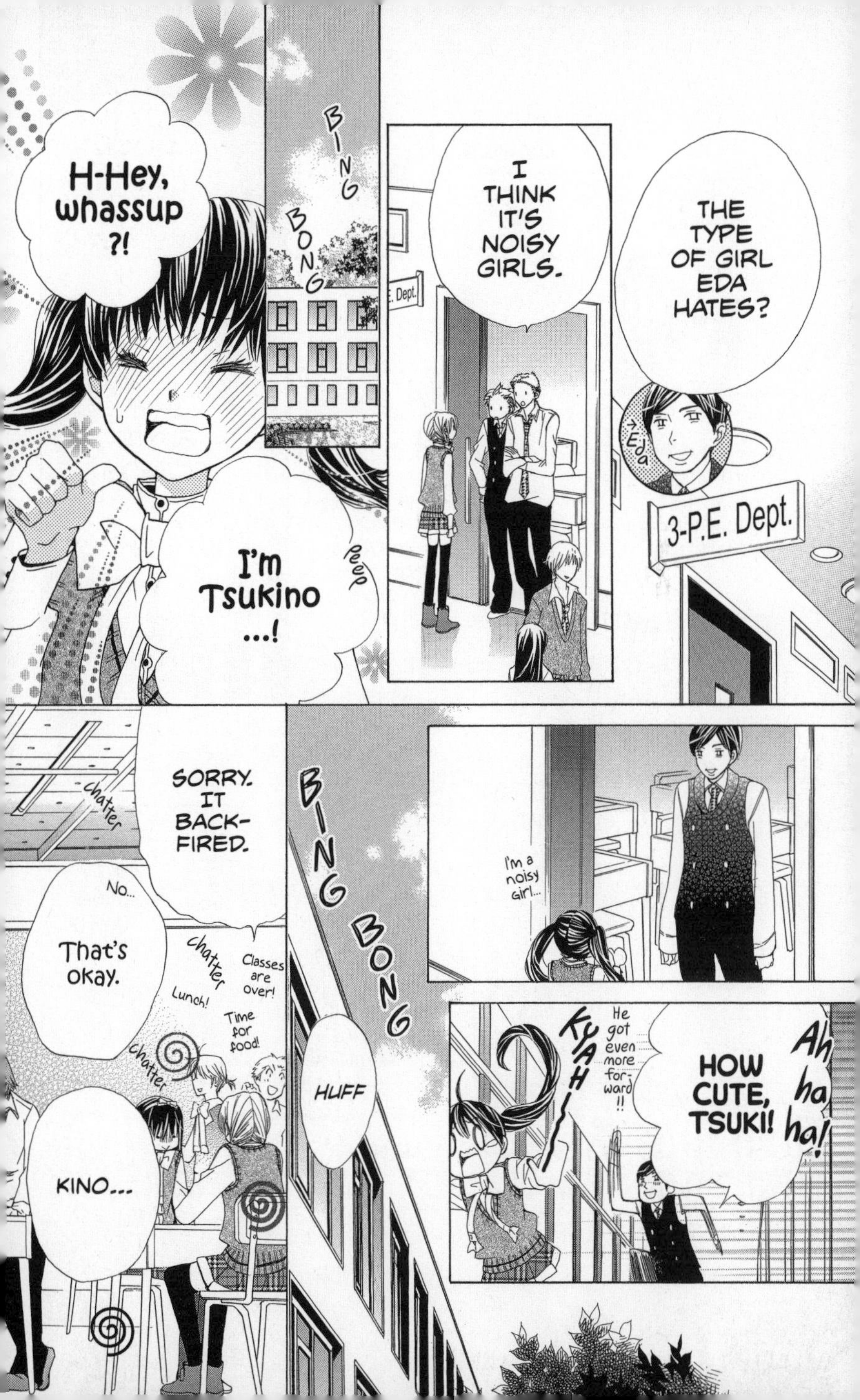
THE TYPE OF GIRL EDA HATES?
→Eda
3-P.E. Dept.
I THINK IT'S NOISY GIRLS.
E. Dept.
BING BONG
H-Hey, whassup?!
I'm Tsukino...!
peep
I'm a noisy girl...
Ah ha ha!
HOW CUTE, TSUKI!
He got even more for-ward!!
KYAH-!
BING BONG
HUFF
SORRY. IT BACKFIRED.
chatter
No...
That's okay.
chatter
Classes are over!
Lunch!
Time for food!
chatter
KINO...

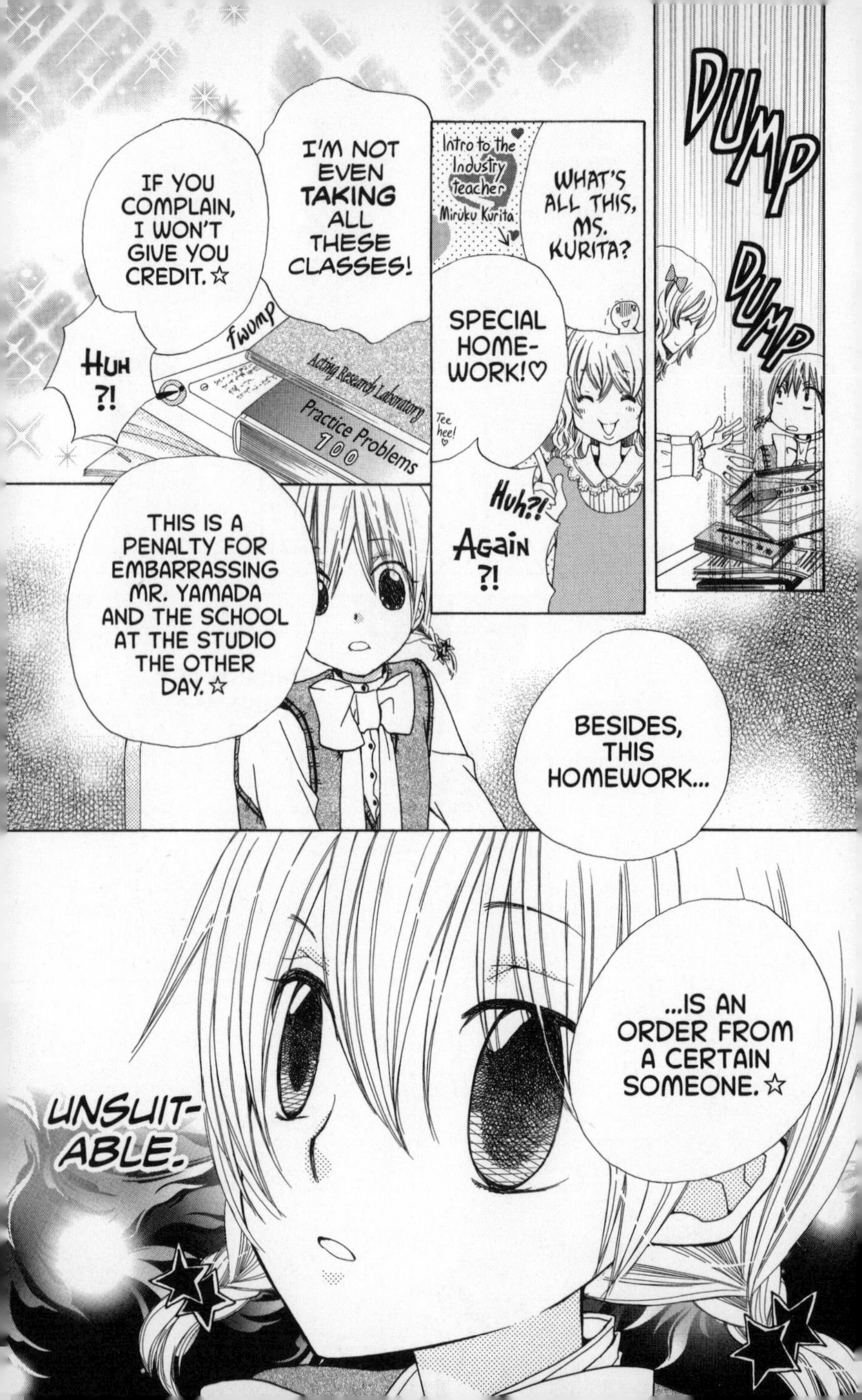
DUMP
DUMP
DUMP
WHAT'S ALL THIS, MS. KURITA?
Intro to the Industry teacher Miruku Kurita
SPECIAL HOMEWORK!♡
Tee hee!
Huh?!
Again?!
I'M NOT EVEN TAKING ALL THESE CLASSES!
IF YOU COMPLAIN, I WON'T GIVE YOU CREDIT.☆
fwump
Acting Research Laboratory
Practice Problems 100
HUH?!
THIS IS A PENALTY FOR EMBARRASSING MR. YAMADA AND THE SCHOOL AT THE STUDIO THE OTHER DAY.☆
BESIDES, THIS HOMEWORK...
...IS AN ORDER FROM A CERTAIN SOMEONE.☆
UNSUIT-ABLE.

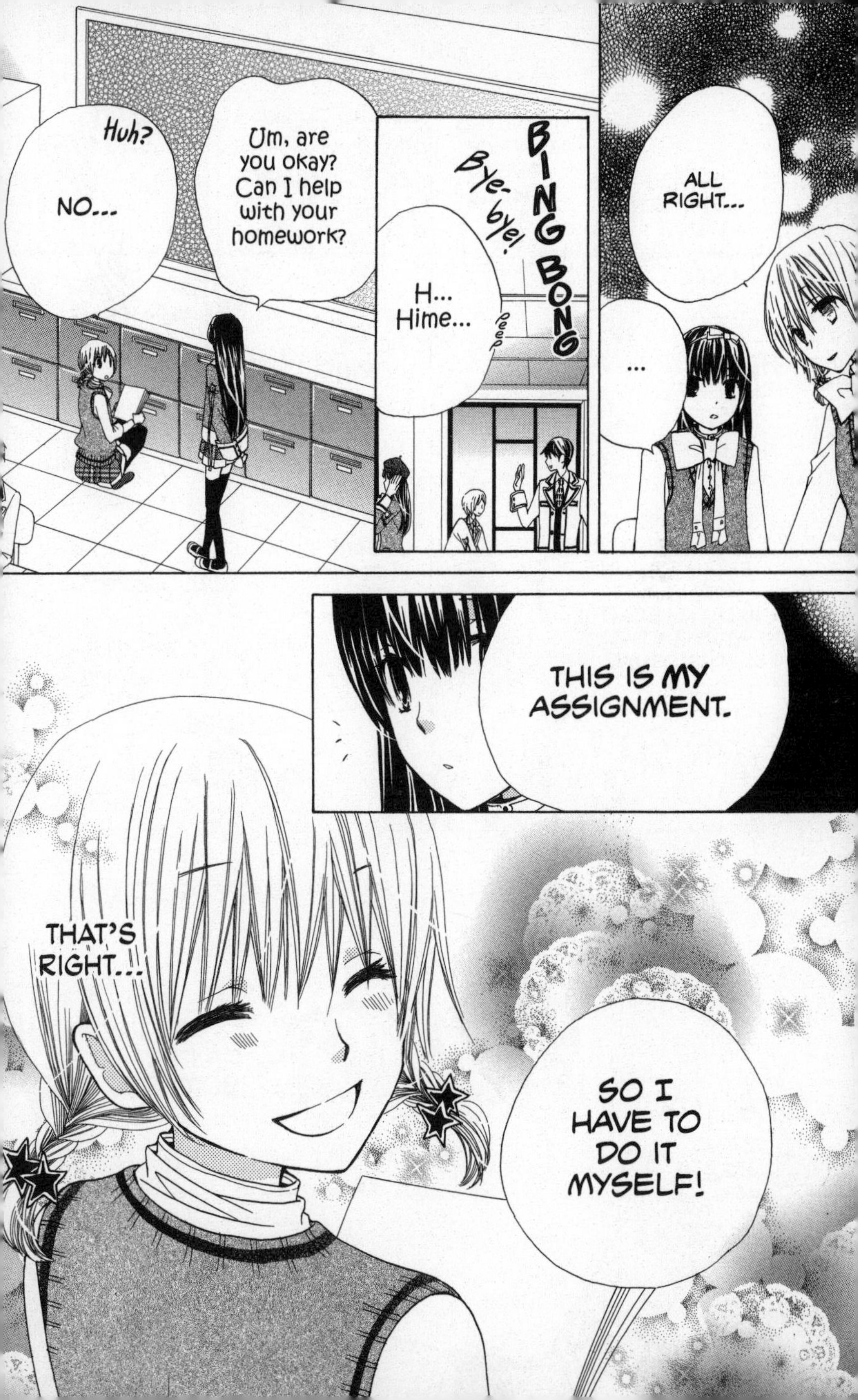
ALL RIGHT...
...
BING BONG
Bye-bye!
H... Hime...
Um, are you okay? Can I help with your homework?
Huh?
NO...
THIS IS MY ASSIGNMENT.
THAT'S RIGHT...
SO I HAVE TO DO IT MYSELF!

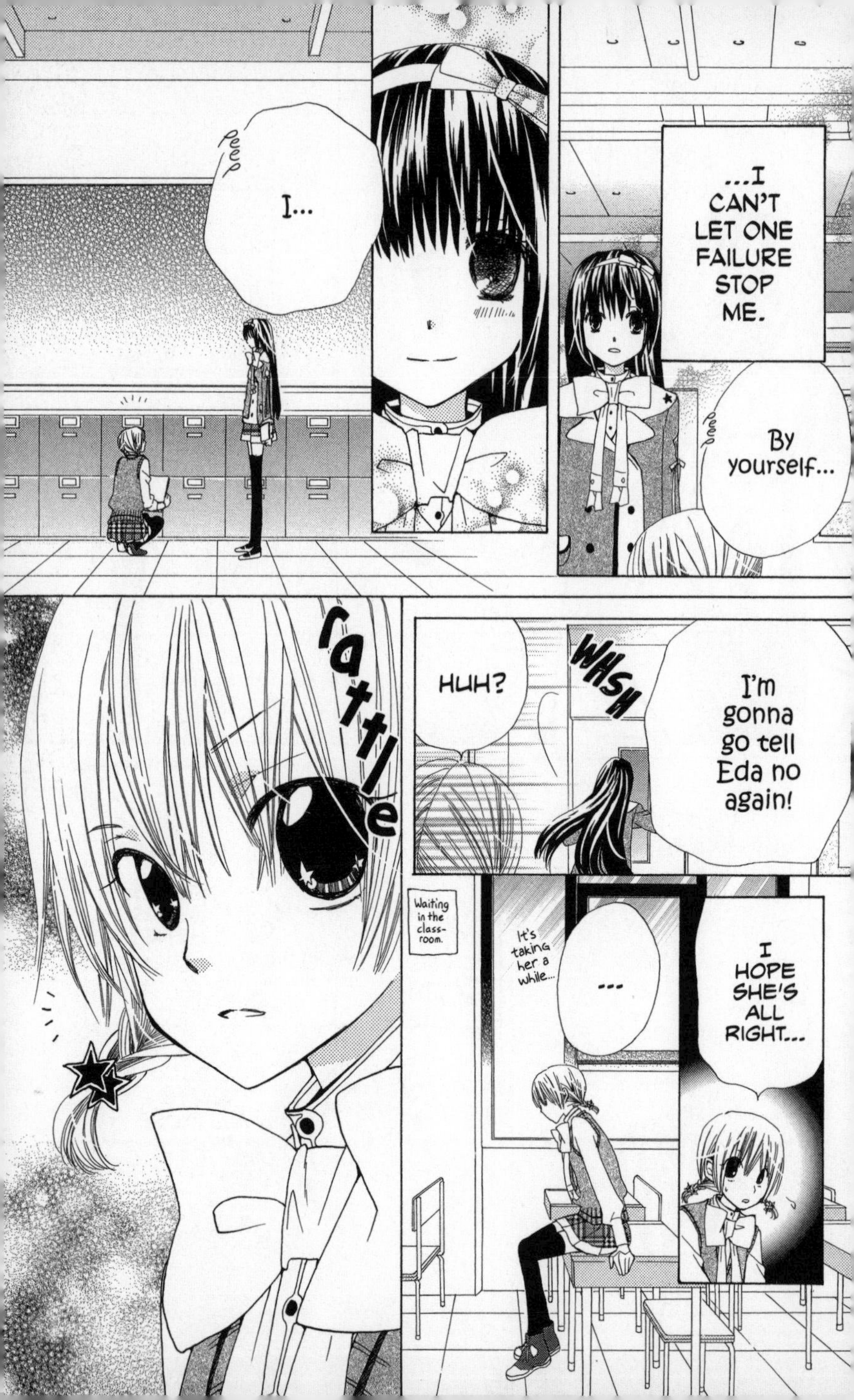
...I CAN'T LET ONE FAILURE STOP ME.
peep
By yourself...
peep
I...
I'm gonna go tell Eda no again!
WHSH
HUH?
I HOPE SHE'S ALL RIGHT...
It's taking her a while...
...
Waiting in the class-room.
rattle

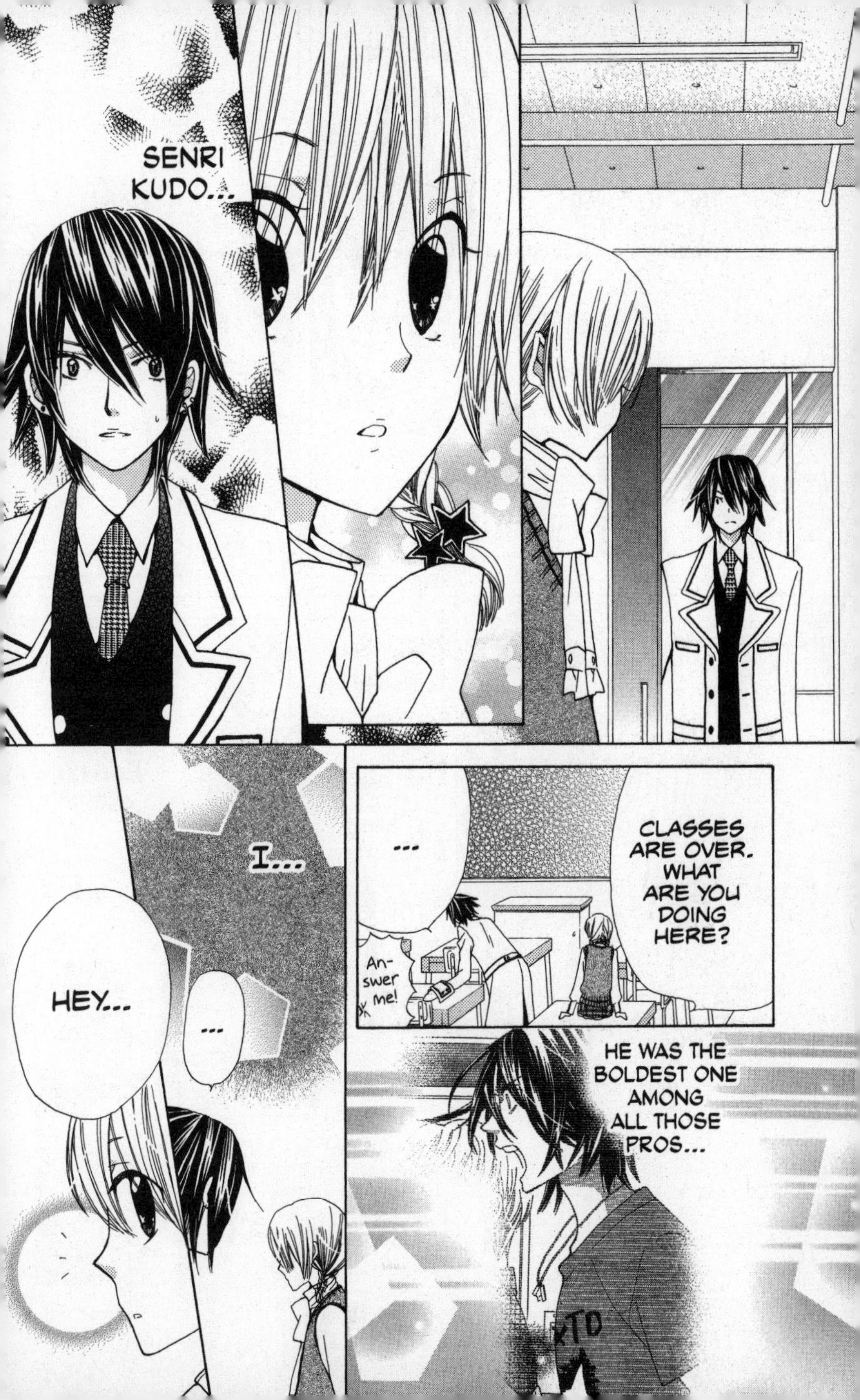
SENRI KUDO...
CLASSES ARE OVER. WHAT ARE YOU DOING HERE?
...
Answer me!
HE WAS THE BOLDEST ONE AMONG ALL THOSE PROS...
I...
...
HEY...

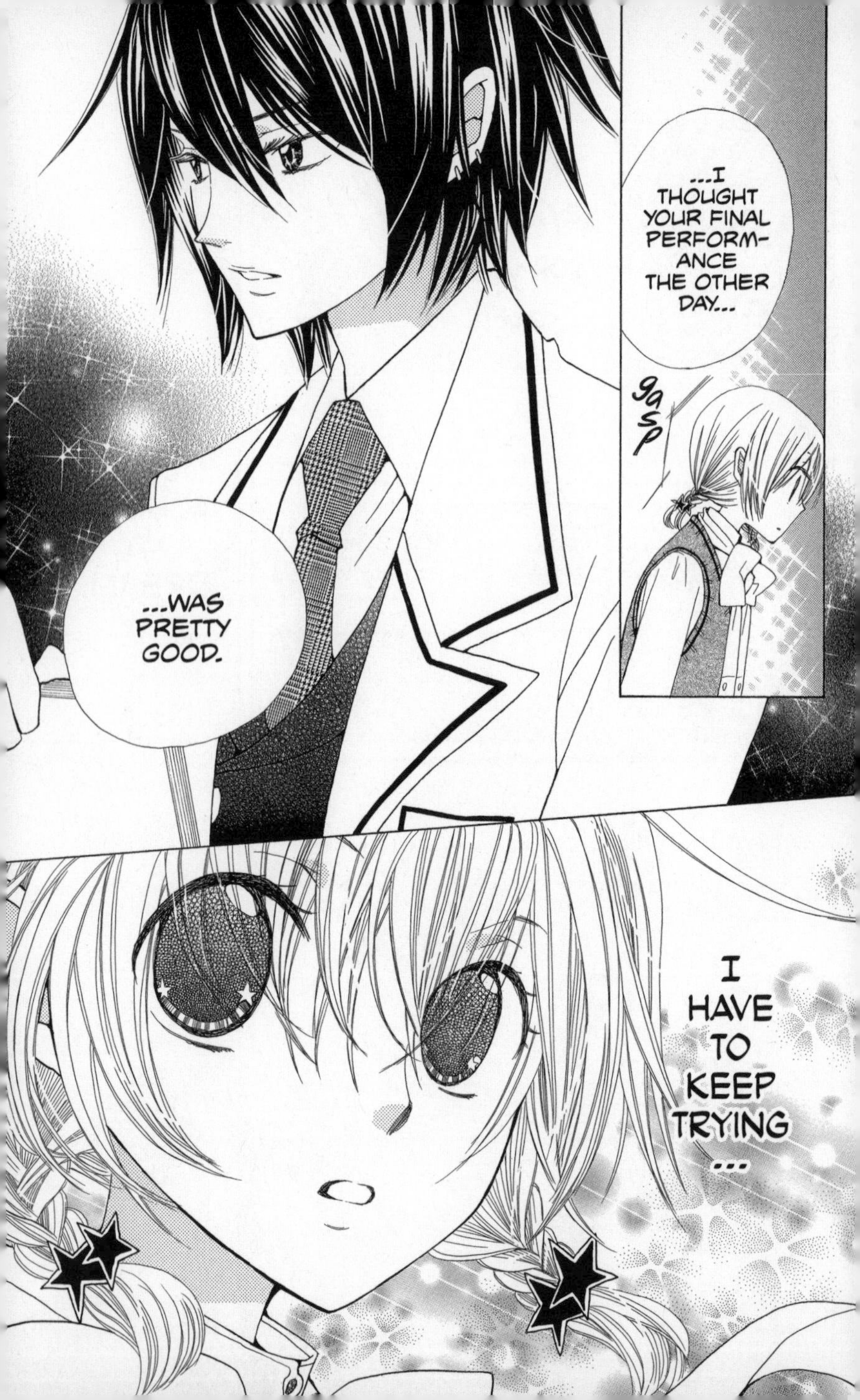
...I THOUGHT YOUR FINAL PERFORM-ANCE THE OTHER DAY...
gasp
...WAS PRETTY GOOD.
I HAVE TO KEEP TRYING...

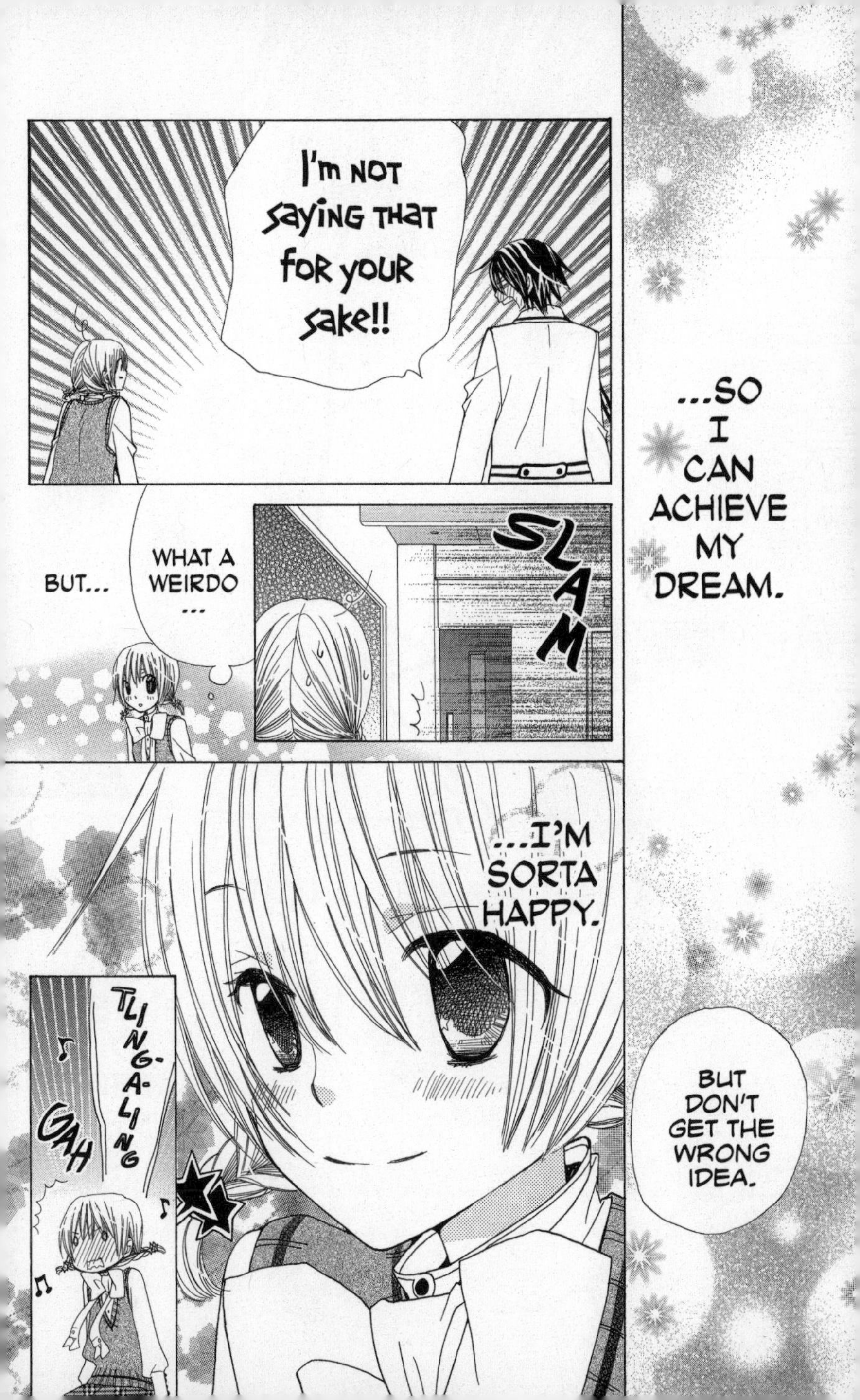
...SO I CAN ACHIEVE MY DREAM.
BUT DON'T GET THE WRONG IDEA.
I'm NOT saying THAT for your sake!!
SLAM
WHAT A WEIRDO...
BUT...
...I'M SORTA HAPPY.
TLING-A-LING
GAH

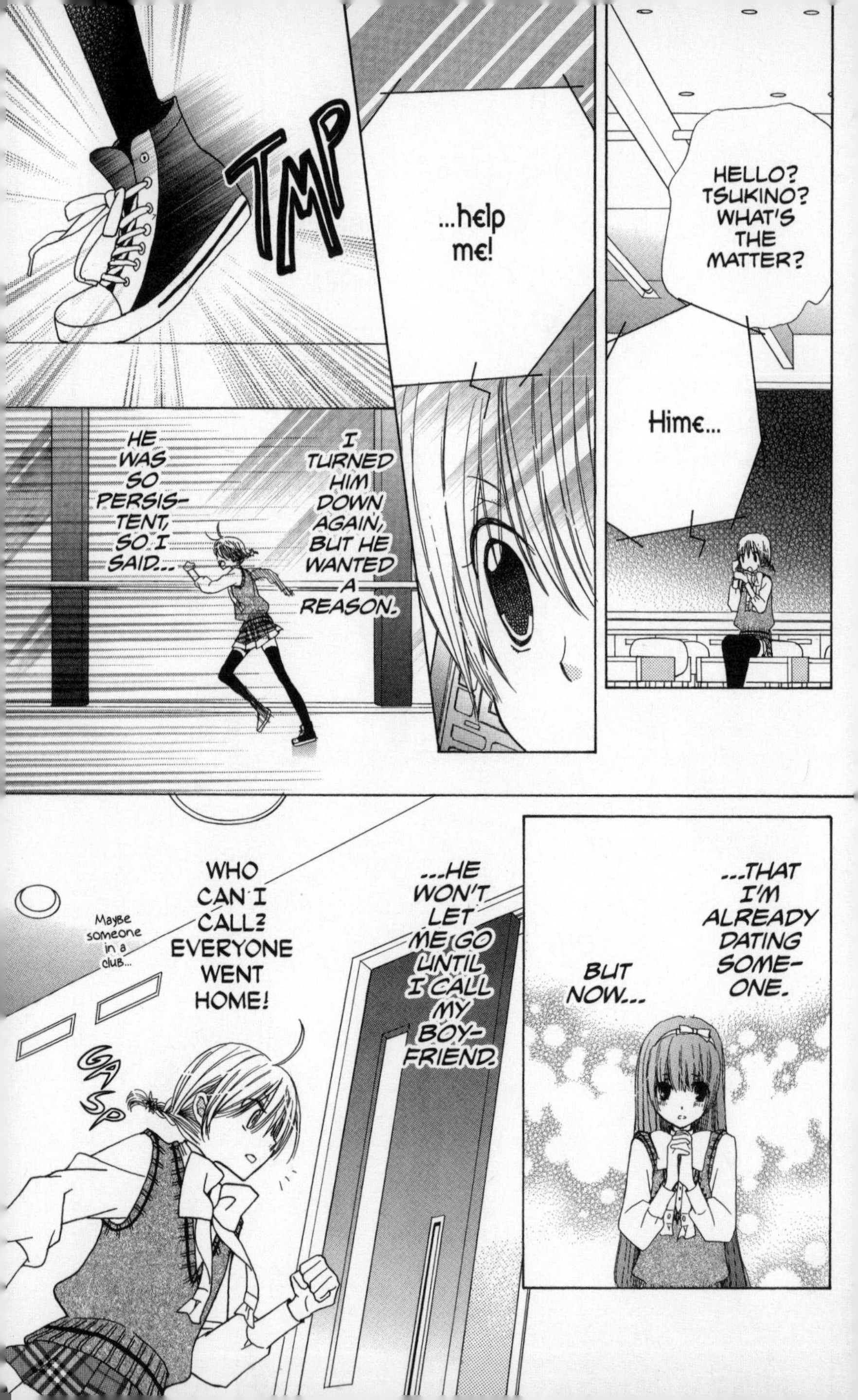
HELLO? TSUKINO? WHAT'S THE MATTER?
Hime...
...help me!
TMP
I TURNED HIM DOWN AGAIN, BUT HE WANTED A REASON.
HE WAS SO PERSIS-TENT, SO I SAID...
...THAT I'M ALREADY DATING SOME-ONE.
BUT NOW...
...HE WON'T LET ME GO UNTIL I CALL MY BOY-FRIEND.
WHO CAN I CALL? EVERYONE WENT HOME!
Maybe someone in a club...
GASP

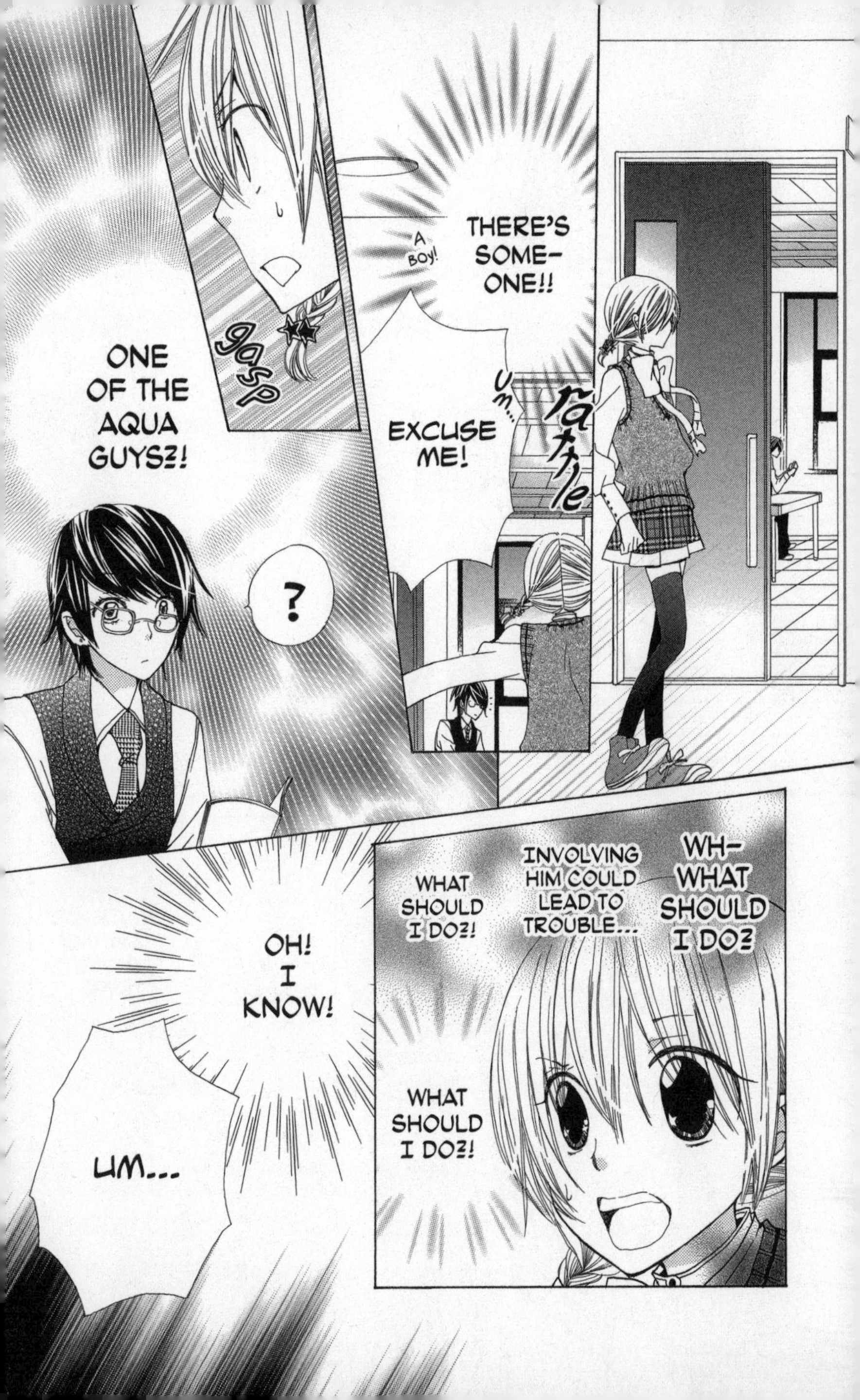
rattle
Um...
EXCUSE ME!
gasp
THERE'S SOME-ONE!!
A BOY!
?
ONE OF THE AQUA GUYS?!
WH-WHAT SHOULD I DO?
INVOLVING HIM COULD LEAD TO TROUBLE...
WHAT SHOULD I DO?!
WHAT SHOULD I DO?!
OH! I KNOW!
UM...

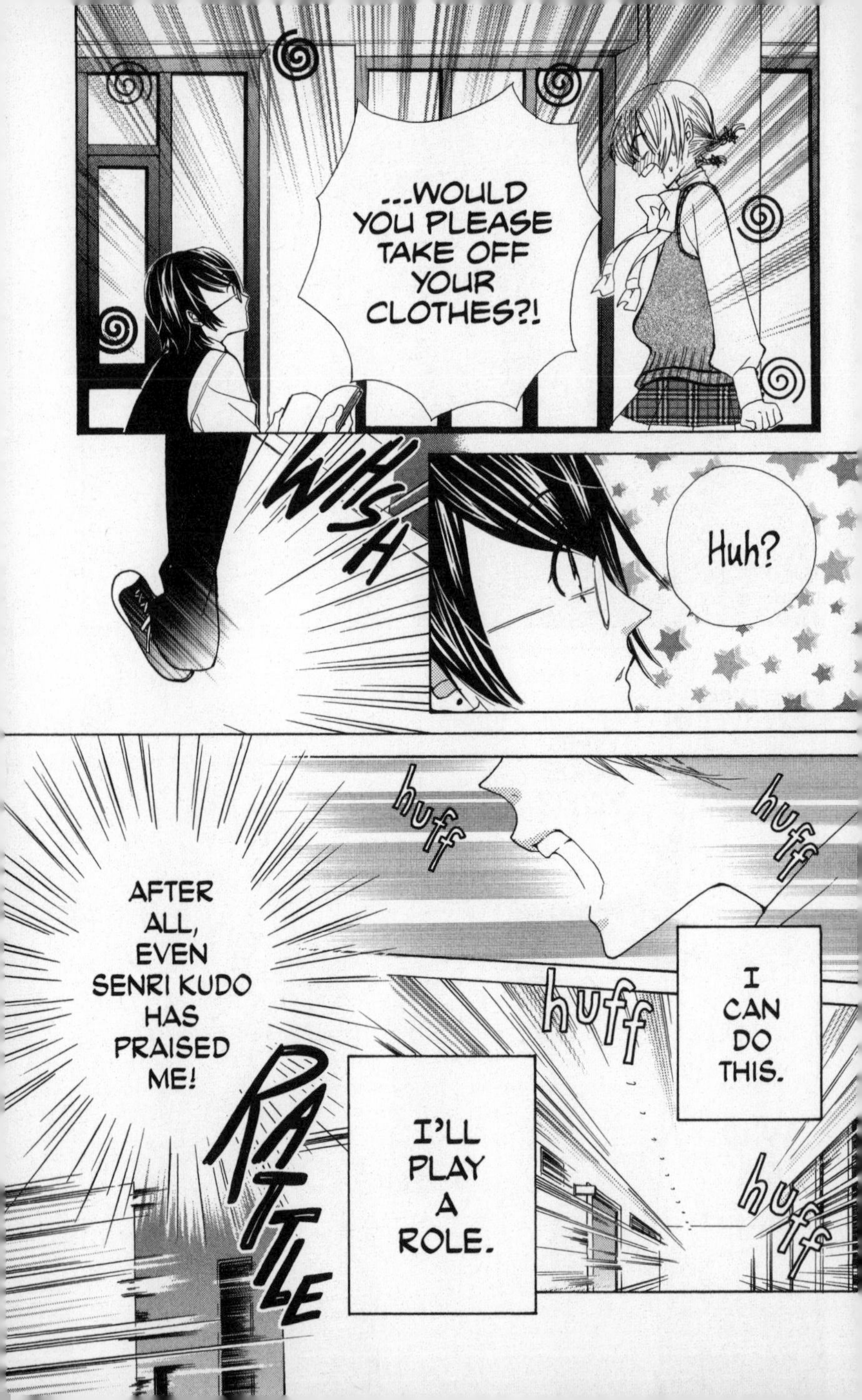
...WOULD YOU PLEASE TAKE OFF YOUR CLOTHES?!
Huh?
WHSH
huff
I CAN DO THIS.
huff
huff
huff
I'LL PLAY A ROLE.
AFTER ALL, EVEN SENRI KUDO HAS PRAISED ME!
RATTLE

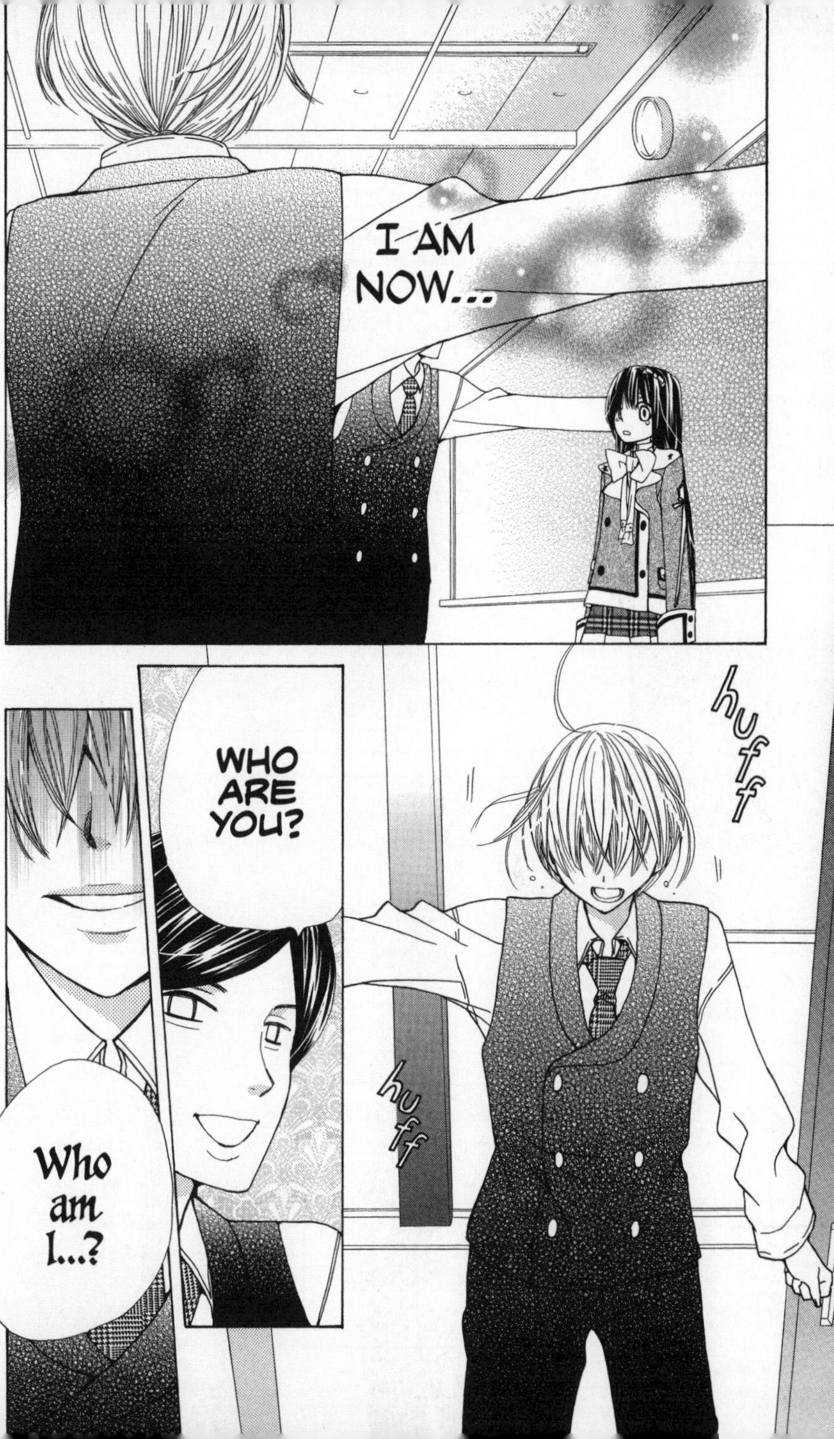
I AM NOW...
huff
huff
WHO ARE YOU?
Who am I...?

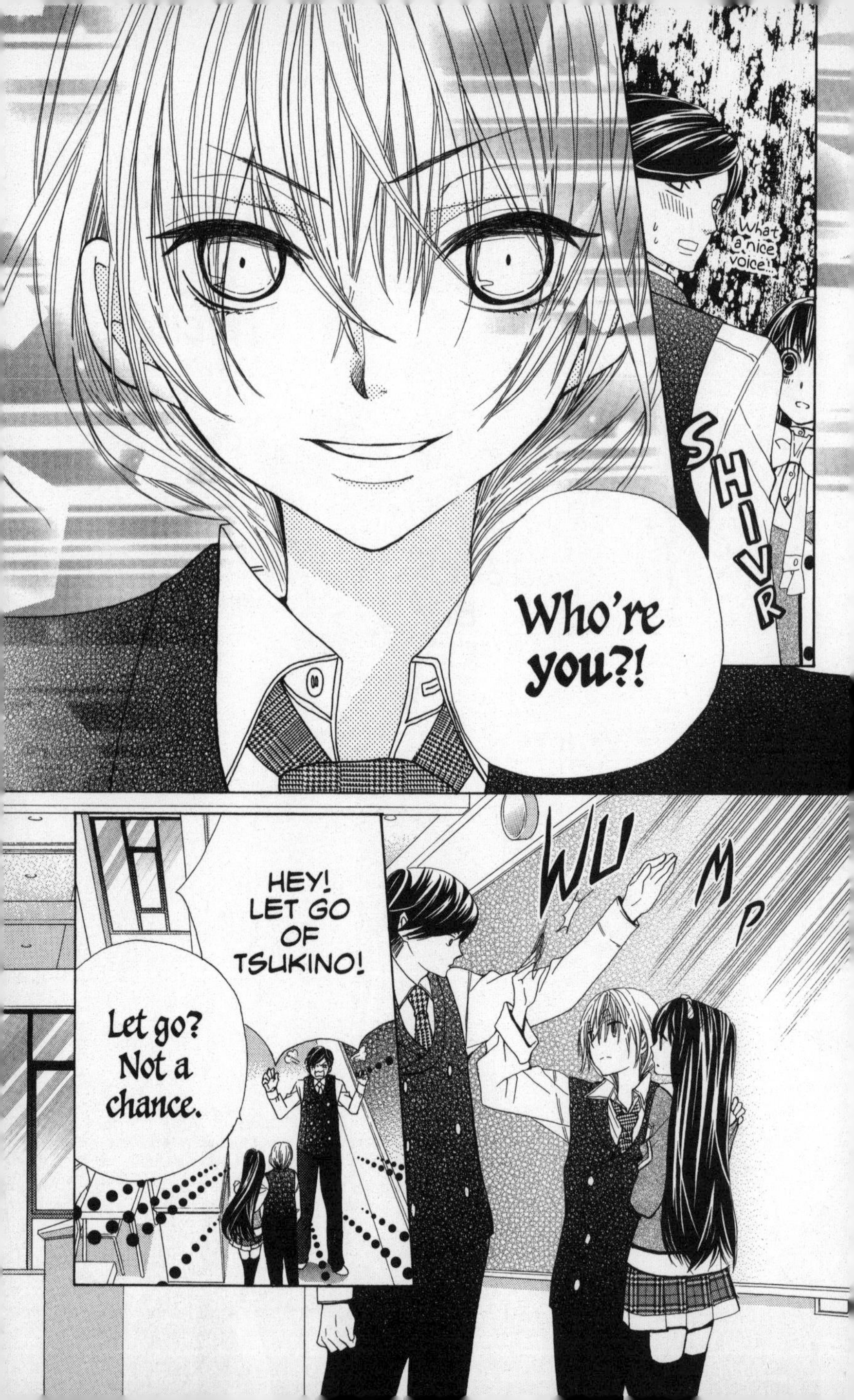
What a nice voice...
SHIVR
Who're you?!
WUMP
HEY! LET GO OF TSUKINO!
Let go? Not a chance.

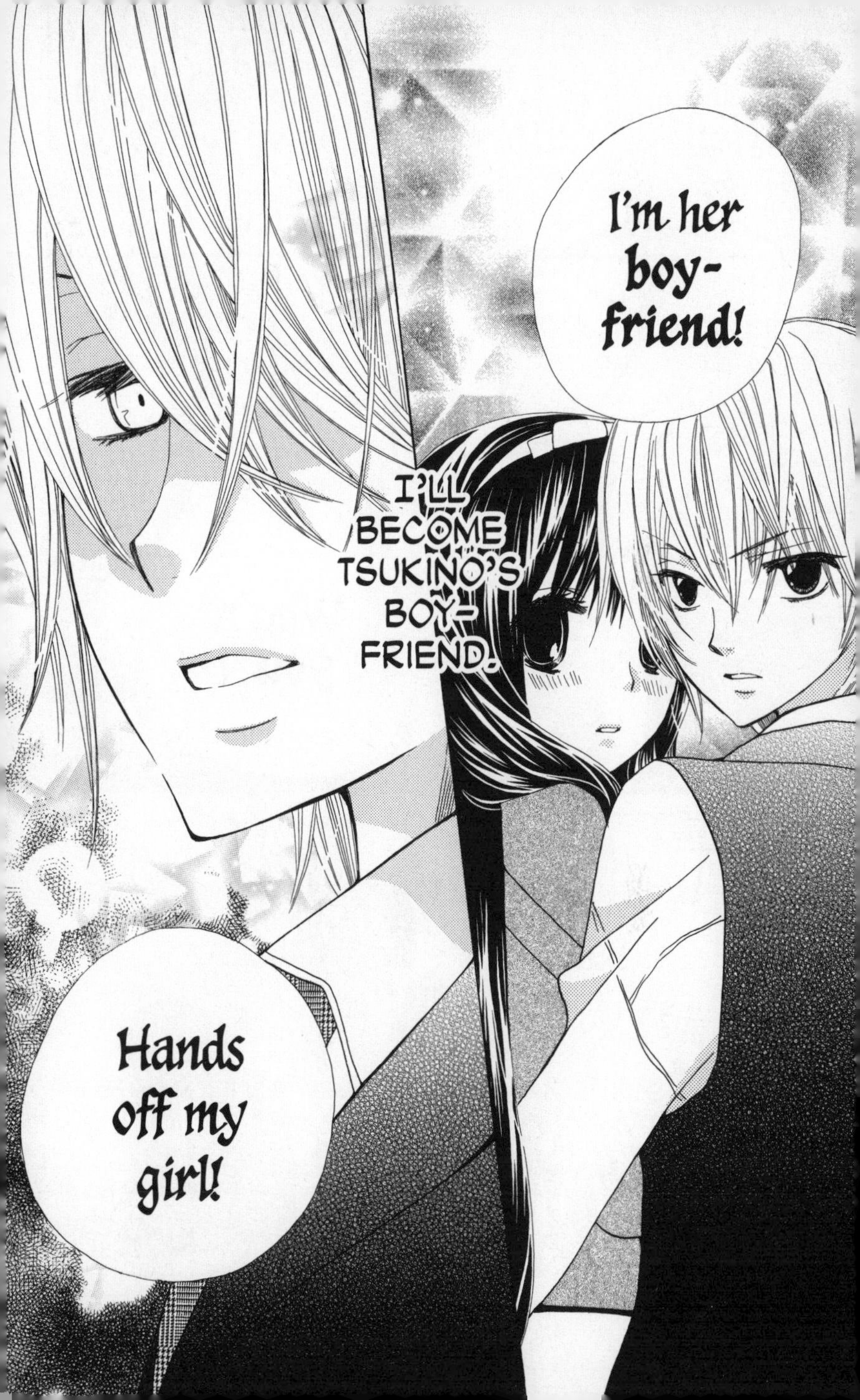
I'm her boy-friend!
I'LL BECOME TSUKINO'S BOY-FRIEND.
Hands off my girl!

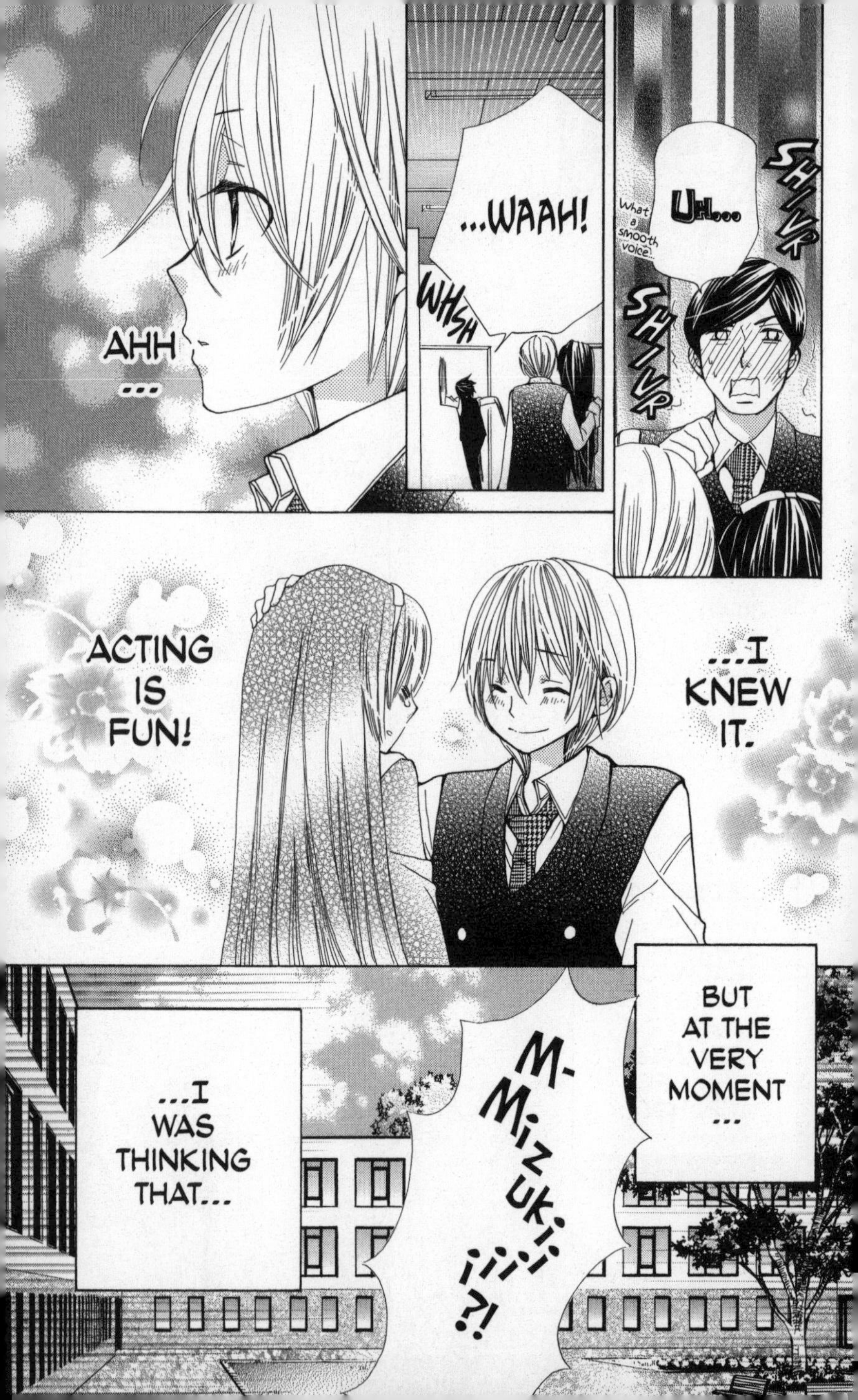
SHIVR
SHIVR
UH...
What a smooth voice...
...WAAH!
WHSH
AHH...
...I KNEW IT.
ACTING IS FUN!
BUT AT THE VERY MOMENT...
M-Mizuki!!?!
...I WAS THINKING THAT...

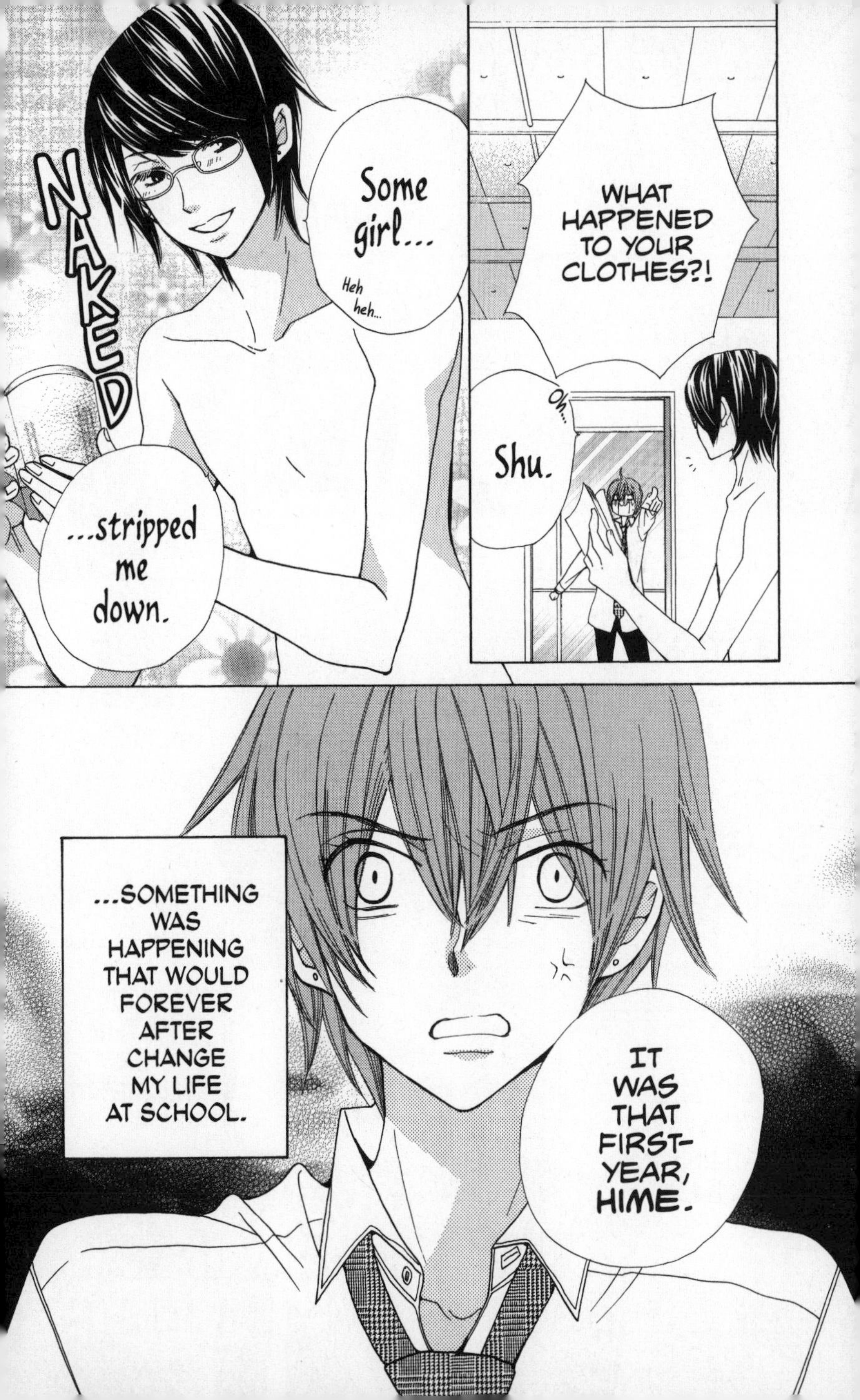
WHAT HAPPENED TO YOUR CLOTHES?!
Oh...
Shu.
Some girl...
Heh heh...
NAKED
...stripped me down.
IT WAS THAT FIRST-YEAR, HIME.
...SOMETHING WAS HAPPENING THAT WOULD FOREVER AFTER CHANGE MY LIFE AT SCHOOL.

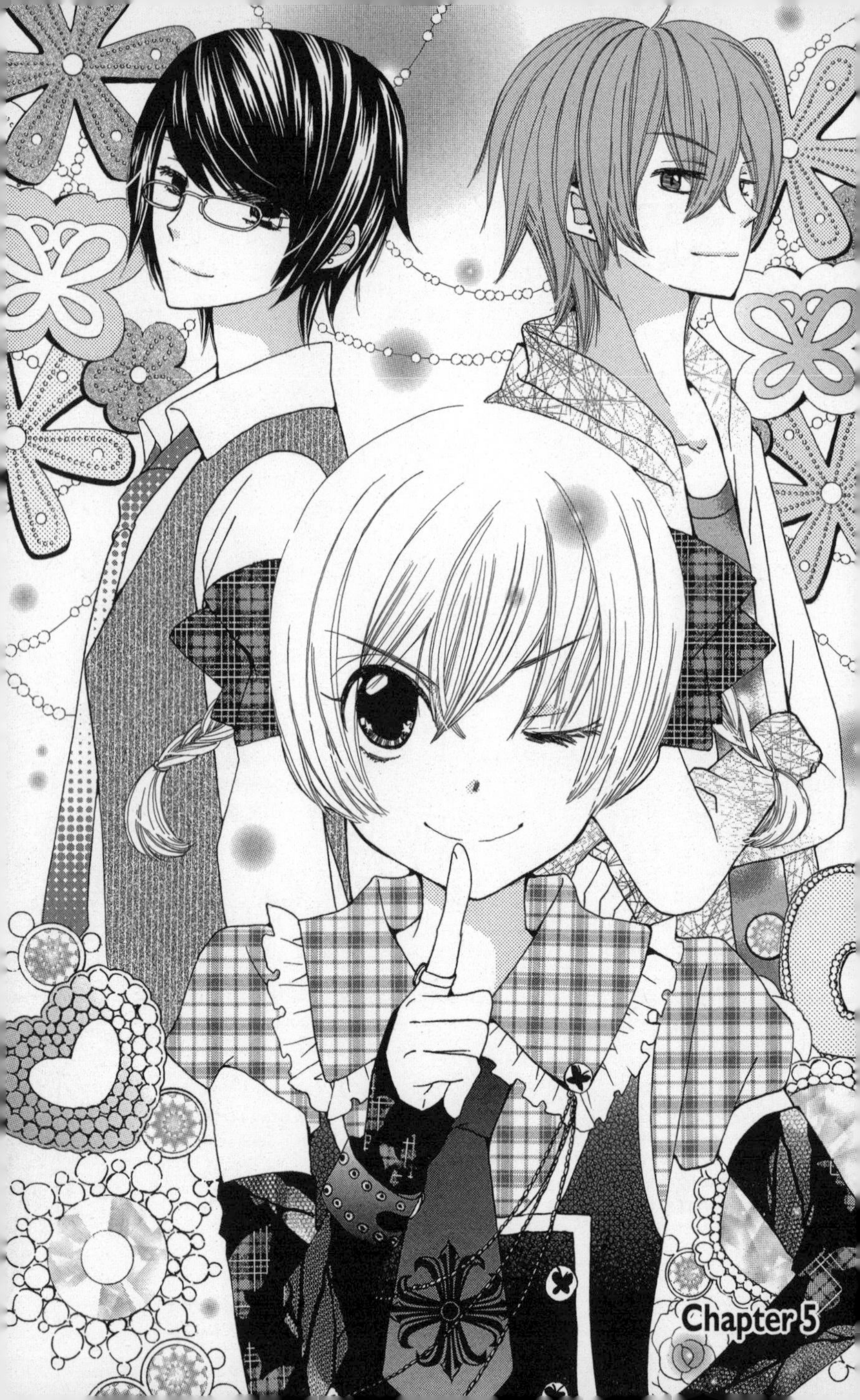
Chapter 5

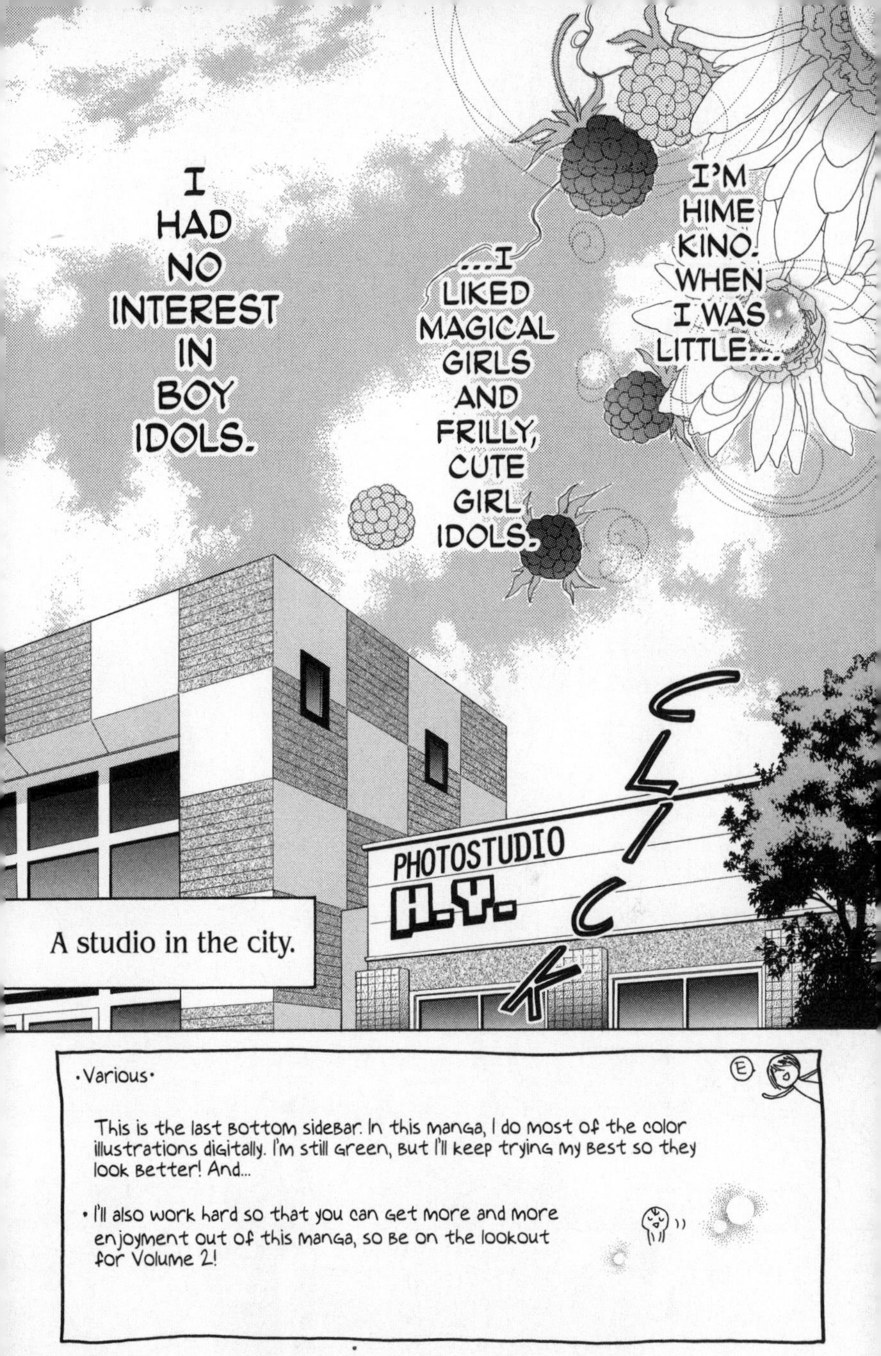
I'M HIME KINO. WHEN I WAS LITTLE...
...I LIKED MAGICAL GIRLS AND FRILLY, CUTE GIRL IDOLS.
I HAD NO INTEREST IN BOY IDOLS.
CLICK
PHOTOSTUDIO H.Y.
A studio in the city.

•Various•

This is the last bottom sidebar. In this manga, I do most of the color illustrations digitally. I'm still green, but I'll keep trying my best so they look better! And...

• I'll also work hard so that you can get more and more enjoyment out of this manga, so be on the lookout for Volume 2!

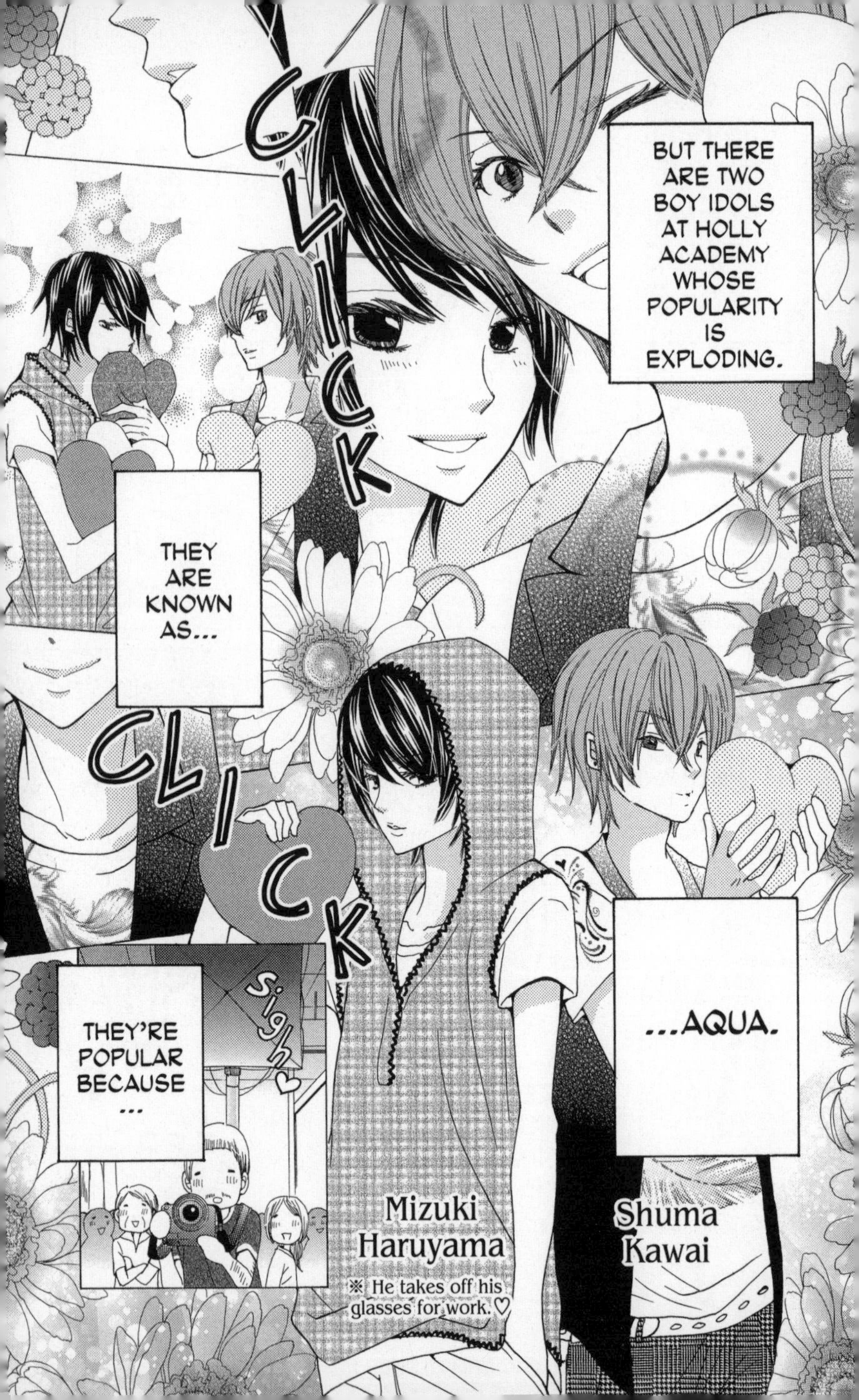
BUT THERE ARE TWO BOY IDOLS AT HOLLY ACADEMY WHOSE POPULARITY IS EXPLODING.
CLICK
THEY ARE KNOWN AS...
CLICK
...AQUA.
Shuma Kawai
Mizuki Haruyama
※ He takes off his glasses for work.♡
sigh♡
THEY'RE POPULAR BECAUSE ...

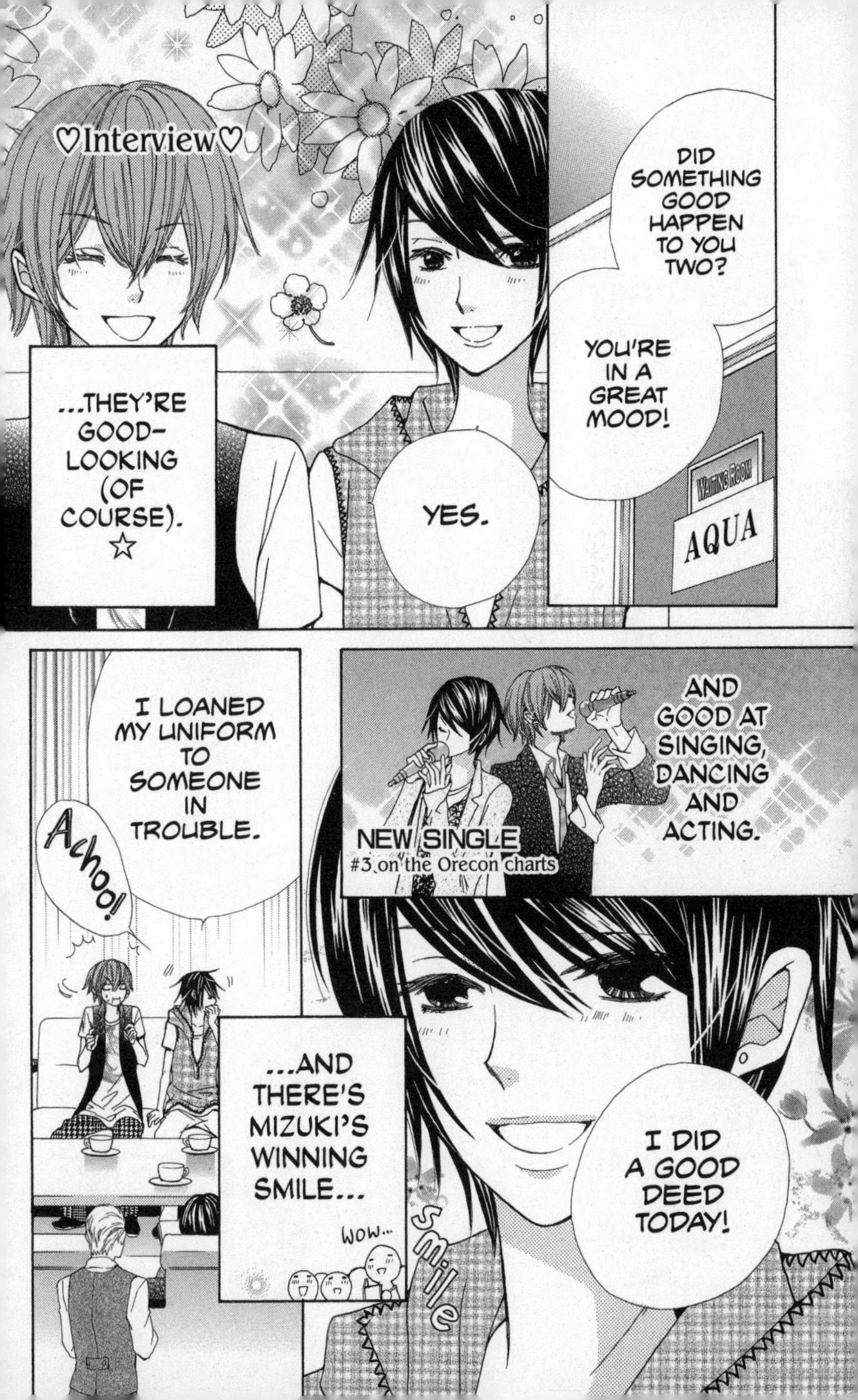
DID SOMETHING GOOD HAPPEN TO YOU TWO?
YOU'RE IN A GREAT MOOD!
WAITING ROOM
AQUA
♡Interview♡
YES.
...THEY'RE GOOD-LOOKING (OF COURSE). ☆
AND GOOD AT SINGING, DANCING AND ACTING.
NEW SINGLE
#3 on the Orecon charts
I DID A GOOD DEED TODAY!
Smile
...AND THERE'S MIZUKI'S WINNING SMILE...
WOW...
I LOANED MY UNIFORM TO SOMEONE IN TROUBLE.
Achoo!

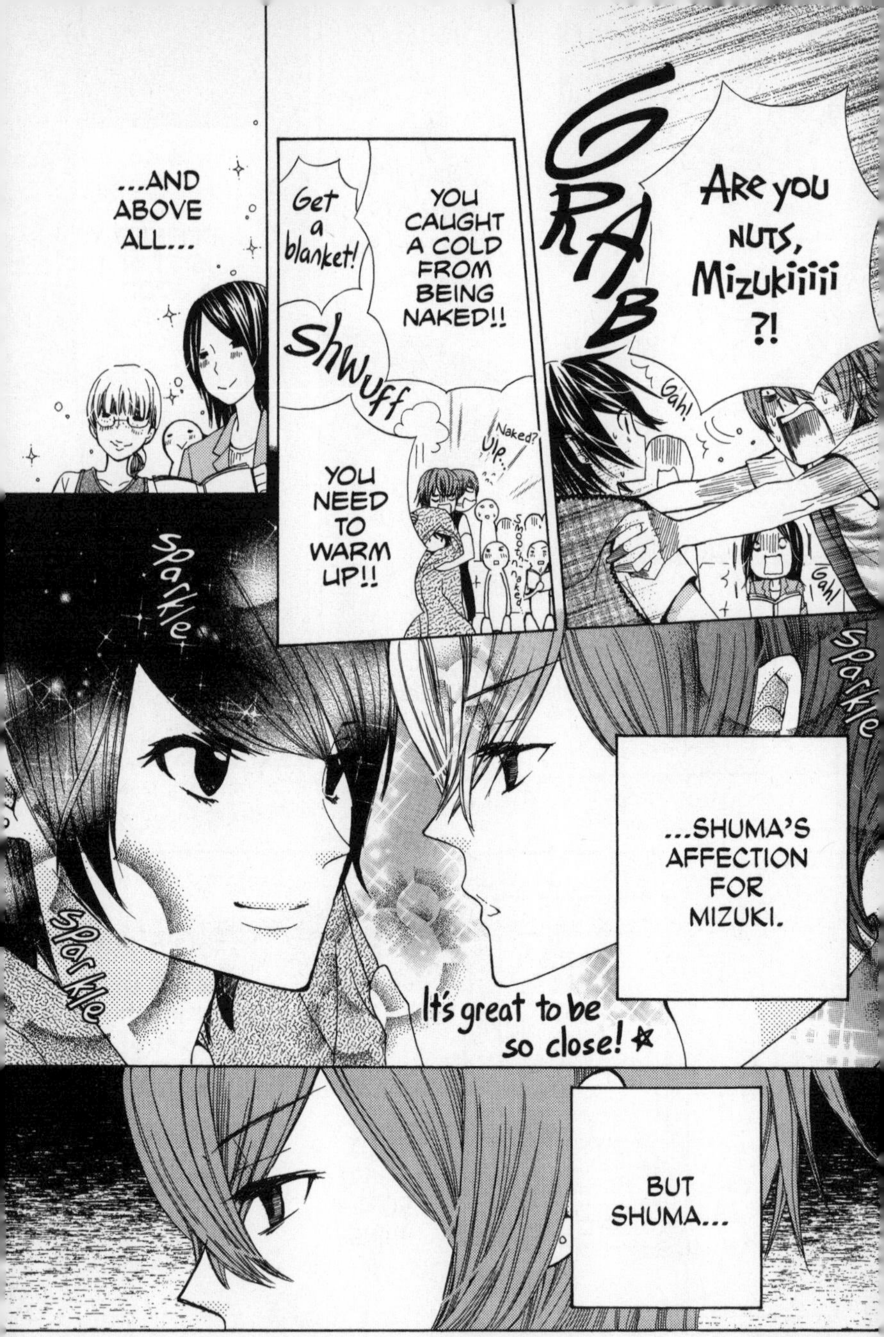
GRAB
Are you NUTS, Mizukiiiii?!
Gah!
Gah!
Get a blanket!
YOU CAUGHT A COLD FROM BEING NAKED!!
SHWUFF
Naked?
Ulp...
Smooth-n-naked...
YOU NEED TO WARM UP!!
...AND ABOVE ALL...
Sparkle
...SHUMA'S AFFECTION FOR MIZUKI.
It's great to be so close! ★
Sparkle
Sparkle
BUT SHUMA...

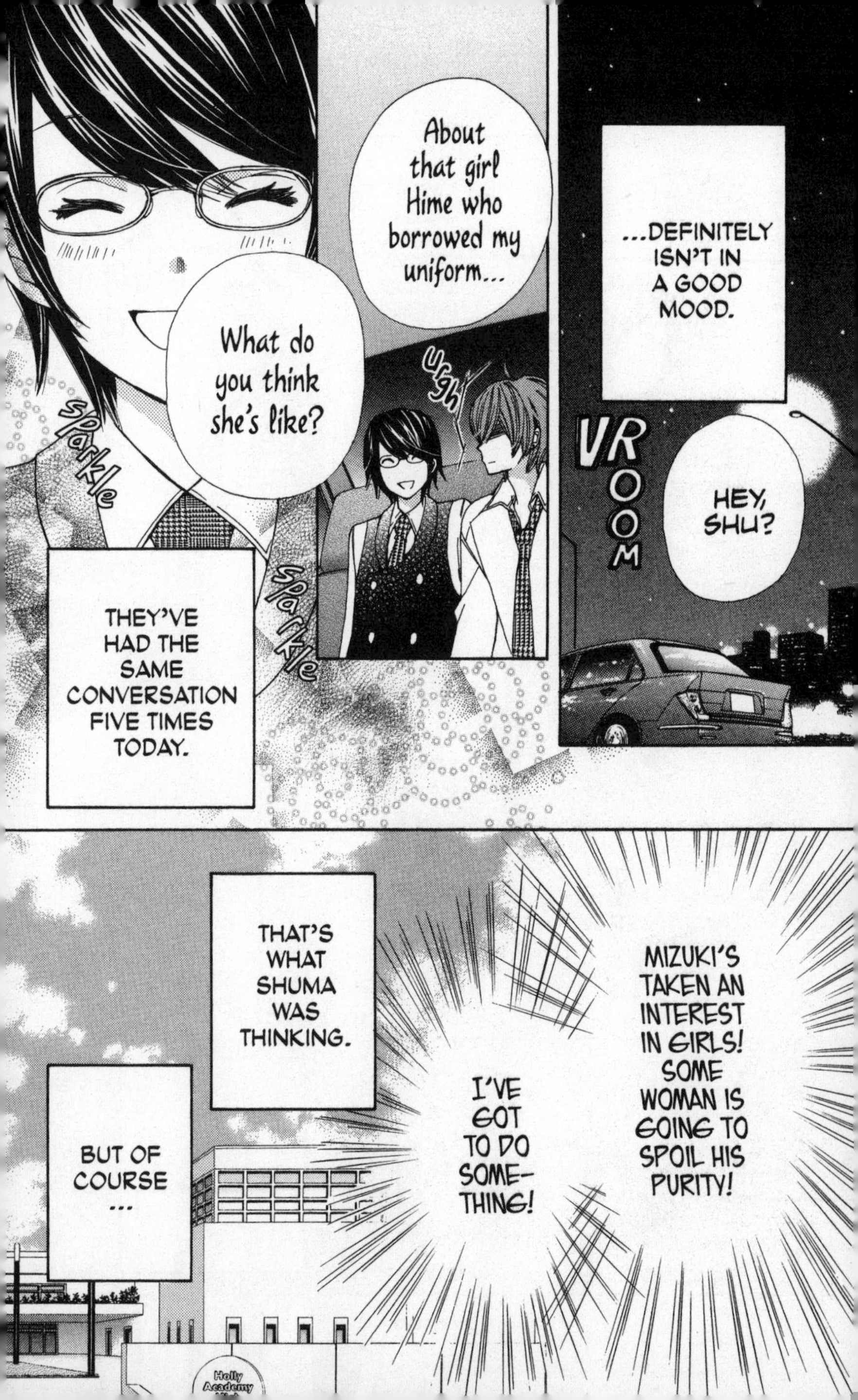
...DEFINITELY ISN'T IN A GOOD MOOD.
VROOM
HEY, SHU?
About that girl Hime who borrowed my uniform...
Urgh
What do you think she's like?
sparkle
sparkle
THEY'VE HAD THE SAME CONVERSATION FIVE TIMES TODAY.
MIZUKI'S TAKEN AN INTEREST IN GIRLS! SOME WOMAN IS GOING TO SPOIL HIS PURITY!
I'VE GOT TO DO SOME-THING!
THAT'S WHAT SHUMA WAS THINKING.
BUT OF COURSE ...
Holly Academy

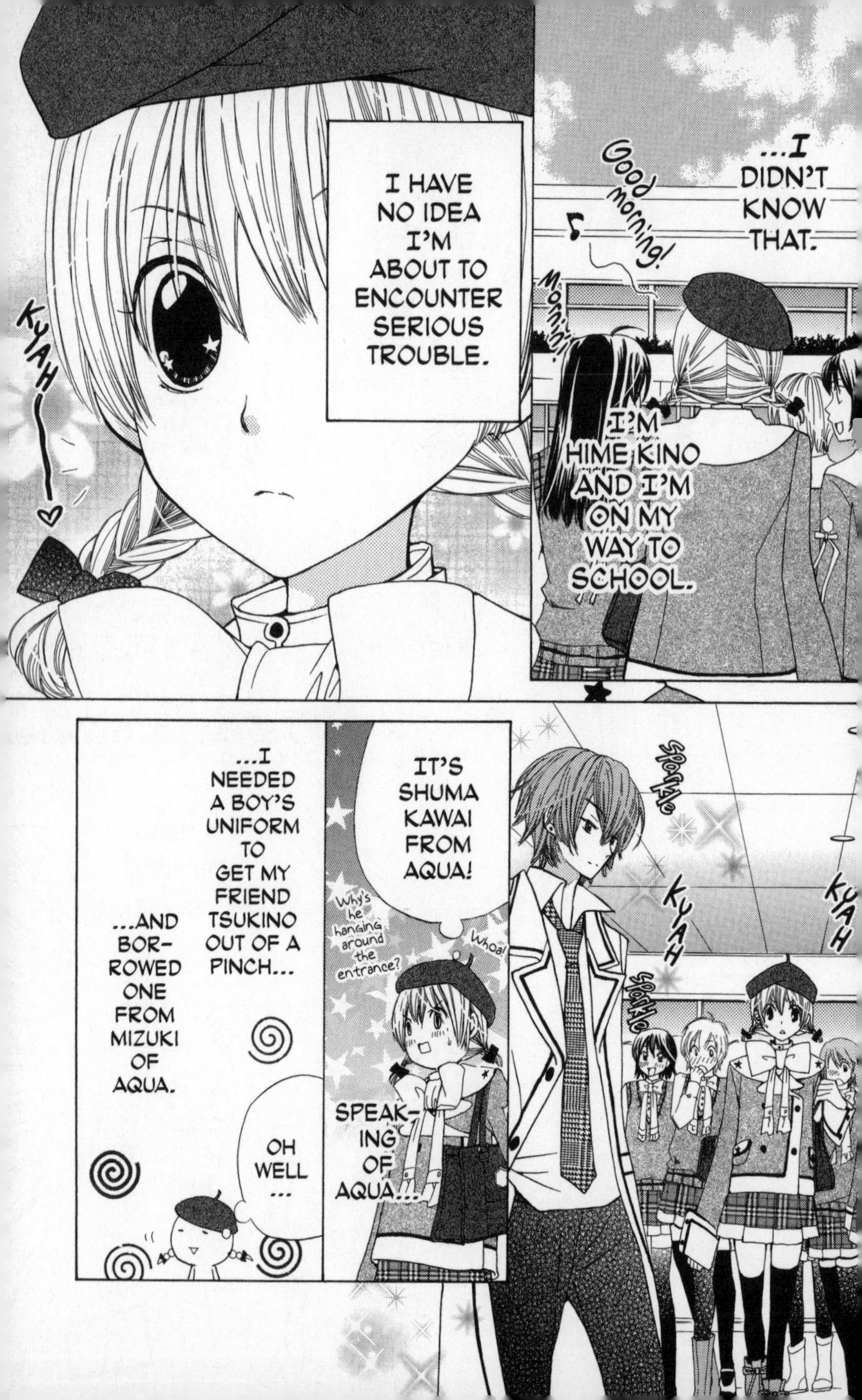
...I DIDN'T KNOW THAT.
Good morning!
Mornin'!
I'M HIME KINO AND I'M ON MY WAY TO SCHOOL.
I HAVE NO IDEA I'M ABOUT TO ENCOUNTER SERIOUS TROUBLE.
KYAH—♥
sparkle
KYAH
KYAH
sparkle
IT'S SHUMA KAWAI FROM AQUA!
Whoa!
Why's he hanging around the entrance?
SPEAKING OF AQUA...
...I NEEDED A BOY'S UNIFORM TO GET MY FRIEND TSUKINO OUT OF A PINCH...
...AND BORROWED ONE FROM MIZUKI OF AQUA.
OH WELL...

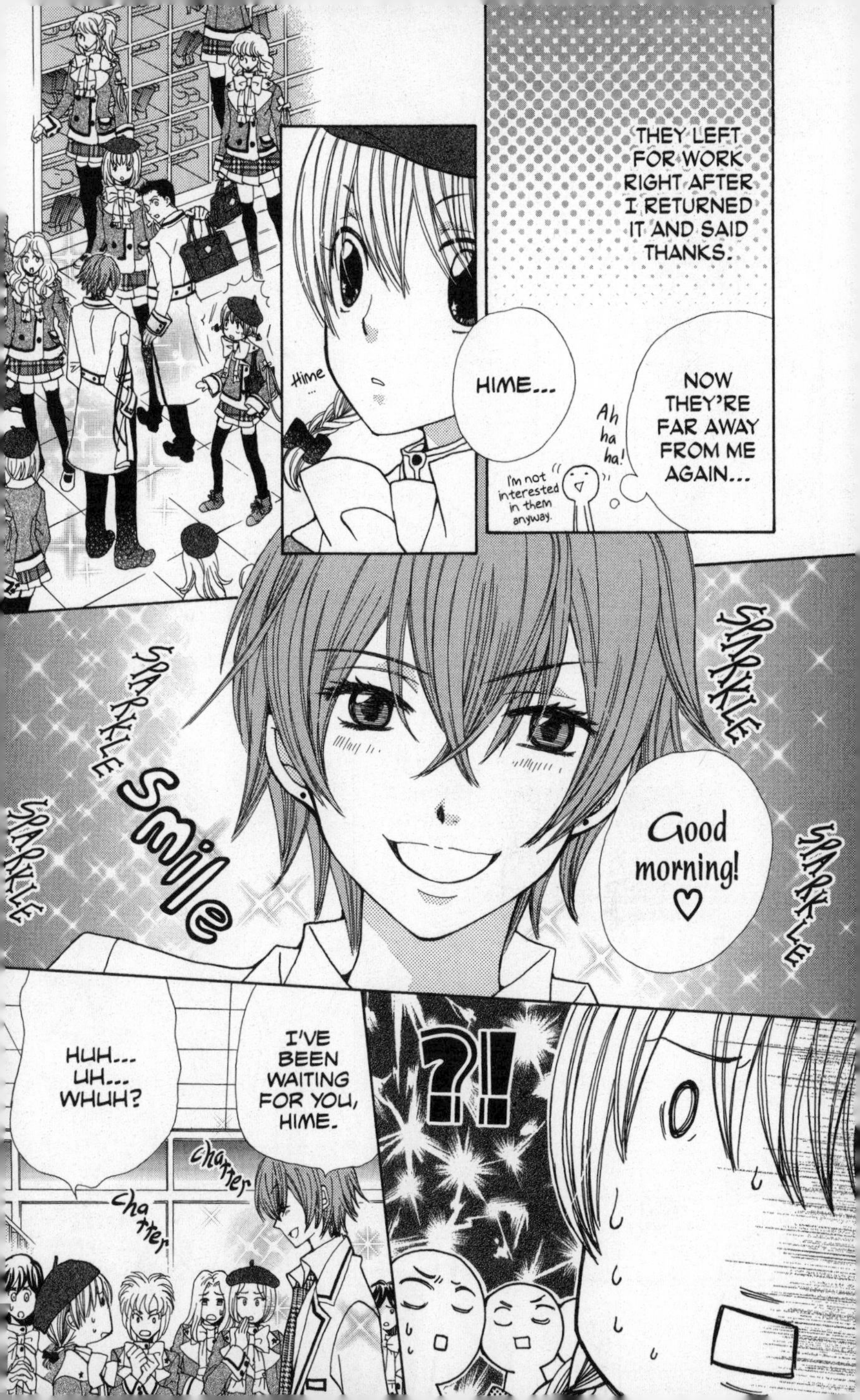
THEY LEFT FOR WORK RIGHT AFTER I RETURNED IT AND SAID THANKS.
NOW THEY'RE FAR AWAY FROM ME AGAIN...
Ah ha ha!
I'm not interested in them anyway.
HIME...
Hime ...
SPARKLE
Good morning! ♡
SPARKLE
Smile
SPARKLE
SPARKLE
?!
I'VE BEEN WAITING FOR YOU, HIME.
chatter
HUH... UH... WHUH?
chatter

• Various •

Thank you for reading this far!!

• If you have any ideas about sidebar illustrations or other new illustrations you'd like to see, just let me know! ♡

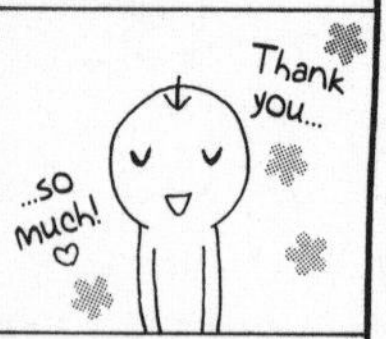
Thank you...
...so much! ♡

And much thanks to everyone who read this, my editor, my assistants, everyone who helped with composition, all the schools and studio personnel who helped with research, my family, my friends, and everyone in charge of the graphic novels!!

♡ If you want, let me hear your thoughts! ♡

Maki Minami c/o
Shojo Beat
P.O. Box 77010
San Francisco, CA
94107

南マキ
Maki Minami

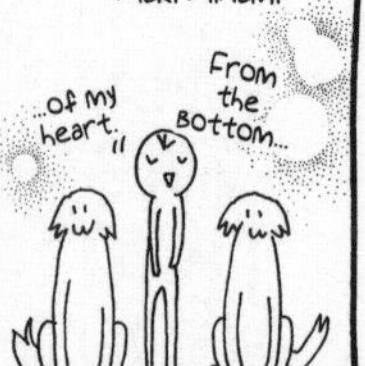
From the Bottom...
...of my heart.

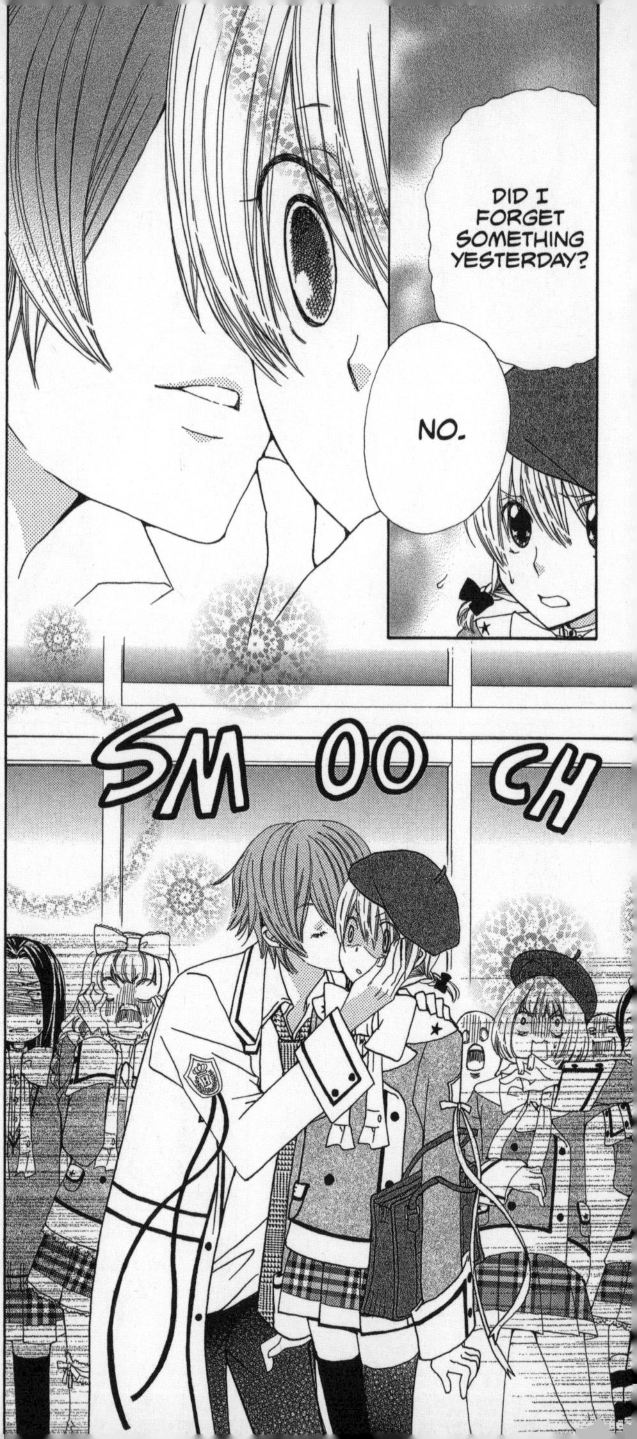
DID I FORGET SOMETHING YESTERDAY?
NO.
SMOOCH

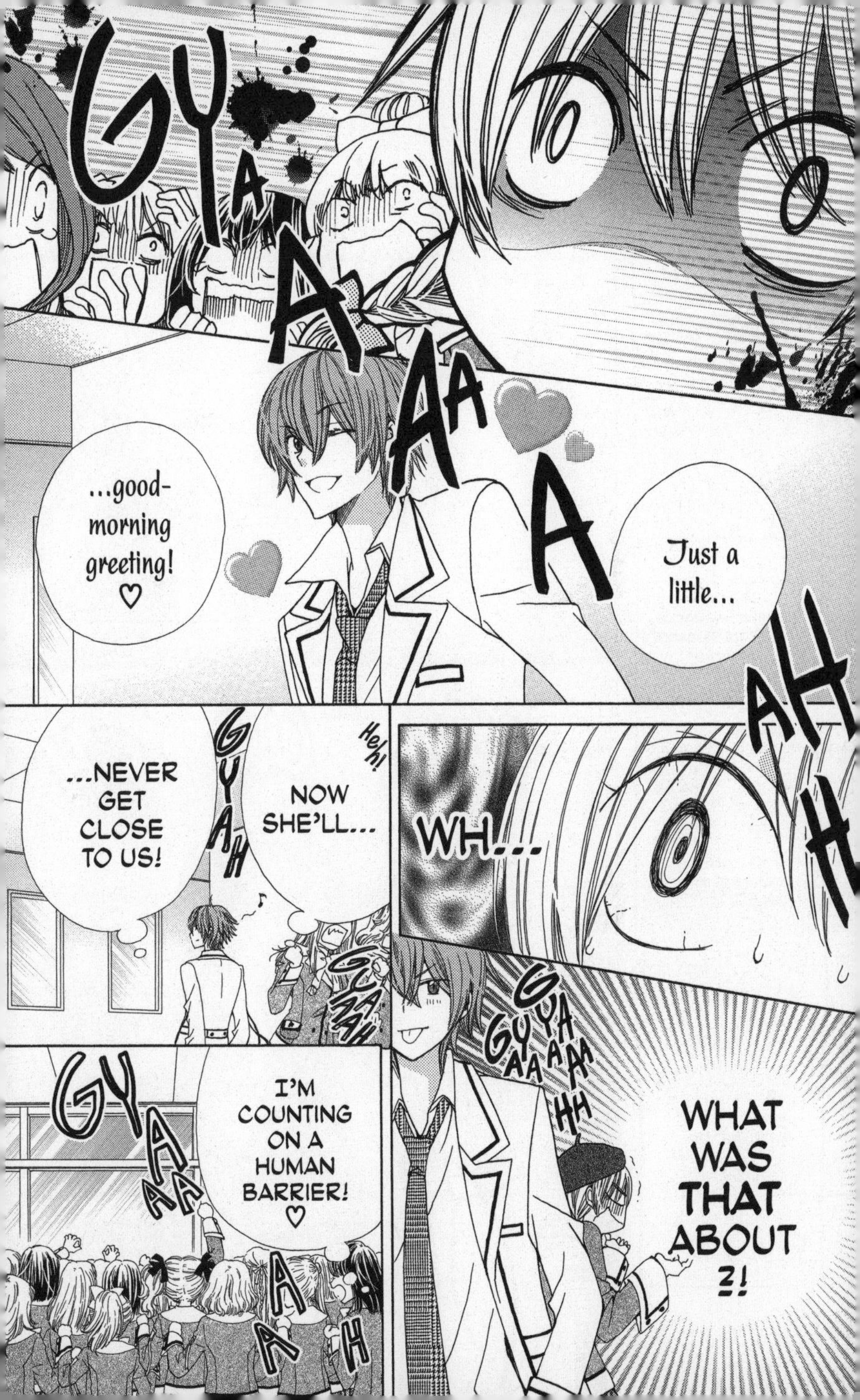
GYAAAAAA
Just a little...
...good-morning greeting! ♡
AHH
WH...
Heh!
NOW SHE'LL...
...NEVER GET CLOSE TO US!
GYAAH
GYAAH
GYAAAAAHH
WHAT WAS THAT ABOUT ?!
I'M COUNTING ON A HUMAN BARRIER! ♡
GYAAAAAH

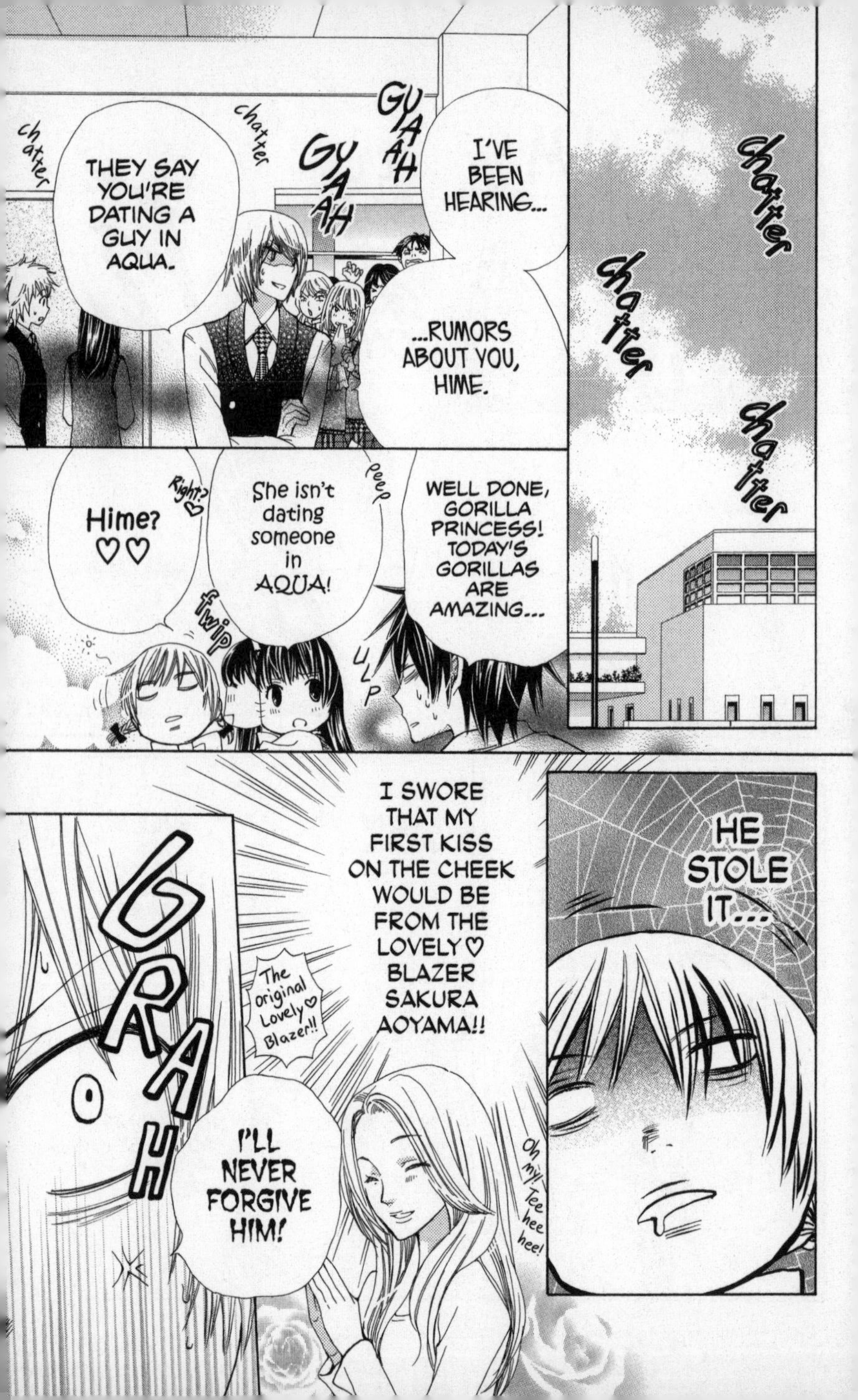
chatter
chatter
chatter
I'VE BEEN HEARING...
GUYAAH
GUYAAH
chatter
...RUMORS ABOUT YOU, HIME.
THEY SAY YOU'RE DATING A GUY IN AQUA.
chatter
WELL DONE, GORILLA PRINCESS! TODAY'S GORILLAS ARE AMAZING...
ULP
peep
She isn't dating someone in AQUA!
twip
Right? ♡
Hime? ♡♡
HE STOLE IT...
I SWORE THAT MY FIRST KISS ON THE CHEEK WOULD BE FROM THE LOVELY♡ BLAZER SAKURA AOYAMA!!
The original Lovely♡ Blazer!!
GRAAH
Oh my! Tee hee hee!
I'LL NEVER FORGIVE HIM!

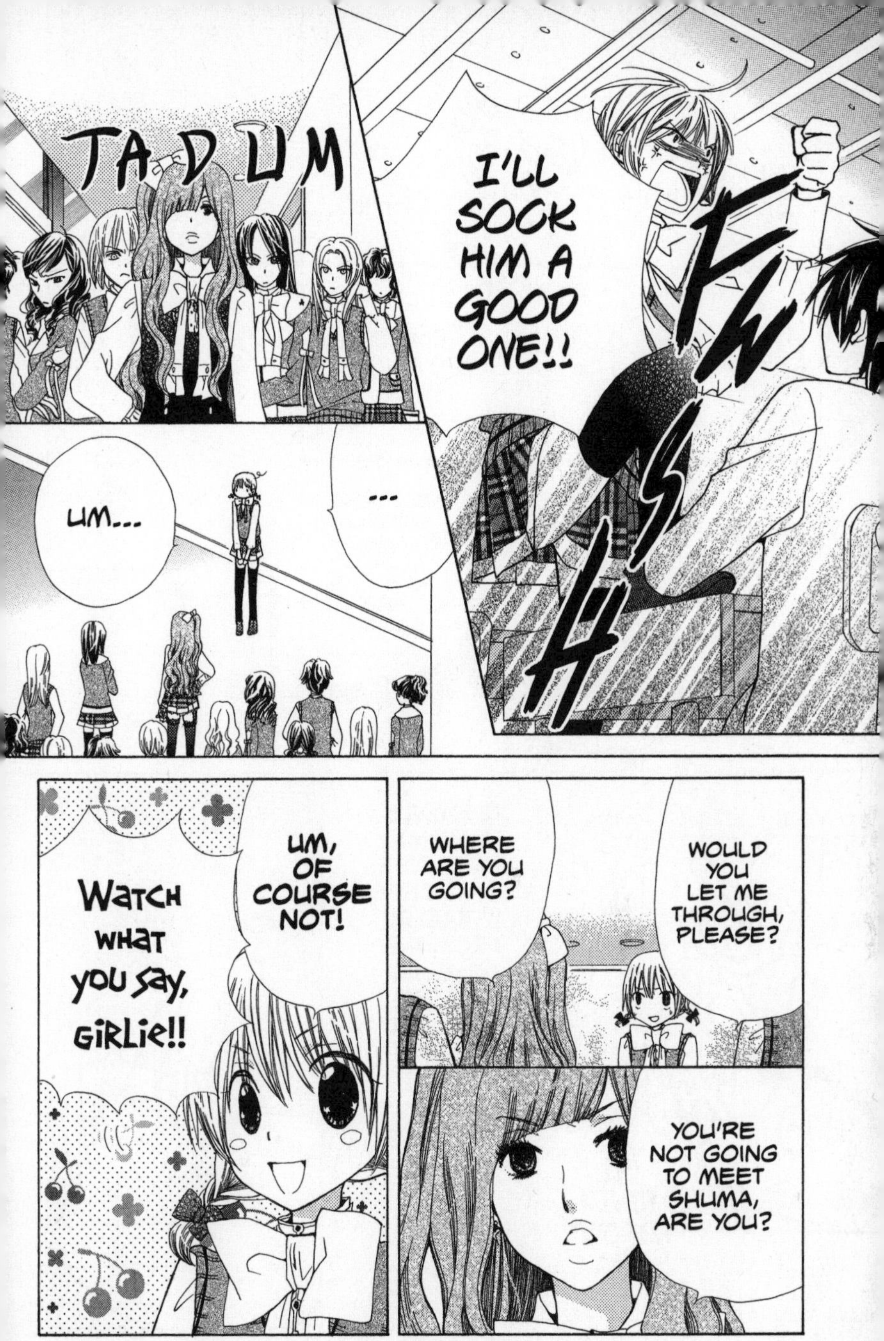
I'LL SOOK HIM A GOOD ONE!!
TA DUM
...
UM...
WOULD YOU LET ME THROUGH, PLEASE?
WHERE ARE YOU GOING?
YOU'RE NOT GOING TO MEET SHUMA, ARE YOU?
UM, OF COURSE NOT!
Watch what you say, girlie!!

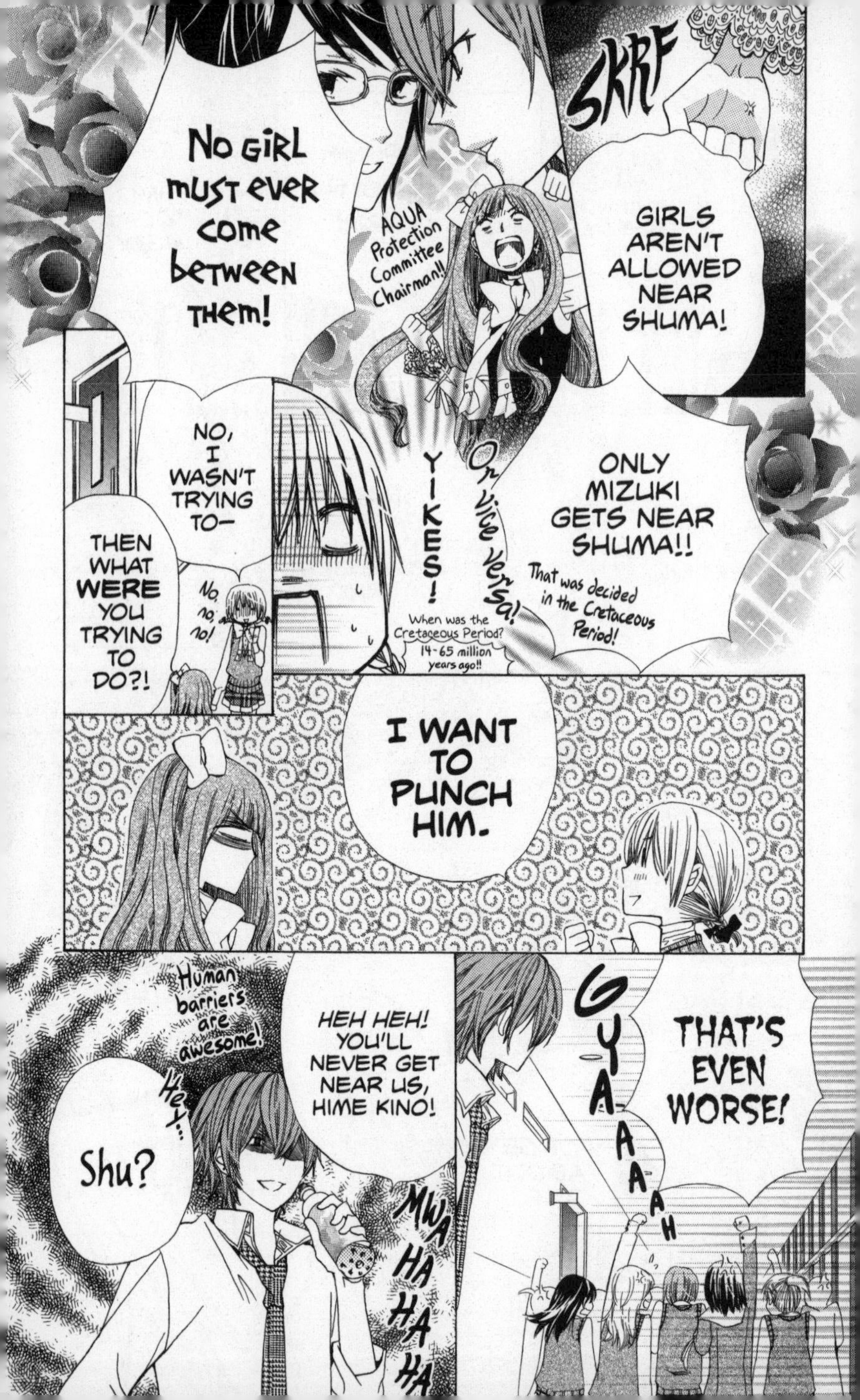
SKRF
GIRLS AREN'T ALLOWED NEAR SHUMA!
AQUA Protection Committee Chairman!!
No girl must ever come between them!
ONLY MIZUKI GETS NEAR SHUMA!!
That was decided in the Cretaceous Period!
Or vice versa!
YIKES!
When was the Cretaceous Period? 14-65 million years ago!!
NO, I WASN'T TRYING TO—
THEN WHAT WERE YOU TRYING TO DO?!
No, no, no!
I WANT TO PUNCH HIM.
THAT'S EVEN WORSE!
GYAAAAAH
HEH HEH! YOU'LL NEVER GET NEAR US, HIME KINO!
MWAHAHAHAHA
Human barriers are awesome!
Hey...
Shu?

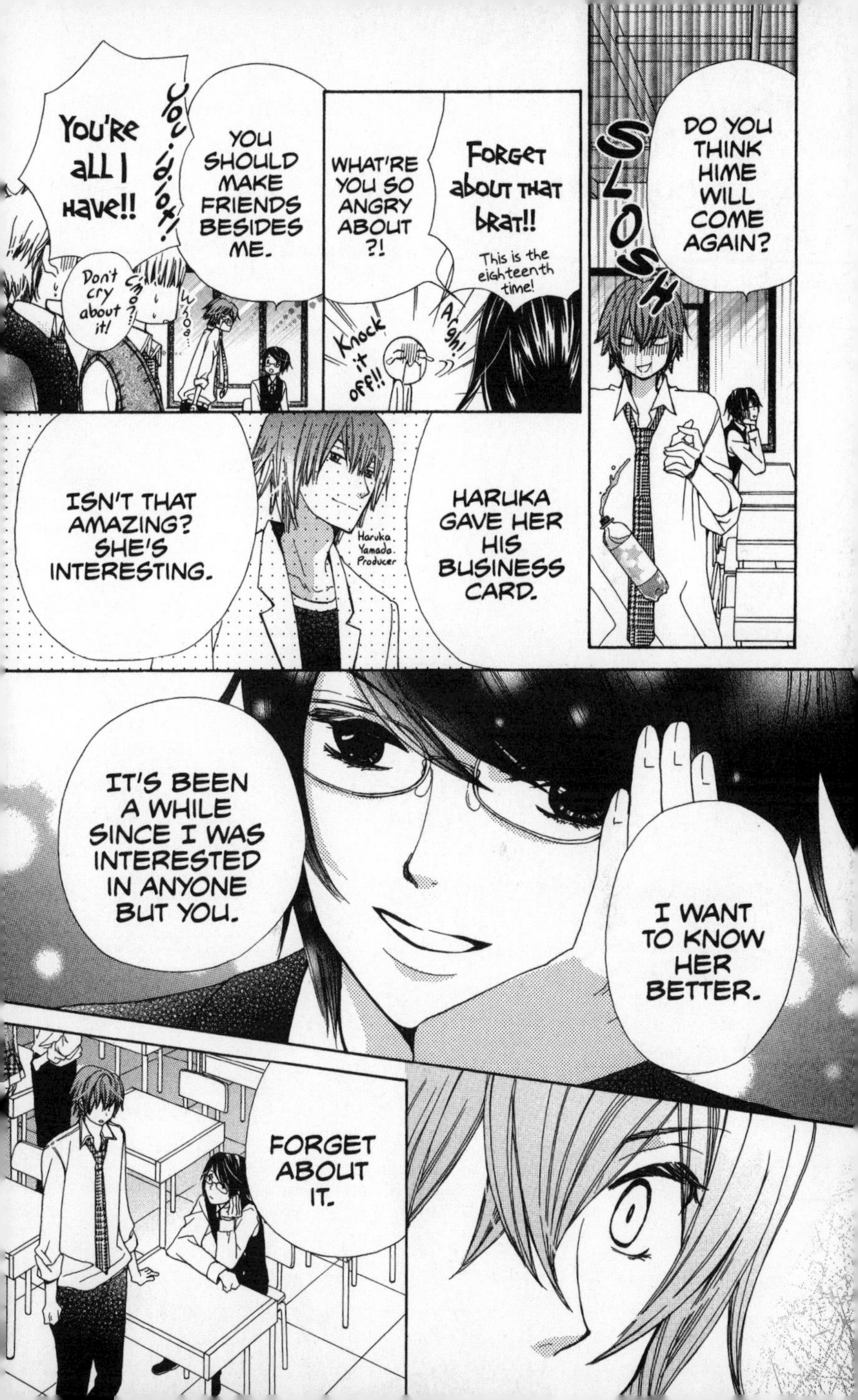

DO YOU THINK HIME WILL COME AGAIN?
SLOSH
Forget about that brat!!
This is the eighteenth time!
WHAT'RE YOU SO ANGRY ABOUT?!
Argh!
Knock it off!!
YOU SHOULD MAKE FRIENDS BESIDES ME.
You idiot!
You're all I have!!
C'mon?
Whoa...
Don't cry about it!
HARUKA GAVE HER HIS BUSINESS CARD.
Haruka. Yamada. Producer
ISN'T THAT AMAZING? SHE'S INTERESTING.
I WANT TO KNOW HER BETTER.
IT'S BEEN A WHILE SINCE I WAS INTERESTED IN ANYONE BUT YOU.
FORGET ABOUT IT.

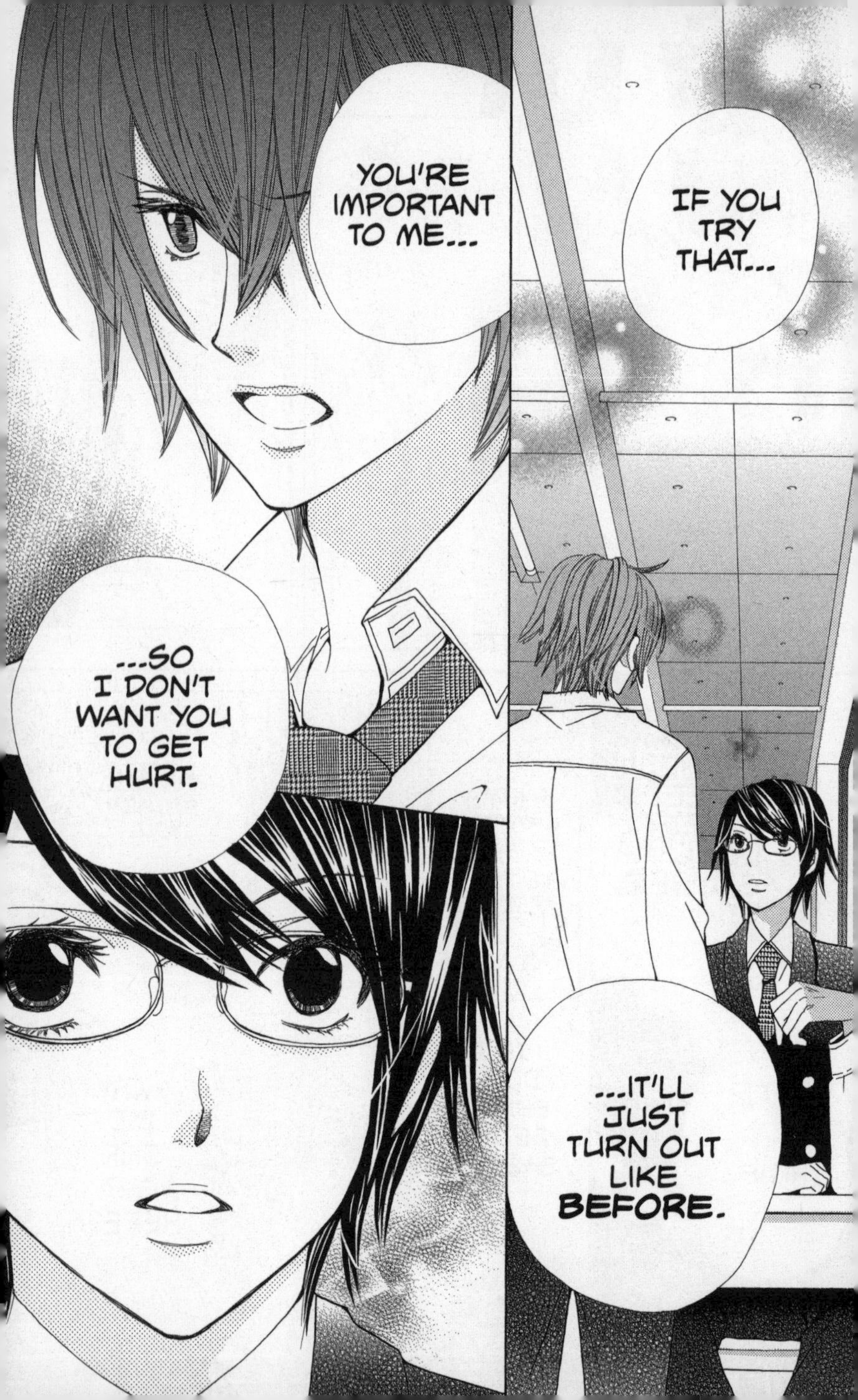
IF YOU TRY THAT...
...IT'LL JUST TURN OUT LIKE BEFORE.
YOU'RE IMPORTANT TO ME...
...SO I DON'T WANT YOU TO GET HURT.

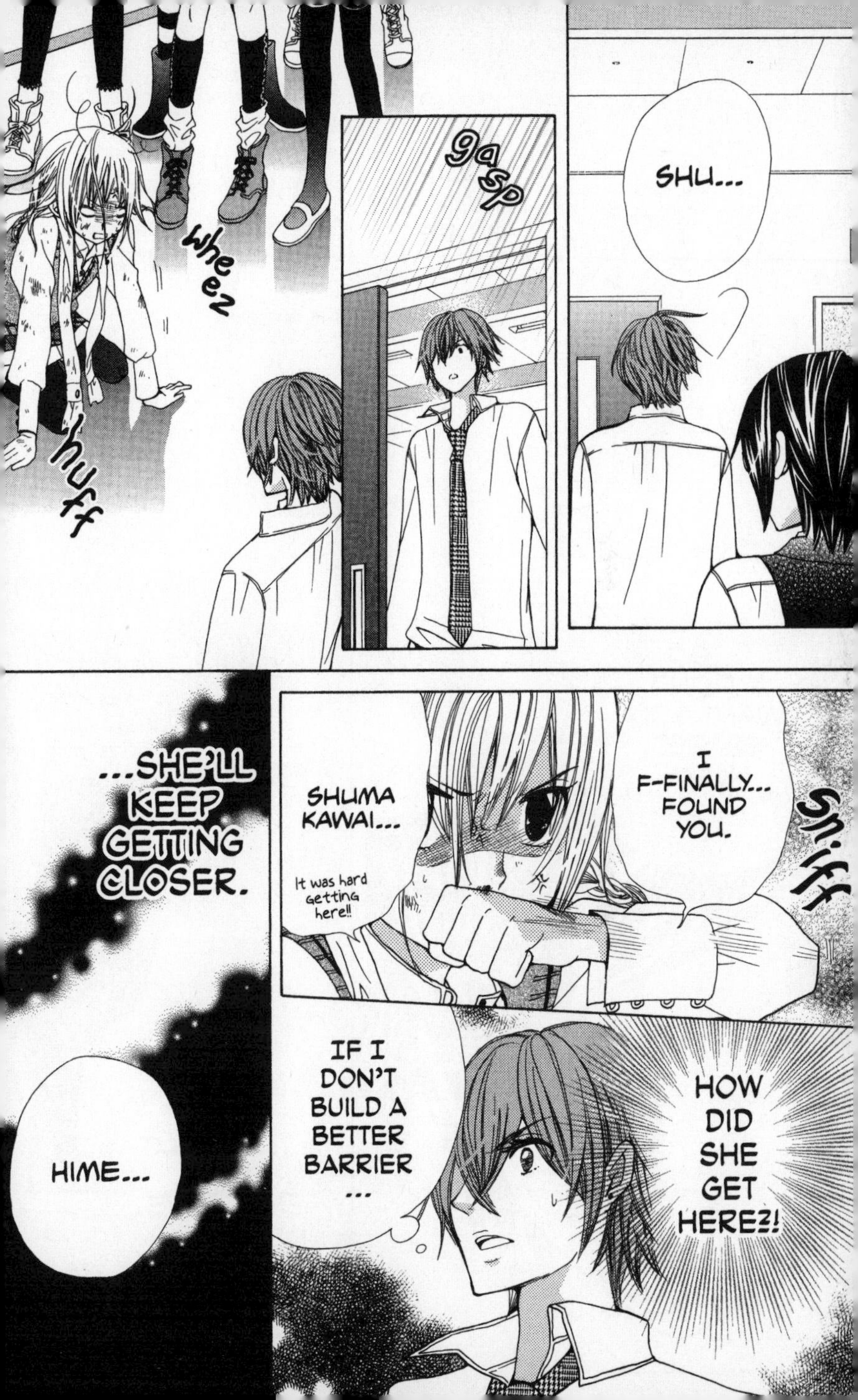
SHU...
gasp
wheez
huff
I F-FINALLY... FOUND YOU.
Sniff
SHUMA KAWAI...
It was hard getting here!!
HOW DID SHE GET HERE?!
IF I DON'T BUILD A BETTER BARRIER ...
...SHE'LL KEEP GETTING CLOSER.
HIME...

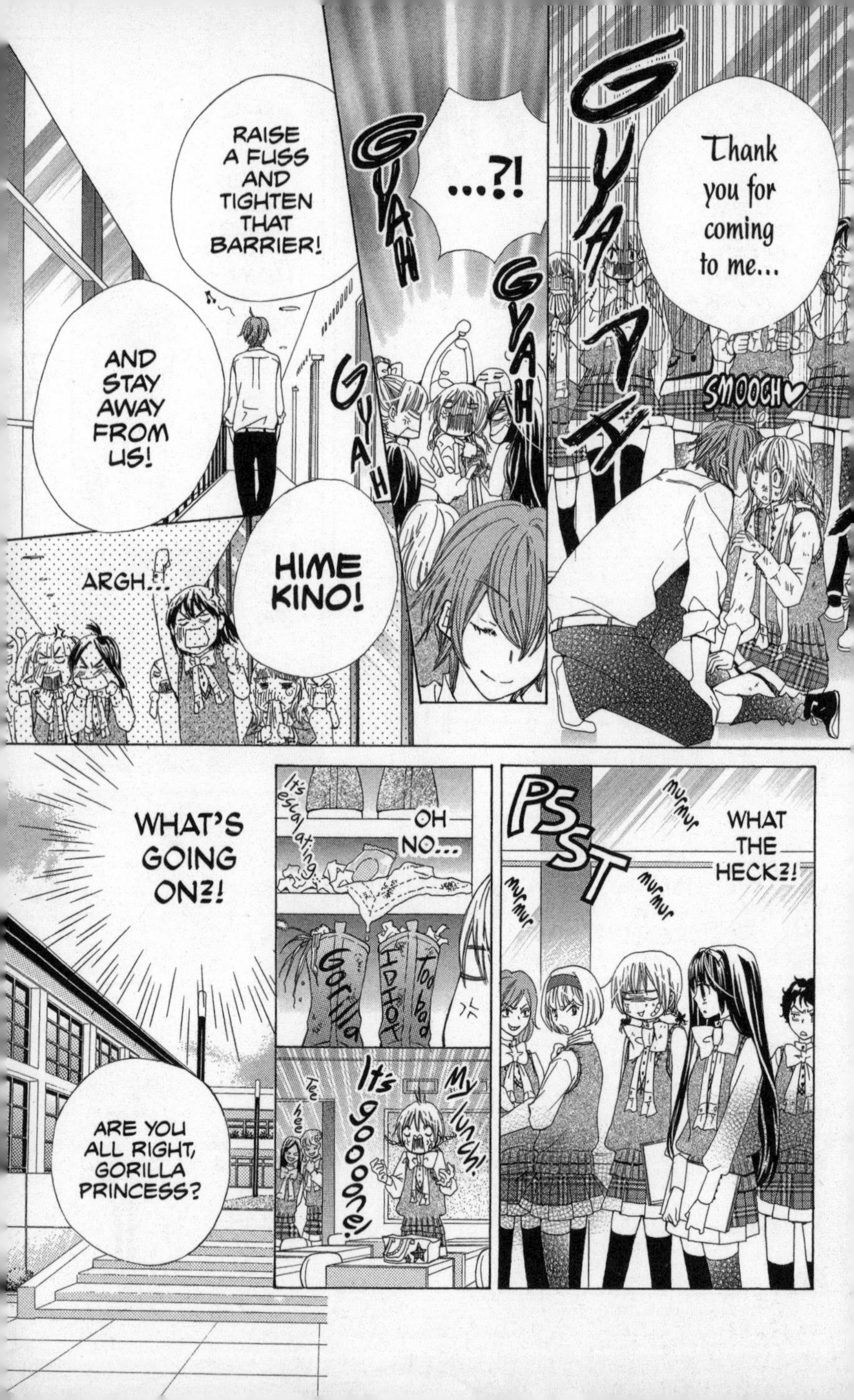
Thank you for coming to me...
GYAAAAH
SMOOCH♥
...?!
GYAH
GYAH
GYAH
HIME KINO!
RAISE A FUSS AND TIGHTEN THAT BARRIER!
AND STAY AWAY FROM US!
ARGH...
PSST
murmur
WHAT THE HECK?!
murmur
murmur
OH NO...
It's escalating...
Gorilla
IDIOT
Too bad
My lunch!
It's goooone!
Tee hee
WHAT'S GOING ON?!
ARE YOU ALL RIGHT, GORILLA PRINCESS?

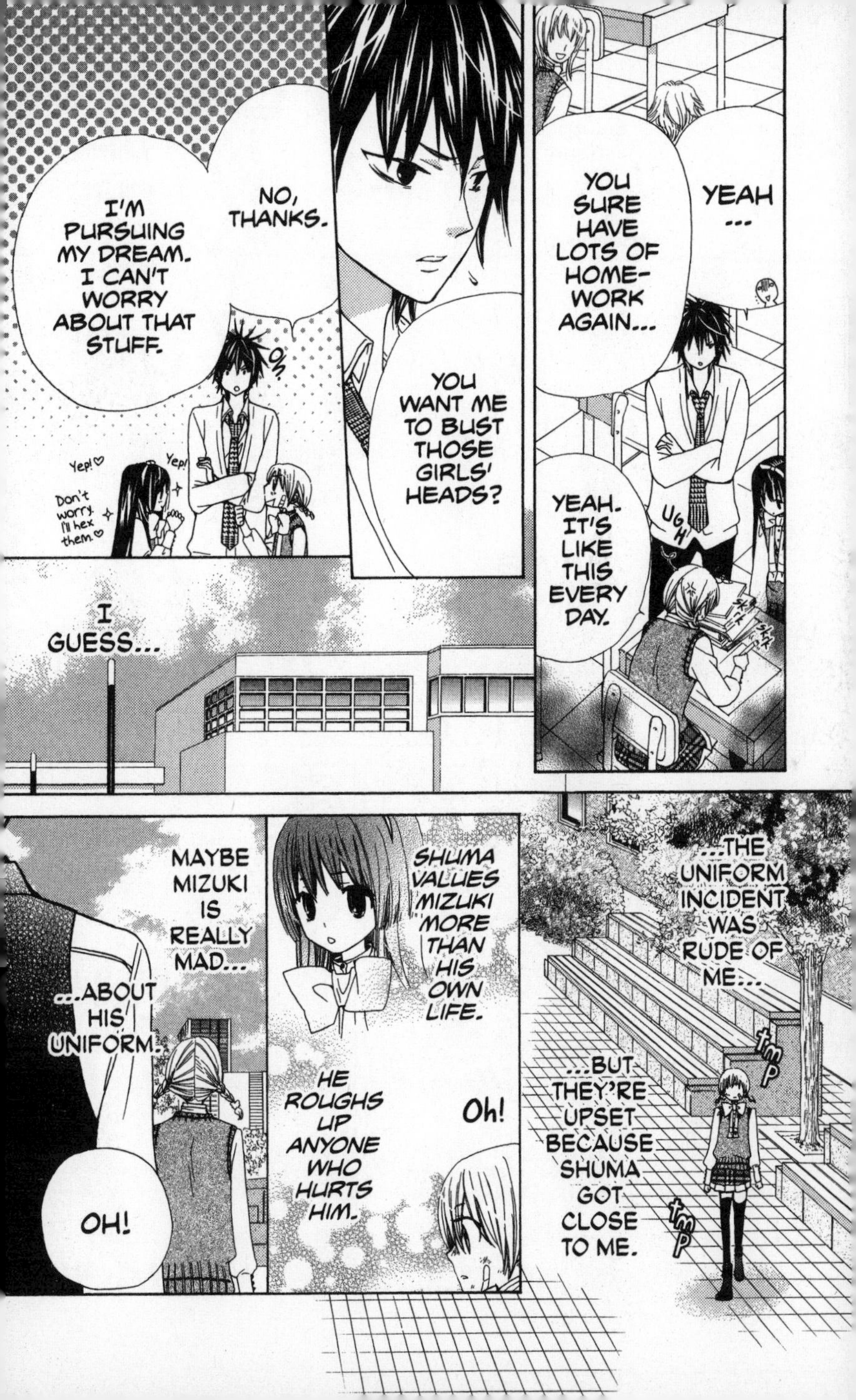
YEAH...
YOU SURE HAVE LOTS OF HOMEWORK AGAIN...
YEAH. IT'S LIKE THIS EVERY DAY.
UGH
skrk
skrk
YOU WANT ME TO BUST THOSE GIRLS' HEADS?
NO, THANKS.
I'M PURSUING MY DREAM. I CAN'T WORRY ABOUT THAT STUFF.
Oh?
Yep!
Yep!
Don't worry. I'll hex them.
I GUESS...
...THE UNIFORM INCIDENT WAS RUDE OF ME...
...BUT THEY'RE UPSET BECAUSE SHUMA GOT CLOSE TO ME.
tmp
tmp
SHUMA VALUES MIZUKI MORE THAN HIS OWN LIFE.
HE ROUGHS UP ANYONE WHO HURTS HIM.
Oh!
MAYBE MIZUKI IS REALLY MAD...
...ABOUT HIS UNIFORM.
OH!

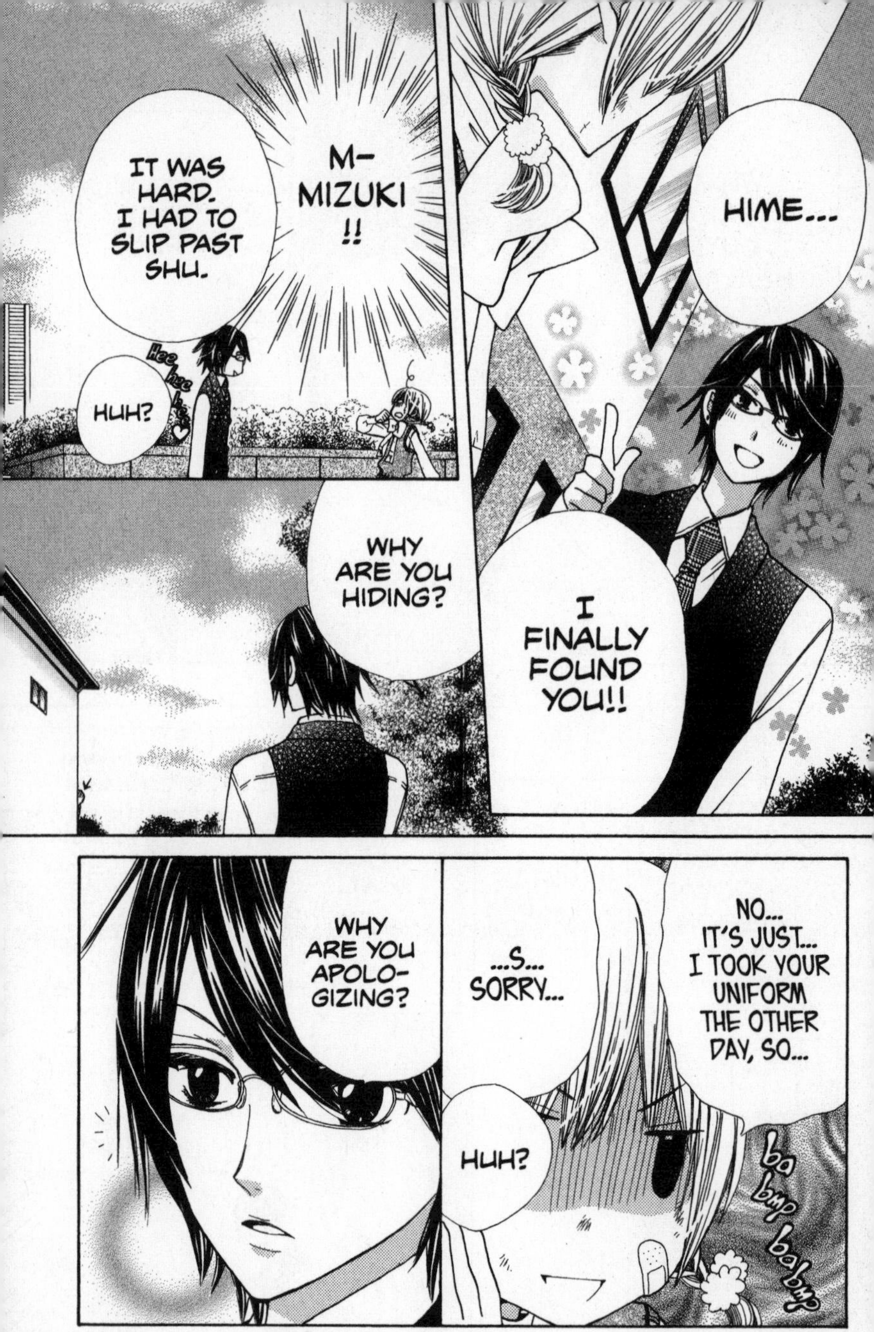
HIME...
I FINALLY FOUND YOU!!
M-MIZUKI!!
IT WAS HARD. I HAD TO SLIP PAST SHU.
Hee hee hee
HUH?
WHY ARE YOU HIDING?
NO... IT'S JUST... I TOOK YOUR UNIFORM THE OTHER DAY, SO...
...S... SORRY...
HUH?
ba bmp ba bmp
WHY ARE YOU APOLOGIZING?

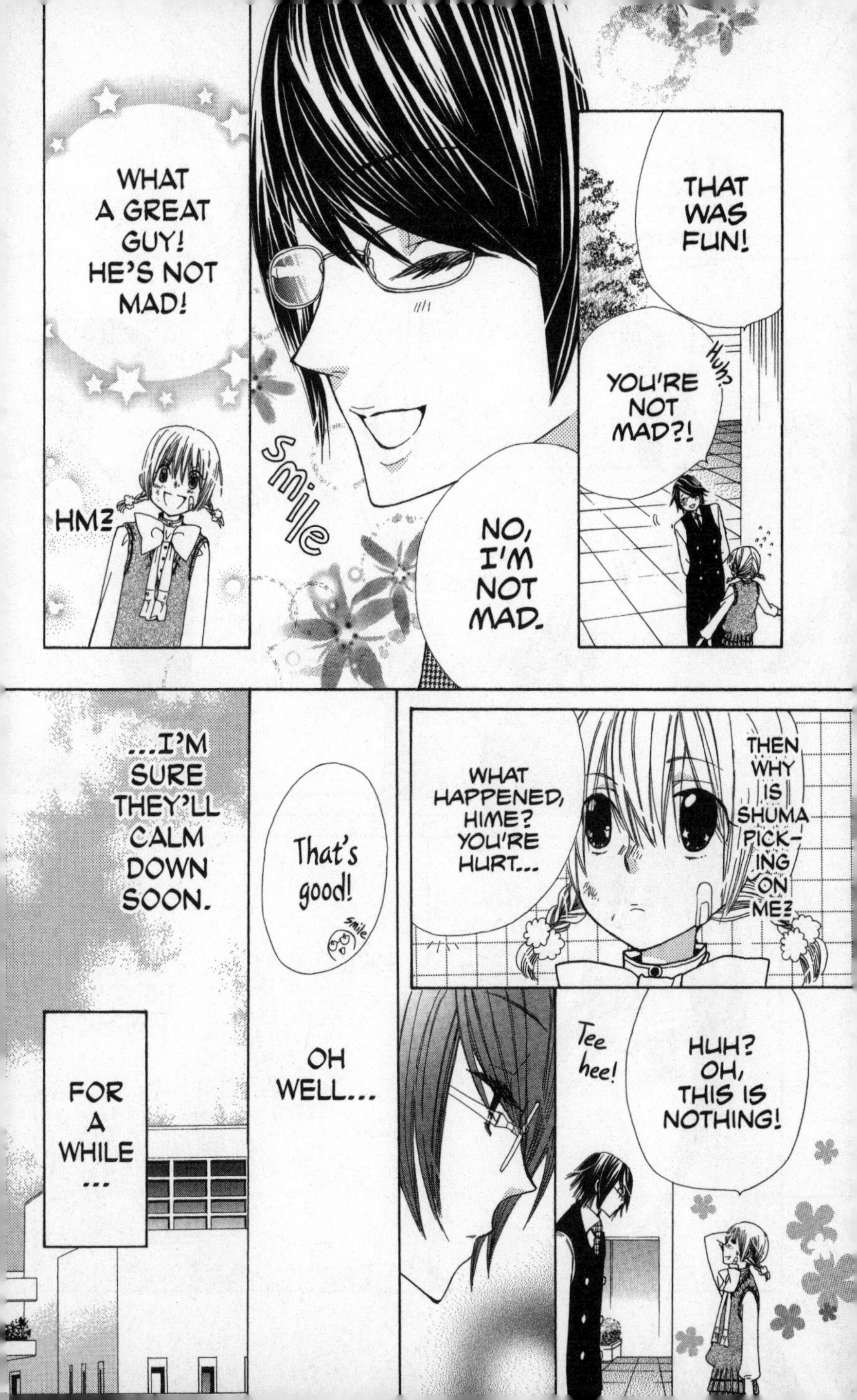
THAT WAS FUN!
Huh?
YOU'RE NOT MAD?!
NO, I'M NOT MAD.
smile
WHAT A GREAT GUY! HE'S NOT MAD!
HM?
THEN WHY IS SHUMA PICKING ON ME?
WHAT HAPPENED, HIME? YOU'RE HURT...
HUH? OH, THIS IS NOTHING!
Tee hee!
That's good!
smile
OH WELL...
...I'M SURE THEY'LL CALM DOWN SOON.
FOR A WHILE...

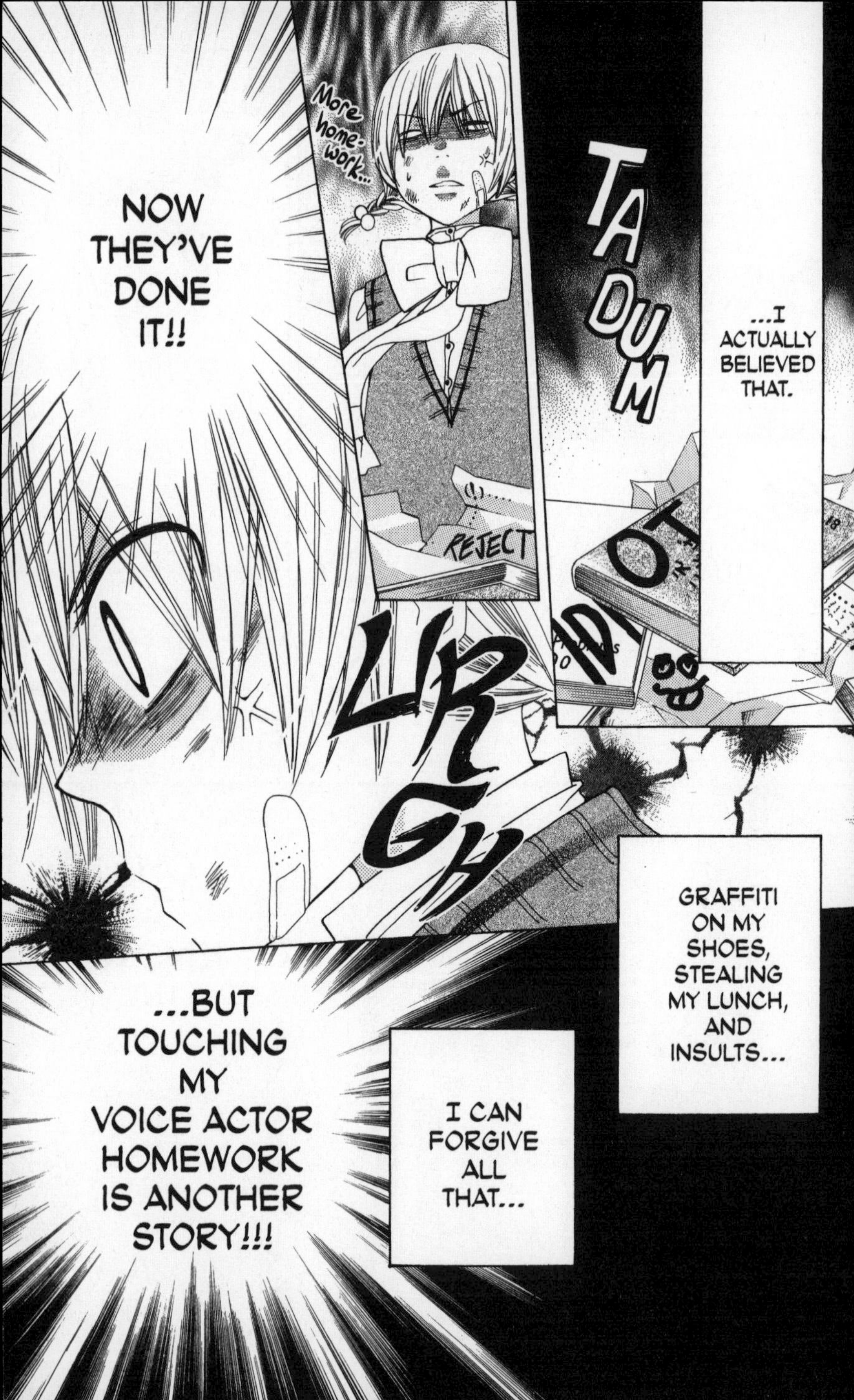
...I ACTUALLY BELIEVED THAT.
TADUM
More home-work...
REJECT
NOW THEY'VE DONE IT!!
URGH
GRAFFITI ON MY SHOES, STEALING MY LUNCH, AND INSULTS...
I CAN FORGIVE ALL THAT...
...BUT TOUCHING MY VOICE ACTOR HOMEWORK IS ANOTHER STORY!!!

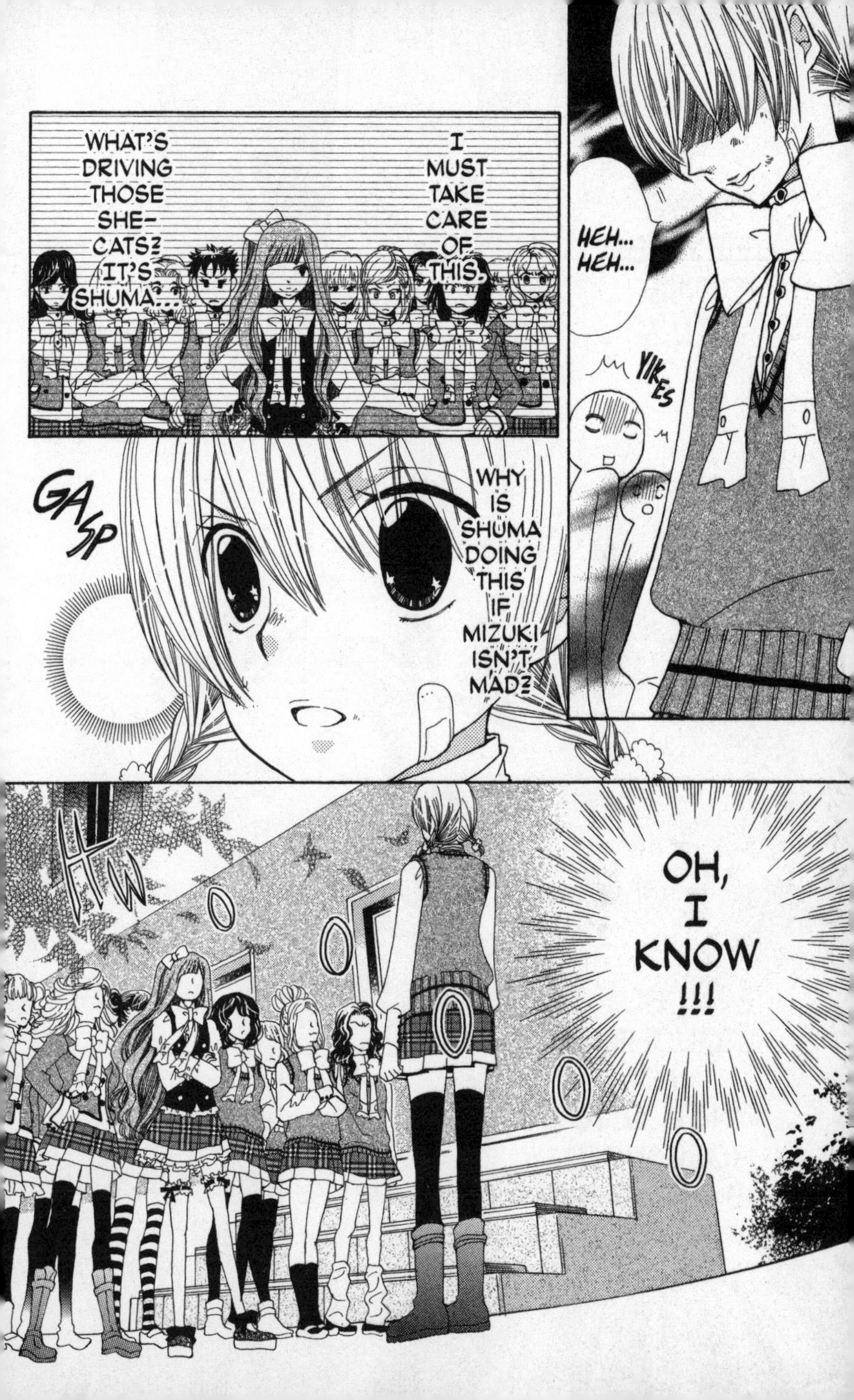
HEH... HEH...
YIKES
I MUST TAKE CARE OF THIS.
WHAT'S DRIVING THOSE SHE-CATS? IT'S SHUMA...
WHY IS SHUMA DOING THIS IF MIZUKI ISN'T MAD?
GASP
OH, I KNOW!!!

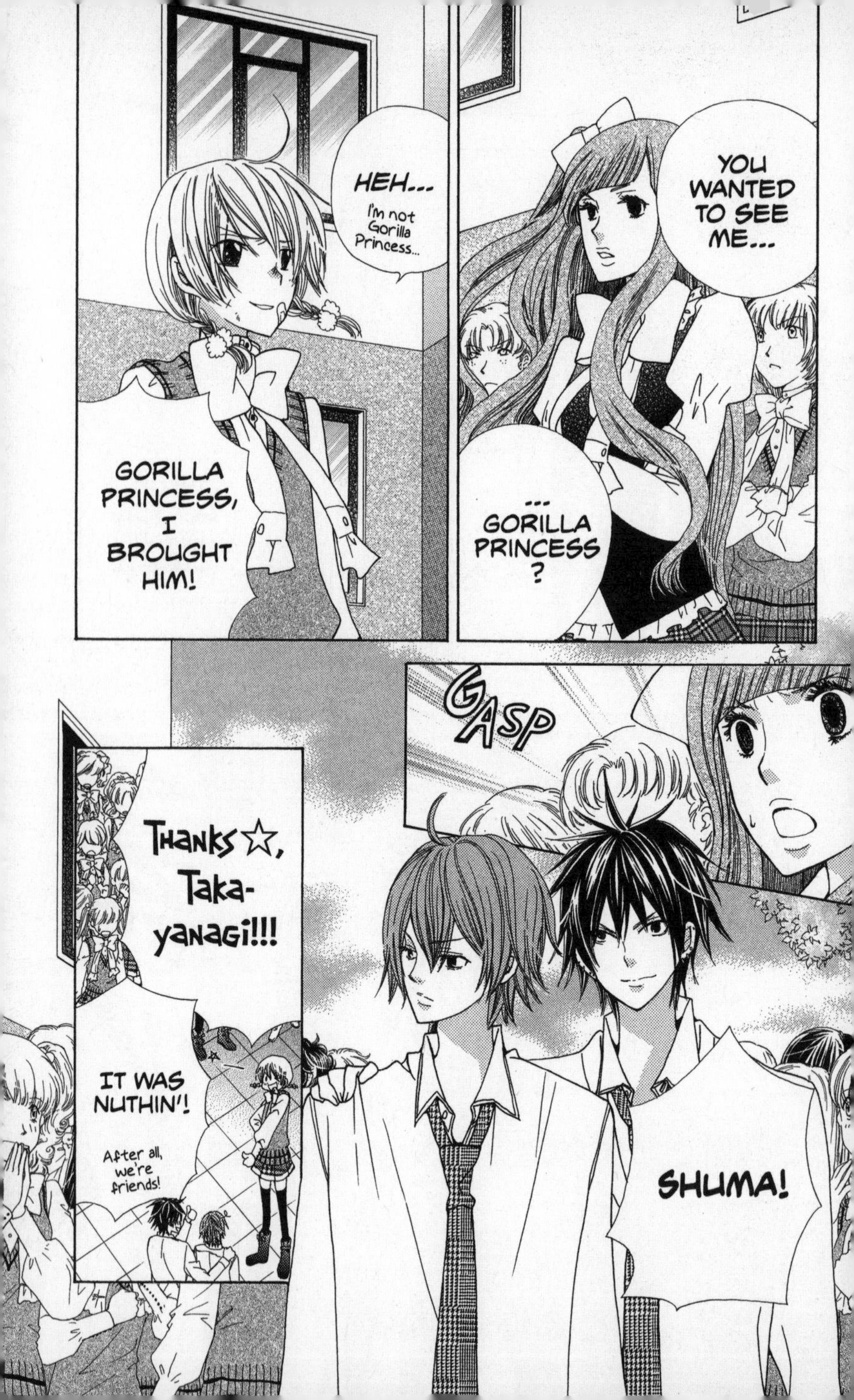
YOU WANTED TO SEE ME...
...GORILLA PRINCESS?
HEH...
I'm not Gorilla Princess...
GORILLA PRINCESS, I BROUGHT HIM!
GASP
SHUMA!
Thanks☆, Taka-yanagi!!!
IT WAS NUTHIN'!
After all, we're friends!

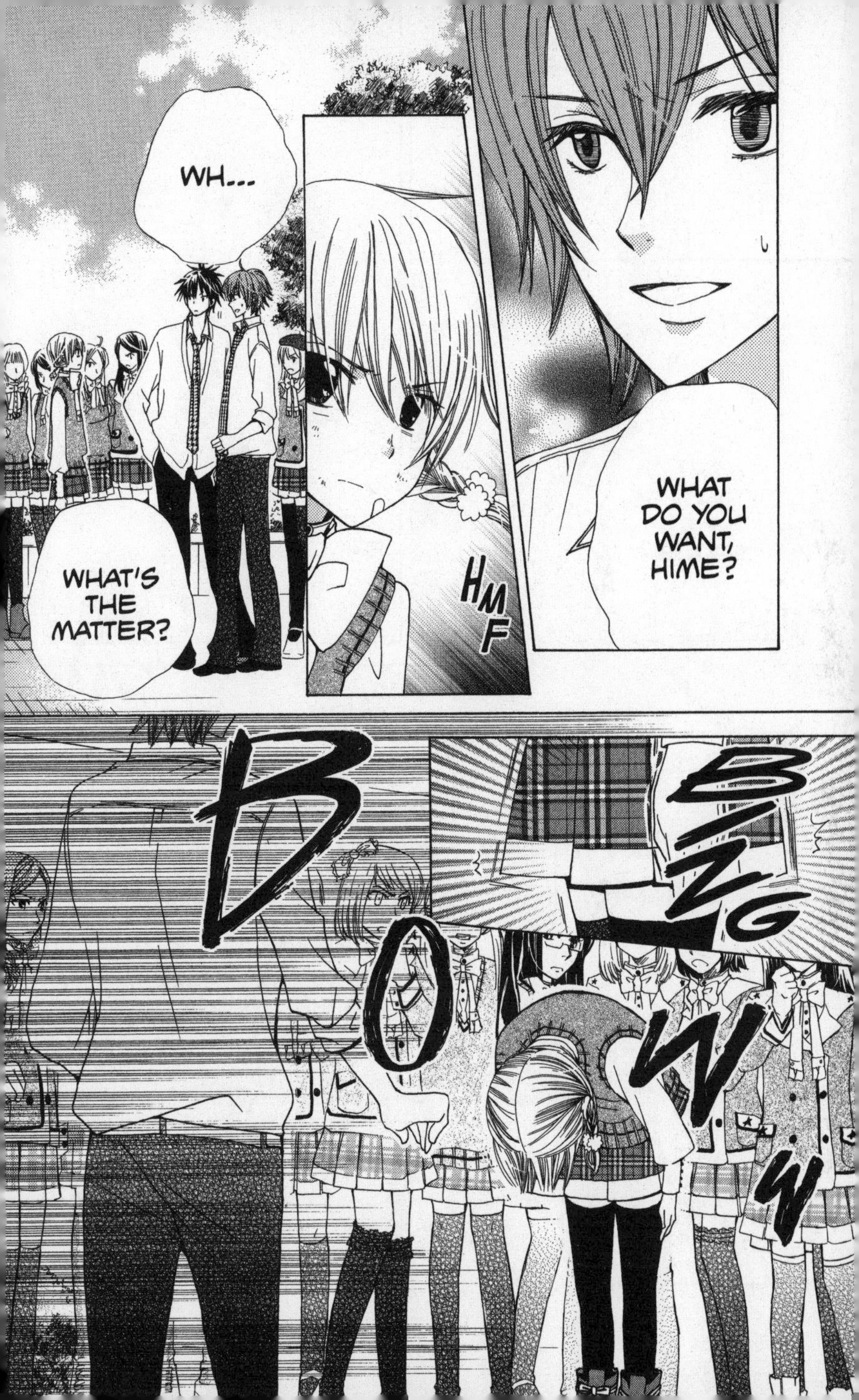
WHAT DO YOU WANT, HIME?
HMF
WH...
WHAT'S THE MATTER?
BING
BOWW

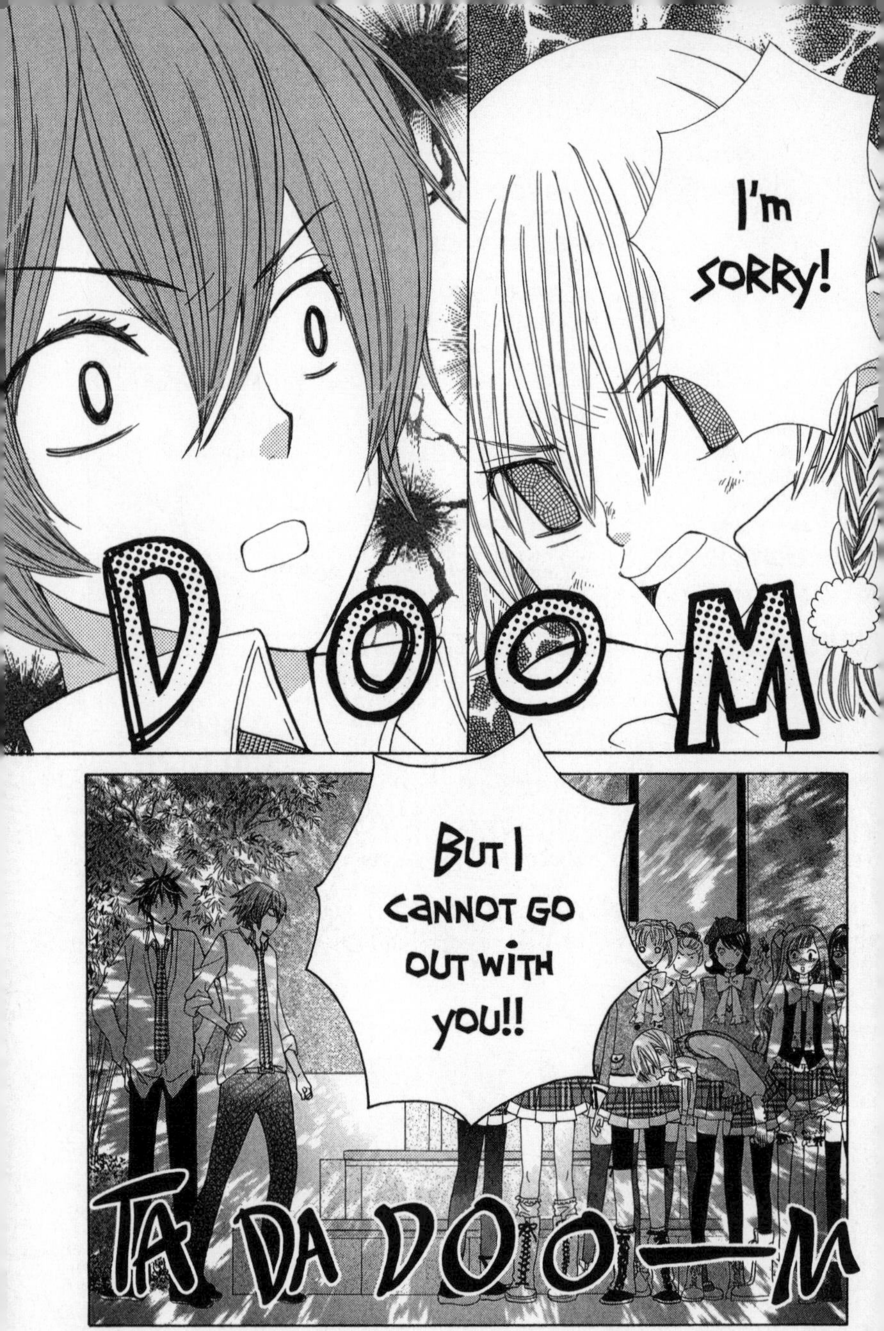
I'm SORRY!
DOOOM
BUT I CANNOT GO OUT WITH YOU!!
TA DA DOO—M

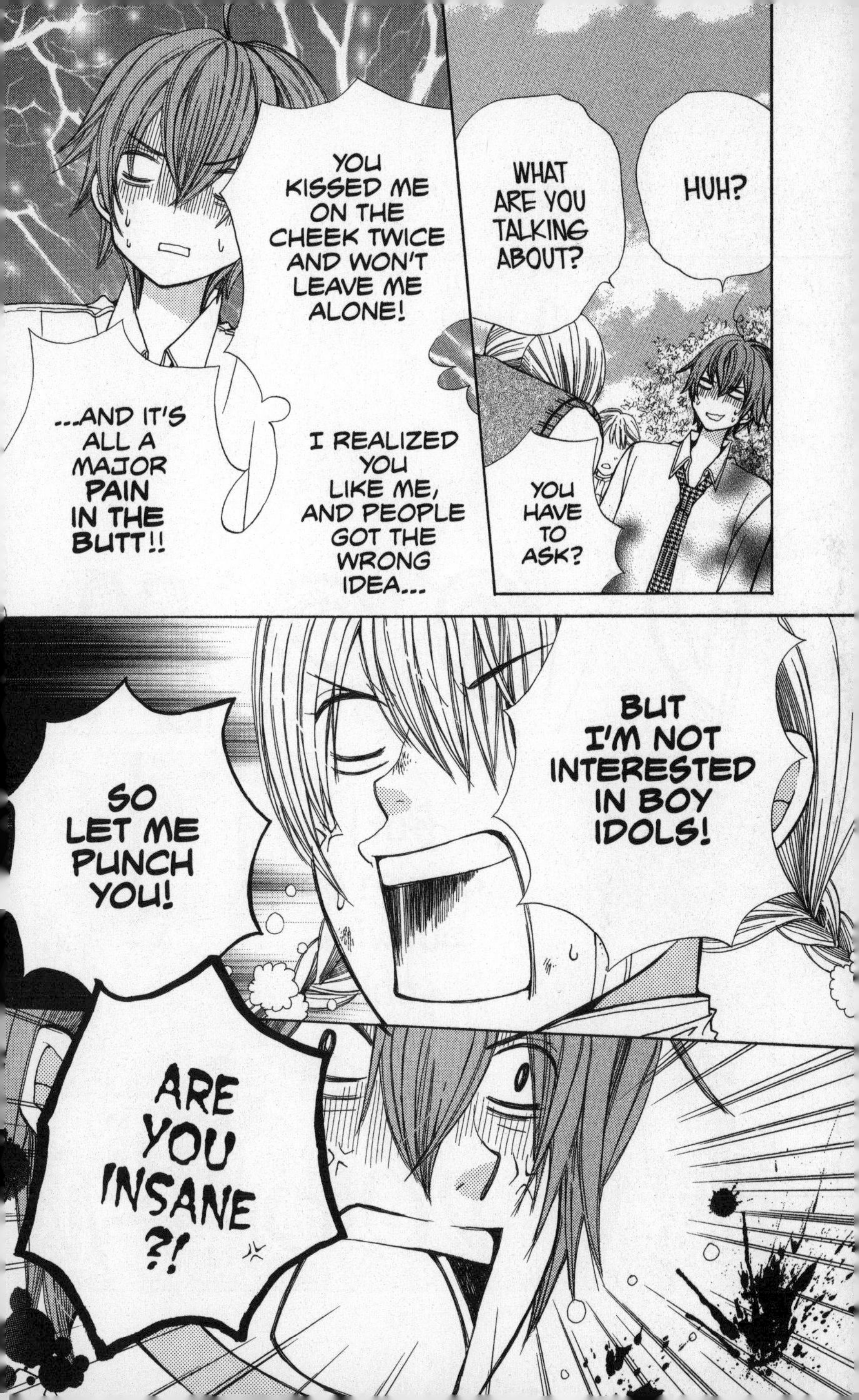
HUH?
WHAT ARE YOU TALKING ABOUT?
YOU HAVE TO ASK?
YOU KISSED ME ON THE CHEEK TWICE AND WON'T LEAVE ME ALONE!
I REALIZED YOU LIKE ME, AND PEOPLE GOT THE WRONG IDEA...
...AND IT'S ALL A MAJOR PAIN IN THE BUTT!!
BUT I'M NOT INTERESTED IN BOY IDOLS!
SO LET ME PUNCH YOU!
ARE YOU INSANE?!

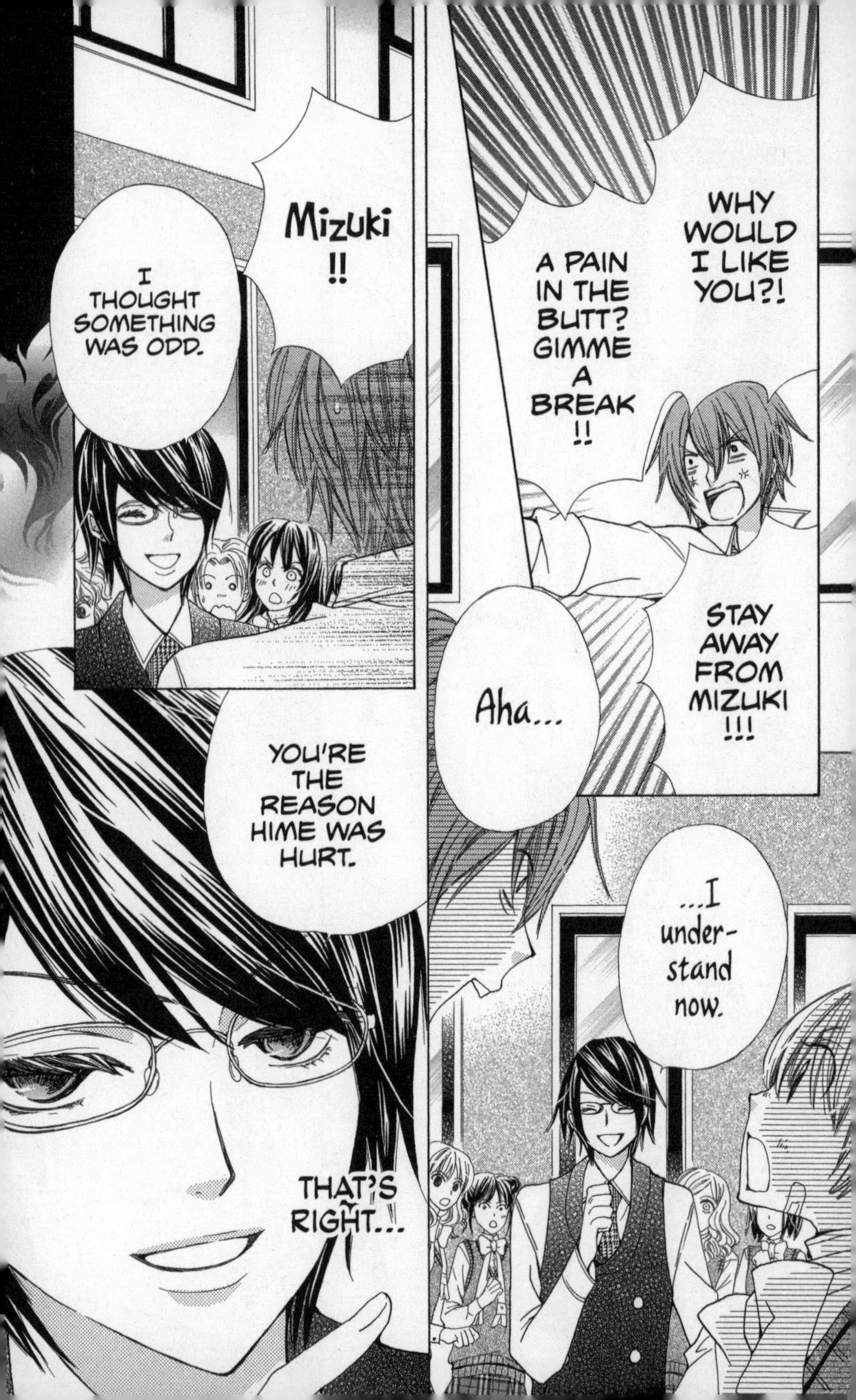
WHY WOULD I LIKE YOU?!
A PAIN IN THE BUTT? GIMME A BREAK!!
STAY AWAY FROM MIZUKI!!!
Mizuki!!
I THOUGHT SOMETHING WAS ODD.
Aha...
...I under-stand now.
YOU'RE THE REASON HIME WAS HURT.
THAT'S RIGHT...

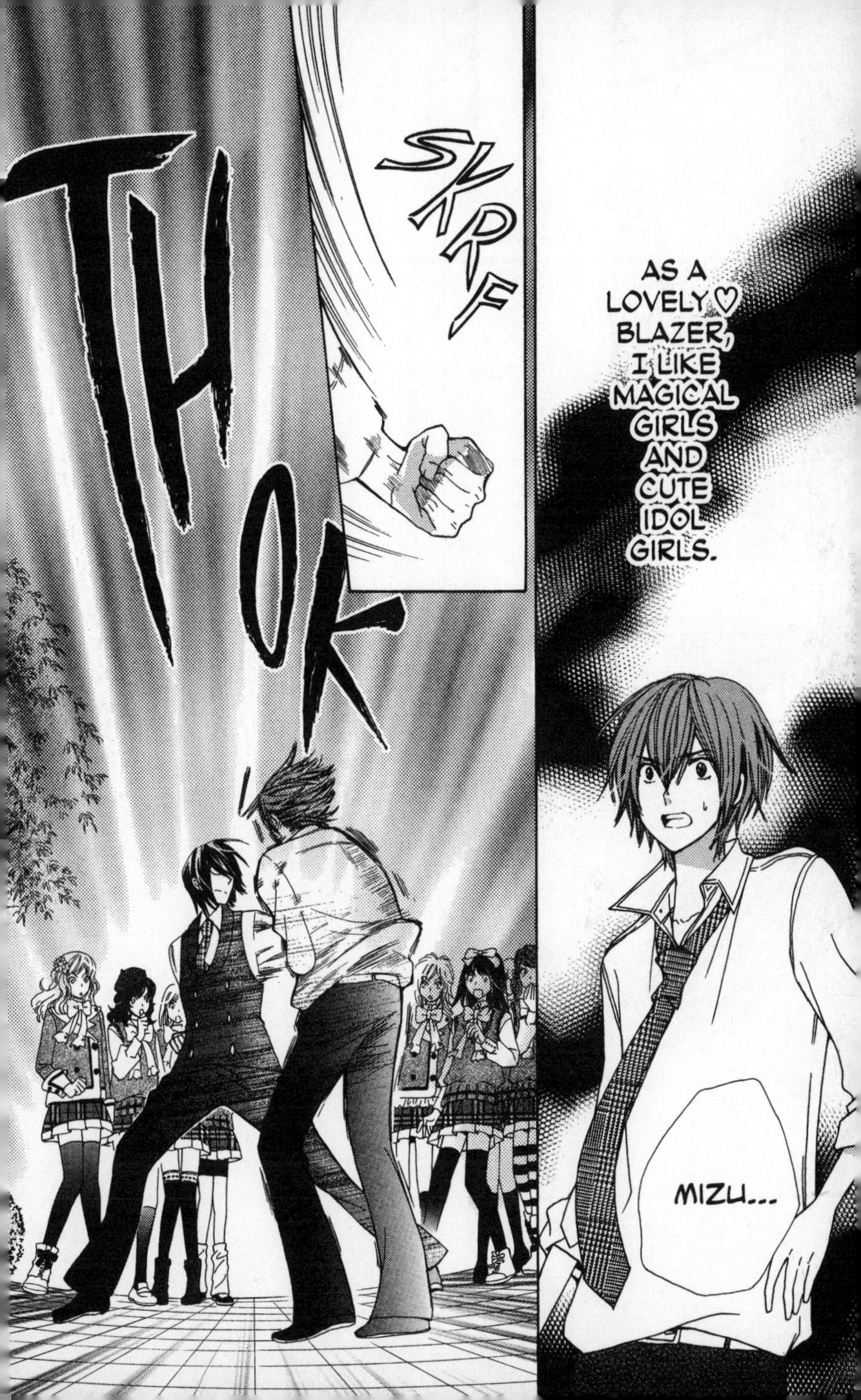
AS A LOVELY♡ BLAZER, I LIKE MAGICAL GIRLS AND CUTE IDOL GIRLS.
MIZU...
SKRF
THOK

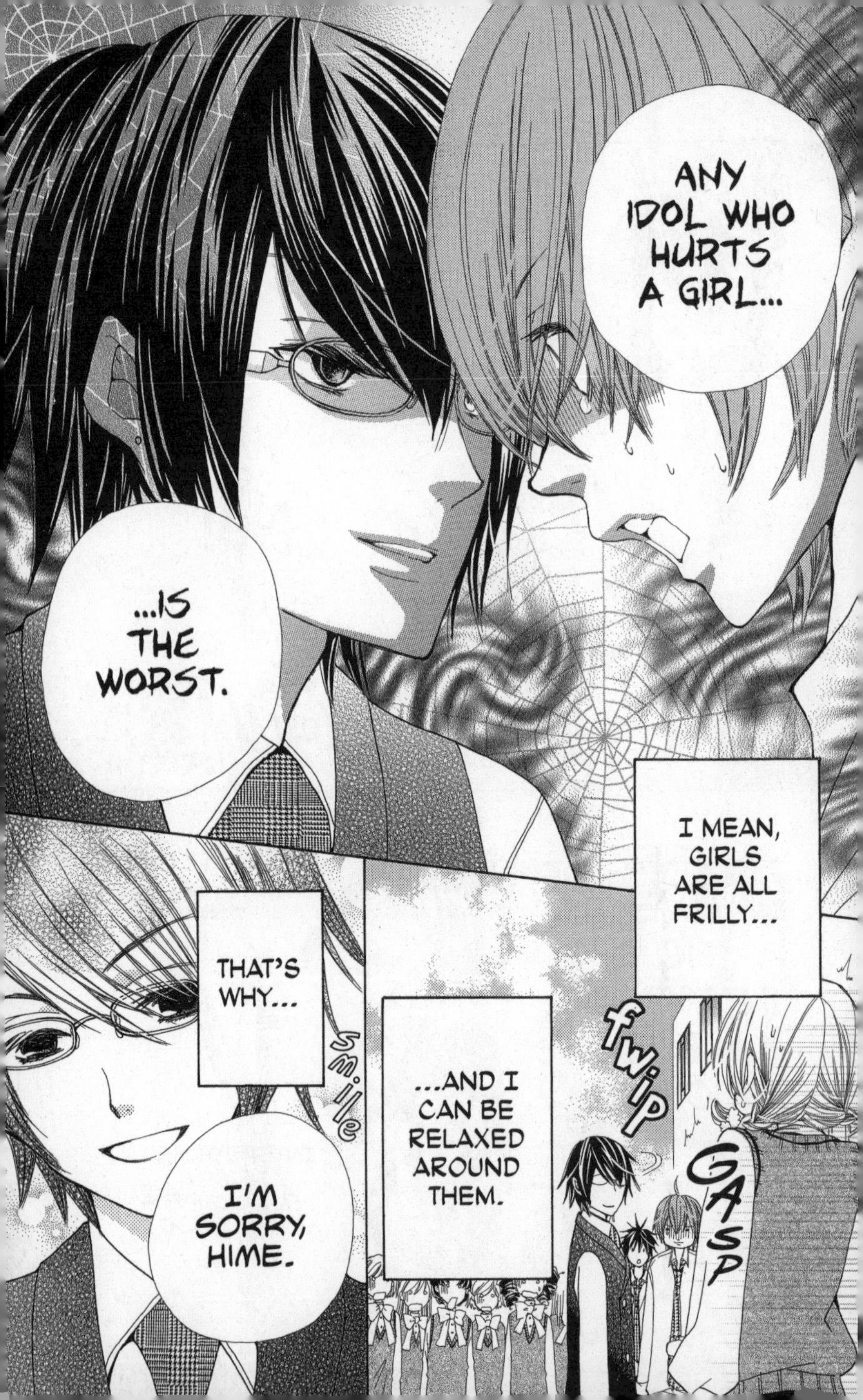
ANY IDOL WHO HURTS A GIRL...
...IS THE WORST.
I MEAN, GIRLS ARE ALL FRILLY...
fwip
GASP
...AND I CAN BE RELAXED AROUND THEM.
THAT'S WHY...
smile
I'M SORRY, HIME.

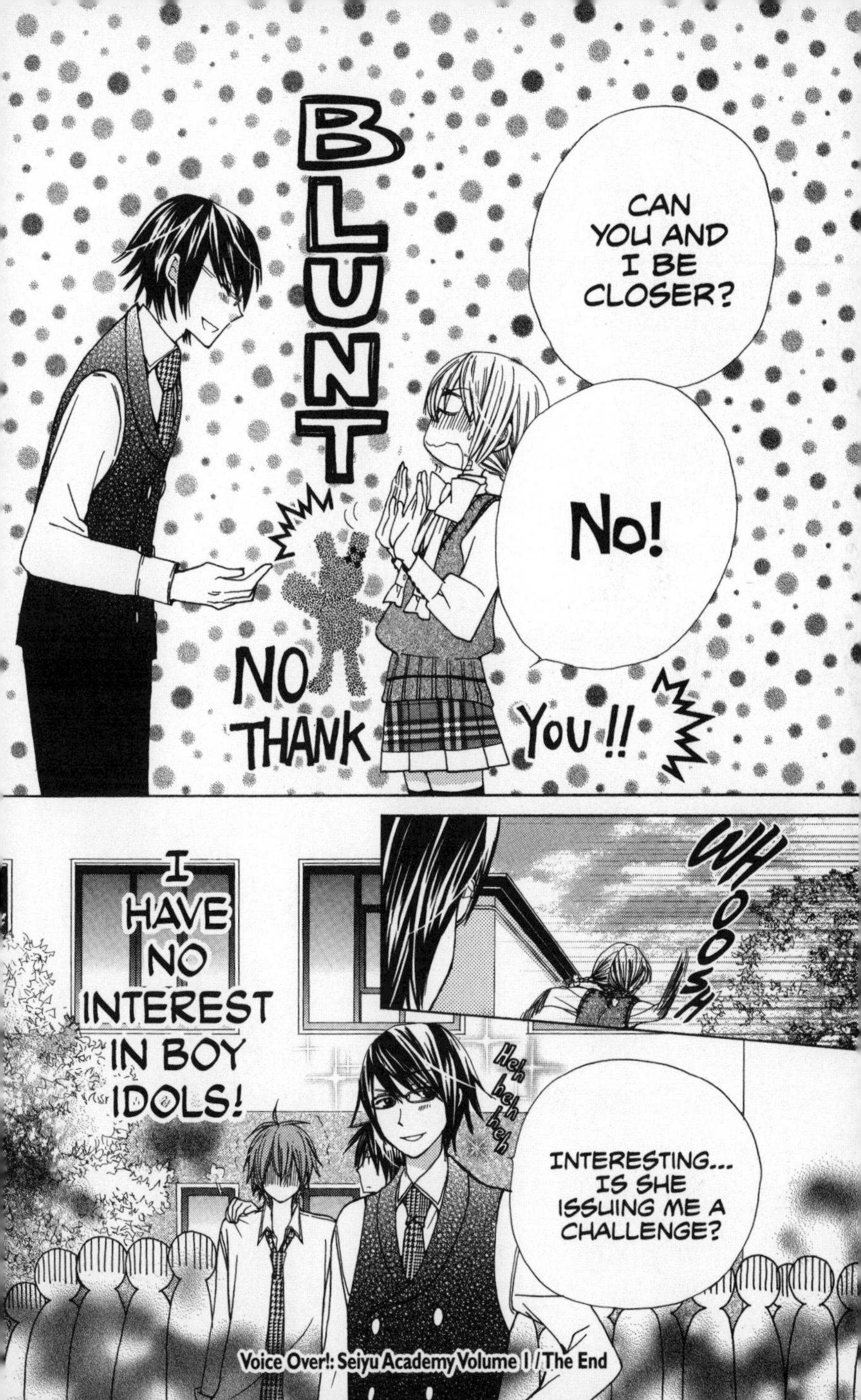
CAN YOU AND I BE CLOSER?
BLUNT
No!
NO THANK YOU!!
WHOOOSH
I HAVE NO INTEREST IN BOY IDOLS!
Heh heh heh
INTERESTING... IS SHE ISSUING ME A CHALLENGE?
Voice Over!: Seiyu Academy Volume 1 / The End

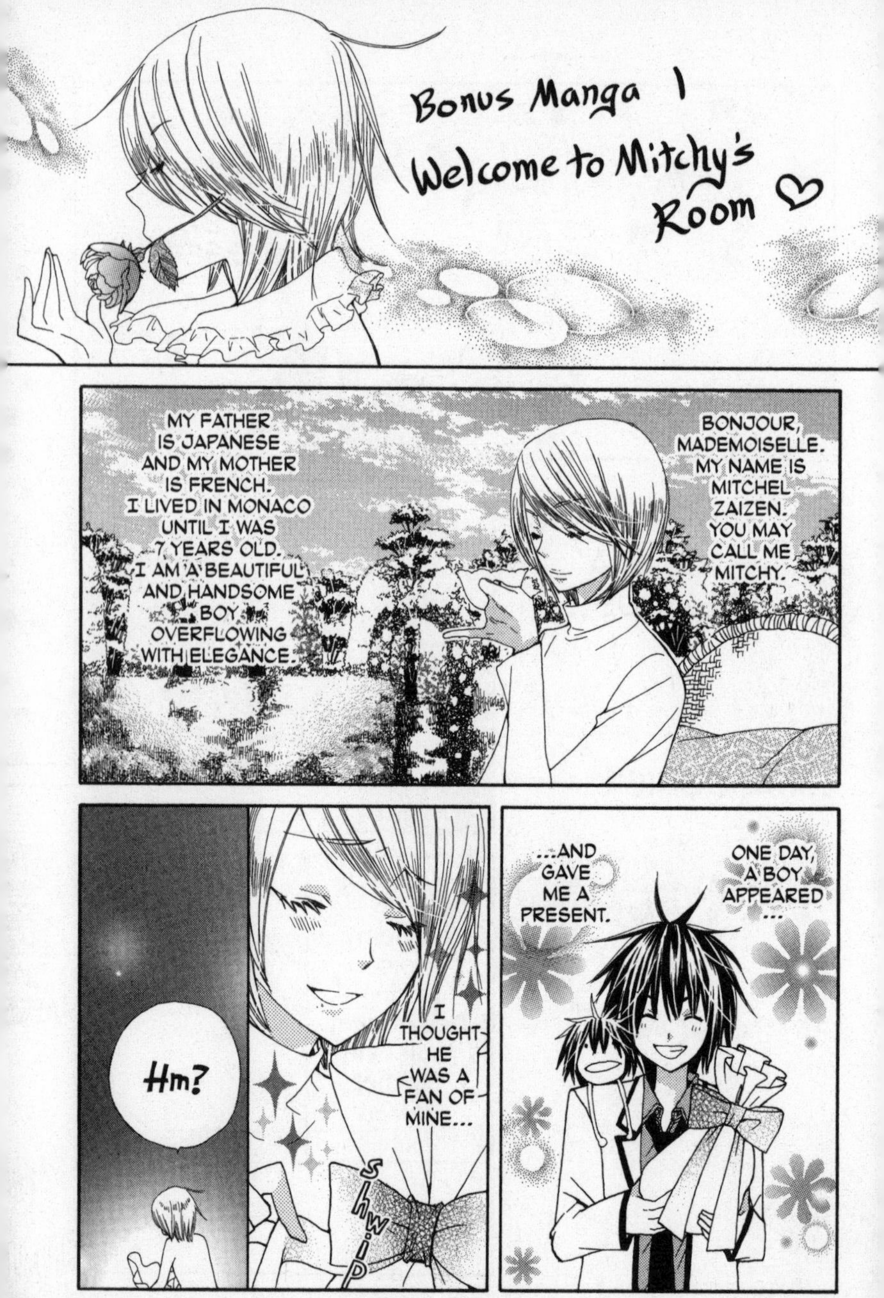
Bonus Manga 1
Welcome to Mitchy's Room ♡
BONJOUR, MADEMOISELLE. MY NAME IS MITCHEL ZAIZEN. YOU MAY CALL ME MITCHY.
MY FATHER IS JAPANESE AND MY MOTHER IS FRENCH. I LIVED IN MONACO UNTIL I WAS 7 YEARS OLD. I AM A BEAUTIFUL AND HANDSOME BOY OVERFLOWING WITH ELEGANCE.
ONE DAY, A BOY APPEARED...
...AND GAVE ME A PRESENT.
I THOUGHT HE WAS A FAN OF MINE...
SHWIP
Hm?

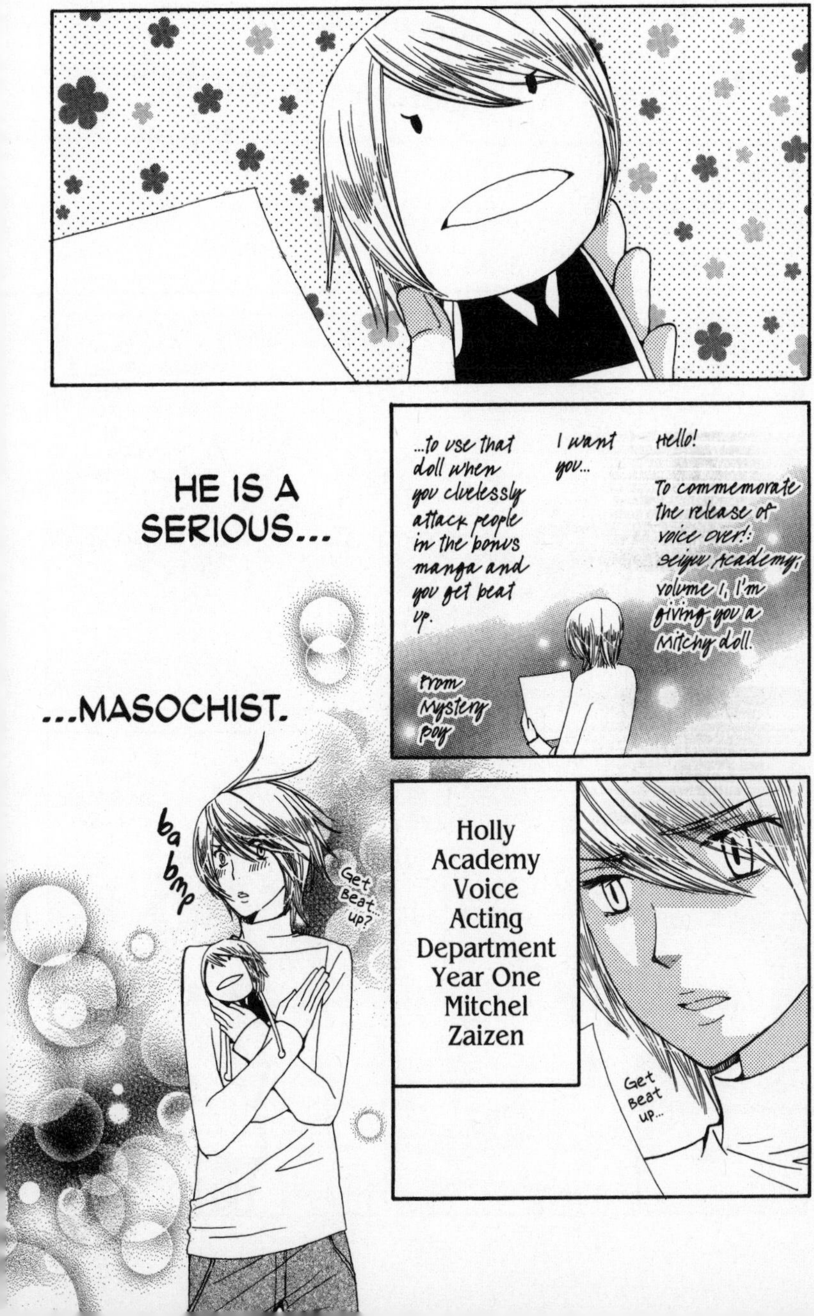
Hello! To commemorate the release of voice over!: seiyu academy, volume 1, I'm giving you a Mitchy doll.
I want you...
...to use that doll when you cluelessly attack people in the bonus manga and you get beat up.
From Mystery boy
Holly Academy Voice Acting Department Year One Mitchel Zaizen
Get Beat up...
HE IS A SERIOUS...
...MASOCHIST.
ba bmp
Get Beat up?

Voice Over! Seiyu Academy

End Notes

Page 11, side bar: Taiyaki
Fish-shaped cakes, usually filled with sweet bean paste.

Page 19, panel 5: Shichi-go-san
Shichi-go-san is a festival for children in Japan. It's for girls who are 3 and 7 years old, and boys who are 3 and 5 years old.

Page 23, panel 5: Jugemu
Jugemu is a Japanese folktale about a boy who is given a ridiculously long tongue twister of a name. The name is sometimes used for vocal training for actors and other entertainers.

Page 75, panel 1: Host
A name for young men who work at "host clubs" entertaining women customers. A kind of modern-day male geisha.

Page 138, sidebar: Saitama
Saitama Prefecture is a suburb of Tokyo.

Maki Minami is from Saitama Prefecture in Japan. She debuted in 2001 with *Kanata no Ao* (Faraway Blue). Her other works include *Kimi wa Girlfriend* (You're My Girlfriend), *Mainichi ga Takaramono* (Every Day Is a Treasure), *Yuki Atataka* (Warm Winter) and *S•A*, which was published in English by VIZ Media.

VOICE OVER!
SEIYU ACADEMY
VOL. 1
Shojo Beat Edition

STORY AND ART BY
MAKI MINAMI

TECHNICAL ADVISORS
Yoichi Kato, Kaori Kagami, Ayumi Hashidate,
Ayako Harino and Touko Fujitani

Special Thanks
81produce
Tokyo Animator College
Tokyo Animation College

English Translation & Adaptation/John Werry
Touch-up Art & Lettering/Sabrina Heep
Design/Yukiko Whitley
Editor/Pancha Diaz

SEIYU KA! by Maki Minami
© Maki Minami 2009
All rights reserved.
First published in Japan in 2009 by HAKUSENSHA, Inc., Tokyo.
English language translation rights arranged with
HAKUSENSHA, Inc., Tokyo.

Printed in the U.S.A.

Published by VIZ Media, LLC
P.O. Box 77010
San Francisco, CA 94107

10 9 8 7 6 5 4 3 2 1
First printing, October 2013

www.viz.com   www.shojobeat.com

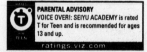

PARENTAL ADVISORY
VOICE OVER!: SEIYU ACADEMY is rated
T for Teen and is recommended for ages
13 and up.
ratings.viz.com

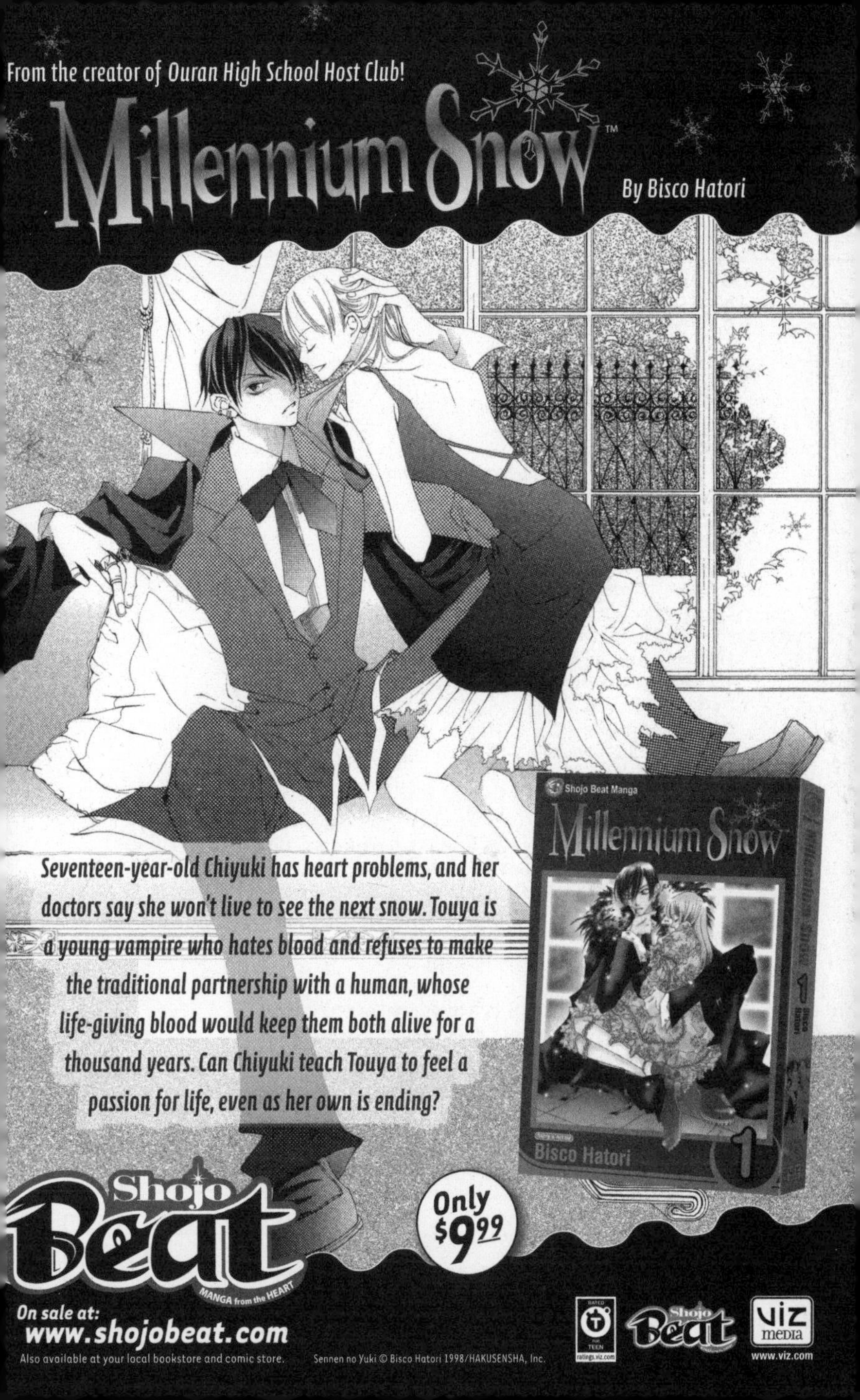
From the creator of Ouran High School Host Club!
Millennium Snow™
By Bisco Hatori
Seventeen-year-old Chiyuki has heart problems, and her doctors say she won't live to see the next snow. Touya is a young vampire who hates blood and refuses to make the traditional partnership with a human, whose life-giving blood would keep them both alive for a thousand years. Can Chiyuki teach Touya to feel a passion for life, even as her own is ending?
Shojo Beat Manga
Millennium Snow
1
Bisco Hatori
Shojo Beat
MANGA from the HEART
Only $9.99
On sale at:
www.shojobeat.com
Also available at your local bookstore and comic store.
Sennen no Yuki © Bisco Hatori 1998/HAKUSENSHA, Inc.
RATED T FOR TEEN
ratings.viz.com
VIZ media
www.viz.com

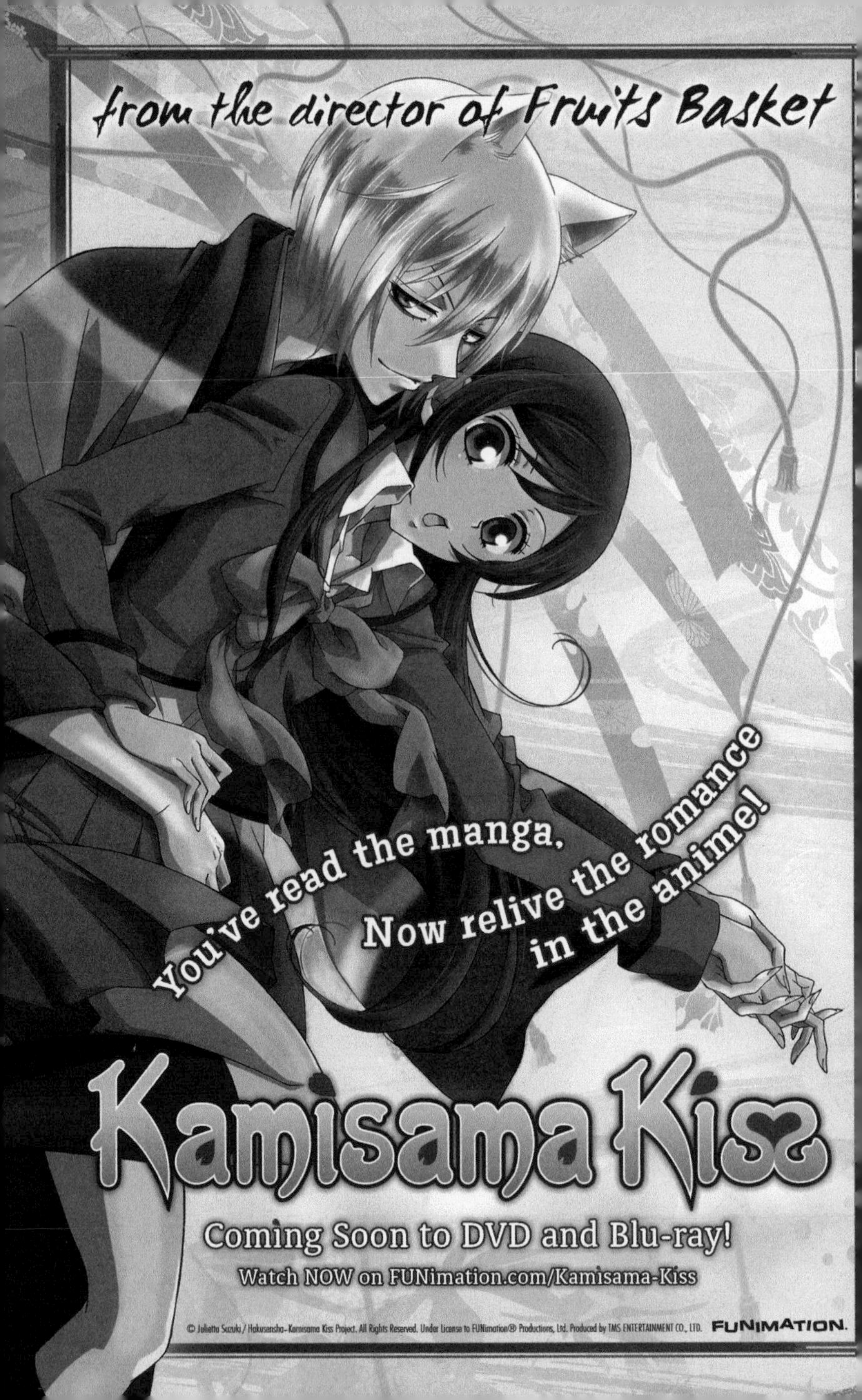
from the director of Fruits Basket
You've read the manga.
Now relive the romance
in the anime!
Kamisama Kiss
Coming Soon to DVD and Blu-ray!
Watch NOW on FUNimation.com/Kamisama-Kiss
© Julietta Suzuki / Hakusensha-Kamisama Kiss Project. All Rights Reserved. Under License to FUNimation® Productions, Ltd. Produced by TMS ENTERTAINMENT CO., LTD.
FUNIMATION.

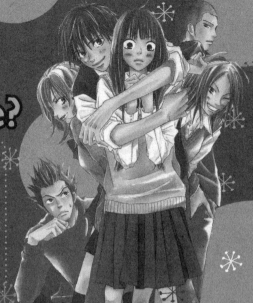
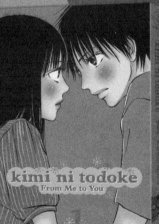
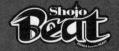

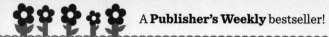
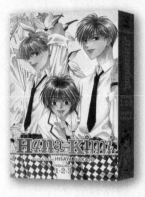 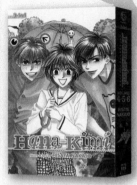 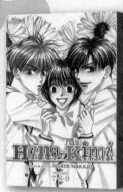

∪IZM∧NG∧
Read manga anytime, anywhere!

From our newest hit series to the classics you know and love, the best manga in the world is now available digitally. Buy a volume* of digital manga for your:

- iOS device (**iPad®**, **iPhone®**, **iPod®** touch) through the **VIZ Manga** app

- Android-powered device (**phone or tablet**) with a browser by visiting VIZManga.com

- **Mac or PC computer** by visiting VIZManga.com

VIZ Digital has loads to offer:

- 500+ ready-to-read volumes
- New volumes each week
- FREE previews
- Access on multiple devices! Create a log-in through the app so you buy a book once, and read it on your device of choice!*

To learn more, visit www.viz.com/apps

* Some series may not be available for multiple devices.
  Check the app on your device to find out what's available.

Aiwo Utauyori Oreni Oborero! Volume 1 © Mayu SHINJO 2010
DEATH NOTE © 2003 by Tsugumi Ohba, Takeshi Obata/SHUEISHA Inc.
NURARIHYON NO MAGO © 2008 by Hiroshi Shiibashi/SHUEISHA Inc.

ratings.viz.com   viz.com/app

This is the last page.

In keeping with the original Japanese comic format, this book reads from right to left—so action, sound effects, and word balloons are completely reversed. This preserves the orientation of the original artwork—plus, it's fun! Check out the diagram shown here to get the hang of things, and then turn to the other side of the book to get started!

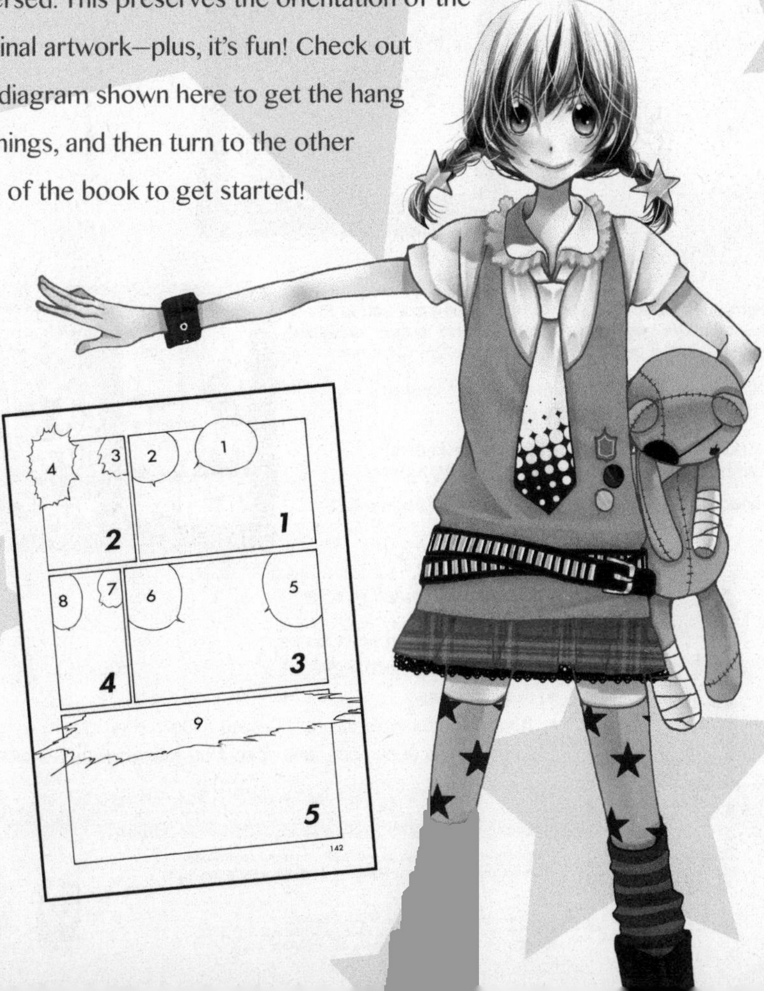
1
2
3
4
1
2
5
6
7
8
3
4
9
5
142